MAC OS X UNIX
101 BYTE-SIZED PROJECTS

Adrian Mayo

Peachpit Press

MAC OS X UNIX 101 BYTE-SIZED PROJECTS
Adrian Mayo

Inside Mac is published in association with Peachpit Press

Peachpit Press
1249 Eighth Street
Berkeley, CA 94710
510/524-2178
800/283-9444
510/524-2221 (fax)

Find us on the World Wide Web at: www.peachpit.com. To report errors, please send a note to: errata@peachpit.com. Peachpit Press is a division of Pearson Education.

Project Editor: Jim Akin
Production Editor: Simmy Cover
Copyeditor: Kathy Simpson
Tech Editor: Dominique Werner
Compositor: Christi Payne
Indexer: Julie Bess
Cover design: Aren Howell
Interior design: Joan Olson

ISBN 0-321-37411-8

9 8 7 6 5 4 3 2 1

Printed and bound in the United States of America

Dedication

Loraine, Ferdinand, and Galadriel.

Thanks to:

My editor Jim Akin for his expert touch and elimination of such sins as passive no-nos.

My technical editor Dominique Werner.

Scott Sheppard of Inside Mac Press for starting the whole deal, and Peachpit for seeing it through.

Janet Forbes for being Janet Forbes, and for allowing me to use text from her Diary Extracts, published on http://jan.1dot1.com.

Glen Carpenter, for being a Unix command-line guinea pig.

iTunes in association with The Cooper Temple Clause, Muse, Rush, The White Stripes, The Zutons, and many others.

My iMac G5 and its 20" LCD screen, which makes writing and proofing so much easier.

Beer.

CONTENTS

Chapter 3: Work with File Content   135

Chapter 4: Edit Files   187

Chapter 5: Keep an Eye on Your Mac   241

Chapter 6: Make the Most of the Shell   281

Chapter 7: Programmatically Change Files   343

Chapter 8: Administer the System 383

Chapter 9: Learn Shell Scripting 439

Chapter 10: Network in Unix   515

Chapter 11: Discover More Commands   561

Appendix: Unix Terminology Reference   593

Index   599

Introduction

This book is for you if you have a problem to solve or a task to complete. Working at the Unix command line often provides the quickest and easiest solution. Although a modern Unix environment such as Mac OS X provides a graphical method of working, the real power still lies in the Terminal and in typing commands. The Unix command line lets you work with your Mac in ways that are difficult or even impossible graphically, unlocking the hidden workings of Apple's OS and unleashing a wealth of powerful free software. Clicking a button may be an easy way to perform a prepackaged action, but it doesn't give you the expressive power of a set of written commands.

By reading the book, you'll learn Unix through doing. Moreover, you'll learn how to *apply* Unix to solve real-world problems. Whether you want to search for files, search file content, use regular expressions, mount disks, create user accounts, configure Apache, or do any of 95 other things, you'll find a project that shows you how.

Philosophy

Plenty of books teach Unix theory, covering a single subject like Unix itself, the Bash shell, shell scripting, the vim or emacs text editor, the awk text-processing language, the Apache Web server, networking, firewalls, and so on. That's a lot of books, a lot of reading, and a lot of theory. Ninety percent of you don't have the inclination or time to follow that route. You learn on demand and want to cut to the chase to get a specific job done. You want to focus on the micro-topic that solves your current problem or gives you the knowledge to work out your own solution. Moreover, because most solutions involve more than a single command, you want to know the relevant techniques, technologies, and commands, and how to use them in combination.

These considerations lead to the book's approach. For 101 of the most common tasks, it explores the most appropriate commands and shows you how to use and combine them in the context of the task. This is different from the traditional theory approach, which considers a command in its own right and then asks, "What can I do with this command?"

The book uses a 90:10 philosophy. Ninety percent of the usefulness of a tool or technology lies in just 10 percent of its functionality. awk (a text-processing language) is a good example—very powerful and commonly used, but rarely stretched beyond its 10 percent headline functionality. By taking the 90:10 approach, we combine 10 books in one; illustrate a broad range of topics that you'll encounter every day; and show techniques used in combination, not isolation.

But I Love My Mouse

Mac OS X provides a powerful and elegant graphical user interface, so you might find it counterintuitive to drop into the Unix command line to get a job done. But as with a powerful car, sometimes you need to get under the hood to squeeze out all the performance it can deliver.

Even if you don't have an immediate need, working through some of the projects in this book is a Unix analog to the pointing, clicking, and dragging way in which most of us learned the Mac OS. It'll help you gain familiarity and confidence in using Unix. When you've made friends with the man pages, practiced stringing commands together, and written a few scripts, you'll begin to know and appreciate the power under the Aqua-colored hood.

What You'll Learn

You'll learn how to apply Unix and achieve results. Along the way, you'll learn Unix commands, techniques, and technologies. Basic Unix is covered in Chapter 1.

From the 101 projects in this book, you'll learn how to:

▶ Locate and then edit many files automatically

▶ Find files and commands anywhere in the file system, as you can with Apple's Spotlight—and process them at the same time.

▶ Write shell scripts that execute a series of commands automatically

▶ Search file content for particular text or patterns of text

- Use the Unix manual to full effect to learn about new commands and technologies

- Manage your Mac's hardware, software, user accounts, and network settings

- Mount local disk drives, removable media, and shares from other machines

- Use and customize the Bash and Tcsh shells—the Unix equivalent of using and customizing your Desktop and the Finder

- Display, edit, sort, compare, compress, and archive files

You'll also learn techniques and technologies such as:

- Globbing and pattern-matching operators that allow you to select many files at the same time, such as all JPEG files or all files starting with `letter-to`

- Scripting commands such as `sed` and `awk` that search for and transform the text content of files

- Redirection and pipelining, which enable you to save the results of commands and use commands in combination

- Users, groups, and Unix file permissions that protect your files from unauthorized access by other users and the system files from being deleted or damaged

- Hard and soft links, which are like Mac OS aliases

- Regular expressions, written to describe patterns of text for which you can search

- Unix text editors

- Scheduling and periodic maintenance to perform particular tasks automatically at specified times

- Server technologies such as the Apache Web server, Unix Network File System (NFS) for sharing files with other Unix machines, File Transfer Protocol (FTP) for transferring files between computers, and the Domain Naming System (DNS) that translates names such as www.apple.com into Internet addresses (IP addresses)

↗ LEARN MORE

Project 22 shows you how to view binary and compressed files.

❦ NOTE

When creating the patch file, be sure that the filenames passed to diff *are in the correct order (name of outdated file, followed by up-to-date version); otherwise, the patch will be applied in reverse.*

Directories and Files

In Unix, the term *directory* is used instead of *folder*. Folder comes from the desktop analogy and the visual representation of directories. The term *file* is often used in a general sense to mean both files and directories. Technically, in Unix, a directory is just a file.

Ţ TIP

To find out which signals a command or daemon respects, check its man page, and search for the section "SIGNALS."

How to Use This Book

Although it can be read sequentially, the book was written for "random access." You'll probably pick it up when you seek a solution to a problem. Each chapter groups projects that cover similar tasks, so start with the table of contents, and choose the chapter that seems closest to your task. Scan the list of projects in the chapter, and choose the project that looks like the closest fit. Then read the introduction to confirm that the project is the right one; each project introduction starts with a typical question that the project will answer and then outlines the material it covers.

Follow the project through, preferably in front of a computer with a Terminal window open so you can try the examples. Projects are written to be self-contained, and except for Chapter 1, most assume some basic knowledge and competence at the command line. If you are new to Unix (or a bit rusty), Chapter 1 is essential reading.

Each project covers just the commands required to complete the task at hand. It may draw on many technologies and techniques, distilling the necessary information for you. It won't give an encyclopedic description of a command or list all its available options. If you want to know more about one of the commands used to complete a task, reach for the Unix manual pages. Pointers directing you to do so appear throughout the book, and the manual is also the focus of Project 3.

Sometimes you want to discover more or have further interest in one of the technologies a project uses. You might want to extend one of the examples. Projects acknowledge this by giving you many links to other projects that discuss a technique or command in detail or that use it in another way. Think of the Learn More links as being like HTML hyperlinks to other projects in the book. You'll see them in the margins, like the example to the left.

The margins also use Notes to give additional and important information, caveats, or problems you might encounter.

Sidebars give additional but nonessential explanatory information.

Finally, the margins are littered with great tips like the one to the left.

Sometimes you'll see a warning where you might encounter problems or potentially do something damaging.

❗ WARNING

This is an example warning. A warning is always in the main body of text and introduced by the warning graphic you see above. Always take care to read and understand warnings.

Project 100 lists a very large number of Unix commands, each with a brief description of its purpose. The commands are organized into categories and grouped together by similar functionality. Where a command is covered by a project in this book, the project number is shown in brackets.

The appendix lists the Unix terminology, techniques, and concepts covered in the book. Each term is cross-referenced to the projects(s) that cover it.

Code Extracts

Code extracts are integral parts of this book. You'll find lots of them, showing you what to type and the results you'll see. Try them for yourself, and try your own variations; it's all good practice.

To help you, the following conventions are employed, illustrated by this code extract.

```
$ sudo renice -15 25132
Password:
$ ps -xc -O pri,nice | grep iPhoto
  PID PRI  NI  TT  STAT     TIME COMMAND
25132  18 -15  ??  S<    0:04.72 iPhoto
```

The $ symbol is the shell's prompt; don't type it or the space that follows. Type what's shown in the **bold fixed-width typeface**. Press Return when you complete each line. The response you get back (if any) follows, shown in `fixed-width typeface` but not bold. In this example, you type two commands, **sudo renice -15 25132** and **ps -xc -O pri,nice | grep iPhoto**, pressing Return at the end of each command.

Sometimes you're required to give your administrator's password before a command can be executed, as shown on the second line of the example. Type your password and press Return, and don't worry when nothing is echoed back as you type. If you are not an administrator, you won't be able to issue such commands.

The output from a command is included in the code extract unless the command line is being illustrated without the need for example output. Sometimes a $ is shown at the end of the results to emphasize that no (more) output is expected. Sometimes the prompt is shown as # which means you should be running as the root user (superuser).

Mostly, output shown in the examples is as you see it in the Terminal. Sometimes it's curtailed, or sections are chopped from the middle, because it's too long and not of great interest.

The book uses an ellipsis (...) to indicated omitted output.

```
$ top -o cpu
...
PID COMMAND        %CPU   TIME    #TH #PRTS #MREGS RPRVT  ...
15931 top          26.4%  0:29.98  1   18    22   1.04M...
14631 Microsoft    20.5%  6:00:56  4   96    368  23.2M...
10898 Terminal      7.3% 20:17.01  8  105    193  3.37M...
14140 Safari        1.3% 38:12.23  7  291    412  24.0M...
   69 WindowServ    1.3%  4:29:47  2  882   2914  34.8M...
...
```

A Terminal window is usually 80 or more characters wide, but typographical limitations mean that examples in the book are only 60 characters wide. It has been necessary, therefore, to edit long lines by using any of four techniques. Where possible, padding (white space) is removed, so the output shown in the book looks more squashed than you'd see in the Terminal. Sometimes lines are truncated, indicated by an ellipsis.

```
$ top
Processes: 125 total, 3 running, 122 sleeping, 391 thre...
Load Avg:  0.93, 0.62, 0.46    CPU usage:  24.7% user,...
```

Sometimes the middle part is chopped because the end is important.

```
$ ps -acux
USER      PID  %CPU %MEM  ... TIME       COMMAND
root    18670  11.0  0.1  ... 0:00.29    sshd
saruman 10898   8.5  1.5  ... 22:58.57   Terminal
```

Finally, sometimes output is wrapped to cover two lines where you'd see it all on one line in the Terminal.

Commands that you type should be on a single line. Where command lines are too long for the width of the book, they are shown broken, but they must be entered as one line. Where a command line has to be broken for layout reasons, the special symbol ¬ is used, and the rest of the command follows on the next line, indented four spaces.

```
$ ipfw add 3010 allow tcp from any to any dst ¬
    1024-65535 in
```

It's very important to note whether a space appears before the ¬ symbol and to include it on your command line. Type the line shown above as

```
ipfw add 3010 allow tcp from any to any dst 1024-65535 in
```

Where no space should be typed, none is shown before the ¬ symbol. For example, type the following line

```
$ ditto -rsrc User\ Template/¬
    English.lproj/ /Users/jan
```

as:

```
ditto -rsrc User\ Template/English.lproj/ /Users/jan
```

In the main text, command names, arguments, options, files, directory names, and whatever you type at the command line is shown in fixed-width typeface.

Supported Systems

This book was written for Mac OS X 10.4 (Tiger), although most examples work in Mac OS X 10.3 (Panther), with differences noted in the text. Most examples work in older versions of Mac OS X, too.

The default shell for accounts created with Panther and Tiger is Bash. Examples are written assuming Bash. There's support for Tcsh (the default shell pre-Panther) via notes or separate projects. If you are running Tcsh, Project 1 shows you how to change your default shell to Bash.

Examples should work on any model of Mac. Although written for Client, they are largely applicable to Mac OS X Server too. Server has extra graphical tools to manage such things as user accounts, the Apache Web server, and FTP administration.

Although not essential, to get the most from Mac OS X, we recommend that you install the X11 windowing system and the Developer Tools. Both are optional installs and can be installed at any time.

To install X11, insert your original Mac OS X install disc; double-click the Optional Installs package; and follow the instructions, selecting X11 from the Applications set in the appropriate screen.

To install the Developer Tools, insert your original Mac OS X install disc, double-click first the Xcode Tools folder and then the Xcode Tools package, and follow the instructions.

Further Reading

There's a companion web site for the book providing further links, contact information, resources, and an errata. Point your browser at http://101.1dot1.com.

Inside Mac Press (http://www.insidemacpress.com).

OSXFAQ – Technical News and Support for Mac OS X (www.osxfaq.com).

Absolute Basics 1

There's stuff you just have to know. Chapter 1 has ten projects to get you started in Unix. Whereas Chapters 2 to 11 are practical exercises focused on specific tasks, "Absolute Basics" covers basic commands and theory, including the following essential topics:

The Terminal application and the command line. These, and the shell, form your day-to-day working environment, so it's good to get to know them well.

Basic Unix commands and concepts. The essentials are covered to get you started.

The Unix manual. All commands are documented in the manual, albeit in a rather terse manner.

Bash and other shells. You'll be talking to the shell more than anything else, so learn its language and take advantage of what the various shells have to offer.

Redirection and pipelining. Two of the cornerstones of Unix power, these concepts are used extensively throughout the projects in this book.

Users, groups, and permissions. Understand and maintain the Unix file system security model.

Shell scripting. Learn to flex your Unix muscle by mastering shell scripting.

Complete these projects if you are new to Unix or do not feel comfortable working at the command line. They guide you through your first encounters, starting from the absolute basics, and arm you with the necessary skills to tackle projects in the remaining chapters. Although subsequent projects don't assume prior knowledge of the subject area they cover, they do assume competence in basic command-line skills: Refer back to this chapter if you get into difficulties completing a project.

"Absolute Basics" has many references to other projects that make practical use of the theory being taught. So as well as teaching the basics, it acts as a road map, or springboard, to the practical use of Unix—"to boldly go beyond the theory."

Now, lose the mouse . . .

What Is Darwin?

Apple's Aqua technology provides all the shiny bits of Mac OS X—those beautiful icons, windows, and menus. However, underneath in the engine room, Darwin, Mac OS X's Unix foundation, is hard at work. There are many variants of Unix, and Apple chose to base Darwin on FreeBSD (Berkeley Standard Distribution, developed at the University of California, Berkeley). FreeBSD, like a great many other Unix distributions, is open-source software; its source code is freely available, and pro-grammers around the world continually improve and update it. In addition to FreeBSD, Darwin takes advantage of many other open-source tech-nologies, including the Mach kernel, Apache, and GCC.

✒ NOTE

The prompt you see may differ from that shown in the screen shot in Figure 1.1, depending on which version of OS X you are running and what the default shell is. Shells are explained a little later in this chapter.

Project 1
Lose the Mouse

. . . but not just yet. Use it to launch Apple's Terminal application, which you'll find in the Utilities folder within Applications at the root of your system disk (`Macintosh HD:Applications:Utilities:Terminal.app`). You'll see a white screen with black text (**Figure 1.1**) welcoming you to *Darwin* (see the sidebar). You may want to Control-click the Termi-nal icon in the Dock and select Keep in Dock: You'll be using it a lot!

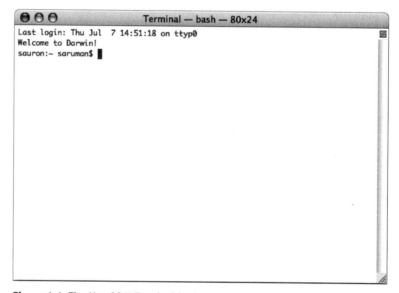

Figure 1.1 The Mac OS X Terminal is the gateway to Unix projects.

Now you can lose the mouse. Why? Unix has been around since the late '60s, long before the era of the graphical user interface (GUI), with its windows, icons, and mice. Everything was text based. You didn't point and click; you typed commands. Although modern Unix environments include a GUI, the real power still lies at the Terminal and in typed commands. Clicking a button may be an easy way to perform a prepackaged action, but it doesn't give you the expressive power of a written set of commands. After all, you don't write scripts by clicking a mouse (even AppleScript scripts); you type them.

On the line following the welcome message, you'll see a *prompt* followed by a cursor. The prompt, as its name suggests, is prompting you, saying, "Terminal is ready and waiting for you to type something."

Your First Commands

You are now expected to type a command on the *command line* and press Return. Unix will then execute the command, and the results, if any, are written back to the Terminal below the command. When a command is not expected to yield any visible results, it will be silent. Accept the philosophy that "no news is good news." Type the following on the command line:

```
$ ls
Desktop      Library      Music       Public
Documents    Movies       Pictures    Sites
$
```

So what have we just done? Typing ls at the prompt launches a Unix *command* (or application) called ls. The lines that follow represent the results, or *output,* of running that command. You should see a list of the files in your home directory. As you might have guessed, *ls* is short for *list*. The output from ls should correspond to what you see in the Mac OS X Finder. It's the same information, presented textually rather than graphically.

Next, display the current working directory (CWD). The CWD is an important concept and is discussed, together with absolute and relative pathnames, in Project 2. Issue the following command:

```
$ pwd
/Users/your-username-here
$
```

The command pwd will print (display on the terminal screen) the CWD and should display the *absolute pathname* to your home directory. In Finder terms, the pwd output says, "the folder your-username-here, inside the folder Users at the top level of the system disk."

Directories and Files

In Unix, the term *directory* is used instead of folder. *Folder* comes from the Desktop analogy and the visual representation of directories by the GUI. The term *file* is often used in a general sense to mean both files and directories. Technically, in Unix, a directory is just a file.

Find Out What the Finder Doesn't Find

Let's try some more commands. Compare the output you get (not shown here) with what you see in the Finder.

First, list the files in the directory /Users—the directory one above your home directory. This example gives one *argument* to ls, which is the directory to list. A command and its argument(s) must be separated by a space.

```
$ ls /Users
```

You may notice that ls lists more files than the Finder shows. The Finder is being slightly dishonest, but in a nice way. It doesn't display Unix system files in which the average user isn't interested.

Next, list files at the top level of the system disk (the Macintosh HD). In Unix, the top level of the system disk is termed the *root* of the file system and is represented by "/". Refer to "Pathnames" in Project 2 for more information.

```
$ ls /
```

Again, you'll notice that ls lists more files than the Finder shows.

List both of the above in one command by giving two arguments to ls, separated by a space.

```
$ ls / /Users
```

Next, list the files in your home directory. The two commands below are equivalent because ls without a pathname argument will assume the CWD.

```
$ ls /Users/your-username-here
$ ls
```

Finally, list files in the directory Documents within your home directory. Again, the two commands below are equivalent. The CWD, relative pathnames, and absolute pathnames are all significant here. See Project 2 for a full explanation.

```
$ ls /Users/your-username-here/Documents
$ ls Documents
```

Command Options

Most Unix commands can be modified with one or more *options*, which change or enhance the command's basic functionality. Options always begin with a dash (-) symbol and are one character long.

Here are some examples of the options available to `ls`. Option `-l` (letter "l") gives a long (more detailed) list.

```
$ ls -l
total 0
drwx------   3 saruman saruman  102  5 May 09:54 Desktop
drwx------  15 saruman saruman  510  4 May 12:11 Documents
drwx------  42 saruman saruman 1428 18 Mar 10:15 Library
...
```

Option `-t` lists files in time order, with the most recently created or modified files shown first. This example shows that many options can be specified together, separated by a space.

```
$ ls -l -t
total 0
drwx------   3 saruman saruman  102  5 May 09:54 Desktop
drwxr-xr-x   5 saruman saruman  170  4 May 22:04 Public
drwx------  15 saruman saruman  510  4 May 12:11 Documents
...
```

Options can be merged, so the following are equivalent.

```
$ ls -l -t
$ ls -lt
```

Cases and Spaces

The Unix file system (UFS) is case sensitive, which means that the file documents is *not* the same file as Documents: The two files can coexist in the same directory. Likewise, Unix commands treat filenames in a case-sensitive manner. For Mac OS X (or, more correctly, Darwin), the situation is complicated somewhat. The default file system is not UFS, but Apple's HFS+, which is *not* case sensitive. However, many of the traditional Unix commands remain case sensitive.

⚓ TIP

Read the Unix manual to find out more about a command and what options it supports. Project 3 shows you how to get the most from the Unix manual.

◣ NOTE

Many code extracts shown in this book are curtailed (to keep the book to a reasonable size). You'll recognize a curtailed extract because it finishes in an ellipsis (...) rather than the dollar prompt.

Multi-letter Options

Commands that originate from the GNU (GNU is Not Unix) Project from the Free Software Foundation have multi-letter options. So as not to confuse these with merged single-letter options, multi-letter options begin with a double-dash (--) and cannot themselves be merged.

⟵ LEARN MORE

**Project 5 tells you more
about the available shells.**

You can ignore case most of the time, but be warned that occasionally you will get caught out.

Spaces in filenames may catch you out, too. Trying to list a directory named `My Directory` will throw an error.

```
$ ls My Directory
ls: Directory: No such file or directory
ls: My: No such file or directory
$
```

Recall that multiple arguments are separated by spaces. To indicate that the space in `"My Directory"` is part of the filename, and not an argument separator, either enclose the file name in quotes, or *escape* the space with a backslash (\) symbol.

```
$ ls "My Directory"
$ ls 'My Directory'
$ ls My\ Directory
```

All About Shells

It's possible to use Unix without being aware of what a shell is, but you won't get the most from your command-line experience if you do not understand this concept. Apple's Terminal application is not a shell; it's an Aqua application that provides a window on your Desktop, a means of reading the keyboard, and a means of displaying text. Terminal then launches a Unix program called a *shell*. The shell displays the prompt. Everything you type at the command line goes to the shell, which interprets what you have typed and acts accordingly. Type `ls /Users`, for example, and the shell will run the command `ls`, passing it the argument `/Users`. The shell will tell `ls` where to send its output (usually back to the Terminal). After `ls` has completed, it stops and returns control to the shell, which then issues another prompt, and the sequence repeats.

The shell performs many other tasks, including setting up redirection and pipelining (Project 6), running shell scripts (Projects 9 and 10), and implementing command-line editing (discussed later in this chapter). Many shells are available, and Darwin comes with most of them.

Have a Bash

You are most likely running the Bash shell if your user account was created by Mac OS X 10.3 or later, or if the prompt ends with a dollar symbol. If your user account was created by an earlier version, or if the prompt ends with a percent (%) symbol, you are most likely running the Tcsh shell. To be absolutely certain which, type the following command and examine the shell name (the part following /bin/ on the output line).

```
$ echo $SHELL
/bin/bash
$
```

Alternatively, use the application NetInfo Manager (see **Figure 1.2**), which you will find in the Utilities folder in Applications at the root of your system disk (Macintosh HD:Applications:Utilities:NetInfo Manager.app).

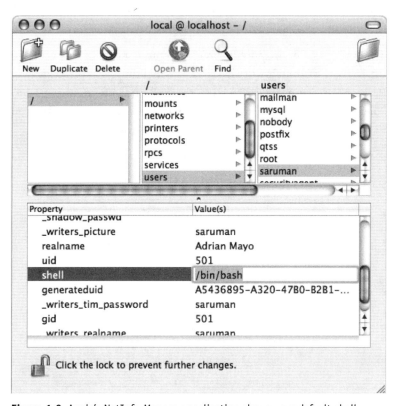

Figure 1.2 Apple's NetInfo Manager application shows your default shell.

ʘ̣ TIP

When you have become familiar with Bash, why not compare it with another shell by simply running the new shell from the command line? For example, explore the Z shell by issuing the following command.

$ zsh

Type exit *when you want to exit Zsh and return to Bash.*

↗ LEARN MORE

Project 4 covers Bash basics and customization.

↗ LEARN MORE

The projects in Chapter 6 help you make the most of your command-line experience.

How to Change the Default Shell

The projects in this book are written assuming the Bash shell. Use NetInfo Manager to change your default shell to Bash permanently. Referring to Figure 1.2, click your username. In the lower pane, scroll down until you see *shell* in the Property pane. Change the value in the Value(s) pane to /bin/bash. You must authenticate first by clicking the lock icon in the lower left corner and entering your administrator password. Press Command-s to save; then click Update this Copy. Close NetInfo and start a new Terminal session. Your prompt should now end with a dollar symbol. If the shell has not changed, quit and restart Terminal.

Command-Line Editing

You'll probably spend a lot of time using Terminal and Bash, so it's worthwhile getting to know more about them. Bash can be customized in many ways to suit your style of working.

The ability to recall and edit previous command lines can be a big time-saver—so much so that it's worth mentioning separately here. Press the up arrow key (cursor-up) to recall previous command lines. The left and right arrow keys, and the Backspace key, work as expected to edit the command line. Useful editing keystrokes include:

- ▸ Control-a to move to the start of the line
- ▸ Control-e to move to the end of the line
- ▸ Control-k to delete from the cursor to the end of line
- ▸ Control-u to delete from the cursor to the start of the line

Project 2
Learn Basic Unix

This project will familiarize you with commands used to view and manipulate files and directories. It also covers Unix concepts such as the current working directory, pathnames, mounted volumes, and recursion.

Pathnames

README.txt is a file. There may be any number of files with that name in the file system. To describe one particular README.txt file unambiguously, it is necessary to give the full pathname to that file. A *pathname* describes the location of a file, starting from the root of the file system, and listing each directory that must be traveled to reach the file. One particular README.txt file can be described unambiguously with the following pathname.

/Users/your-username-here/Documents/importantinfo/README.txt

A pathname that starts at the root of the file system is termed an *absolute pathname.* However, absolute pathnames require much typing. When one gives directions in real life, especially to local places, it makes sense to assume that the starting point is "right here." Similarly, Unix has a "right here" called the Current Working Directory (CWD). If a pathname does not begin with a slash (/) symbol, the starting point is assumed to be the CWD instead of the file-system root. When you start a new Terminal window, CWD is set to be your home directory (/Users/your-username-here). Thus, the absolute pathname given above is equivalent to the *relative pathname.*

Documents/importantinfo/README.txt

Absolute and relative pathnames can be used wherever a command requires a filename as an argument. For example, let's display the CWD using the command pwd. (My username is saruman.)

```
$ pwd
/Users/saruman
```

The / and : Dilemma

Unix uses a forward slash (/) symbol as a separator, so it is not possible to use it in a filename. The Finder uses a colon (:) symbol, and similarly, this cannot be used in a filename. You might see a dilemma here, where one system creates a filename that is illegal in the other. What happens is that the two characters are transposed as the filename is written or viewed in the different systems.

Next, let's list the contents of my Documents directory, using an absolute pathname.

```
$ ls /Users/saruman/Documents
AppleWorks User Data    HouseHold        iChats
Connections             Job              importantinfo
Letters
```

This time, we'll use a relative pathname on the assumption that the CWD is /Users/saruman.

```
$ ls Documents
AppleWorks User Data    HouseHold        iChats
Connections             Job              importantinfo
Letters
```

Finally, by preceding Documents with a "/" symbol, we are specifying an absolute pathname implying that the directory lies in the file-system root, which it doesn't.

```
$ ls /Documents
ls: /Documents: No such file or directory
```

Basic Commands

This section gives a brief overview of the most essential Unix commands. To find out more about these and others, use the Unix manual (see Project 3). Most projects in this book are task-focused rather than command-focused and teach how to use a command, or many commands together, to complete a particular task.

Changing the CWD

Sometimes the files you are working on are not in your home directory or are a couple of directories into it. In this situation, it's convenient to set up a new base camp by moving your CWD. Use the command cd to achieve this. Naturally, the argument to cd can be either a relative or an absolute pathname, but must be a directory name and not a filename. First, let's display the CWD and list the directory Sites/images. We use a relative pathname and assume that Sites lies in the current directory.

```
$ pwd
/Users/saruman
$ ls Sites/images
apache_pb.gif  macosxlogo.gif  web_share.gif
```

Next, we change the CWD to Sites/images, enabling us to issue a simple ls command without specifying the directory name.

```
$ cd Sites/images
$ pwd
/Users/saruman/Sites/images
$ ls
apache_pb.gif  macosxlogo.gif  web_share.gif
```

View Files with less and cat

Use the command less to view text files on the Terminal. It displays them a pageful at a time. The command less is not an editor; it only displays files.

```
$ cd ~
$ less Sites/index.html
...
```

To move forward through the file a page at a time, press the spacebar. To move back and forth one line at a time, use the cursor keys (up arrow and down arrow). To finish viewing and return to the command line, press q. Other useful keystrokes include

▶   u and d to move up and down a half-page

▶   Control-g to display a status line

▶   /word and then Return to forward-search for word

▶   ?word and then Return to backward-search for word

▶   n to search for the next occurrence of *word*

The command cat displays a file all in one go, without pausing at each pageful.

☀ TIP

Issue the command cd *with no arguments to change the CWD to your default home directory.*

☀ TIP

The tilde (~) symbol is shorthand for the absolute pathname of your home directory. The command ls ~/Art *lists the contents of directory* Art *in your home directory, no matter what the CWD is set to. It's always equivalent to the command* ls /Users/[username]/Art.

⟋ LEARN MORE

Projects 13 and 14 tell you more about changing your CWD.

⟋ LEARN MORE

The projects in Chapter 4 tell you more about editing files in Unix.

⟋ LEARN MORE

Projects 21 and 22 tell you more about viewing files.

ℹ TIP

Use option -p *with* copy *to preserve file metadata such as the time stamp, the file owner, and file permissions.*

Copy Files

The command cp makes a copy of a file, taking as arguments the pathname of the file to be copied and the pathname of the new copy, in that order and separated by a space. The copy can be placed in the CWD or any other directory.

If the file copy is being placed in the same directory as the original file, you must give it a name different from the original's. Here, we create a copy of index.html named index2.html. Let's check what files we have and then apply the copy command.

```
$ cd ~/Sites
$ ls
images  index.html
$ cp index.html index2.html
$ ls
images  index.html  index2.html
```

To copy to another directory, and perhaps rename the copied file too, specify a pathname including a new filename.

```
$ cp index.html /Users/Shared/home.html
```

If you're copying to another directory, use that directory's name as your final argument instead of a filename, and the copied file will keep the same name as the original. This procedure makes it easy to copy many files at once to a new directory: Just list all the filenames to be copied as arguments, followed by the name of the directory into which all the files are to be copied.

```
$ cd images
$ ls
apache_pb.gif macosxlogo.gif  web_share.gif
$ cp apache_pb.gif macosxlogo.gif /Users/Shared/
$ ls /Users/Shared/
GarageBand Demo Songs   apache_pb.gif       macosxlogo.gif
SC Info                 home.html
```

Delete Files

Use the command rm to delete (remove) a file. These examples delete the files created by the cp examples above.

```
$ cd ~/Sites
$ ls
images   index.html   index2.html
$ rm index2.html
$ rm /Users/Shared/home.html
$ rm /Users/Shared/apache_pb.gif /Users/Shared/macosxlogo.gif
```

Move Files

Use the command mv to move or rename a file. To move a file, simply give the original pathname and the new pathname as arguments.

First, let's set the CWD to be Sites and see what files it contains.

```
$ cd ~/Sites
$ ls
images   index.html
```

Now let's move index.html to the directory /Users/Shared.

```
$ mv index.html /Users/Shared/index.html
```

Check that the file has moved.

```
$ ls
images
$ ls /Users/Shared/
GarageBand Demo Songs   SC Info            index.html
```

A file can be renamed as it is moved.

```
$ mv index.html /Users/Shared/home.html
```

The command mv is also used to rename a file *without* moving it, so it is the command we use to rename files.

```
$ mv index.html home.html
```

TIP

With mv, *you need not name the destination file if it has the same name as the source file. To move the file* index.html *to* /Users/Shared/index.html, *simply type*

```
$ mv index.html ¬
    /Users/Shared/
```

Touch Me

Touch is an easy way to create a new (empty) file, although its real purpose is to alter the timestamp of an existing file.

As with copying, many files can be moved to a destination directory in one go.

```
$ cd images
$ mv apache_pb.gif macosxlogo.gif /Users/Shared/
```

If you follow these examples, don't forget to move the files back to their original locations.

```
$ mv /Users/Shared/index.html ~/Sites/
$ mv /Users/Shared/apache_pb.gif ~/Sites/images/
$ mv /Users/Shared/macosxlogo.gif ~/Sites/images/
```

It's Goodbye, Not Au Revoir

❗ WARNING

Unix assumes you know what you are doing. If you remove a file, for example, that file will be removed; it won't be placed in the Trash, and you won't be asked for confirmation. The file will never been seen again. It's goodbye, not au revoir. (This assumes you have the necessary permissions to delete the file.) If you copy file-one to file-two, and file-two already exists, file-two will be overwritten. Gone. The same applies to moving files. Move file-one to file-two, and if file-two already exists, it will be overwritten. The old file-two will be gone. If this behavior makes you a little nervous, option -i may help calm you.

Create two files.

```
$ touch x y
```

Try to rename x to y, with and without the option -i. The first line will prompt you, asking whether you really want to overwrite y; the second line won't. (The second line will fail if you previously allowed the first to proceed.)

```
$ mv -i x y
$ mv x y
```

Using the -i option with the copy command also generates a confirmation prompt.

```
$ cp -i x y
$ cp x y
```

It works for file removal, too.

```
$ rm -i x y
$ rm x y
```

In the above examples, option -i specifies interactive mode.

! WARNING

The Mac OS X file system (called HFS+) allows each file two *forks*: the *data fork*, which is the normal data contents of the file, and a special *resource fork*. The resource fork contains file metadata, such as the creator application, a custom icon, and perhaps a preview if the file holds an image. Unix does not recognize resource forks, so if you were to copy a file using the Unix cp command, only the data fork would be copied: The resource fork is lost.

Having said that, as of Mac OS X 10.4 (Tiger), many Utilities have been written to understand resource forks. To quote the Apple documentation on the subject:

> *Extended attributes. Tiger introduces a new level of file system sophistication with vfs-level support for extended attributes, inspired by the POSIX.2e proposal. These include *xattr routines to read, write, list, and delete extended attributes. Extended attributes are stored natively on HFS+ as forks and emulated on other file systems via the AppleDouble format (that is, "._filename"). This provides a consistent, Darwin-level API for managing resource forks, metadata, security information, properties, and other attributes.*
>
> *cp, mv, scp, emacs, vim, pico. Properly handle HFS+ resource forks using the new extended attribute APIs, as do archivers such as tar, rsync, gzip, bzip2, and cpio.*

⚓ TIP

Use the command echo *as an easy way to create a short file containing a line of text. For example,*

```
$ echo "This is file ¬
    one" > file1
```

creates file1 *containing the specified text. Project 10 has more examples that use* echo.

↗ LEARN MORE

Projects 11 and 12 explain the concept of globbing or wildcard expansion.

Multiple Files

Most commands are happy to operate on more than one file at a time, as shown in the examples above. Sometimes it's handy to be able to say "all files" or "all JPEG files" instead of naming them individually. This concept comes under the strange name of *globbing* or *wildcard expansion* and is implemented by all shells.

Commands for Directories

The use of directories to organize and manipulate multiple files is an important Unix skill. Some commands operate on directories the same way they do other files, but there are also some directory-specific commands you must know.

Create a Directory

Use the command mkdir to create a new, empty directory.

```
$ ls
Desktop     Library    Music      Public
Documents   Movies     Pictures   Sites
$ mkdir Projects
```

The command ls will show a new directory called Projects.

```
$ ls
Desktop     Library    Music      Projects   Sites
Documents   Movies     Pictures   Public
```

Remove a Directory

Use the command rmdir to delete (or remove) an *empty* directory.

```
$ rmdir Projects
```

The command rmdir won't remove a directory that is not empty. You must use the command rm recursively (see "Recursion" later in this chapter).

Copy and Move a Directory

The commands cp and mv, described earlier in this chapter, can be applied to directories. The command mv can be used for directories in exactly the same way as it is used for files and can move and/or rename a directory. The command cp must be used recursively (see the following section, "Recursion").

Recursion

Recursion occurs when an operation applied to a directory is reapplied to each item it contains. The recursive use of ls on your home directory, for example, will list the files and directories it contains, the contents of *those* directories and any directories *they* contain, and so on until it lists every one of your files. The commands cp and rm have a recursive option where they can be used to copy and remove whole directory hierarchies.

The following example illustrates the use of recursion with ls.

First, we use mkdir to create two directories: outer and, inside it, inner.

```
$ mkdir -p outer/inner
```

Now we use the touch command to create files called file1 and file2 in the outer directory and file3 and file4 in the inner directory.

```
$ touch outer/file1 outer/file2
$ touch outer/inner/file3 outer/inner/file4
```

Now we list the contents of outer, using ls and activating recursion with option -R.

```
$ ls -R outer
file1   file2   inner

outer/inner:
file3   file4
$
```

Notice that ls did not stop once it had listed the contents of outer but continued with inner and listed its contents, too. Many other commands operate recursively, using option -R or -r.

Copy a Directory

To copy the entire contents of a directory, including nested directories and their contents too, use cp in recursive mode by specifying option -R. Here, we copy outer and all of its files, including inner and all of its files, to a new directory called outer-new.

```
$ cp -R outer outer-new
$ ls -R outer-new
file1    file2    inner

outer-new/inner:
file3    file4
$
```

Remove a Directory

To remove a nonempty directory, use a recursive remove by specifying option -R or -r.

```
$ rm -ri outer-new
examine files in directory outer-new? y
remove outer-new/file1? y
remove outer-new/file2? y
examine files in directory outer-new/inner? y
remove outer-new/inner/file3? y
remove outer-new/inner/file4? y
remove outer-new/inner? y
remove outer-new? y
$
```

Remember that rm removes a file completely and does not prompt for confirmation. The recursive use of rm can be very destructive if you accidentally give it the wrong directory to remove. Here, we have used option -i to be on the safe side. If you feel confident, remove outer, too, without the safety net.

```
$ rm -r outer
```

Dotty Files

Issue the following commands in your home directory.

```
$ touch .hidden
$ ls
```

The file you just created is not there! Why? Files that begin with a dot (period) are hidden. A hidden file is no different from a normal file, other than the fact that its name begins with a dot and the fact that ls does not show it. A hidden file is often used to hold configuration information that does not need to be viewed or changed regularly. Hiding prevents visual clutter in the directory listing. View hidden files by applying the -a option to ls.

```
$ ls -a
.                       .bash_history       Movies
..                      .hidden             Music
.CFUserTextEncoding     Desktop             Pictures
.DS_Store               Documents           Public
.Trash                  Library             Sites
```

Now you see .hidden. You will also notice that the first two files listed are dot and dot-dot. There may be other files that start with a dot too, like .Trash, which is used by the Finder to hold items you have put in the trash. The files dot and dot-dot are present in every directory and are shorthand (akin to Finder aliases) for the current directory (dot) and its parent directory (dot-dot). When you type dot at the start of a pathname, it's equivalent to typing the absolute pathname of the current directory. When you type dot-dot, it's equivalent to typing the absolute pathname of the directory just above the current directory. Issue the following commands from your home directory (the output is not shown).

```
$ ls .
$ ls ..
```

↗ LEARN MORE

The dot and dot-dot files are actually hard links to their respective directories. Project 19 tells you more about Unix links.

↗ LEARN MORE

If you wish to know more about permissions, users, and groups, read Projects 7 and 8.

The command `ls .` lists the contents the current directory and is equivalent to a simple `ls`. The command `ls ..` lists the contents of the parent directory, which, from your home directory, should be `/Users`. Dot and dot-dot can be used anywhere an absolute pathname can. Dot comes in handy when you want to say "here." The three lines below are equivalent.

```
$ mv Sites/index.html .
$ mv Sites/index.html index.html
$ mv Sites/index.html ./index.html
```

Dot-dot is handy when you want to move the CWD up a level . . .

```
$ cd ..
```

. . . or two.

```
$ cd ../..
```

How to Become the Root User

You are no doubt aware of the concept of file permissions in Mac OS X. You may have tried to edit or delete a file and been denied permission, or have had to install a new application using an administrator account.

With respect to permissions, users can be divided into three groups:

▶   Normal (nonadministrative) users, who are able to modify files in their home directories but only view or execute files outside them.

▶   Administrative users, who are also able to create and modify files in certain directories outside their home directory, such as `/Applications`.

▶   The all-powerful root user, who can override permissions and who has the power to change everything except your bank balance.

Some projects require write access to system files, so you must become the root user temporarily. You achieve this in one of two ways. To become the root user for the duration of a single command, use the command `sudo`. Simply type `sudo` before the command you wish to issue as root. For example, only root can write to the `crontab` file in `/etc`.

```
$ touch /etc/crontab
touch: /etc/crontab: Permission denied
$
```

That attempt failed, so let's do the same operation, but running as user root.

```
$ sudo touch /etc/crontab

We trust you have received the usual lecture from the
Administrator. It usually boils down to these two things:

        #1) Respect the privacy of others.
        #2) Think before you type.


Password:
$
```

At the password prompt, type your administrator password. Nothing will be echoed back as you type. (You'll not be prompted for the password again if you issue another sudo command within the next five minutes.) The touch command will now (silently) succeed.

A nonadministrator user cannot use sudo. This is by design to prevent normal users from escalating their privileges.

```
$ sudo touch /etc/crontab
Password:
loraine is not in the sudoers file.
This incident will be reported.
```

Naughty!

The second way to become the root user is to start a root shell, again using sudo.

```
$ sudo -s
Password:
#
```

Option -s tells sudo to start a new shell running as user root. You'll notice no difference except that you are now root, and your every command will be honored. Unless you have altered the default prompt, it will end with a hash (#) symbol to indicate (warn you of) a root shell. You may now delete essential system files and completely hose Mac OS X. I wouldn't recommend that you do so, but when you're root, nothing is going to argue with you!

Having attained a root shell, do what you need to do, *thinking before you type*. When you have completed your task, type exit to exit the root shell. Now you can relax and reflect on the fact that in the days before Mac OS X, you effectively did everything as root!

! WARNING

Running as root gives you full access to Mac OS X system files. Incorrect or ill-advised commands can seriously damage the health of your Mac.

Partitions and Disks

As we've seen, the *path separator* in Unix, used in pathnames to denote levels in directory hierarchy, is the forward slash (/) symbol. The first level of every absolute pathname, the system disk, has no name; that's why an absolute path always starts with /. In fact, in Unix, no volume (disk or partition) has a name. This is at odds with the Mac OS X Finder, which gives all volumes names. Another difference between Unix and the Finder, and one that can lend confusion, is the way volumes other than the active system disk appear in pathnames. In the Finder, mounted volumes such as CD-ROMs, external drives, and file servers are represented on a peer level with the system hard drive. In Unix, nothing is on a peer level with the system disk; all other volumes are mounted within it, and their pathnames are listed under its root. This leads to an obvious question: "How do I view a mounted disk from the command line?"

When a disk is mounted, it's mounted into a directory, which can be any directory anywhere on the file system but is generally one created specifically for the mount and named appropriately. Darwin automatically mounts all volumes at /Volumes/name-of-vol-in-finder. If you have a mounted volume named Backup, it will appear as /Volumes/Backup. Just treat it like you would any other directory.

```
$ ls /Volumes
Macintosh HD        Backup
$ ls /Volumes/Backup
Music               System              Users
$ cd /Volumes/Backup/Users
$ ls
Shared              saruman
```

Further Projects

Refer to these projects to see other essential Unix commands in action:

▶ grep Project 23

▶ find Projects 15, 17, 18, and 20

▶ awk Projects 60 and 62

Refer to these projects to learn more essential Unix:

▶ Globbing Projects 11 and 12

▶ Regular expressions Projects 77 and 78

▶ Hard and soft links Project 19

▶ Editing files Chapter 4

Refer to these projects to gain practical experience in some commonly performed tasks:

▶ Finding files Projects 15, 17, 18, and 20

▶ Searching files by content Project 23

▶ Compressing files Project 27

⚓ TIP

The man *command itself has a manual page!*

Project 3
Get the Most from
the Unix Manual

This project introduces the Unix manual—the system of "help files" that explains Unix commands. It shows how the manual works, how to use it most effectively to learn commands, and how to discover new ones.

Without the visual clues afforded by a graphical interface, Unix commands can be difficult to use. Fortunately, all (almost all) commands include documentation on what they do, the options they provide, and how to use them. When a Unix command is installed, a manual page is installed too. All manual pages are accessible via the command man. If you are not sure how to use a command, read its manual page. Let's have a look at the man page for ls.

```
$ man ls
LS(1)              BSD General Commands Manual              LS(1)


NAME
     ls -- list directory contents


SYNOPSIS
     ls [-ABCFGHLPRTWZabcdefghiklmnopqrstuwx1] [file ...]


DESCRIPTION
     For each operand that names a file of a type ...
     -A        List all entries except for . and ...
...
```

A manual page is displayed a screenful at a time. Press Return to scroll line by line, the spacebar to scroll screen by screen, and q to quit. The style of manual pages is more reference than tutorial. The pages do not make light reading, but the necessary information is there. Almost all man pages have the same basic format:

- SYNOPSIS. Lists the available options followed by mandatory and optional arguments. Items enclosed in [square brackets] are optional, and those followed by an ellipsis (...) can be repeated any number of times.

- DESCRIPTION. Includes a list of options that may be given to the command. This is probably the most useful part of the man page.

- EXAMPLES. Useful but generally underused. If the rest of the man page is hard going, refer to this section.

- SEE ALSO. If the command does not quite hit the spot, check this section for related commands.

- FILES. Where a command reads system files, perhaps for configuration information, this section will name them.

Search by Keyword

You may want to perform a certain task but cannot think of a suitable Unix command that might do so. You might flip through this book looking for a suitable project. Alternatively, man provides a search option -k to locate a suitable command by keyword lookup. There's also a command called apropos that's equivalent to man -k; either can be used.

As an example, locate commands to change the owner of a file thus.

```
$ man -k owner
Tk_OwnSelection(3tcl) - make a window the owner of ...
chown(2), fchown(2), lchown(2) - change owner and g...
chown(8)                - change file owner and gr...
XSetSelectionOwner(3), XGetSelectionOwner(3), Xconv...
XtOwnSelection(3), XtDisownSe... - set selection owner
```

You'll notice that each command name has a bracketed number after it. The number is the manual section in which the command is documented. Manual sections are covered later; for now, consider just commands from sections 1 and 8. The command we want is chown, but chown(8), not chown(2). Look up the chown variant from Section 8 by specifying the section number.

```
$ man 8 chown
```

TIP

The job of displaying man pages is given to the command less. *Refer to Project 2 for more information on using* less. *Alternatively, just type* man less. *To save scrolling through the manual looking for a particular section, use search. Type* /SEE ALSO; *then press Return to jump straight to the SEE ALSO section. Because* man *uses* less *to display its results, you are able to search a manual page by typing* /searchterm *and then pressing Return.*

NOTE

The results you see from running man -k *and* whatis *may vary if you have not installed Apple's Developer Tools or X11.*

NOTE

In versions of Mac OS X prior to 10.4 (Tiger), whatis *searches the entire synopsis line like* apropos *but matches only whole words.*

makewhatis.local

There's also a command called makewhatis.local that operates only on locally mounted file systems. It's not prudent to rebuild the databases on another machine.

LEARN MORE

Project 72 tells you more about periodic maintenance, and Projects 70 and 71 cover execution of scheduled commands.

TIP

The keyword given to apropos *and* whatis *is treated as a regular expression, so you can realize more selective searches by using a (quoted) regular expression instead of a plain word. Project 77 covers regular expressions.*

When you request a keyword search, man searches the synopsis line of every manual page, attempting to match the keyword. The match is not case sensitive, and the keyword may match either a complete word or a partial word. Try searching for own instead of owner, and you'll get a lot more matches.

whatis

The command man -f or its equivalent, whatis, displays the synopsis line of the given command, making for a quick reminder as to what the command does.

```
$ whatis chown
chown(2), fchown(2), lchown(2) - change owner and grou...
chown(8)                       - change file owner and group
```

Whereas apropos matches a complete or partial word across the entire synopsis line, whatis matches only complete command names.

The whatis Database

To speed searching, man, apropos, and whatis do not read man pages directly, but rely on a prebuilt database containing all synopsis lines. The database is rebuilt automatically each week, but only when your Mac is switched on during the early hours of Saturday. If this is not the case, or if you have recently added new commands, you may have to build or update the whatis database manually.

You will most likely have whatis databases in the following directories:

▶ /usr/share/man for standard OS X commands

▶ /usr/local/man for commands you have installed yourself

▶ /usr/X11R6/man for X11 commands

Rebuild any or all of the above databases with the command makewhatis. To rebuild /usr/share/man/whatis (/usr/share/man/ whatis.db pre 10.4, or Tiger), use the following command, typing your administrator password when prompted.

```
$ sudo /usr/libexec/makewhatis /usr/share/man
Password:
$
```

The Nine Manual Sections

The Unix manual is divided into nine sections, and the manual page for a command is listed in the section most appropriate to the command's function. These are the sections, listed in order of general usefulness:

▶ Section (1) user commands

▶ Section (8) system commands

▶ Section (5) configuration file formats

▶ Sections (6), (7) miscellaneous

▶ Sections (2), (3), (4) library calls for programmers

▶ Section (9) kernel developer's manual

The command man searches for a command section by section and returns the first entry it finds. Therefore, if a command of the same name lies in more than one section, man will display only the first one it finds. Although the command chown appears in sections (2) and (8), only the variant from section (8) is displayed. The command man searches sections in order of general usefulness, which may or may not correspond to the order given above. Unless you are a developer looking for library calls, man will return the command you want. If necessary, tell man to consider a specific section by specifying the section number or to return results from all sections by specifying option -a.

```
$ man 2 chown
$ man -a chown
```

Find out more about a manual section with

```
$ man <section number> intro
```

🛈 TIP

Generate a list all the commands in a particular section by clever use of apropos. To list the commands in section (1), sorting them in order, type

```
$ apropos "(1)" | ¬
    sort -df
```

The Man Pager

Pager refers to the command used to display man pages on the Terminal. By default, it's the command `less -is` (or the command `more` on Mac OS X 10.2 and earlier). Set the environment variable MANPAGER to change it. To use the vim editor, for example, set MANPAGER as follows.

```
$ declare -x MANPAGER="
col -b | vim -"
```

Refer to Project 4 if you wish to learn more about environment variables.

In pre-10.4 versions of Mac OS X, set PAGER instead of MANPAGER.

↗ LEARN MORE

Project 6 tells you all about redirection and pipelining.

ᴛ̈ TIP

Some useful man *entries are*

```
$ man hier
$ man ascii
$ man re_format
$ man samba
```

Many commands have entries in the GNU info *system. Try the following:*

```
$ info ls
$ info info
```

Example of man Use

Here's a brief example of using the manual to answer the question "How do I mount a file system?" First, use `apropos` on the term mount.

```
$ apropos mount
...
mount(8)                        - mount file systems
```

The most appropriate candidate is `mount` from section (8). Next, read the man page for `mount`.

```
$ man 8 mount
MOUNT(8)          BSD System Manager's Manual          MOUNT(8)
...
DESCRIPTION
     The mount command .....  If either special or node...
     the information is taken from the fstab(5) file.
...
FILES
     /etc/fstab   file system table
SEE ALSO
     mount(2), fstab(5), mount_afp(8), mount_cd9660(8)...
...
```

The DESCRIPTION section refers to the file fstab(5), and you'll also see a reference to this in the SEE ALSO section. The reference includes (5); this is a clue saying that more information on the format of fstab can be found by issuing the command `man 5 fstab`. Looking at the FILES section also tells us the absolute pathname of fstab.

```
$ man 5 fstab
FSTAB(5)          BSD File Formats Manual          FSTAB(5)

NAME
     fstab -- static information about the filesystems
...
```

Project 4
Learn Bash Shell Basics

This project provides an overview of the Bash shell and its features, and introduces techniques for customizing it to enhance your command-line experience. Awareness of the Bash basics will increase your productivity and improve life at the command line.

You'll spend much of your Unix time talking to Bash through Terminal. Both can be customized, and Bash has many features and facilities to help increase your productivity and make your command-line experience more pleasant. This is a large and important subject area—so much so that an entire chapter, Chapter 6, is devoted to it. This project covers enough Bash for everyday use and for tackling the projects in this book. Follow the links given to projects in Chapter 6 when you need more detailed knowledge of a particular subject area.

Entering Commands

Entering a command is the most basic and frequent task you'll perform in Bash, so it makes sense to simplify it as much as possible. To this end, Bash provides auto completion, command-line history, and command-line editing. This section will get you started on all three.

Auto Completion

Auto completion will probably save you more time and typing than any other feature. You need type only the first few characters of a command or filename, enough to make it unambiguous, and Bash will complete the rest for you. For this exercise, change into your home directory. We are going to list Documents, using autocompletion to do most of the typing for us. Type ls and just Do for documents, and then press the Tab key. Bash will complete the directory name for you, and you need only press Return. Seven keystrokes versus thirteen is a big savings.

```
$ cd
$ ls Do<tab>
$ ls Documents/
```

↗ LEARN MORE

Autocompletion is case sensitive, and typing `ls do<tab>` **will not work as you might expect. Project 45 shows you how to make autocompletion case insensitive.**

If the filename you type is ambiguous—D, for example, could be Desktop or Documents—pressing Tab will have no effect. Continue typing until the filename is unambiguous; then press Tab. If you need a hint, press Tab twice, and Bash will list the possible completions for you.

```
$ ls D<tab><tab>
Desktop    Documents
$ ls Do<tab>
$ ls Documents/
```

Command names can also be autocompleted by pressing Tab, with the same rules applying for ambiguity and case sensitivity. Thus, the command apropos can be abbreviated apr<tab>.

Command-Line History

Bash remembers every command you type in its *command-line history*. Press the up arrow key (cursor-up) to recall previous command lines and the down arrow key (cursor-down) to move in the opposite direction. When you exit a shell, all the commands you typed are saved to a file in your home directory called .bash_history, and when you return, they are read back in again. You can view the history by typing

```
$ history
    1  ls -R
    2  cd
    3  ls
    4  ls Documents/
    5  history
$
```

Previous command lines can be recalled and edited. Press Control-r; then start typing a command. As you type, the history will be reverse-searched for the first line that matches what you have typed so far. For example, press Control-r and then type ls. Assuming that you issued command ls Documents recently, Bash will complete the command line for you. Press Return to execute it.

```
$ Control-r
(reverse-i-search)`ls': ls Documents/
```

If this is not the command you are looking for, either type more characters to identify the command fully or press Control-r repeatedly until the desired command is found. Each press of Control-r causes Bash to search farther back in history for a matching command.

Command-Line Editing

Any command recalled from the history can be edited. After pressing Control-r to recall a command, press Escape to edit it instead of Return. The left and right arrow keys, and the Backspace keys, work as expected. Useful editing keystrokes include

▶ Control-a to move to the start of the line

▶ Control-e to move to the end of the line

▶ Control-k to delete from the cursor to the end of line

▶ Control-u to delete from the cursor to the start of the line

Aliases and Functions

Bash supports the definition of aliases and functions. An *alias* can be defined to be a complete or partial command line. When it's used as the first word on a command line, Bash replaces it with its definition.

Here's an alias called ll that creates a shortcut for the command ls -al. Enclose the definition in single quotes to ensure that the shell doesn't interpret the definition before it's assigned to the alias.

```
$ alias ll='ls -al'
```

To use the alias, simply type its name and press Return.

```
$ ll
total 280
drwxr-xr-x  45 saruman   saruman 1530 May 10 14:13 .
drwxrwxr-t  18 root      admin    612 Apr  9 18:22 ..
...
drwx------  13 saruman   saruman  442 Apr 14 13:25 Pictures
drwxr-xr-x   5 saruman   saruman  170 May  4 22:04 Public
drwxr-xr-x  25 saruman   saruman  850 Apr 16 15:24 Sites
```

TIP

It's not necessary to type the first letters of the command you wish to search for. Pressing Control-r and typing Doc *will initiate a search for previous commands that contain* Doc, *not just those that begin with* Doc.

LEARN MORE

Project 48 shows you how to increase the number of commands saved in the command-line history and how to stop sensitive commands from entering it. Project 49 gives you more ways to recall information from the command-line history.

LEARN MORE

Project 53 tells you more about command-line editing.

TIP

Project 80 teaches you the black art of shell quoting.

✎ NOTE

A Bash alias is not the same as a Finder alias.

An alias need not form the complete command line. It will accept arguments and option settings that work with the command it's based upon.

```
$ ll Sites
. . .
```

If you always use a particular command with a specific set of its options turned on, an alias can save typing: Just make the generic command name an alias for the option-enabled version. This technique is used below to make sure the safe -i option is used by default with commands cp, mv, and rm. (See "It's Goodbye, Not Au Revoir" in Project 2 for a recap of why this is a good precaution.)

Type the following lines of code.

```
$ alias cp='cp -i'
$ alias mv='mv -i'
$ alias rm='rm -i'
```

Used without options or arguments, the alias command displays the definitions of aliases you've set up.

To remove an alias you've created, you can use the unalias command. Use it to delete the ll alias you made earlier.

```
$ unalias ll
```

Fun with Functions

Functions are similar to aliases, but they can include arguments as well as commands and are often more complex. As an example, a good candidate for use in a function is this command sequence.

```
$ ls -al <directory> | less
```

The sequence performs a handy task: It generates a long listing of the specified directory and hands the list off to command less, which ensures that the list is displayed one page at a time without overflowing the length of the Terminal window.

Our new function, which we'll call lll, encapsulates this useful sequence as a custom command, which takes a directory pathname as its argument. After we've defined it, simply typing lll <directory> will display the directory's long listing in less.

Type the following carefully to define the function. Don't worry too much about the unfamiliar characters; we'll discuss them at greater length later on. And don't panic when Bash changes its prompt from $ to > when you start a new line; that's its way of saying, "You pressed Return, but I don't have enough information to execute a command, so keep typing."

```
$ lll() {
> ls -al $* | less
> }
$
```

List all currently defined functions, using command declare -f, and you'll see that Bash now recognizes our new function:

```
$ declare -f
lll ()
{
    ls -al $* | less
}
$
```

The final example shows how lll could be defined in a single line: Note that the space after the first brace and the semicolon after less are necessary.

```
$ lll() { ls -al $* | less;}
```

To use the function, simply type its name followed by any arguments.

```
$ lll Sites Documents Library
```

Make them Permanent

An alias or function is good only for the current shell session. If you start a new shell session, all alias and function definitions are lost. To make them permanent, you must define them during the shell's

⤴ **LEARN MORE**

Project 51 explores Bash aliases at greater length, and Project 52 explores Bash functions.

startup sequence by adding the definitions to one of Bash's startup files. See "Bash Initialization" later in this chapter.

Shell and Environment Variables

Shell and environment variables hold values that can be recalled and used later. Shell variables are local to the current shell session. If you run another command, like `ls`, `bash`, or `zsh`, that command does not inherit (cannot see) shell variables from the current shell session. Environment variables, however, *are* inherited by new commands, which means they *can* be seen.

Shell Variables

A *shell variable* is used to record, and later recall, a value. The command line `var='value'` sets shell variable *var* to the value *value*. Introducing a variable with a dollar symbol, using format `$var`, causes the shell to *expand* the variable, replacing it with its value. Here's how to set and use a shell variable called `sites`.

```
$ sites='/Users/saruman/Sites'
$ ls $sites
images          index.html
```

In the example above, Bash expands the command

```
$ ls $sites
```

to

```
$ ls /Users/saruman/Sites
```

Use echo to display the contents of a variable.

```
$ echo $sites
/Users/saruman/Sites
```

Shell variables are most often used in *shell scripts,* which are discussed in detail in Chapter 9. A shell variable is visible only to the shell in which it was set. Other commands launched by the shell do not have visibility to those variables.

Use either `set` or `declare` to list all shell variables and their values. (The `set` and `declare` commands list environment variables too.) To remove a variable, use the `unset` command. You'll notice that many shell variables are already set, including `HOME`.

You may use existing variables within the declarations for new ones, as in this example, which uses the preset variable `HOME` to reset the variable `sites` you just created.

```
$ sites="$HOME/Sites"
```

Run the `echo` command on `sites` again, and you'll see that it expands the same way, whether it's set using the `HOME` variable short-cut or the full pathname to the `Sites` directory. Using preset variables like `HOME` not only saves typing, but also lets you set variables in a way that will work for all users, no matter what their home directory is.

```
$ echo $sites
/Users/saruman/Sites
```

The shell expanded `$HOME` when the variable `sites` was initialized. Notice the use of double quotes here, versus single quotes in previous examples. Bash *does not* look inside single quotes to expand variables and therefore would not have expanded `$HOME`. Bash *does* look inside double quotes and hence *does* expand `$HOME`.

Environment Variables

What differentiates a shell variable from an environment variable is its *scope*. Whereas shell variables are particular to the defining instance of Bash (or whatever shell you are running), environment variables are part of the environment inherited by all commands launched by the shell. When you set an environment variable in Bash, any command run from that shell (like `man` or `ls`) inherits the variable and can read its value. This also applies when you run Bash itself, or `zsh`, as they are just regular commands too.

Traditionally, environment variables are in uppercase, and user-defined shell variables are in lowercase. The command `env` lists all environment variables and, unlike `set` and `declare`, does not list shell variables or functions.

⬈ LEARN MORE

Project 80 explores the mysterious world of shell quoting.

To turn a shell variable into an environment variable, it must be exported from the shell (made part of the environment). Use either the export command

```
$ SITES="$HOME/Sites"
$ export SITES
```

or the declare command. Option -x says to export the variable just declared.

```
$ declare -x SITES="$HOME/Sites"
```

Issue command env to check that SITES has been correctly defined and exported as an environment variable.

```
$ env
TERM_PROGRAM=Apple_Terminal
TERM=xterm-color
SHELL=/bin/bash
SITES=/Users/saruman/Sites
...
```

LESS is a good example of an environment variable in action. It's read by the command less, where its value is taken as the default list of options that less should assume. The line below will cause less to assume it has been issued as command less -iqM. This is particularly useful when man calls less to display a man page. It gives you a way to influence the way less behaves when called from man.

```
$ declare -x LESS="-iqM"
```

Other notable environment variables are PWD, which records the current working directory, and PS1, which holds the prompt. Try this.

```
$ PS1="What next master? "
What next master?
```

Scope

Scope is best explained by example. In the extract below, we declare and initialize a shell variable (sv) and an environment variable (EV). Then we run a command and examine the environment inherited by the command. In this example, the command is Bash, to make it easy to display the environment, but it could be any command. You'll see that the environment variable is inherited and the shell variable is not.

First, set the two variables, and export EV to make it an environment variable. Note that EV is just a shell variable until it is exported.

```
$ sv="Shell variable"
$ EV="Environment variable"
$ export EV
$ echo "sv="$sv", and EV="$EV
sv=Shell variable, and EV=Environment variable
```

Next, start a new command (the Bash shell), and display the variables as seen by the new command. We see that shell variable sv loses its value (or, rather, it's not defined in the new shell), whereas environment variable EV is inherited.

```
$ bash
$ echo "sv="$sv", and EV="$EV
sv=, and EV=Environment variable
$
```

Next, we change the values of both sv and EV and then exit the command (the new Bash shell), retuning to the original shell. You'll notice that the environment of the original shell is unchanged—in particular, EV has its original value. Although a command inherits the environment from its parent, it's free to modify its own environment without affecting that of its parent. Environment variables are inherited but not passed back. This behavior is by design, to prevent a child process from trashing the environment of its parent.

```
$ sv="Shell variable two"
$ EV="Environment variable two"
$ export EV
$ echo "sv="$sv", and EV="$EV
sv=Shell variable two, and EV=Environment variable two
$ exit
exit
```

↗ LEARN MORE

Project 47 tells you more about Bash initialization on startup.

Back in the original shell, we have the original values of sv and EV.

```
$ echo "sv="$sv", and EV="$EV
sv=Shell variable, and EV=Environment variable
$
```

Bash vs. Tcsh

The Tcsh shell employs a different syntax for setting shell and environment variables. If you ever use it, here's what you need to know.

To set a shell variable:

```
% set sv="Shell Variable"
% echo $sv
Shell Variable
%
```

To set an environment variable:

```
% setenv EV "Environment Variable"
% echo $EV
Environment Variable
%
```

Bash Initialization

When a Bash shell starts up, it executes a number of scripts written to set up and customize its environment. Some of these are global and are executed for all users; others are individual to each user. Additionally, Bash can be started as a *login shell* or a *non-login shell,* and this affects which scripts are executed. Apple's Terminal application starts a new window with a login shell, while whereas typing **bash** at the command line starts a non-login shell.

A login shell (opening a new Terminal window starts a login shell) *sources* (executes) these scripts, and in this order:

▸ /etc/profile This is a global file sourced for all users.

▸ ~/.bash_profile Every user has his own version of this.

A non-login shell (typing `bash` at the command line starts a non-login shell) sources these scripts, and in this order:

▶ `/etc/bashrc` This is a global file sourced for all users.

▶ `~/.bashrc` Every user has his own version of this.

Finally, an *interactive shell*, which is launched to run a shell script and exits when the script completes, does not source any initialization scripts. Thus, it inherits environment variables but does not configure any settings of its own.

What Goes in Which Script?

The question arises as what to put into each of the four script files. Those in `/etc` are sourced for all users and therefore would include global customization. All users have their own customization scripts in their home directories (those starting with `~/`). The login scripts should contain all customization (setting environment variables, shell variables, functions, aliases, and shell options). The non-login scripts should do all this except setting environment variables. Why do the non-login scripts not need to set environment variables? Remember that environment variables are inherited, and so the non-login shell, which is launched from the command line, will inherit its parent's environment variables.

It's possible to avoid the duplication described above (setting shell variables, functions, aliases, and shell options in both login and non-login scripts). Simply add a line in `/etc/profile` to say, "Now execute `/etc/bashrc`", and similarly add a line in `~/.bash_profile` to say, "Now execute `~/.bashrc`". Now the login scripts will simply fetch the appropriate settings from the non-login scripts. (The default `/etc/profile` supplied with Mac OS X already does this.)

Here's what to do.

Add this line to the end of `/etc/profile`.

source /etc/bashrc

Add this line to the end of `~/.bash_profile`.

source ~/.bashrc

❗ NOTE

Remember that the tilde (~) symbol is used as shorthand for the absolute pathname of your home directory. ~/.bashrc means the file .bashrc in your home directory.

↗ LEARN MORE

Project 9 tells you more about writing simple shell scripts.

↗ LEARN MORE

Project 6 covers redirection.

Editing Script Files

The best way to make and change scripts is to use one of the Unix editing tools discussed in Chapter 4. For now, just type along to use the echo and cat commands, along with a technique called redirection, to create some user customization scripts.

The following sequence of commands sets ~/.bash_profile to call ~/.bashrc and defines the aliases described in "Aliases and Functions" earlier in this project.

First, we create a login script in ~/.bash_profile and tell it to execute the non-login script in ~/.bash_rc. Don't worry if ~/.bash_profile already exists; the commands will be added to the end of it.

```
$ echo 'source ~/.bashrc' >> ~/.bash_profile
```

Now check the contents of ~/.bash_profile .

```
$ cat ~/.bash_profile
source ~/.bashrc
```

Next, create the non-login script, and add the commands to define the alias and functions.

```
$ echo "alias cp='cp -i'" >> ~/.bashrc
$ echo "alias mv='mv -i'" >> ~/.bashrc
$ echo "alias rm='rm -i'" >> ~/.bashrc
$ echo "alias ll='ls -al'" >> ~/.bashrc
$ echo 'lll() { ls -al $* | less;}' >> ~/.bashrc
```

Finally, check the contents of ~/.bashrc.

```
$ cat ~/.bashrc
alias cp='cp -i'
alias mv='mv -i'
alias rm='rm -i'
alias ll='ls -al'
lll() { ls -al $* | less;}
```

Start a new login shell with a new Terminal session (or start a non-login shell by simply typing bash), and verify that the shell is configured as expected.

Check that the aliases and the function exist.

```
$ alias
alias cp='cp -i'
alias ll='ls -al'
alias mv='mv -i'
alias rm='rm -i'
$ declare -f
lll ()
{
    ls -al $* | less
}
```

Try out the new commands.

```
$ touch x y
$ cp x y
overwrite y? (y/n [n]) y
$ ll
total 56
drwxr-xr-x  20 saruman   saruman   680 11 May 10:17 .
drwxrwxr-t  18 root      admin     612  9 Apr 18:22 ..
...
drwxr-xr-x   5 saruman   saruman   170 10 May 10:07 Sites
$ lll Sites
...
```

X11 and xterm

If you use X11 and xterm, be warned that xterm, unlike Apple's Terminal, does not start a login shell. To force a login shell, either invoke xterm with the option -ls or add this line to the file ~/.Xdefaults:

XTerm*.LoginShell: True

⟋ LEARN MORE

Project 46 gives information on the Tcsh shell.

Project 5
Discover Other Shells

This project tells you more about the different Unix shells available and how they compare.

The concept of a shell is hard-wired into Unix, but the actual shell program is not. Consequently, all Unix installations provide a variety of shells and let you choose your favorite. A shell has two primary functions:

▸   To provide an interactive experience (the user interface). In this role, we call it an interactive shell. This is where you type a command and the shell executes it. A good interactive experience will make your life at the command line easier.

▸   To provide a shell scripting language and execute shell scripts.

Darwin provides all the popular shells:

▸   The Bourne shell (command sh) was the first major Unix shell. Several system features depend on this shell and its scripting language. All other shells listed here, except the C and the TENEX C shells, fully support the Bourne shell's scripting language. The Bourne shell provides a primitive interactive experience upon which all the other shells improve.

▸   The C shell (command csh) was one of the first shells to improve on the interactive experience of the Bourne shell. Written by Bill Joy at the University of California, Berkeley, it incorporated command history, completion, and job control. Its name comes from similarities between the C programming language and the shell's scripting language. That scripting language, which is widely regarded as flawed, is incompatible with the Bourne shell.

▸   The TENEX C shell (command tcsh) is an enhanced but compatible version of the C shell that fixes most of the flaws in that shell's scripting language. It adds a command-line editor, programmable completion, and command/filename spelling correction.

▶ The Korn shell (command ksh), written by David Korn, is compatible with the Bourne shell. It includes command-line editing and job control, and is highly customizable. It also enhances the scripting language of the Bourne Shell. Note: The ksh shell was not included in Mac OS X until version 10.4 (Tiger).

▶ The Bash shell (command bash) is compatible with the Bourne shell and has a much-improved interactive experience. It incorporates useful features from the Korn and C shells, and enhances the scripting language of the Bourne shell. It's the default shell for Mac OS X and Linux, and the shell assumed throughout this book. Bash stands for Bourne Again Sh!

▶ The Z shell (command zsh) is compatible with the Bourne shell. The Zsh shell most closely resembles Ksh but includes many enhancements. It has command-line editing, built-in spelling correction, programmable command completion, shell functions (with autoloading), a history mechanism, and many more features. Paul Falstad originally wrote Zsh.

The default shell in Mac OS X is Bash if your user account was created by Mac OS X 10.3 or later. If your user account was created by an earlier version, you are most likely running Tcsh. To be certain which, or to change your default shell, see "All About Shells" in Project 1. Remember, you can change your current interactive shell temporarily by simply running a new shell.

You can run a script written for any of the above shells no matter which shell you are running interactively. The first line of a script should say which shell is to execute it, and your interactive shell will launch the stated shell to do so.

⚐ LEARN MORE

Project 4, and the projects in Chapter 6, teach the Bash shell.

Project 6
Use Redirection
and Pipelining

Redirection and pipelining are techniques for using Unix commands in combinations to perform a particular task. Many of the projects in this book use, and assume knowledge of, redirection and pipelining.

The concepts of redirection and pipelining lie at the core of Unix and take advantage of the central idea that set Unix apart from many other computer operating systems. The central idea has input and output (IO) as streams of (usually human readable) characters. This is true for all IO, whether it is file-based, console-based (terminal screen and keyboard) or interprocess communication (communication between running commands). Other operating systems break this symmetry by doing file-based IO in blocks. In Unix, information can flow as it is generated. The symmetry among file, console, and interprocess IO makes it easy to plug any output stream into any input stream.

A Unix command that normally takes input from the keyboard and writes output to the screen, for example, can easily be made to read from and write to a file instead. This is termed *redirection*. A command can also be told to take its input from the output of a previous command, and in this way, many commands can be chained, each reading the output from its predecessor. This is termed *pipelining*. Pipelining enables a task to be performed by combining lots of small, specialized tools, each doing its own thing on the data stream. You don't have to rely on a few monolithic applications, hoping they do exactly what you require. Instead, you combine small tools to create your own customized application, tailored to do exactly as you require.

Much of the skill in getting the most from Unix lies not just in employing the right commands, but also in being able to combine them in the right manner to achieve your goal. This is the practical application of Unix and, in a nutshell, is what this book and most of its 101 projects are about.

Redirection and pipelining work without any special effort from the commands involved; the shell does all the work. A command sees three streams:

- Standard in (`stdin` or stream 0) The source from which it reads input text

- Standard out (`stdout` or stream 1) The destination to which it writes output text

- Standard error (`stderr` or stream 2) To which it writes error message text. The `stderr` stream exists because it's usually not desirable to mix error messages with normal output.

The shell regards the keyboard as the `stdin` device and the Terminal screen as the `stdout` and `stderr` devices. Normally, these three streams are inherited by the command when it is launched by the shell. When redirection is applied, the shell opens the specified file(s) and reassigns them as `stdin`, `stdout`, and `stderr` as appropriate before executing the command. This process is transparent to the command, which does not treat the streams any differently.

When pipelining is applied, the shell opens a special stream called a *pipe*, assigning this as `stdout` of the first command and also as `stdin` of the second command. A pipe just channels its input to its output.

To use redirection and pipelining, all you need understand is the shell's syntax. The syntax given here is good for Bourne and Bash.

⤷ LEARN MORE

Be sure to learn about shell scripting; it's another tool essential to getting the most from Unix. Refer to Projects 9 and 10, and the projects in Chapter 9.

Redirection of stdout and stderr

We'll get started with redirection by having a command that normally writes to the screen send its output to a file instead. Let's redirect output from the command `ls` to the file `list.txt` and then display that file. To specify redirection of `stdout` to a file, simply use `> filename`.

```
$ ls > list.txt
```

The file `list.txt` will contain the text that would otherwise have been written to the Terminal screen.

↘ NOTE

You might notice that the text looks different from ls *output sent to the screen. The appearance is different because* ls *was aware of the redirection and, even though the principles of redirection don't require it, formatted its output differently for use in a text file.*

↘ NOTE

The stderr *stream is stream 2; hence,* 2> *redirects* stderr. *Similarly,* 1> *redirects to* stdout; > *is shorthand for* 1>.

Let's view it using the cat command.

```
$ cat list.txt
Desktop
...
Sites
list.txt
```

The next example demonstrates that error messages go to stderr and not to stdout, then illustrates redirection of stderr, using the syntax 2> filename.

We'll start by intentionally generating an error message, using the redirection sequence from the previous exercise to list the contents of a nonexistent directory.

```
$ ls zzz > list.txt
ls: zzz: No such file or directory
$ cat list.txt
```

Now add a 2 before the > symbol to redirect stderr to the list.txt file. You'll notice that nothing is written to the Terminal screen this time because we have sent stderr to a file.

```
$ ls zzz 2> list.txt
```

View the text file with cat to confirm that stderr output has been written to it.

```
$ cat list.txt
ls: zzz: No such file or directory
```

To redirect both stdout and stderr, just combine the two examples above.

```
$ ls zzz Sites >out.txt 2>error.txt
```

Sometimes, you may want to redirect both stdout and stderr to the same file. To accomplish this, first redirect stdout; then merge stderr (stream 2) into stdout (stream 1). The second line shown below is equivalent to the first but reverses the way stdout and stderr are merged.

```
$ ls zzz Sites >out.txt 2>&1
$ ls zzz Sites 2>out.txt 1>&2
```

In Bash, but not Bourne, there's a shorter syntax:

```
$ ls zzz Sites &> out.txt
```

As you may have noticed when we redirected `stderr` to `list.txt`, use of the character > causes the specified file to be overwritten if it exists. Use a double arrow, >> or 2>>, if you want to add, or *append*, output to an existing text file instead.

```
$ ls > list.txt
$ echo "--------------" >> list.txt
$ ls Sites >> list.txt
$ cat list.txt
Desktop
...
Sites
list.txt
--------------
images
index.html
```

Try the following experiment. Issue the command `cat` with no file to read, and redirect `stdout` to `letter.txt`. The command `cat` will wait for you to type something at the keyboard; it assumes that you meant it to read from `stdin` because you did not specify an input file. When you've finished, type `Control-d` (Control-d means end of file), and display the file.

```
$ cat > letter.txt
Hello,
I am writing...
<Control-d>
$ cat letter.txt
Hello,
I am writing...
```

ᴛᴛ TIP

Throw away output or errors by redirecting to `/dev/null`. *This is a special file akin to a bottomless pit.*

```
$ cat janets-tax-¬
    return.txt > ¬
    /dev/null
```

ℹ TIP

Because the command tr *processes a line at a time, it's impossible to write output back to the file being read. The following trick, which uses a semicolon to separate two commands on a single line, produces that effect: The command before the semicolon redirects translated output from* mac-file *to a new file,* tmp. *When that command completes, the* mv *command renames* tmp *to* mac-file, *overwriting the original file with a translated replacement.*

```
$ tr '\r' '\n' <
mac-file > tmp; mv tmp
mac-file
```

What's the Difference?

What is the difference between

```
$ cat letter.txt
```

and

```
$ cat < letter.txt
```

To the user, there is no difference. In the first example, cat opens letter.txt and reads from it. In the second, the shell opens letter.txt, passing it as stdin to cat, while cat, seeing no input filename, reads stdin.

Redirection of stdin

The real value of using stdin lies in pipelining, described later in this chapter, but redirection of stdin is useful where a command takes no filenames, expecting to use the keyboard and the screen. A command that normally reads from the keyboard, for example, can be made to read from a file by means of redirection. One such command is tr, which translates one character to another. To see how this works, try this example, which changes every occurrence of the letter *i* to the letter *u*. First, let tr read from the keyboard and write to the screen.

```
$ tr i u
big
bug
<Control-d>
$
```

A typical use for tr is to translate files that have Mac-style end-of-line characters (Return) into files that have Unix-style end-of-line characters (Newline). In this example, stdin is redirected so it's read from mac-file, and stdout is redirected so it's written to unix-file. The character sequence \r represents Return, and \n represents Newline. To specify redirection of stdin, simply use < filename.

```
$ tr '\r' '\n' < mac-file > unix-file
```

Pipelining

The concept of standard in and standard out streams lets us chain Unix commands, where a command takes its input from the output of the previous command. Such *pipelines* are set up by the shell, which arranges for the standard input of command #n to be taken from the standard output of command #(n-1).

Here's an example of pipelining that uses the commands ps and grep. The command ps displays the status of all processes running on your Mac, and grep picks out lines that match a regular expression.

First, try `ps` on its own. Options `-cx` tell `ps` to list the names of all commands you are running.

```
$ ps -cx
  PID TT  STAT      TIME COMMAND
  196 ??  Ss     3:02.28 WindowServer
...
  389 std Ss     0:00.16 -bash
  478 p2  S      0:00.12 -bash
```

Now pipe the results to `grep`, which we'll tell to pick out lines containing "Terminal". This should leave just the status line for process Terminal.

```
$ ps -xc | grep "Terminal"
  476 ??  S      0:24.52 Terminal
```

The three-digit number at the start of the line is the process identification (PID) of `Terminal`, a number that changes each time you quit and re-launch it. Let's add another stage to the pipe to return just the PID. We can use the command `awk` to do this. The command `awk` displays particular fields of each line it reads. In the following example, we display just field 1 (`$1`).

```
$ ps -xc | grep "Terminal" | awk '{print $1}'
476
```

Ordinarily, `stderr` output is not included in a pipeline. To pipe it too, first combine `stderr` with `stdout` by using `2>&1`; then pipe as normal.

A Time to Kill

Finally, let's write a command line that will kill (abort) the Terminal. We use the command `kill` to achieve this. The command `kill` takes a PID as its argument, which we'll furnish using the pipeline we just built. (It outputs Terminal's PID, you'll recall.) We'll enclose the pipeline sequence in `$()`, which tells Bash to execute it, write the result back to the command line, and then execute the remainder of the command line.

⏎ LEARN MORE

Project 23 tells you more about using the command grep, and Project 39 covers the command ps.

Projects 60 and 62 tell you more about the command awk.

❦ NOTE

Other shells, such as Tcsh, use the syntax `` `command` `` instead of `$(command)`.

ℹ **TIP**

Use the Unix manual to find out about the command
killall*.*

Before we do any actual killing, use echo to demonstrate that the expression enclosed by $() still outputs Terminal's PID.

```
$ echo $(ps -xc | grep "Terminal" | awk '{print $1}')
476
```

Now run kill.

```
$ kill $(ps -xc | grep "Terminal" | awk '{print $1}')
```

(At this point, Terminal will vanish!)

When Terminal restarts, it will have a different PID, but the command above will still work. As an exercise, write a generic kill command that takes a name instead of a PID. The new command will take one argument, so a Bash function seems an obvious solution. If you would like to have a go at this, you can find all the required information in Project 4.

The pipelining example above shows how a task can be accomplished by combining a few Unix commands and even how you can create your own custom command. This nicely illustrates an important point. To achieve what we did took a lot of Unix knowledge and the ability to pick the correct commands and combine them in the right manner. You could read 500 pages on Unix and still not be able to craft the command line you require from a blank sheet. This is precisely why the majority of projects in this book are task focused. Pick a chapter and a project that looks closest to your needs, and you'll learn how to *use* Unix, not just *about* Unix.

Syntax Summary

Table 1.1 and **Table 1.2** summarize Bash and Tcsh syntax for redirection and pipelining.

Table 1.1 Bash Syntax for Redirection and Pipelining

Function	Syntax
redirect stdout	command > filename
redirect stderr	command 2> filename
redirect stdout appending	command >> filename
redirect stderr appending	command 2>> filename
redirect both to the same file	command &> filename
redirect both to different files	command > outfile 2> errorfile
redirect stdin	command < filename
pipe stdout	command1 | command 2
pipe both	command1 2>&1 | command2

Table 1.2 Tcsh Syntax for Redirection and Pipelining

Function	Syntax
redirect stdout	command > filename
redirect stderr	(command > /dev/tty) >& filename
redirect stdout appending	command >> filename
redirect stderr appending	(command > /dev/tty) >>& filename
redirect both to the same file	command >& filename
redirect both to different files	(command > outfile) >& errorfile
redirect stdin	command < filename
pipe stdout	command1 | command2
pipe both	command1 |& command2

Just for Fun

Create a trick file.

```
$ cat haha.txt 2> tmp;
mv tmp haha.txt
$ cat haha.txt

cat: haha.txt: No such
file or directory
```

Project 7
Know Your Users and Groups

This project covers users and groups, and how they affect your access to the file system. Permissions, covered in Project 8, are intimately related to users and groups.

Unix and its *file system* (its method of organizing and storing information) were designed from the ground up to keep data secure on computers shared by multiple users. Users, Groups, and Permissions form the foundation of this secure file system (and that of Mac OS X as well). Unix employs users and groups to identify you and associate you with the files you own and the files you share. Permissions (see Project 8) are assigned to each file individually. They mark out your personal "turf" and the extent of your access to the remainder of the file system —that is, which files and directories you can see and change, and which programs you can run.

Every Unix file is owned by a specific user and is associated with a specific group. Three sets of permissions are applied to each file: one for the owner, one for members of the associated group, and one for everyone else. Each set of permissions allows or forbids the file to be read, written, and executed.

Users

A *user* is someone who has an account on a Unix machine. A user has a name and a password, and is able to log in. Each user has a numeric user identity (UID) on that machine and a home directory in which to place personal files. The user name is used only for logging on; thereafter, you are identified to Unix by your UID.

There are two classes of user: those created as user accounts and *daemonic* users created for the purpose of running daemons, such as user www, under which the Apache web server runs. There's also the root user, an all-powerful user with a UID of 0 to which permissions and restrictions do not apply.

Creating a user account using Mac OS X System Preferences also creates a new Unix user account. In fact, the two are one and the same, as the same account information is shared between Aqua and the command line.

Groups

Many users can belong to the same group. Every user belongs to at least one group (a self-named primary group) and can be added to any number of other groups at any time. Like a user, a group has a name and a numeric group identity (GID).

The idea behind groups is to associate a set of users with a set of files. Group file permissions can be set to allow access to members of the group and to prevent access by nonmembers. Without the concept of groups, no mechanism would exist by which a file can be shared among selected users.

Groups are used in OS X to distinguish administrative users from normal (staff) users; administrative users belong to the group admin, for example. There are also groups such as www, which serve as the primary group of the corresponding daemonic users.

Root's primary group is called wheel and has a GID of 0.

Unix Commands

Because the concept of users and groups is so central to Unix, it's important to learn some commands that let you identify and specify user and group information for files and directories.

☰ TIP

Use System Preferences to create a second administrative user. If you run into a problem such that your regular administrative user becomes unusable, you can log into the spare one to diagnose and ideally correct the problem.

Display Your Details

To display your user and group information, use the command id. It displays your UID and user name, your primary GID and group name, and then a list of all the groups to which you belong. The command groups lists the groups to which you belong. In the following example, saruman is an administrative user, and loraine is a standard user.

```
$ id
uid=501(saruman) gid=501(saruman) groups=501(saruman),
81(appserveradm), 79(appserverusr), 80(admin)
$ groups
saruman appserveradm appserverusr admin
$ id
uid=504(loraine) gid=504(loraine) groups=504(loraine)
$ groups
loraine
```

In case of severe amnesia, recall who you are by typing either of the following.

```
$ whoami
saruman
$ who am i
saruman   ttyp1     Jul 17 19:31
```

Display a File's Details

Use the familiar command ls, with its -l option, to display the owner and associated group of a file.

```
$ ls -l letter.txt
-rw-r--r-- 1 saruman saruman 100 12 May 19:27 letter.txt
```

From this, we can see that letter.txt is owned by user saruman and is associated with group saruman. The very first character describes the file type, - for file, d for directory, and so on (see the man page for ls). The next nine characters, -rw-r--r--, describe the file permissions for the user, for members of the associated group, and for everyone else (see Project 8 for an explanation of permissions). At the end we see the file size (100 bytes), the date of last modification, and the filename.

On the other hand, `mach_kernel` is owned by user root and is associated with group wheel.

```
$ ls -l /mach_kernel
-rw-r--r-- 1 root wheel 4308960 31 Mar 05:11 /mach_kernel
```

Change Groups and Owners

Use command `chgrp` to change the group associated with a file. You must be the owner of the file to change its group, and the new group must be one to which you belong. Only root has the power to change the group arbitrarily.

```
$ chgrp admin letter.txt
$ ls -l letter.txt
-rw-r--r--  1 saruman  admin  100 12 May 19:27 letter.txt
$
```

Command `chown` will change the owner of a file and optionally the group too. You must be root to change the owner of a file, for obvious security reasons.

```
$ chown loraine letter.txt
chown: letter.txt: Operation not permitted
$ sudo chown loraine letter.txt
Password:
$ ls -al letter.txt
-rw-r--r--  1 loraine  admin  100 12 May 19:27 letter.txt
$
```

Check out the Unix man pages for `chgrp` and `chown`. Both have a recursive mode when you need to modify all files in a directory hierarchy. (See "Recursion" in Project 2.)

List Users and Groups

Use the command dscl to maintain and query Mac OS X Directory Services, where much of the account information is held. The command dscl is a comprehensive utility, but here we use it just to display a list of users and groups.

```
$ dscl / -list /Users
amavisd
appowner
...
root
saruman
...
xgridcontroller
$ dscl / -list /Groups
accessibility
admin
amavisd
...
saruman
...
```

Default Users and Groups

When you create a new file or directory, the owner is always you, the user who created the file. The associated group is not as you may expect; it has nothing to do with your primary group or any of the groups to which you belong. It is in fact the group of the containing directory (which is often your primary group anyway). This behavior is not the same in all variants of Unix; others use the primary group of the user who creates the file. The way Mac OS X does it makes good sense when you create a file in a directory outside your home, such as /Users/Shared.

Project 8
Manage File Permissions

This project covers permissions and how they affect your access to the file system. You'll learn how to interpret permissions and how to modify them. Users and groups, covered in Project 7, are intimately related to permissions.

Unix and its *file system* (its method of organizing and storing information) were designed from the ground up to keep data secure on computers shared by multiple users. Users, Groups, and Permissions form the foundation of this secure file system (and that of Mac OS X as well). Unix employs users and groups (see Project 7) to identify you and associate you with the files you own and the files you share. Permissions are assigned to each file individually. They mark out your personal "turf" and the extent of your access to remainder of the file system —that is, which files and directories you can see and change, and which programs you can run.

What are Permissions?

Every file (including directories and executables) is owned by a particular user and has an associated group. Permissions define those files you may view (read), write to, and execute.

Three sets of read/write/execute (rwx) permissions are defined: one for the owner, one for members of the associated group, and one for everyone else. (The root user has read, write, and execute permissions on all files.) Your permissions for a given file are determined as follows:

▶ If you are the owner of the file, you have the permissions stated for the owner.

▶ If you do not own the file but belong to the associated group, you have the permissions stated for members of the group.

▶ If neither of the above applies, you have the permissions stated for everyone else (others).

Execute Permission on Directories

You may be wondering what execute permission means for a directory. Read permission allows listing of the directory contents. But without execute permission, you cannot create a new file, edit a file, or cd into the directory.

Permission Triplets

Permissions are displayed in three sets of triplets. Reading from left to right, they apply to the owner, members of the associated group, and everyone else. They are interpreted as r for read access granted, w for write access granted, and x for execute permission granted. A dash (-) means permission is not granted.

As an example, list the contents of your home directory.

```
$ ls -l
total 0
drwx------   4 saruman saruman   136 12 May 18:59 Desktop
drwx------  15 saruman saruman   510  4 May 12:11 Documents
...
drwxr-xr-x   5 saruman saruman   170  4 May 22:04 Public
...
```

The directories Desktop and Documents are private to saruman, whereas Public can be read and executed (but not written to) by members of group saruman and in fact by everyone. This is consistent with Public's being a directory that others can view but cannot change. Note that if an enclosing directory does not grant read/write permissions, the files in that directory cannot be accessed, no matter what permissions they themselves may carry.

Permissions on Mac OS X System Files

The file system in Mac OS X can be split into three areas with regard to permissions:

▶ Home directories. Normal users maintain only their own home directories.

▶ Applications and the shared library. Administrator users also maintain the shared library and applications.

▶ The Unix core. This is the domain of the root user.

The split works well: Demarcation of the Unix core allows the non-expert Mac user to be an administrator, but without any danger of hosing the core installation.

This users/administrators/root split is achieved by using groups. An administrator user is made a member of the group admin. Any file that is to be writable by administrators, but not by normal users, is associated with admin, and write permission is granted to the group.

Viewing permissions in /Applications confirms this.

```
$ ls -ld /Applications
drwxrwxr-x  28 root  admin  952 13 May 11:18 /Applications
$ ls -l /Applications
total 0
drwxrwxr-x  3 root admin 102 15 May  2004 Address Book.app
drwxrwxr-x  7 root admin 238 24 Apr 06:47 AppleScript
...
drwxrwxr-x  3 root admin 102 11 Aug  2004 iSync.app
drwxrwxr-x  4 root admin 136 13 May 11:18 iTunes.app
```

A normal user is able to execute all applications but cannot modify them; no write access is granted to others. However, the associated group is admin with read and write access granted. An administrative user, being a member of group admin, can therefore modify an application (install or update it).

The directory /System/Library contains the Unix core and is protected from administrative users. Only root may modify this area.

```
$ ls -ld /System/Library
drwxr-xr-x  52 root  wheel  1768 24 Apr 06:49
/System/Library/
$ ls -l /System/Library
total 90144
drwxr-xr-x 228 root wheel 7752 Apr  8 01:59 Automator
drwxr-xr-x  11 root wheel  374 Apr  8 01:57 CFMSupport
drwxr-xr-x   9 root wheel  306 Jun 12 21:45 Caches
...
```

ᵢ TIP

To learn the attributes of a directory (total size, permissions settings, etc.), use ls *with the* -ld *option pair. Option* d *tells* ls *to report on a directory itself, rather than on its contents.*

Permissions in Octal

As shorthand for the nine-letter triplet designations, file permissions can be specified using *octal* numbers as arguments for chmod (in absolute mode) or umask (described later in this chapter). To determine a file's octal number, convert each of its permission triplets to a three-digit number by substituting 1 for each letter and 0 for each dash. (Permission rwxr-xr-- translates to 111 101 100.) Next, read each three-digit set as a binary number and convert it to its base-10 (or, more strictly, base-8) equivalent (picking up on the earlier example, 111=7; 101=5; 100=4). String the resulting digits together to get the octal number. (For the example, it's 754.) Initial zeroes are optional in octal numbers (066 is the same as 66). We then apply the permissions using

```
$ chmod 754 file
```

Take Command of Permissions

Use the command chmod to change file modes (permissions). You must specify to whom the new permissions apply by using the following encoding:

▶ u for user (the owner)

▶ g for associated group

▶ o for others

▶ a for all, equivalent to ugo

what permissions are to be applied:

▶ r for read

▶ w for write

▶ x for execute

and how they are to be applied:

▶ = to set the permissions exactly as stated (absolute mode)

▶ + to add permissions to those already granted (relative mode)

▶ - to remove permissions from those already granted (relative mode)

Here are some examples.

Set permissions to rwx r-x r-- (rwx for users, r-x for group, r-- for others):

```
$ chmod u=rwx,g=rx,o=r file
```

Remove read access from others, and add write access to the group.

```
$ chmod o-r file
$ chmod g+w file
```

Add execute permission for everyone. Use one of these.

```
$ chmod +x file
$ chmod a+x file
$ chmod ugo+x file
```

Finally, set the group permissions to equal those of the owner.

```
$ chmod g=u file
```

Check out the Unix man page for chmod. It has a recursive mode when you need to modify all files in the directory hierarchy. (See "Recursion" in Project 2.)

Set Default Permissions

New files are created with the permissions rw- rw- rw- *minus* the permissions specified by the umask. New directories are created with the permissions rwx rwx rwx *minus* the permissions specified by the umask. Use the command umask to display and set it. To see the current value of umask, type

```
$ umask
0022
```

0022 is in octal and means --- -w- -w-. (See the sidebar "Permissions in Octal.") Therefore, after the umask value is applied, a file is created with permissions rw- r-- r--, and a directory is created with permissions rwx r-x r-x. Setting the mask to 077 (--- rwx rwx) causes new files to be created with permissions rw- --- --- and new directories with permissions rwx --- ---. To set the umask to the new value, type

```
$ umask 077
```

Append-Only Directories: The Sticky Bit

A user who has write permission for a directory can delete any file from that directory, whether or not she has write permission on the file itself. This may seem odd (the reason is that deletion changes directory contents without changing any actual file contents), and it's certainly not always desirable. Everybody has read and write permission for the shared directory /Users/Shared, for example, but users shouldn't have a license to delete one another's files arbitrarily. To address this concern, Unix permissions feature something called the sticky bit.

↗ **LEARN MORE**

For information on sudo, see "How to Become the Root User" in Project 2.

The secret to preventing unwanted file removal lies in making a directory *append-only*. Unprivileged users may add files to an append-only directory but may not delete them. Such a directory is termed *sticky* and has the *sticky bit* set.

For example, the Shared directory is sticky.

```
$ ls -ld /Users/Shared
drwxrwxrwt  10 root  wheel  340  6 May 20:57 /Users/Shared
```

Stickiness is indicated by a t, replacing what would normally be an x in the others' permissions triplet. If x were not set, the sticky bit would be displayed as T instead. Command chmod sets and clears the sticky bit.

```
$ chmod u+t directory
```

You may also use g+t, which has exactly the same effect; o+t has no effect. A file in a sticky directory may be removed only by the owner of the file; the owner of the directory, provided that he has write access for the directory; and (of course) root.

Executing as Another User

When you execute a command such as rm, you can remove only files for which you have the appropriate permissions. Another user issuing the same command sees a different set of permissions and can remove only files for which they have the appropriate permissions. The mechanism that makes a particular command behave differently depending on who invoked it is *inheritance.* When a command is executed, it inherits the UID and GID of the user who executed it. It runs on behalf of that user and enjoys the same file-system permissions (and restrictions).

Under certain circumstances, a command may inherit a UID or GID different from that of the executing user. Commands issued by the command sudo (short for *substitute user do*) are one such example. Running sudo as an intermediate lets a user confer the UID and GID of the super-user (or any other user) to a command instead of his own. (Indiscriminate use of sudo would create obvious security concerns, so only users with Administrator privileges can run it.)

The s-Bit

The s-bit is best explained by example. The ability of sudo to change the UID of its user is related to the permissions set on the sudo program file itself and a special permission setting known as the s-*bit*. To see it in action, let's examine the sudo executable:

```
$ ls -l /usr/bin/sudo
 -r-s--x--x  1 root wheel 101028 4 May 11:59 /usr/bin/sudo
```

The presence of an s in place of an x in the owner's permissions triplet indicates that the s-bit—the *set user ID on execution (S-UID)* bit—is set. When sudo is executed, instead of inheriting the UID of the user by whom it was executed, it inherits the UID of the user who owns the file. In this case the owner is root, and sudo runs with root permissions. When sudo invokes a command, that command inherits the UID, so it too has root status.

Use chmod to set the S-UID bit.

```
$ chmod u+s my-command
```

You can set an s-bit in a file's group-permissions triplet as well.

```
$ chmod g+s my-command
```

As you'd expect, this *set group ID on execution (S-GID)* bit allows execution of a file using the GID (and related group permissions) of its associated group.

Commands Inherit Permissions, Too

Use of the S-UID and G-UID bits has serious security implications. If the file my-command in this example were written to delete some of my files, any user who can execute it can now delete those files regardless of their native permissions. The command is running with my UID and GID; it is effectively running as me. The command may call another command such as rm, and rm in turn inherits my UID and GID. In the general case, any command invoked by the S-UID-enabled my-command, and any command invoked by that runs as me.

If my-command is part of a pipe, the S-UID and S-GID bits do not influence commands farther along the pipe, because subsequent commands are called by the shell and not by my-command.

S-UID on Scripts

For security reasons, S-UID on scripts is ignored. There are too many covert ways in which to turn a script to the Dark Side.

More Octal

The s- and t-bits can be specified using octal format. Pass a four-digit octal number to chmod, where the first digit specifies the s- and t-bits, and the remaining three specify permissions as described previously. To determine the top octal digit, convert the s- and t-bits to a three-digit binary number, using 1 to set a bit and 0 to clear it. The bits are in this order: S-UID S-GID Sticky.

To set the S-UID and the S-GID bits but clear the Sticky bit, use 110 or 6 octal. One might use

```
$ chmod 6755 my-command
```

To set the Sticky bit only, use 001 or 1 octal.

```
$ chmod 1755 my-¬
    directory
```

↗ LEARN MORE

Refer to the projects in Chapter 9 when you crave more scripting power.

↗ LEARN MORE

The projects in Chapter 4 cover Unix text editors at greater length.

Project 9
Learn About Shell Scripts

In this project, you'll learn how shell scripts are used to automate a series of Unix commands, and you'll study the anatomy of a basic shell script.

A *shell script* is a sequence of commands written in a shell *scripting language* and stored in a file the shell can read. When a shell script is run, the shell reads the file and runs the commands it contains in much the same way as it reads and executes commands you type at the command line. Of course, the same file can be executed many times.

The components of a shell script fall into two categories:

▶ Normal Unix commands as you would issue them on the command line, such as cd, ls, mv, and so on. This project focuses on them.

▶ Features of the shell scripting language itself, such as variables, and control constructs that enable techniques like loops and conditional processing. We might have the script test to see whether a file exists, rename it if it does, and display an error message if it doesn't. We'll look at scripts that use these techniques in Project 10.

Any serious attempt at scripting requires the use of a text editor, and you'll need to use one to complete the examples in this project. If you're not familiar with any of the available Unix text editors, such as Nano, Emacs, and Vim, use Apple's TextEdit, but remember to save the file as plain text. In TextEdit, select menu Format and then item Make Plain Text. If you see the item Make Rich Text instead, the file is already in plain text.

A Simple Script

Let's look at a ready-made script called info that illustrates the basics. This sample script does nothing more than invoke a few Unix commands, exactly as you could do interactively on the command line. It doesn't exist on your Mac, so you're going to have to create it by typing it in a text editor and saving it. You can save it anywhere—Documents might be a good place to choose. This is how it looks displayed in cat.

```
$ cat info
#!/bin/bash
# A simple Bash shell script
echo "Information produced on " $(date)
echo "Host information"
hostinfo
echo; echo "Hostname"
hostname
echo; echo "Uptime"
uptime
```

The first line of the script (and it must be the very first line) is #!/bin/bash. It says this is a Bash script and that it should be passed to /bin/bash for execution. When you execute a shell script, it doesn't run in your interactive shell directly; instead, your shell launches a new shell, inside itself, to run the script. This approach lets users run scripts that weren't written for their preferred shell; a Z shell user, for example, can run a Bash shell script, relying on the first line of the script to tell the Z shell to find and launch /bin/bash. The approach also has advantages with scripts written in the "native" language of the user's interactive shell. Running in a shell-within-the-shell (or *subshell*), a script can set its own environment settings without affecting those of the user's current shell. (See "Scope" in Project 4.)

The second line is a comment, denoted by a hash (#) symbol and not immediately followed by an exclamation point. The shell ignores lines that start with #; *comments* are notes describing what the script does and how it does it.

The remainder of the script simply runs Unix commands echo, date, hostinfo, hostname, and uptime. Several commands can be placed on the same line if they are separated by a semicolon.

↗ LEARN MORE

Refer to Project 8 for more on permissions and how to set them. See Project 50 to understand why the script name must be preceded by an absolute pathname or ./.

Sourcing a Script

If you want a script to run directly in your interactive shell, not a new shell inside it, use the command source. A script run using "source script-name" or the equivalent of ". script-name" can affect the environment of the current interactive shell (see "Scope" in Project 4) and may be used to set environment variables and shell options and variables.

You may recall that we used this command in our login scripts in "Bash Initialization" in Project 4; the script /etc/profile sources the script /etc/bashrc.

Executing the Script

To execute the script, type its full pathname or precede it with ./. Let's see what happens when we do so.

```
$ ./info
-bash: ./info: Permission denied
```

Oops! Before a script can be run, it must have execute permission. We'll fix that with chmod.

```
$ chmod +x info
```

Permissions set, let's try it again.

```
$ ./info
Information produced on  Mon Jul 18 16:55:15 BST 2005
Host information
Mach kernel version:
        Darwin Kernel Version 8.2.0: Fri Jun 24 17:46:54...
Kernel configured for a single processor only.
1 processor is physically available.
Processor type: ppc970 (PowerPC 970)
Processor active: 0
Primary memory available: 1.00 gigabytes
Default processor set: 86 tasks, 271 threads, 1 processors
Load average: 1.64, Mach factor: 0.24


Hostname
sauron.mayo-family.com


Uptime
16:55 up 3 days, 4 hrs, 2 users, load aves: 1.04 0.68 0.73
```

That's about all there is to writing and running a simple shell script.

Project 10
Write Shell Scripts

In this project, you'll write a simple shell script using arguments, shell variables, and control constructs.

In Project 9, we learned that a *shell script* is a sequence of commands, written in a shell *scripting language* and stored in a file the shell can read, and we wrote a simple script of the kind runs a series of normal Unix commands, just as you would issue them on the command line, such as cd, ls, mv, and so on.

Now we'll take a look at a more advanced kind of shell script, one that takes advantage of features of the shell scripting language itself. These advanced features include variables and a variety of control constructs, and they enable techniques like loops and conditional processing. In combination with standard Unix commands, these scripting features allow the creation of sophisticated scripts that can adapt their behavior to different system conditions. A script might test for the presence of necessary support files before installing software— and install any missing files before continuing.

We won't be that ambitious with our first conditional script; we'll just have it test to see whether a file exists, rename it if it does, and display an error message if it doesn't.

Once again, scripting requires the use of a text editor. If you're not familiar with any of the available Unix text editors, use Apple's TextEdit, but remember to save the file as plain text. In TextEdit, select menu Format and then item Make Plain Text. If you see the option Make Rich Text instead, your file is already in plain text.

Shell Arguments

Most Unix commands take arguments. In the command cp file1 file2, for example, cp is passed two arguments. Shell scripts, too, can take arguments, and this section shows how a script processes them.

⤢ LEARN MORE

This project covers the subject only briefly. Refer to the projects in Chapter 9 for shell script basics.

⤢ LEARN MORE

The projects in Chapter 4 cover Unix text editors at greater length.

↗ LEARN MORE

Refer to Project 9 if you are
unsure of the basics of shell
scripts.

↗ LEARN MORE

See Project 76 when you
wish to learn more about
parameter expansion in
Bash.

Looking at it from the inside (when writing a script as opposed to running it), arguments are often called *parameters*, so that's the term I'll use throughout this project.

Let's look at a ready-made script called rename that illustrates the basics. It doesn't exist on your Mac, so you're going to have to create it by typing it in a text editor and saving it. You can save it anywhere—Documents might be a good place to choose. This is how it looks displayed in cat.

```
$ cat rename
#!/bin/bash
# Usage: extension filename
mv $2 $2.$1
$
```

This script expects to see two parameters: an extension and a filename. It adds the extension to the filename. A parameter is accessed using the notation $n, where n=1 for the first argument passed, 2 for the second, and so on. This is termed *parameter expansion*. The script is very primitive and doesn't do any more than command mv does, but we shall improve it over the course of the project. Let's give it execute permission and run it.

```
$ chmod +x rename
$ ls
f1        rename
$ ./rename txt f1
$ ls
f1.txt    rename
$
```

The script does what it should but has a flaw: If it is passed a filename with spaces, it fails. In this example

```
$ ./rename txt "my file"
usage: mv [-f | -i | -n] [-v] source target
       mv [-f | -i | -n] [-v] source ... directory
```

the line

```
mv $2 $2.$1
```

expands to

```
mv my file my file.txt
```

To prevent this type of problem, it's prudent to enclose parameter expansion in double quotes. By doing so we preserve spaces in file names. Don't use single quotes, because single quotes stop parameters from being expanded.

Here's the new version of the script. Enclosing "$1" in quotes ensures that whatever $1 is expanded to, it will be treated as a single item, never as two space-separated items.

```
$ cat rename
#!/bin/bash
# Usage: extension filename
mv "$2" "$2"."$1"
$ ls
my file          rename
$ ./rename txt "my file"
$ ls
my file.txt      rename
$
```

Conditional Processing

Conditional processing says to do something only if particular conditions are met and possibly to do something else if they are not. One improvement to the rename script is to ensure that at least two arguments are passed.

```
$ cat rename
#!/bin/bash
# Usage: extension filename
if [ $# -ne 2 ]; then
  echo "Usage: $0: extension filename"
else
  mv "$2" "$2"."$1"
fi
$
```

↗ LEARN MORE

See Project 80 to learn more about the black art of shell quoting.

NOTE

The white space after the open bracket and before the close bracket is necessary, as is the semicolon. Get the syntax wrong, and Bash will complain. It is permissible to miss out the semicolon and put the then *statement on a new line.*

TIP

To learn about the sorts of conditions that can be used, read the man page for [. *Issue command* help test.

LEARN MORE

Project 81 covers Bash conditions in greater depth.

An if construct evaluates the condition that follows in [square brackets]. If the condition turns out to be true, the statements between then and else are executed; if it turns out to be false, the statements between else and fi are executed. Any number of statements is allowed in either part of the if statement, even other if-then-else-fi statements. Notice that within the if and else parts, other statements are indented to make the structure of the script easier to read.

The special parameter expansion $# expands to the number of arguments passed, and within a condition, -ne means *not equal to.* So the condition is testing "if the number of arguments is not equal to 2." The special parameter expansion $0 on the next line expands to the name of the shell script itself, as typed on the command line.

The else part is optional, and this is perfectly legal.

```
if [ condition ]; then
  statements
fi
```

Running the improved rename with too few parameters gives

```
$ ./rename txt
Usage: ./rename: extension filename
$
```

Multiple Conditions

An if statement may have multiple conditions, each additional condition being introduced by elif.

```
if [ "$1" = "positive" ]; then
  echo "Yes"
elif [ "$1" = "negative" ]; then
  echo "No"
else
  echo "Not sure"
fi
```

Alternatively, if all the conditions test for alternative values of a single variable, use a `case` statement. Each alternative should be terminated by ;; . Otherwise, processing *falls through* to the next alternative instead of going to the end of the case. The very last alternative should be *), which catches all other possibilities.

```
case "$1" in
  "positive")
    echo "Yes"
  ;;
  "negative")
    echo "No"
  ;;
  *)
    echo "Not sure"
  ;;
esac
```

ᵼ TIP

A case alternative does not have be exact. It's possible to specify a pattern such as Y*|y*) *to match Y, y, Yes, yep, and so on. See "Pattern Matching" in the Bash man page.*

Loops

The `rename` script would be actually useful if it could take an arbitrary number of filenames onto which the extension is added. Doing this requires some sort of loop that will process all the parameters. In shell speak, "all the parameters" is represented by the special parameter expansion $*. Bash provides several looping constructs, of which the `for` loop is the most appropriate here.

```
$ cat rename
#!/bin/bash
# Usage: extension filename
if [ $# -lt 2 ]; then
  echo "Usage: $0: extension filename"
else
  # loop to process each parameter
  for file in $*; do
    # rename the file
    echo mv "$file" "$file"."$1"
  done
fi
```

The `for` loop repeats for each value given in a list of values and assigns the next value to variable `file` each time around the loop. You may use any variable name here instead of `file`, of course. In this example, the list is `$*`, which expands to all parameters (all arguments passed to the script).

As a precaution, the line that does the actual moving is preceded by `echo`.

```
echo mv "$file" "$file"."$1"
```

The `move` command will not be executed—just displayed on the terminal. In this way, we can check that it will do as we expect, and if everything looks good, we remove `echo` .

Let's run the script.

```
$ ./rename txt "file 1" "file 2"
mv txt txt.txt
mv file file.txt
mv 1 1.txt
mv file file.txt
mv 2 2.txt
```

D'oh! You will notice two problems, or *bugs*, with the script, First, we did not want to process the extension name within the loop; second, parameters with spaces are being split. A useful command called `shift` drops the first parameter off the list, which we can use after first saving the extension name in a shell variable. A shell variable is assigned with the syntax

```
variablename=value
```

and the value is recalled by

```
$variablename
```

To solve the second bug, we need only surround `$*` in double quotes, as we did with `$1`.

```
$ cat rename
...
else
  # save the extension then drop it from the parameter list
  extension="$1"
  shift
  # loop to process each parameter
  for file in "$*"; do
    echo mv "$file" "$file"."$extension"
  done
fi
$ ./rename txt "file 1" "file 2"
mv file 1 file 2 file 1 file 2.txt
```

D'oh! Again! Quoting $* has created one big long parameter. Solving this problem would be tricky were it not for a neat feature of Bash. Enter "$@", which expands to "$1" "$2"... instead of "$1 $2...", which is what "$*" expands to.

```
$ cat rename
...
  # loop to process each parameter
  for file in "$@"; do
    if [ -r "$file" ]; then
      mv "$file" "$file"."$extension"
    else
      echo "No such file: $file"
    fi
  done
fi
```

Now let's run the script.

```
$ ls
f2      file 1      file 3      rename
$ ./rename txt file\ 1 f2 rubbish "file 3"
No such file: rubbish
$ ls
f2.txt  file 1.txt  file 3.txt  rename
```

Don't Forget the Quotes

A condition such as

```
if [ $1 = Yes ]
```

will cause a shell script error if $1 is empty. The condition will become

```
if [ = Yes ]
```

Use quotes so that the condition is always syntactically valid.

```
if [ "$1" = "Yes" ]
```

becomes

```
if [ "" = "Yes" ]
```

ᵢ TIP

Learn more about a Bash built-in command by using the command

```
$ help nameofcommand
```

That looks better. Notice that an extra `if` condition has been added to check that the file we are trying to rename does exist and is readable. Check out the man page for `test` for a list of possible conditions.

A `while loop` loops continually while a specified condition is true. The condition is formed in exactly the same way as for an `if` statement.

```
#!/bin/bash
read -p "Give a filename: " fn
while [ "$fn" != "" ]; do
  if [ -e "$fn" ]; then
    file "$fn"
  else
    echo "File $fn does not exist"
  fi
  read -p "Give a filename: " fn
done
```

This script prompts you to enter a filename, then displays the content type of the file you named (if it exists). It accepts filenames that contain spaces, without requiring that they be quoted.

Bash also provides an `until` loop, which simply uses the keyword `until` instead of `while`. As you might guess from the linguistic sense of the construct, the condition for exiting the loop is reversed.

Browse and Search the File System   2

Surfing the file system is something you'll do a lot, browsing directories and searching for specific files. Chapter 2 has ten projects that do just that, covering the following topics:

Globbing and wildcard expansion. Learn how to say "all files" or "all text files" in shell-speak. It's easier and quicker than listing them individually.

File system navigation. Learn how to move quickly from directory A to directory Z and then back again.

Finding files. Sometimes you need to root out a group of files and then list them or process each file. Unix puts some powerful commands at your disposal.

Unix links and Finder aliases. Don't get confused between hard and soft links, and find out why Unix doesn't understand Finder aliases.

The projects in this chapter show you how to move around the file system more efficiently and illustrate advanced file-finding techniques. If you need to process a set of files, finding them is usually the first step.

Project 11
Globbing with [^*?]

"How do I list all JPEG files?"

This project illustrates globbing and introduces the pattern-matching operators. It uses filename patterns written to match specific sets of filenames.

The Power of Pattern Matching

The widely used Unix technique of *globbing* lets you specify an ambiguous filename and has the shell find all files with names that match it. Globbing lets you operate on multiple files at the same time without having to name them individually (or even know their names in the first place).

We specify a *filename pattern* such as *.jpg by using *pattern-matching operators* (also known as *wildcards*) such as * ^ ?. The shell performs an operation known as *globbing* or *wildcard expansion*, expanding the pattern into a list of filenames that match the pattern. Each wildcard operator has its matching rules. A filename pattern may contain more than one wildcard, including multiple instances of the same one.

Star Globbing

Use the star pattern-matching operator to select all files. Bash expands a command line such as file * by replacing star with a list of all files in the current directory. In the example that follows, the filenames are passed to command file — a handy utility to determine what type a file is (directory, executable, text, empty, and so on).

```
$ cd ~
$ file *
Desktop:     directory
Documents:   directory
Library:     directory
...
```

List All JPEG Files

Star is matched by any sequence of characters, including none. The filename pattern in the command line

```
$ ls *.jpg
```

is matched by all filenames that end in `.jpg`.

A star can be used anywhere and many times. The pattern `A*B*C*` is matched by `ABC` and `AxBCyy` but not `AxCyy`, because it has no `B` to match against.

❗ WARNING

Be very careful not to add a stray space in a command such as

```
$ rm *.jpg
```

An erroneous space after the star causes `rm` to remove *all* nonhidden files (because a lone star matches all filenames) and then to try to remove the file `.jpg`. I've seen it done!

Glob the Path

Globbing is not limited to filenames; you may use wildcards anywhere in the pathname. In the next example, the star pattern-matching operator is used in two directory names as well as the filename.

```
$ ls 101*/dir*/file*
101-projects/dir1/file1    101-projects/dir1/file2
101-projects/dir2/file3    101-projects/dir3/file4
```

Match One Character

The query (?) pattern-matching operator matches exactly one character. All characters match query. The two comparative listings on the following page first show *all* files in the directory and then just those that match the filename pattern. The second listing is space-padded to make it easier for you to see which files matched.

ⓘ TIP

Star is not matched by filenames that begin with dot (hidden files). That's usually what you want, but if not, match the dot explicitly by using dot-star.

```
$ file .*
```

"Dotglob" in Project 12 shows you how to change this behavior.

What Globs?

The shell does the globbing when it interprets a command line, searching the current directory (or the given pathname) for all filenames that match the pattern. It expands the command line by replacing a pattern with the filenames that match the pattern. The command itself never sees the pattern—only the filenames. If a command cannot process many filenames, globbing will not work with it.

ⓘ TIP

To include a] *symbol in a list of characters, put it first in the list. Pattern* x[][]z *matches* x[z *and* x]z *but nothing else.*

To include a dash symbol in a list of characters, put it first or last in the list. To include both a dash and]*, put the bracket first and the dash last. Pattern* x[][-]z *matches* x-z, x[z, *and* x]z.

✎ NOTE

Although all shells have the same basic globbing rules, this project is written specifically for Bash. You might encounter different behavior in other shells; check their man pages.

```
$ ls
baag    bag     bags    bfg     bg      big     blag    bug
$ ls b?g
        bag             bfg             big             bug
```

A list of characters in square brackets is matched by any one of those characters (and exactly one, not zero and not two). The examples below should illustrate this.

```
$ ls
baag    bag     bags    bfg     bg      big     blag    bug
$ ls b[aeiou]g
        bag                     big             bug
$ ls b[aeiou]g*
        bag     bags            big             bug
```

Reject specific characters by starting the list with a caret (^) operator. Here, any character *other* than those listed matches.

```
$ ls
baag    bag     bags    bfg     bg      big     blag    bug
$ ls b[^aeiou]g
                bfg
```

Match Character Ranges and Classes

You may shorten a continuous sequence of characters by using a range. Specify the start and end characters of the range separated by a dash (-). For example:

- ▶ [a-z] matches any lowercase letter and is equivalent to [abcdefghi...xyz].

- ▶ [0-9] matches any digit and is equivalent to [0123456789].

- ▶ [A-Z0-9] matches any uppercase letter or digit.

Pattern-matching operators may be combined. Here, we match file-names that start with either *m* or *t* ([mt]), followed by any number of intervening characters (*), ending in literally **day** followed by exactly one digit ([0-9]).

```
$ ls [mt]*day[0-9]
-rw-r--r--  1 saruman   saruman   0 18 May 13:05 monday1
-rw-r--r--  1 saruman   saruman   0 18 May 13:05 thursday1
-rw-r--r--  1 saruman   saruman   0 18 May 13:05 tuesday3
```

Bash provides character classes using the syntax [[:class-name:]]. Character classes can be used in place of ranges. The following pattern matches any letter followed by exactly two digits.

```
$ ls [[:alpha:]][[:digit:]][[:digit:]]
A23
```

Bash character classes include alnum, alpha, ascii, blank, cntrl, digit, graph, lower, print, punct, space, upper, word, and xdigit.

Escape from Globbing

You may wish to specify a file that contains one or more pattern-matching operators as part of its name. Filenames may be protected from shell interpretation by escaping either the entire filename or the particular characters that have a special meaning to the shell. Special characters include the pattern-matching operators and the escape characters themselves: single quote, double quotes, and backslash. Here are some examples applied to the following (oddly named) files.

```
$ ls a*
a"*'b   a"b   a'b   a*b   a\b
```

Escape a backslash:

```
$ ls "a\b"
a\b
$ ls a\\b
a\b
```

ⓘ TIP

If you wish to know exactly which characters are included in a particular class, check out the Section 3 man page for the corresponding library function. The library function is named like the class but starts with is. *To read about character class* [:space:], *for example, look at the man page for* isspace *by typing*

```
$ man 3 isspace
```

✎ NOTE

An illegally formed pattern will not be recognized as such, but as an attempt to form a filename. The shell won't report an error message (other than perhaps "No such file or directory"). Consider

```
$ ls [A-Z][0-9][0-9]
A23
```

versus

```
$ ls [A-Z0-90-9]
ls: [A-Z0-90-9]: No such
file or directory
```

Similarly, [[:alpha:]][[:digit:]] *is a legal pattern, whereas* [[:alpha:][:digit:]] *is not.*

↗ **LEARN MORE**

**Project 12 shows you how
to control and customize
globbing in Bash.**

Escape double quotes and single quote:

```
$ ls 'a"b'
a"b
$ ls "a'b"
a'b
$ ls a\"b
a"b
```

Finally, escape the combination of special characters in the filename
a"*'b by using a combination of techniques. The double quotes are
escaped by backslash, whereas the star and single quote are escaped by
enclosing them in double quotes.

```
$ ls a\""*'b"
a"*'b
```

Some commands, such as find, do their own expansion of pattern-
matching operators. When using such a command, you must escape
the operators to prevent the shell from expanding them before they
are passed to the command. Here, the shell expands an unescaped star,
confusing find.

```
$ find . -name *
find: bag: unknown expression primary
```

Escaping the star allows it to be passed to find.

```
$ find . -name "*"
.
./baag
./bag
...
```

Shrink Big Command Lines

When many files, in the order of thousands, match a pattern, the command line gets too big, causing an error to be thrown. Suppose you have a command `scale` that you want to apply to the thousands of JPEG files in the current directory. You may issue the command

```
$ scale *.jpg
bash: /usr/local/bin/scale: Argument list too long
```

Note: The `scale` command is given as an example of a command you might employ; you won't necessarily have the command on your system.

You'll notice that Bash has thrown an error because `*.jpg` expanded to too many files. We use the `find` command to solve this problem. The command does its own wildcard expansion independent of the shell (remember to escape pattern-matching operators). Pipe the output from `find` (that's the list of files) to the `xargs` command. The `xargs` command constructs an argument list from its input and passes the list to the target command.

```
$ find . -name "*.jpg" | xargs scale
```

Run this command line as is, and you may wonder how it improves on our original: It has merely pushed the long-argument-list problem onto `xargs`, which will be forced to construct a command line with thousands of arguments. That's fine, however, because `xargs` has a few tricks up its sleeve. Using its option -n, you can specify the maximum number of arguments to use in each invocation of the target command, thus limiting the maximum size of a command line. In this example, we invoke `scale` repeatedly in batches of 1,000 until all arguments have been processed.

```
$ find . -name "*.jpg" -print0 | xargs -0 -n1000 scale
```

The extra options -print0 and -0 are there to cope with spaces in filenames.

⤴ LEARN MORE

Projects 15, 17, and 18 tell you all about using commands find **and** xargs.

Project 6 explains how to pipe output from one command to another.

Project 12
Power Globbing

"Globbing is great, but how do I customize the way it works to my own liking?"

This project shows you how to extend your globbing skills beyond the basics. It gets Bash to reveal the list of filenames before they are processed, customizes the way Bash expands filename patterns, and reveals more powerful pattern-matching operators.

Check Completion

Imagine typing the command

```
$ rm some-filename-pattern
```

and getting the filename pattern wrong or forgetting about some essential files that happen to match it. Not good. It's wise to dry-run a pattern first, using a neutral command such as echo or ls.

```
$ ls some-filename-pattern
<visually check the list of files>
$ rm some-filename-pattern
```

Even better is to use Bash's *glob list expansion*. Type the pattern, press and release Control-x, and then press g to get Bash to list the expansion.

Let's dry-run an rm command and then issue it:

```
$ rm b?g<Control-x>g
bag  bfg  big  bug
$ rm b?g
```

Alternatively, type Control-x * to get Bash to expand directly onto the command line.

```
$ rm b?g<Control-x>*
$ rm bag bfg big bug
```
If the dry run looks good, press Return to execute the command. Otherwise, press Control-u to delete the command line.

(This is similar to the more familiar technique of simply pressing the Tab key. Tab differs in that it either completes if a single match is found, or, after a second Tab, lists all the matches, if many matches are found.)

Customize Completion

Bash's globbing can be controlled and customized through shell options, which are settings that control the way Bash works. You can switch them on and off with the shopt command, specifying the command-line option -s (set) to switch on an option or -u (unset) to switch off an option. Issued without command-line options, shopt displays the current settings of all the shell options. Only the options relevant to globbing are shown in the example below (by filtering out unwanted options with grep). By default, all options are off.

```
$ shopt | grep glob
dotglob        off
extglob        off
nocaseglob     off
nullglob       off
```

Set nocaseglob

You may make globbing case insensitive (that is, get it to ignore case) by setting the shell option nocaseglob. (This does not affect tabbed completion in cases where globbing is not involved.)

With option nocaseglob switched off (the default setting), the pattern *a does not match files ending in A.

```
$ echo *a
smalla
```

If we switch on nocaseglob by typing

```
$ shopt -s nocaseglob
```

we'll see that globbing no longer considers case.

```
$ echo *a
bigA smalla
```

⊤ TIP

Type help shopt *to learn more about Bash shell options.*

↗ LEARN MORE

Project 45 covers Bash shell options and the shopt **command in more detail, also showing how to make tabbed completion case insensitive.**

Set nullglob

When no files match a pattern, Bash leaves the pattern unexpanded. In this example, there are no files beginning in zzz.

```
$ ls zzz*
ls: zzz*: No such file or directory
```

This is fine for interactive use, where you probably want to know that no files match, but often not what is wanted in a shell script. The example script below will try to process a nonexistent file called bz*.

First, we try a pattern that does match and expands to a list of filenames. The for loop simply echoes the name of each file to the screen for illustrative purposes.

```
$ for file in ba*; do echo "Processing file: $file"; done
Processing file: baag
Processing file: bag
Processing file: bags
```

Next, we try a pattern that is not matched by any file. Bash does not expand the pattern but leaves it verbatim on the command line.

```
$ for file in bz*; do echo "Processing file: $file"; done
Processing file: bz*
```

We'd prefer bz* to expand to nothing. Perhaps this point isn't obvious to you right now, but when you start writing shell scripts you'll understand that this is not usually what's wanted. (It doesn't matter either way in this simple example, because we are just echoing the name, but in a real scenario we will process the filenames in some way.) To this end, Bash provides the shell option nullglob. Switch on this option by typing

```
$ shopt -s nullglob
```

Now rerun the previous example. The for loop no longer tries to process bz* but exits silently, having processed no files.

```
$ for file in bz*; do echo "Processing file: $file"; done
```

Now switch the option off again.

```
$ shopt -u nullglob
```

One word of warning: Although `nullglob` works well in this example, it can cause unexpected results for other commands. When used with the `ls` command, for example, expansion to nothing causes `ls` to list all files in the current directory. To be safe, turn `nullglob` on when it is required and off again when it's not required.

The dotglob Option

The star pattern-matching operator is not matched by filenames that begin with a dot (hidden files). This is usually what's wanted, and the dot should be matched explicitly when required. For example:

```
$ file .*
```

Change this behavior by setting the shell option `dotglob`, after which star will be expanded to include hidden files (but not the dot and dot-dot directory entries).

Without `dotglob` we get

```
$ echo *
baag bag bags bfg bg big blag bug
```

Turn on `dotglob`, and we get

```
$ shopt -s dotglob
$ echo *
.hidden baag bag bags bfg bg big blag bug
```

Set GLOBIGNORE

You may tell Bash to ignore particular filenames when expanding filename patterns by setting the shell *variable* (not option) `GLOBIGNORE`. It should contain a colon-separated list of filenames and filename patterns. Bash will perform the expansion as normal and then remove any filenames that match any of those in the `GLOBIGNORE` pattern list.

This is best illustrated by an example. First, let's see which files match.

```
$ echo *
baag bag bag.tmp bags bfg bg big blag bug bug.bak
```

⟁ LEARN MORE

Projects 9 and 10 cover basic shell scripting, and the projects in Chapter 9 cover more advanced scripting.

⤴ LEARN MORE

**Refer to Project 4 to learn
about shell variables.**

Now tell Bash to ignore all `.tmp` and `.bak` files.

```
$ GLOBIGNORE="*.tmp:*.bak"
$ echo *
.hidden baag bag bags bfg bg big blag bug
```

The `.tmp` and `.bak` files are no longer matched. Notice, however, that
`.hidden` shows up (even if `dotglob` is turned off). This is because setting `GLOBIGNORE` turns on `dotglob`. When `GLOBIGNORE` is set, Bash pre-
sumes you'll use it rather than `dotglob` when you want to ignore
hidden files. To ignore hidden files, add `.*` to the ignore list.

```
$ GLOBIGNORE=".*:*.tmp:*.bak"
$ echo *
baag bag bags bfg bg big blag bug
```

Activate Extended Globbing

The final shell option listed in "Customize Completion" is `extglob`,
which enables *extended globbing*. Extended globbing lets you list alternative patterns to match, and specify how many occurrences of each
pattern to match. The alternative patterns are regular filename patterns and may include any of the usual pattern-matching operators,
like star, query, ranges, and classes.

The alternative matching patterns are enclosed in parentheses and
separated by a vertical bar (|). One of four operators (@, *, ?, and +)
must be placed immediately before the enclosing parentheses to specify how many repetitions of each pattern are necessary to match.

First, let's match exactly one from a number of patterns. The *at* (@)
symbol says to match exactly one of the patterns.

Let's create some test files.

```
$ touch monmonday monday tuesday
$ touch wednesday thursday friday day
```

Next, enable extended globbing.

```
$ shopt -s extglob
```

Finally, write a pattern to match `monday` and also `t` followed by anything and then *day*.

```
$ ls @(mon|t*)day
```
monday   thursday   tuesday

Another might match `monday` and also `t` or `u` or `v` or `w` followed by anything and then `day`.

```
$ ls @(mon|[t-w]*)day
```
monday   thursday   tuesday   wednesday

Notice that `monmonday` does not match. Only one repetition of the pattern is allowed, specified by the @ pattern prefix.

The star prefix allows zero or more repetitions of the pattern to match. Notice that both `monmonday` and `day` now match.

```
$ ls *(mon|t*)day
```
day   monday   monmonday thursday   tuesday

The query prefix allows zero or one repetitions of the pattern to match, so we still see `day` but not `monmonday`.

```
$ ls ?(mon|t*)day
```
day   monday   thursday   tuesday

Finally, the plus prefix allows one or more patterns to match, so we now see `monmonday` but not `day`.

```
$ ls +(mon|t*)day
```
monday   monmonday thursday   tuesday

Here are some more examples in which we assume the following files.

```
$ echo *.txt
a.txt a1.txt a11.txt a111.txt a12.txt a2.txt a21.txt
 a22.txt a222.txt a3.txt a33.txt a333.txt
$ echo a?(1|2).txt
a.txt a1.txt a2.txt
$ echo a*(1|2).txt
a.txt a1.txt a11.txt a111.txt a12.txt a2.txt a21.txt
 a22.txt a222.txt
$ echo a+(1|2).txt
a1.txt a11.txt a111.txt a12.txt a2.txt a21.txt
 a22.txt a222.txt
```

❧ NOTE

Although monmonday *does not match, a stuttering* ttttttttttuesday *does match, but only because* t* *is allowing the* t *to repeat, not the* @ *prefix.*

↗ LEARN MORE

Refer to "Bash
Initialization" in Project 4
to learn more about the
Bash startup sequence.

Finally, the exclamation point matches anything *except* one of the patterns.

```
$ echo a!(1|2).txt
a.txt a11.txt a111.txt a12.txt a21.txt
 a22.txt a222.txt a3.txt a33.txt a333.txt
```

The easiest way to understand extended globbing is to play with it.

Make It So

To set shell options and shell variables permanently, place the commands in a Bash startup file. To change settings for all users, put the commands in /etc/bashrc and ensure that /etc/profile sources /etc/bashrc. To change settings for just yourself, put the commands in ~/.bashrc and ensure that ~/.bash_profile sources ~/.bashrc.

Project 13
Change Your Working Directory

"Can I reduce the amount of typing I have to do to change my current working directory?"

This project shows you how to squeeze the last drop from the cd command. It covers the use of aliases with command cd, the cd path, and some quick cd tricks.

Popular Destinations

You probably have a number of frequently visited directories, so speeding the process of getting to them can save time and typing. Here are a few ways of doing this in which we use the directory /var/log/httpd as an example.

Use Aliases

The simplest form of shortcut is to define an alias that switches you to a frequently visited directory.

```
$ alias cdhtl='cd /var/log/httpd'
$ cdhtl
$ pwd
/var/log/httpd
```

Another method is to make an alias for the directory. Unfortunately, this will not work, because only the first word on a command line is a candidate for alias expansion, whereas our alias is the second word. The alias htl will not be expanded in this example.

```
$ alias htl='/var/log/httpd'
$ cd htl
-bash: cd: htl: No such file or directory
```

↗ **LEARN MORE**

Project 51 covers aliases.

We can employ a clever trick, however, that defines an alias for the `cd` command itself, the alias being defined as `cd` followed by a space.

```
$ alias cd='cd '
$ cd htl
$ pwd
/var/log/httpd
```

Why this works is not obvious; it's explained in Project 51.

Teleport Using a CD Path

When given a relative pathname, the `cd` command will assume that the pathname is relative to the current working directory. Bash lets you specify a number of directories that the `cd` command should try instead. Set the variable `CDPATH` to contain a colon-separated list of directories. You must add dot to the start of the list; otherwise, the current directory will be tried last, which can be confusing. The `cd` command considers the directories in the order in which they are listed, stopping at the first for which the relative pathname leads to a valid directory. Let's set the `CDPATH`.

```
$ CDPATH=".:/var/log:~/Documents"
```

Next, change to the directory `/var/log/httpd` by typing simply

```
$ cd httpd
/var/log/httpd
```

This works because `/var/log` is in the search path.

Similarly, the directory `Letters` is in `~/Documents`, so we need type only

```
$ cd Letters
/Users/saruman/Documents/Letters
```

Beware Tilde Expansion

Follow the example below, and consider why the alias works but the shell variable doesn't. We have defined an alias and a shell variable to help move quickly to the directory ~/Documents.

```
$ alias docs
alias docs='cd ~/Documents'
$ echo $docs
~/Documents
```

Try the alias method

```
$ docs
$ pwd
/Users/saruman/Documents
```

Try the variable method

```
$ cd $docs
-bash: cd: ~/Documents: No such file or directory
```

Why does the second method fail? The shell is doing a lot of expansion—aliases, tilde (~) expanded to your home directory, and variables, and in that order. The *alias* docs is expanded to include a tilde and then the tilde is expanded to be the full pathname of your home directory. The *variable* docs, however, expands to include a tilde *after* tilde expansion has been completed; it's too late now to expand the tilde itself.

If there's a moral to this example, it's to avoid setting up shortcuts that themselves contain shortcuts. You'll have fewer unpleasant surprises if the contents of aliases and variables are fully expanded as they are assigned, so they don't have to be expanded as they are used.

↗ LEARN MORE

Project 14 discusses more directory-navigation tricks.

↗ LEARN MORE

Refer to "Bash
Initialization" in Project 4
to learn more about the
Bash startup sequence.

cd Quickies

Finally, some common cd tricks are listed in **Table 2.1**.

Table 2.1 Features of cd

Command	Effect
cd or cd ~	Change to the directory given by $HOME
cd ~username	Change to the home directory of user username
cd - or cd ~-	Change to the previous working directory given by $OLDPWD
cd -P	Try cd -P /etc versus cd /etc and issue command pwd
cd directory	Set $PWD to be directory
help cd	Display information on Bash's built-in command cd

Make It So

To set shell options and environment variables permanently, place the commands in a Bash startup file. To change settings for all users, put the commands in /etc/bashrc and ensure that /etc/profile sources /etc/bashrc. To change settings for just yourself, put the commands in ~/.bashrc and ensure that ~/.bash_profile sources ~/.bashrc.

Project 14
Navigate the File System

"How do I move around the file system and then get back to where I was ten minutes ago?"

This project is useful if you have a tendency to hop from one directory to another and forget where you came from. It covers the commands pushd, popd, and dirs.

Pushing and Popping

Bash implements a *directory stack*. You *push* directories onto the stack in the order A, B, C and then *pop* them off the stack in the reverse order C, B, A. It's like leaving a trail of breadcrumbs so you can retrace your steps. Instead of using the cd command, use pushd to change to a new directory and stack the old one; then use popd to return to a previous directory. Use the dirs command at any time to display the directory stack. All three are Bash built-in commands.

As an example, let's start in our home directory.

```
$ pwd
/Users/saruman
```

Next, we move to the directory /etc/httpd, stacking our home directory. The pushd command also echoes the current directory stack.

```
$ pushd /etc/httpd
/etc/httpd ~
```

Then we move to the directory /var/log and from there to /Volumes.

```
$ pushd /var/log
/var/log /etc/httpd ~
$ pushd /Volumes
/Volumes /var/log /etc/httpd ~
```

ℹ TIP

Use the pushd *command with no parameters to flip back and forth between the last two directories. This is equivalent to typing* cd -.

❦ NOTE

The cd *command overwrites the top (last) stack entry, thereby changing the return path that will be followed by* popd.

Use the `dirs` command to display the current directory stack, which should trace back to where we started. The verbose option -v tells `dirs` to list the directory stack line by line, numbering each entry.

```
$ dirs -v
 0   /Volumes
 1   /var/log
 2   /etc/httpd
 3   ~
```

Now use `popd` to retrace our steps. The `popd` command also echoes the current directory stack.

```
$ popd
/var/log /etc/httpd ~
$ pwd
/var/log
$ popd
/etc/httpd ~
$ pwd
/etc/httpd
$ popd
~
```

Manipulate the Directory Stack

The directory stack is a Bash array variable and can, therefore, be read and written just like any other. You may use the `pushd` and `popd` commands to manipulate the stack and jump directly to any directory on the stack. Given the following stack

```
$ dirs -v
 0   /
 1   /usr/local/bin
 2   /etc/httpd
 3   /var/log
```

we can jump straight to the directory /etc/httpd (entry number 2), rotating the stack appropriately, by using

```
$ pushd +2
/etc/httpd /var/log / /usr/local/bin
$ pwd
/etc/httpd
$ dirs -v
 0  /etc/httpd
 1  /var/log
 2  /
 3  /usr/local/bin
```

Mimic a Tcsh Shell Feature in Bash

The Tcsh shell also has built-in pushd, popd, and dirs commands. These commands have a few extra features, such as saving the directory stack from one shell session to the next and a silent mode in which the directory stack is not echoed back in the command line each time pushd and popd are used.

If you'd like to silence the pushd and popd commands in Bash, you can do so easily. Just define a couple of aliases that discard the standard out generated by pushd and popd.

```
$ alias pud='pushd >/dev/null'
$ alias pod='popd >/dev/null'
```

Errors will still show because they are sent to standard error.

Let's test the aliases.

```
$ dirs
/Users/saruman
$ pud /etc/httpd
$ pud /var/log
$ dirs
/var/log /etc/httpd /Users/saruman
$ pod
$ pod
$ dirs
/Users/saruman
```

TIP

Find out more about the pushd, popd, *and* dirs *commands from Bash help. For example, type*

`$ help pushd`

LEARN MORE

Refer to Project 6 for more information on redirection.

TIP

You can name the aliases to be pushd *and* popd*, even though there are built-in commands of the same name. Bash expands aliases before it considers commands.*

LEARN MORE

Refer to "Bash Initialization" in Project 4 if you wish to make the aliases permanent.

Project 15
Find Files by Name

"How do I search the file system a file named my lost letter.txt?*"*

This project shows you how to search the file system for specific files based on filename and pathname. It uses the locate command to find public files quickly and the find command to find any file. See Projects 17 and 18 when you need to employ more advanced file-finding techniques. Project 20 gives some handy find tips.

Locate with locate

The locate command searches the file system for files of a given name. Here are the results we get locating the file httpd.conf.

```
$ locate httpd.conf
/private/etc/httpd/httpd.conf
/private/etc/httpd/httpd.conf.applesaved
/private/etc/httpd/httpd.conf.bak
/private/etc/httpd/httpd.conf.default
```

(If you don't get any results, see "The Locate Database" a little later in this project.) To confine the search to named directories, we include a partial pathname. The following example locates files named system.log in any directory named log.

```
$ locate log/system.log
/private/var/log/system.log
/private/var/log/system.log.0.gz
/private/var/log/system.log.1.gz
```

From the examples above, you'll notice that

▶   The locate command matches against the entire pathname, not just the filename. You can search for files, directories, and path-names.

> ▸ Pathnames match if they contain the search term; they don't have to equal it. To use shell globbing terminology, the search term is effectively *search-term*.

> ▸ The locate command is fast (although it's not apparent from reading this book ☺).

The Locate Database

The locate command is fast because it doesn't search the file system; instead, it searches a prebuilt database of all public files. *Public* files are those for which "others" are granted read permission, ensuring that locate won't reveal the names (or the existence) of your private files. To be completely accurate, locate reveals only files that are accessible to the user nobody; see the sidebar "User Nobody" for more details.

The locate command will not find my private file template.rtf.

```
$ ls Documents/Letters
template.rtf
$ locate template.rtf
<no results - this is to be expected>
```

So how is the locate database built in the first place? It's (re)built automatically as part of weekly maintenance during the early hours of Saturday. If you've recently added new public files, you may have to rebuild the locate database manually. The best way to do this is to run the weekly maintenance scripts by typing

```
$ sudo periodic weekly
```

Use Globbing with locate

The locate command lets you specify a filename pattern as the search term, using the same pattern-matching operators as for shell globbing—namely, [^*?]. In fact, locate automatically converts a bare search term such as httpd.conf to *httpd.conf*. If you use any pattern-matching operator in your search term, you override this default behavior, and no star characters are added.

User Nobody

The user nobody is a special user with a UID of -2. It has a primary group called nobody that has a GID of -2. This user is an unprivileged user who does not (usually) own any files and is restricted to the permissions assigned to *others*. Refer to Projects 7 and 8 for more information on users, groups, and permissions.

```
$ id nobody
uid=4294967294(nobody)
gid=4294967294(nobody)
groups=4294967294(nobody)
```

If you are curious, or even if you are not, 4294967294 is also -2 interpreted as a 32-bit unsigned number.

TIP

To avoid automatic globbing when searching for a filename such as httpd.conf, *use the search term* */httpd.conf.

↗ LEARN MORE

Refer to Project 11 to learn about globbing.

Periodic Maintenance

Your Mac runs daily, weekly, and monthly maintenance scripts in the early hours. If your Mac isn't running at that time, the scripts will be run later, but only in Mac OS X 10.4 (Tiger). Before Tiger, missed schedules were simply skipped.

↗ LEARN MORE

See Project 71 to learn more about periodic maintenance, and Project 70 to learn more about execution of scheduled commands.

The next example locates all the Unix man-page directories. A search term such as */man/man? matches pathnames .../man/man1, .../man/man2, and so on. The query character must be escaped from the shell; otherwise, it will be expanded before it is passed to locate. Also, because the search term now includes a pattern-matching operator in the query symbol, a star is not implicitly added to the start and so must be added explicitly (and escaped from the shell).

```
$ locate '*/man/man?'
```

Rebuild Manually

You may build the locate database manually and without having to run periodic maintenance scripts. It's not that easy, though; in particular, you must do it as the user nobody to avoid revealing the names of private files. Here are step-by-step instructions for doing so. Even if you don't need to perform a manual rebuild, the procedure is interesting, as it includes some clever "geekery."

First, become nobody (not as sad as it sounds). This is not so simple, because the user nobody does not have a password. In fact, the password is not even nothing. It has a hash value of star, for which there is no possible plain-text password.

```
$ su nobody
Password:
su: Sorry
```

The trick is to become root (the ultimate Somebody). Root can become any other user without the need for a password, neatly sidestepping the problem.

```
$ sudo -s
Password:
#
```

Let's rebuild the database now. First, we must ensure that the database exists by touching it (which has the effect of creating it, if it does not exist).

```
# touch /var/db/locate.database
```

Then we make it writable by user *nobody* by making the owner *nobody* and giving the owner write permission.

```
# chown nobody /var/db/locate.database
# chmod 644 /var/db/locate.database
```

Now switch to user *nobody*. This doesn't seem to do anything. Why? Because user *nobody* is not permitted to log in.

```
# su nobody
# whoami
root
```

The trick is to use option -m, which switches users without going through the normal login process:.

```
# su -m nobody
$ whoami
nobody
```

Now we can run the update script, located at /usr/libexec/locate.updatedb. It's wise to throw away "Permission denied" errors ; there'll be lots of them, for obvious reasons. To do this, we pipe standard error to the grep command and filter out the appropriate lines.

```
$ /usr/libexec/locate.updatedb 2>&1 | ¬
    grep -v "Permission denied"
```

Finally, we tighten the permissions and exit from users *nobody* and then root.

```
$ chmod 444 /var/db/locate.database
$ exit
exit
# exit
exit
```

⟁ LEARN MORE

Refer to Projects 7 and 8 to learn about users, groups, and permissions.

⟁ LEARN MORE

Refer to Project 6 if you need to brush up on redirection and pipelining.

⟁ LEARN MORE

See Project 23 to learn more about the grep command.

↗ LEARN MORE

Projects 17 and 18 cover the advanced features of find, **showing how it can be combined with other commands to process a list of files or the files themselves.**

Primaries

A *primary* introduces a new search criterion. The find command uses primaries combined with *operators* such as AND and OR to build complex criteria specifying which files should match and which should not (Projects 17 and 18 cover primaries and operators in greater depth.)

Read the man page for find for a full list of primaries and operators.

ᵢ̈ TIP

If you get bored waiting for find *to complete and want to do something more interesting, simply press* Control-c *to abort it.*

Find with find

Unlike the locate command, which searches a prebuilt database, the find command does a *live* search of the file system. The find command is very powerful and able to search for files based on many criteria. This project shows searches based only on filename and pathname.

Find by Name

Let's find all files named letter.txt located in *(rooted in)* our home directory. The find command is inherently recursive, so you need to specify only the root of the search. The command *requires* a search root as its first argument; it can't be omitted, because find won't assume the current directory. To search by name, specify the *primary* -name and follow it with the search term. For example:

```
$ find ~ -name letter.txt
/Users/saruman/Documents/Letters/letter.txt
...
```

To search the current directory, simply replace tilde with dot. To search the entire file system, use forward slash and the sudo command. A search of the entire file system can take a while to complete.

```
$ sudo find / -name letter.txt
Password:
/Users/saruman/Documents/Letters/letter.txt
...
```

The find command uses a case-sensitive comparison against the search term. To ignore case, use the primary -iname.

Use Globbing with find

You may specify a filename pattern as the search term by using the same pattern-matching operators as in shell globbing—namely, [^*?]. Unlike with the locate command, a bare search term like httpd.conf is *not* automatically converted to *httpd.conf*.

The next example finds all .txt files rooted in the current directory. The star character must be escaped from the shell; otherwise, it will be expanded before it is passed to find.

```
$ find . -iname "*.txt"
./Letters/letter.txt
...
```

Search by Pathnames

Use the primary -path (or -ipath, to be case insensitive) to search against the whole pathname, not just the filename. Compare the following two examples. The first finds all files named test anywhere. The second finds files named test rooted in directories named test.

First, match filenames. Only pathnames ending in test will match.

```
$ find . -iname test
./test
./test/test
./Trial/One/Test
./Trial2/test
./Trial2/version1/test
./Trial2/version1/test/a/test
```

Second, match pathnames. Any pathname containing the sequence /test/ and ending test will match.

```
$ find . -ipath "*/test/*test"
./test/anewtest
./test/test
./Trial2/version1/test/a/test
```

The second example fails on a file called anewtest. We wanted to match only files named exactly test. The easiest way to correct this is to combine primaries. Use -ipath to match pathnames and -iname to match filenames. Both primaries must match. Because anewtest does not match the filename test, it is eliminated from the search results.

```
$ find . -ipath "*/test/*" -iname test
./test/test
./Trial2/version1/test/a/test
```

Running find in the Background

You may want to run a lengthy find operation in a new Terminal window or in the background. The example below demonstrates a search of the root disk run in the background (the -b option applied to sudo does this). Output is redirected to the file search.out, and the whole command is *niced* (run at a lower priority) to avoid hogging resources.

```
$ nice -n 10 sudo -b ¬
    find / -name ¬
    "search-term" &> ¬
    ~/search.out
```

ℹ TIP

Combine many primaries to suit your search requirements. In particular, primaries can be combined with AND and OR. See Project 17 to learn more about complex conditions.

↗ LEARN MORE

Projects 77 and 78 cover regular expressions in detail.

Use Regular Expressions

You may search pathnames by employing regular expressions instead of the pattern-matching operators used in shell globbing. Use the primary -regex (or -iregex, to be case insensitive) to search against the pathname. Notice the use of the regular expression operator *dot-star* versus the shell globbing operator *star* from previous examples.

```
$ find . -iregex ".*/test/.*test"
./test/test
./Trial2/version1/test/a/test
```

This simple example is equivalent to using the primary ipath. Regular expressions are more powerful than globbing, however, so you may need to consider this alternative for more complex requirements. If you're familiar with regular expressions, take note that matching is against the *whole* pathname. Without the leading dot-star, the file ./Trial2/version1/test/a/test would not match.

Option -E enables *extended* regular expressions, telling the primary -regex to interpret its argument as an extended regular expression. Without this option, -regex would assume a basic regular expression.

Project 16
Find Unix Commands

"When I type ls, *where is the executable found, and will it be overridden by a Bash built-in command or function of the same name?"*

Unix is susceptible to confusion over different entities with the same name. Unix commands, built-in shell commands, and user-defined functions and aliases, for example, might have a common name. This project helps you understand and control the shell's use of these same-name functions and commands, whether you're calling them interactively or writing scripts that use them.

Use Type to Identify a Command

Suppose you wish to discover in which directory a particular Unix command lives. In a script, for example, you might want to call the command by its full pathname to avoid relying on the PATH variable (see "The PATH" later in this project). Alternatively, you may wish to see which instance of a command will be executed in the case where several exist. Bash's built-in command type tells you this. Here, we discover that mkdir is to be found in the directory /bin.

```
$ type mkdir
mkdir is /bin/mkdir
```

The name *type* doesn't make sense until you realize what type actually does. It reports on how Bash will interpret a command in terms of its type, the type being one of the following:

▸ An alias

▸ A keyword like if or for

▸ A function

▸ A shell built-in command

▸ A Unix executable command

The list order corresponds to Bash's search order. When a same-name command exists in many forms, an alias form will override a built-in, and a built-in will override a Unix executable. Here are some examples.

```
$ type pushd
pushd is a shell builtin
$ type cd
cd is aliased to `cd '
```

(This assumes you have defined such an alias.)

Use option -a to reveal all possible types that a command currently has. The types are listed in the order in which Bash considers them. In this example, the cd command will be interpreted as an alias. If the alias is deleted, the built-in command will be used.

```
$ type -a cd
cd is aliased to `cd '
cd is a shell builtin
```

Override Bash's Order

Three Bash built-in commands are available to override the natural order in which commands are considered. They are particularly useful when employed in functions and scripts.

▶ The command command forces a command to be considered as either a built-in or a Unix executable. If the command is an alias or function too, the alias or function will be ignored, even though aliases and functions are normally considered first.

▶ The builtin command forces a command to be considered as a built-in only. No other types will be considered.

▶ The enable command enables and disables built-in commands. See the example of using enable below.

Here's an example using command. We define a function called ls to be shorthand for ls -al argument-list. The following attempt will not work because it gets stuck in a loop: *Function* ls attempts to call the Unix *command* ls, but because Bash considers function names ahead of Unix commands, the function ends up calling itself instead. Futile attempts to call command ls continue forever—or until we interrupt the process by pressing Control-c.

```
$ ls () { ls -al $*; }
$ ls
^C
```

Our second attempt works. When we employ the command command, function ls is made to call the Unix command ls instead of itself.

```
$ ls () { command ls -al $*; }
$ ls
total 560
drwxr-xr-x  47 saruman   saruman    1598 19 May 19:04 .
drwxrwxr-t  18 root      admin       612  9 Apr 18:22 ..
-rwxr-xr-x   1 saruman   saruman   15364 18 May 16:52 .DS_Store
...
```

Here's an example of using the enable command. We see that the command pwd is both a Bash built-in command and a Unix executable by typing

```
$ type -a pwd
pwd is a shell builtin
pwd is /bin/pwd
```

Let's disable the Bash built-in version by using command enable and specifying option –n to disable.

```
$ enable -n pwd
$ type -a pwd
pwd is /bin/pwd
```

Now we restore the built-in version by typing

```
$ enable pwd
$ type -a pwd
pwd is a shell builtin
pwd is /bin/pwd
```

Can One Disable enable?

And how is it enabled again? This is presented purely as fun. Something for you to think about:

```
$ enable -n enable
$ enable enable
enable: Operation
failed: client-
error-not-found
$ builtin enable enable
-bash: builtin: enable:
not a shell builtin
$
```

We can no longer get at the built-in enable.

⚓ TIP

A quick way to override an alias and run the original command is to precede it with a backslash (\) symbol.

```
$ \cd
```

TIP

Run a script or command that resides in the current directory by typing

$ ./script-command-name

LEARN MORE

Project 50 shows how to add directories to the search path.

The PATH

When searching for a Unix command, type checks all directories listed in the PATH environment variable in the order listed. You can view the path by typing

```
$ echo $PATH
/bin:/sbin:/usr/bin:/usr/sbin
```

An executable in any directory outside the path is invisible to type and therefore to Bash too. Bash will not run such a command if you simply type its name; you must use the command's full pathname to invoke it.

If a command of the same name exists in several directories listed in PATH, Bash will invoke the first one it encounters. To invoke a different variant, specify a full pathname. We might have a version of ls in /usr/local/bin as well as the more usual location of /bin, and we may have /usr/local/bin earlier in our PATH. We use type with option -a to identify all versions, which will list them in the order in which Bash considers them.

```
$ type -a ls
ls is /usr/local/bin/ls
ls is /bin/ls
```

The Tcsh Shell

The Tcsh shell does not have command type but instead uses a built-in command called which.

```
% which ls
ls:     aliased to ls --color=tty
% which mkdir
/bin/mkdir
% which which
which: shell built-in command.
```

Tcsh allows alias commands to be overridden temporarily in favor of Unix commands by escaping them with a backslash character, exactly as Bash does. In fact, `which` recognizes this too.

```
% which \ls
/bin/ls
```

If you're using the Tcsh built-in command `which`, be aware that there's a Unix command of the same name.

```
% which \which
/usr/bin/which
```

The Unix `which` command should not be used. It searches only the standard path and misses out on aliases. It's written for use with the csh shell.

When Tcsh starts up, it searches the directories listed in PATH, building a cache of command names. If you install a new command, `which` and the Tcsh shell ordinarily can't find it until you begin a new shell session. Remedy this problem by typing the command `rehash` to tell the current shell to rebuild its command-name cache.

❧ NOTE

Bash rehashes automatically and does not need, or have, a `rehash` *command.*

Project 17
Get Clever Finding Files

"What files have I modified today, and do I have any larger than 20 MB?"

This project shows you how to search the file system for specific files based on file type, size, timestamp, and permissions. It uses find to find files and perform simple processing on them. Project 15 uses locate and find to search for files by name. Project 18 shows how to process the files that were found. Project 20 gives some handy find tips.

Search Criteria

The find command is very powerful. It recursively searches an entire directory structure for files that match a given set of criteria. The criteria are based on:

▶   File name and pathname with pattern matching (see Project 15)

▶   File type and size

▶   Timestamp for last access and modification times

▶   Permissions including file owner, associated group, permissions, and flags

▶   Complex conditions that combine criteria with AND, OR, NOT, and parentheses

The find command generates a list of files that match the specified criteria. Sometimes this is all you want, but often you'll need to process either the list itself or each file named in the list. There are several ways in which you can do this:

▶   Pipe to another command to process the file list

▶   Use find itself to process the files

▶   Use -exec to invoke another command to process each file (see Project 18)

▶   Use pipelining and xargs to invoke another command to process each file (see Project 18)

Find Criteria

When working with Unix files and directories, it's often helpful (or necessary) to identify files that meet one or more criteria, either as a means of simply locating desired information or content, or as the first step in a process that involves comparing, sorting, or performing other operations based on those criteria. The key to many criteria-based searches are in the option settings for command find.

Find by Filename and Pathname

Refer to Project 15, which shows you how to search the file system for specific files based on filename and pathname.

Find by Type

The find command normally considers all files, but if you want to limit the search to a specific type of file, use the primary -type. The type can be a regular file, a directory, a symbolic link, or a special type such as a socket.

To search for directories only (-type d), type

```
$ find . -type d -iname test
./test
./Trial/One/Test
./Trial2/version1/test
```

To search for files only (-type f), type

```
$ find . -type f -iname test
./test/test
./Trial2/test
./Trial2/version1/test/a/test
```

Find by Size

The find command can search for files whose size is equal to, greater than, or less than a given size. Precede the given size with plus to search for files bigger than that size and minus to search for files smaller than

TIP

Using find *with option* -d *causes the lowest-level directory to be listed first, which can be useful sometimes.*

Small Files

The size of a file is always rounded up to the nearest 512-byte block. Therefore, a file of 1 byte will be treated as though it were one 512-byte block. In particular, the file will not be found by specifying -size 0 (as expected) or -size -1 (perhaps not as expected).

✎ NOTE

Primary -print tells find to print (display) the name of each file it finds. Modern versions of find do this anyway, so it's not usually required.

that size. The size is specified as the number of 512-byte blocks (that is, it's specified in units of 512 bytes). To give some examples:

▶ -size 2 means 1K bytes (2 times 512); 1K bytes equals 1024 bytes.

▶ -size 2048 means 1M bytes; 1M bytes equals 1024K bytes.

▶ -size +2048 means greater than 1M bytes.

▶ -size -2048 means less than 1 M bytes.

To find all pictures bigger than 10 M bytes, we would type

```
$ find ~/Pictures -size +20480
```

To find all empty files, we could use either of the following.

```
$ find . -size 0
$ find . -size -1
```

For teensy-weensy files, for which blocks are too coarse a measure, specify the size in bytes (characters) by appending c to the size. Here, we find all files of exactly 19 bytes.

```
$ find . -size 19c -ls
996343  8 -rw-r--r--  1 saruman saruman ... ./Im19Bytes
```

The primary -ls tells find to list the file's details instead of just its name.

Find by Timestamp

The find command can search for files based on their time stamp, either

▶ Time of last access

▶ Time of last modification

▶ Time of creation, which seems always to be the time of last modification in Mac OS X's HFS+ file system

The find command works by units of time. A *unit* can be either a minute or a day (24 hours). Time is calculated as the difference between the time stamp of a file and the time find itself was started. The difference is rounded up to the next unit when testing for equality (last modified one minute ago) but is not rounded otherwise (last modified *less than* one minute ago). Therefore, we can specify criteria such "last accessed one minute ago," "last modified less than two days ago," or "last modified more than seven days ago."

The primaries are -amin, -mmin, -atime, and -mtime. a means access time, and m means modification time; min means units of minutes, and time means units of days. As with size, units of time that are preceded by plus mean a number of units greater than the amount specified, and units of time that are preceded by a minus mean fewer units than the amount specified.

As an example, let's create two files and check that they were both modified/created less than one minute ago. The primary -mmin -1 is formed by m, meaning modified, and min, meaning units of minutes. The value -1 means a time less than one unit before find was invoked.

```
$ touch f-mod f-access
$ find . -mmin -1
./f-access
./f-mod
```

Repeat the find command until it reports no files; then proceed. (If you're a very slow typist, change the time period to two minutes.)

Now let's use the command touch -a to access (but not modify) file f-access and thereby change its access time stamp. Then we'll check to see which files were accessed, and which files were modified, less than one minute ago.

```
$ touch -a f-access
$ find . -mmin -1
$
$ find . -amin -1
./f-access
```

✎ NOTE

Read the man page for the touch *command.*

↗ LEARN MORE

Projects 7 and 8 cover users, groups, and permissions.

Next, we use the command `touch -m` to change the modification time of the file `f-mod` (we could have achieved the same thing by editing it, but `touch`ing it is easier) and then check which files were accessed, and which files were modified, less than one minute ago. Depending on how long we take to type the commands, the file `f-access` may or may not be reported as being accessed less than a minute ago.

```
$ touch -m f-mod
$ find . -mmin -1
./f-mod
$ find . -amin -1
./f-access
```

Finally, wait a few minutes and try again.

```
$ find . -mmin -1
$ find . -amin -1
```

Here are a couple more examples.

Find all files in your home directory modified within the last 24 hours —useful when you want to perform a daily backup.

```
$ find ~ -mtime 1
```

Find files you've forgotten about.

```
$ find ~ -atime +1000
```

Find by Owner, Associated Group, and Permissions

The `find` command accepts search criteria including file owner (or *user owner*, in Unix terminology), associated group, and permissions. Here are a few examples of how they work.

To find all files owned by the user `saruman` in the directory `/Users/saruman`, we use the primary `-user` as our search criterion.

```
$ find /Users/saruman -user saruman
```

(This is user `saruman`'s home directory, so we'll omit the long list of matching files.)

To find all files in the same directory that *aren't* owned by the user saruman, we use the primary -not to invert the sense of any criteria that follow (in this case, the primary -user again). Not surprisingly, the results list is much shorter this time.

```
$ find /Users/saruman -not -user saruman
/Users/saruman/Development/c32-1
```

Let's find all pictures that are *not* associated with the group saruman. A group criterion is introduced by the primary -group.

```
$ find /Users/saruman/Pictures -not -group saruman -ls
871501 6368 -rw-r--r-- 1 saruman admin 320911 Mar 12 09:41
/Users/saruman/Pictures/people/Domi/sledges2photo1.psd
823934  320 -rw-r--r-- 1 saruman admin 123297 Feb 10 19:06
/Users/saruman/Pictures/web-site/jan/home
```

As you may have noticed, the preceding command uses yet another primary of the find command called -ls. Not to be confused with Unix command ls, it instructs find to display a file's details instead of just its name.

To specify permissions as search criteria, we use the primary -perm and express permissions in the octal or symbolic formats expected by command chmod. (If you are unfamiliar with these concepts, refer to Project 8.)

The following examples use find in a directory containing just one file, xxx. Each example uses permissions as search criteria to see whether file xxx matches. Follow them carefully to understand how the criteria are matched.

First, we'll use ls to display the permissions for file xxx. You'll see that the permissions grant write access to owner saruman and read access to group saruman and everyone else (others):

```
$ ls -l xxx
--w-r--r--  1 saruman  saruman  0 20 May 23:42 xxx
```

Our first example seeks files with permissions set *exactly as stated* in our search criteria. Files will match only if their permission settings match the -perm criteria *and* all unspecified permissions are unset. The permissions in this example match those of xxx exactly.

```
$ find . -perm u+w,g+r,o+r
./xxx
```

If we modify the search criteria, additionally specifying write access to others, find no longer locates file xxx. Its permissions no longer match the search criteria *exactly*.

```
$ find . -perm u+w,g+r,o+rw
$
```

We can find files that have *one or more* of the stated permissions set by preceding the permissions with a plus sign (+). File xxx now matches again.

```
$ find . -perm +u+w,g+r,o+r
./xxx
```

We can find files that have *all* of the stated permissions set (but may also have others set) by preceding the permissions with a minus sign (-).

```
$ find . -perm -u+w,g+r,o+r
./xxx
```

Changing the permissions on file xxx to remove "others read" will cause find to fail. The file no longer has *all* of the stated permissions.

```
$ chmod 240 xxx
$ ls -l xxx
--w-r----- 1 saruman  saruman  0 20 May 23:42 xxx
$ find . -perm -u+w,g+r,o+r
$
```

This example will find file xxx because a plus sign means *one or more* permissions, not *all* permissions.

```
$ find . -perm +u+w,g+r,o+r
./xxx
```

When specifying an *exact* match or *all* (but not *one or more*), you may specify that particular permissions should *not* be set. o-r, for example, means that "other read" should not be set.

```
$ find .   -perm u+w,g+r,o-r
./xxx
$ find .   -perm -u+w,g+r,o-r
./xxx
```

Use Complex Conditions

The find command has a very powerful syntax that lets you combine primaries into *expressions* by using AND (-and), OR (-or), and NOT (! -false -not) operators, thereby creating complex search criteria. You enclose expressions in parentheses, which must be escaped from the shell. Here are some examples:

Find all .html and .ws files in ~/Sites:

```
$ find ~/Sites -name "*.ws" -or -name "*.html"
```

Find files modified less than one day ago AND bigger than 5 MB:

```
$ find . -mtime -1 -and -size +10240
```

Find files modified more than one day ago AND smaller than 5 MB:

```
$ find . -mtime +1 -and -size -10240
```

Find files modified less than one day ago AND bigger than 5 MB:

OR

modified more than one day ago AND smaller than 5 MB:

(The following command must be on one line, with a space between the first expression in parentheses and the –or operator.)

```
$ find . \( -mtime -1 -and -size +10240 \) ¬
    -or \( -mtime +1 -and -size -10240 \)
```

↗ LEARN MORE

Project 23 tells you more about the grep command.

Note the use of parentheses (escaped from the shell by backslash symbols) to ensure that the AND and OR expressions are evaluated in the correct order: The two ANDs will be evaluated; then their results will be ORed.

When primaries are grouped in an expression, find assumes by default that AND is the intended operator, so the expressions in this case can be shortened to

```
$ find . \( -mtime -1 -size +10240 \) ¬
    -or \( -mtime +1 -size -10240 \)
```

Also, find evaluates AND operators before OR operators, allowing us to omit the parentheses too.

```
$ find . -mtime -1 -size +10240 -or -mtime +1 -size -10240
```

Process Each File

You may process the list of files returned by find in one of three ways:

▶ Process the list itself, not the files or their contents.

▶ Process each file named in the list with one of find's built-in file-processing primaries.

▶ Process each file named in the list with another command.

It's important to be aware of these three different methods and how to realize each. The next three sections illustrate each technique using a simple example.

Process the List

We may want to process the list of filenames by sorting it alphabetically or filtering it with grep. To display each filename that includes the text *hello,* we can use the following:

```
$ find ~ -iname "*.txt" | grep -i "hello"
/Users/saruman/Documents/Letters/hello.txt
```

Process the Files with find

The `find` command itself has a couple of primaries for processing files directly. The first is `-ls` to display file details, used in some of the examples above. The second is `-delete` to delete every file in a list. Naturally, caution is recommended with this one. Let's delete all files in our home directory that match the pattern `*letter.txt`.

Dry-run the command first.

```
$ find ~ -iname "*letter.txt"
/Users/saruman/Documents/Letters/my_letter.txt
```

Now delete the files, and check what's left.

```
$ find ~ -iname "*letter.txt" -delete
$ find ~ -iname "*letter.txt"
$
```

Process the Files with -exec and xargs

If we wish to search the *contents* of each file for the text *hello,* we must hand each filename off to an external command such as `grep`. In this example, `grep` is given a list of files to search. Compare this with the first example, in which the text of the list itself was searched by `grep`, not the contents of each file in the list.

```
$ find ~ -iname "*.txt" | xargs grep "hello"
/Users/saruman/Documents/Letters/letter-to-jan.txt:Hello Jan,
```

↗ LEARN MORE

Project 18 shows how to process the files returned by find **by using the** -exec **primary and the** xargs **command.**

Project 18
Use find, -exec, and xargs

"How do I delete all my .bak *files and all the empty files too?"*

This project shows how to process the files returned by the find command. It uses first the primary -exec and then the xargs command to process each file in the list. Project 15 uses locate and find to search for files by name. Project 17 shows how to find files by more complex criteria. Project 20 gives some handy find tips.

Do Something With What You Found

The find command is very powerful. It recursively searches an entire directory structure for files that match a given set of criteria. This project examines techniques for processing files identified in a find search, building on concepts discussed in previous projects.

In Project 15, we explored the use of pattern matching with the locate and find commands for searches based on filenames and pathnames.

Project 17 focused on the use of find with additional search criteria, including file type and size; time stamp for last access and modification times; permissions including file owner, associated group, and specific permission settings; and complex conditions that combine criteria using the AND, OR, and NOT operators.

The find command generates a list of files that match the specified criteria. Sometimes this is all you want, but often you'll need to process either the list itself or each file named in the list. Project 17 addresses the limited ability of the find command to process files named in such a list.

In this project, we'll look at file-processing techniques that invoke other commands to process the files identified by find. These methods include pairing find with the primary −exec and pipelining output from find to the xargs command.

Use the -exec Primary

When you've used the power of find to root out a group of files—all the HTML files in your Sites directory, for example—you can narrow your search further by using the primary -exec with the grep command to search the content of files. In the next example, find locates all HTML files; then -exec invokes grep to identify only those files that contain the text *osxfaq.com*.

```
$ find ~/Sites -name "*.htm" -or -name "*.html" ¬
    -exec grep -il "osxfaq.com" {} \;
/Users/saruman/Sites/calendar/data/index.html
/Users/saruman/Sites/mayo-family/frames/links-r.html
/Users/saruman/Sites/osxfaq/index.html
/Users/saruman/Sites/saruman/data-base/tipsandtricks.html
/Users/saruman/Sites/unix/index.html
```

How does this work? The portion of the command line preceding -exec tells find to search the directory ~/Sites for HTML files (which are denoted by filenames ending with .htm or .html). Each time find identifies a matching filename, the -exec primary hands it off to the grep command by creating this command line.

```
grep -il "osxfaq.com" filename
```

The command line tells grep to check the contents of filename and, if it finds the text string "osxfaq.com", to write the file's name to the screen.

The placeholder symbol {} tells -exec where to place the filename when it creates a command line. The semicolon at the end of the command is required by the -exec primary; it signals the end of an argument list. The backslash that precedes the semicolon escapes it from the shell.

⬈ LEARN MORE

The grep **command is discussed at greater length in Project 23.**

◣ NOTE

Piping the list of filenames to grep *without using the primary* -exec *is very different. The* grep *command sees the list of files as its standard input and processes this text. It is not invoked with the name of each file to process.*

The primary -ok does the same thing as -exec but asks for confirmation before processing each file. This is demonstrated by the following command line, which locates and removes backup (.bak) files after confirmation.

```
$ find ~/Sites -name "*.bak" -ok rm {} \;
"rm /Users/saruman/Sites/calendar/jan-index.bak"? y
"rm /Users/saruman/Sites/projects/index.bak"? y
...
```

Process Each File via xargs

Instead of using the primary -exec, we can process each file by piping the output from find to the xargs command. A Unix command in its own right, xargs forms a command line from its parameters, which in this case includes the output from find.

You can see for yourself how it works by modifying the -exec-based command line we used to process HTML files. Our original command line was

```
$ find ~/Sites -name "*.htm" -or -name "*.html" ¬
    -exec grep -il "osxfaq.com" {} \;
```

We replace the -exec primary with a pipe to xargs. Note that xargs doesn't need the {} placeholder or the closing semicolon-with-backslash. Run the command, and you'll see a familiar file list.

```
$ find ~/Sites -name "*.htm" -or -name "*.html" ¬
    | xargs grep -il "osxfaq.com"
/Users/saruman/Sites/calendar/data/index.html
/Users/saruman/Sites/mayo-family/frames/links-r.html
/Users/saruman/Sites/osxfaq/index.html
/Users/saruman/Sites/saruman/data-base/tipsandtricks.html
/Users/saruman/Sites/unix/index.html
```

This represents a different technique but yields the same results.

xargs vs. -exec

So which should you use: xargs or -exec?

▸ The xargs command wins on speed, as it's much faster than -exec. In the comparison above, xargs performed ten times as fast. You may think piping to xargs is less efficient than using the built-in primary. This is not so. Why? Because -exec will execute grep once for each file found. The xargs command, on the other hand, absorbs all the arguments and passes them to grep in one go. This is fine assuming that grep, or whatever command you are invoking, can handle multiple arguments and expects them to be at the end of the command line.

▸ The xargs command wins on options. Use option -t (trace) to echo each command line before it is executed, for example.

▸ The xargs command fails when too many files are found. Because xargs processes all files in one command line, the resulting command line can become too big, and you may see an error message about "too many arguments." This problem can be corrected, as shown later in this project.

▸ The xargs command fails if filenames contain spaces. Again, this problem can be corrected, as shown later in this project.

Cope with Too Many Files

When many files match, in the order of thousands, the command line formed by xargs gets big, causing an error to be thrown. To solve this problem, use option -n, which tells xargs the maximum number of arguments to include on a command line. It will issue the target command repeatedly until all filenames have been processed.

```
$ find ~/Sites  -name "*.htm" -or -name "*.html" ¬
    | xargs -n1000 grep -il "osxfaq.com"
/Users/saruman/Sites/calendar/data/index.html
/Users/saruman/Sites/mayo-family/frames/links-r.html
/Users/saruman/Sites/osxfaq/index.html
/Users/saruman/Sites/saruman/data-base/tipsandtricks.html
/Users/saruman/Sites/unix/index.html
```

❧ NOTE

After some experimentation, I found that 1,000 is a good, safe, round number to choose as the maximum number of filenames. The length of the command line formed by xargs is obviously dependent on the average length of a filename. A higher number increases the risk of the command's failing; a lower number makes the command run slower. The choice is yours.

Spaces in Filenames

Spaces in filenames are not a problem when you use the -exec primary, which passes filenames one at a time to the utility being called. When you use xargs, the filenames are piped to xargs in a batch of arguments, with spaces separating the filenames. The command xargs can't distinguish spaces within filenames from spaces between them, so the distinction between a space *in* a filename and a space *separating* filenames is lost.

Handle Filenames with Spaces

When filenames include spaces, the find | xargs combination will fail. The xargs command cannot tell when a space is part of a filename or an argument separator. In the following example, we encounter a file named *a space.html*.

```
$ find ~/Sites -name "*.htm" -or -name "*.html" ¬
    | xargs -n1000 grep -il "osxfaq.com"
grep: /Users/saruman/Sites/calendar/a: No such file or  ...
grep: space.html: No such file or directory
...
```

The solution is to tell both find and xargs to use a different argument separator, such as the null character instead of a space. The null character should not be part of any filename. Specify the primary -print0 to find and the option -0 (number zero, not letter *O*, in both cases) to xargs.

```
$ find ~/Sites -name "*.htm" -or -name "*.html" -print0 ¬
    | xargs -0 -n1000 grep -il "osxfaq.com"
/Users/saruman/Sites/calendar/a space.html
...
```

Limit find's Scope

Command find is often plagued by an excess of success: If you're looking for one specific file, a search that returns hundreds of matches is as useless as one that turns up nothing. One remedy is to limit the extent of find searches, to prevent it from looking in places where you know your target file won't be found.

Limit Recursion

Suppose that we initiate a search for all index files in the directory Sites by typing

```
$ find Sites -name "index.*"
Sites/albums/index.html
Sites/calendar/data/index.html
Sites/calendar/index.php
Sites/osxfaq/index.html
Sites/osxfaq/index.ws
Sites/sqmail/sqmail/class/deliver/index.php
Sites/sqmail/sqmail/class/index.php
Sites/webdav/index.php
```

Perhaps there are unwanted results, and we wish to eliminate particular directories from the search—for example, those starting with sq* and os*. The find command provides a way to prevent searching of (or recursion into) selected directories by using the primary -prune. Like all primaries, -prune is applied to each file as it is found, starting with the root of the search.

We require three expressions: one to match files named index.* as we already have above, and one for each of sq* and os* telling find not to search any directory that matches either of the patterns. These look like this:

```
-name "sq*" –prune
-name "os*" -prune
```

The complete command looks like this:

```
$ find Sites -name "index.*" -print -or -name "sq*" ¬
    -prune -or -name "os*" –prune
Sites/albums/index.html
Sites/calendar/data/index.html
Sites/calendar/index.php
Sites/webdav/index.php
```

You'll immediately notice three things: One, it worked; two, the expressions are ORed, not ANDed; and three, there's a -print primary after the name expression. Why?

Short answer: These are little tricks one learns.

Long answer: If you were to AND the terms instead of ORing them, you wouldn't get any results. No filename can match all three expressions—index.*, sq*, and os*—at the same time. Second, the primary

-print is always implied and always displays a matched filename. So we'll see filenames that match sq* and os* as well as those that match index.*. The find command is matching them to -prune, but it still prints a filename when it matches. This is unfortunate, but it is a result of -print being implied. By stating -print explicitly, however, we can position it after the -name primary but before the others. The result is that only matches from the -name primary are printed.

If you don't follow this, don't worry. I had to spend a lot of time reading the man page for find to understand in detail how it worked. Accept the short answer. After all, this book is about how to do it, not necessarily about spending several hours studying theory.

Set the Maximum Recursion Depth

Primary -maxdepth limits the number of directory levels covered by a recursive search. Place a number (1 or greater) after the -maxdepth primary to specify the number of search levels. A -maxdepth value of 1 limits the search to files at the search root level; -maxdepth 2 looks inside directories at that level (but not any directories they enclose), and so on.

```
$ find ~/Sites -maxdepth 1 -name "*.htm" -or -name "*.html"
/Users/saruman/Sites/index.html
```

Next, the depth of recursion is limited to two directory levels. Compare the results with those from earlier examples.

```
$ find ~/Sites  -maxdepth 2 -name "*.htm" -or -name "*.html"
/Users/saruman/Sites/albums/albums.html
/Users/saruman/Sites/albums/index.html
/Users/saruman/Sites/index.html
/Users/saruman/Sites/webdav/index.html
```

Avoid Other File Systems

Use option -x (this is an option, not a primary) to stop find from looking inside mounted file systems. In this example, mounted file systems (usually in /Volumes) will not be searched.

```
$ sudo find -x / -name "index.html"
```

Project 19
Understand Links
and Aliases

"What's with symbolic links, hard links, and Finder aliases?"

This project explains Unix links, the difference between hard and symbolic links, and how Finder aliases fit in. It also covers the ln command.

Get a Few Pointers

A *link* is one file that points to another. The link points to the original file, and accessing the link usually accesses the original file. Editing the link will edit the original file. Some commands do not *follow* links by default. The rm command, for example, doesn't follow links. This is a good thing; otherwise, there'd be no way to delete a link without deleting the original file.

Links come in two varieties: *symbolic* links (sometimes called *soft links*) and *hard* links. As you'll see, each type has advantages and limitations.

Create Soft Links

Here is an example of creating a symbolic link.

We have a file called orig. Let's make a symbolic link to that file, using the ln command and specifying option -s for *symbolic*. Specify the original file and a name for the link, in that order.

```
$ ln -s orig sym-pointer
```

Use ls and option -l or -F to show the symbolic link as a link.

```
$ ls -l
-rw-r--r-- 1 saruman saruman 23 ... orig
lrwxr-xr-x 1 saruman saruman  4 ... sym-pointer -> orig
$ ls -F
orig          sym-pointer@
```

ⓘ **TIP**

To remove the symbolic link
home, *which links to the*
directory /Users/saruman,
type

$ **rm home**

not, as would be gotten
by tabbed completion,

$ **rm home/**

Next, display both the original file and the link file. The files should contain the same text. If you edit the original file and display both files again, the link file will have changed too.

```
$ cat orig
I am the original file
$ cat sym-pointer
I am the original file
```

How do symbolic links work? File `sym-pointer` is a file that contains the relative pathname of the target file `orig` and is flagged as a link. When a soft link is followed, the pathname is read from the file and replaces the pathname of the symbolic link.

If you move `orig`, the link will break. If you move `sym-pointer` to another directory, the link will also break; the pathname is relative, not absolute.

```
$ mv orig orig.bak
$ cat sym-pointer
cat: sym-pointer: No such file or directory
```

You can make a link to a file in another directory by giving a pathname (either relative or absolute) as the first argument.

```
$ ln -s /Users/saruman home
$ ls -l
lrwxr-xr-x 1 saruman saruman 14 ... home -> /Users/saruman
...
```

An interesting point to note: In this example, we have used an absolute pathname in /Users/saruman. Therefore, the symbolic link home will contain an absolute pathname. If the symbolic link is moved, the link *will not* be broken, unlike in the first example. If the original file is moved, however, the link *will* be broken.

Create Hard Links

A hard link is different from a symbolic link in that it isn't a file; it's a new directory entry. Both the original and the new directory entries point to the same file. In fact, Unix uses an *i-node* to describe a file, and both directory entries mention the same i-node. Here's an example of a hard link.

```
$ ln orig hard-pointer
$ ls -l
-rw-r--r-- 2 saruman saruman 23 ... hard-pointer
-rw-r--r-- 2 saruman saruman 23 ... orig
lrwxr-xr-x 1 saruman saruman  4 ... sym-pointer -> orig
```

Passing option -i to ls tells it to display a file's i-node number. Here, you can see that both hard-pointer and orig have the same i-node number : 999822.

```
$ ls -i
999822 hard-pointer     999822 orig        999825 sym-pointer
```

Both directory entries have equal claim over the file, and (other than my obvious naming conventions) it's not possible to say which is the original file and which is the hard link. Unlike a soft link, a hard link will not break when either of the linked files is moved, because although the directory entries may change, the i-node number and the file itself remain unchanged. However, hard links cannot point across file systems (disks, partitions, or mounted file systems), because i-node numbers are unique within a file system but not across file systems.

When a hard-linked file is copied, a new file is created, not a new hard link. If you clone a file system by copying all files, the cloned version will have separate files instead of hard links.

```
$ cp hard-pointer new-file
$ ls -i
999822 hard-pointer  999829 new-file  999822 orig ...
```

NOTE

Applying the rm command to a hard-linked file may not actually delete the file. Only its directory entries are removed until the last link to the file has been deleted. Only then will rm delete the file itself.

↗ LEARN MORE

Refer to "Recursion" in Project 2 if you are unfamiliar with recursion.

Symbolic Links vs. Hard Links

Use hard links instead of symbolic links when the linked files may move or be renamed, and you wish the link to remain intact.

Use symbolic links instead of hard links when the link spans disks, partitions, or file systems, or when you wish the link to be recognizable as a link.

Links and Other Commands

Many commands take options -H, -L, and -P, which generally mean the following:

▶ -H. If option -R is specified, symbolic links on the command line are followed. (Symbolic links encountered in the tree traversal are not followed.)

▶ -L. If option -R is specified, all symbolic links are followed.

▶ -P. If option -R is specified, no symbolic links are followed.

Such commands include chflags, chgrp, chmod, chown, cp, du, and find.

Aliases

A Finder alias is like a hard link in that renaming does not break it, but it *can* span file systems. Aliases are not recognized or followed by Unix because the link information is held in the resource fork, and Unix commands do not recognize resource forks. To Unix, an alias looks like an empty file. The Finder does recognize Unix links, however.

Here, we have created a Finder alias called orig alias pointing to orig.

```
$ ls -l
-rw-r--r-- 2 saruman saruman 23 ... hard-pointer
-rw-r--r-- 2 saruman saruman 23 ... orig
-rw-r--r-- 1 saruman saruman  0 ... orig alias
lrwxr-xr-x 1 saruman saruman  4 ... sym-pointer -> orig
```

Displaying orig alias does not follow the alias to orig.

```
$ cat orig
I am the original file
$ cat orig\ alias
```

Project 20
File Finding Tips

What other criteria can I use when searching for files?

This project will add to your arsenal of find techniques, with some powerful tips and suggestions for more nuanced searches. Projects 15, 17, and 18 show you how to use the command find.

Find Files Since

These tips use the find command's ability to compare the timestamps of different files. Primary -newerXY is used to compare the timestamp of each file found to see whether it is newer than a reference file. Both X and Y can be a for access time or m for modification time. X is the found file, and Y is the reference file. Primary -newer is equivalent to -newermm. (You can also specify c for creation time, but this always seems to be equivalent to modification time.) Some examples will clarify the use of newer.

Since Last Restart

List all files modified/created since the last restart. This example finds all files in your home directory that are newer than /mach.sym. (/mach.sym is a file that's created anew each time OS X boots.)

```
$ find ~ -newer /mach.sym
```

Since a Marker File

Create a file at the start of the day to keep track of all files you have edited. This example also shows how to check file modification and access times against a marker file.

First, create two files that will be older than the marker file.

```
$ touch old1 old2
```

Now create the marker file.

```
$ touch ref
```

Finally, create a file that is newer than the marker file.

```
$ touch new
```

Let's find all files that have a modification time later than the modification time of the marker file . . .

```
$ find . -newermm ref
./new
```

. . . and all files that have an access time later than that of the marker file.

```
$ find . -neweram ref
./new
```

Now modify old1 by using command touch -m, and you see that its modification time is now later than that of the marker file.

```
$ touch -m old1
$ find . -newermm ref
./new
./old1
$ find . -neweram ref
./new
```

Now access old2 using command touch -a, and you see that its access time is now later than that of the marker file.

```
$ touch -a old2
$ find . -newermm ref
./new
./old1
$ find . -neweram ref
./new
./old2
```

▲ NOTE

Read the man page for the command touch.

⚓ TIP

The command line

`$ find . -size 0`

will not find empty directories because an empty directory does not have a zero size—just no files in it.

Find Empty Files

The following command finds all empty files and directories.

`$ find . -empty`

To remove them use:

`$ find . -empty -delete`

The `delete` option removes files *and directories*. If a directory contains just empty files, the files will be deleted; then the directory, which is now empty, will also be deleted. Nice!

Remove the Full Pathname

The primary `-execdir` will execute its command from the directory that holds the current file. In contrast, `-exec` executes its command from the directory in which `find` was launched. Therefore, `-execdir` need not, and does not, pass the full pathname of current file when it invokes its command, in exactly the same way that you are able to avoid passing the full pathname when you execute a command from the directory containing the file you pass to it. You can use this feature in other ways, too, as in the following example, which uses `echo` to show exactly what `-execdir` passes to its command.

```
$ find ~/Pictures -name "*.psd" -execdir echo {} \;
ferdi-coll3.psd
ferdi-cool.psd
ferdi-gala.psd
```

Compare this with the usual form.

```
$ find ~/Pictures -name "*.psd"
/Users/saruman/Pictures/complete/ferdi-coll3.psd
/Users/saruman/Pictures/complete/ferdi-cool.psd
/Users/saruman/Pictures/complete/ferdi-gala.psd
```

Follow Symbolic Links

Make find follow symbolic links. /etc is a symbolic link to /private/
etc, and if you use find on /etc, it will not follow the link.

Rather unexpectedly, the following finds no files.

```
$ find /etc
/etc
```

Use either

```
$ find -L /etc
/etc
/etc/6to4.conf
/etc/afpovertcp.cfg
...
```

or

```
$ find /private/etc
/private/etc
/private/etc/6to4.conf
/private/etc/afpovertcp.cfg
...
```

Option -H will work too. It's slightly different in that it tells find to
follow the symbolic link given on its command line, rather than the
symbolic links found during the search.

↗ LEARN MORE

**Project 19 helps you
understand Unix links.**

Work with
File Content

3

This chapter is all about file content and what you can do with it from the Unix command line. The nine projects cover the following topics:

View text files. Learn how to display text files page by page and view them dynamically as they are being written.

View nontext files. View binary and compressed files.

Search files. Say hello to grep and friends—the Unix equivalent of Spotlight.

Sort and compare files. Unix has some handy utilities to process text files.

Compress files. Discover tar-balls for archiving, and learn how to zip and unzip.

These projects show you how to search the file system for specific content, view files, process them, and compress them. For related projects, see Chapter 4 on Unix text editors, and Chapter 7, which shows how to change file content programmatically.

TIP

Create a short text file quickly and easily by using cat *and redirection. Type the text you want to be in the file, and, when you've finished, press* Control-d *(interpreted as end of input).*

```
$ cat > letter.txt
Dear Janet,
How are you these days?
<Control-d>
```

Project 21
Display Text Files

"How do I view a file quickly?"

This project introduces commands to display the contents of a file in the Terminal window and to browse quickly through it. It covers cat, vis and unvis, less, head, and tail.

Reading Files with cat and vis

The simplest way to display a file on the screen is to cat it. Let's illustrate this by displaying one of the system files called /etc/ftpusers.

```
$ cat /etc/ftpusers
# list of users disallowed any ftp access.
# read by ftpd(8).
Administrator
administrator
root
uucp
daemon
unknown
www
```

The cat command pours the whole file onto the screen in one go. If the file is too big, it will overflow the Terminal window, leaving only the tail end visible. The name cat is short for *concatenate* and was originally written to join many files sequentially to form one large file. For example:

```
$ cat part1 part2 part3 > all-parts
```

The cat command has a few useful options. Option -n displays line numbers.

```
$ cat -n letter.txt
    1  Dear Janet,
    2  How are you these days?
```

Option -s squeezes multiple blank lines into a single blank line, while option -v displays nonprinting characters visibly. A file containing control characters can look a mess when displayed on the screen; worse, it can put the terminal into a peculiar mode.

Command vis provides a better way of dealing with control characters, being written specifically to display nonvisible characters. To illustrate, let's display a file that contains four control characters: Control-a, Control-b, Control-c, and Control-d.

```
$ vis control
Here are four control characters: \^A\^B\^C\^D
```

The output generated by vis has each nonvisible character represented by a unique sequence of visible characters. Because the sequences are unique, this human-readable output can be turned back into its original binary form. The unvis command does just this, taking the output from vis and restoring the original file—handy when you need to process or transmit a file in which control characters might cause problems. We might redirect the output from vis to the file safe, which is transmitted and then used as the input to unvis, thereby re-creating the original file contents.

```
$ vis control > safe
$ # and sometime later
$ unvis safe > control
```

Use the cat command as a simple filter to tidy up a messy file. We can remove unnecessary blank lines from a file by using the following commands.

```
$ cat -s messy.txt > tmp
$ mv tmp messy.txt
```

Note that this places the cleaned-up contents of messy.txt in a new file called tmp, and then replaces the original file by renaming tmp to messy.txt. As discussed in Project 6, trying to redirect output back into the original input file can trash the file or cause an infinite loop.

---

‡ TIP

If the terminal suddenly starts spitting out weird-looking characters, try resetting it by typing reset *or* tput reset.

‡ TIP

To view the ASCII character set, including all control and other nonvisible characters, type

```
$ man ascii
```

⤴ LEARN MORE

Project 22 shows you how to view binary files and compressed files.

↗ LEARN MORE

Chapter 4 introduces Unix text editors.

ᵢ TIP

man *uses the* less *command to display man pages, and it's such a useful command that it's worthwhile getting to know well.*

Make a Hard Copy

Printing is beyond the scope of this book, but it's worth mentioning a few key commands. The lp command sends a document to the printer, using CUPS (Common Unix Printing System, a resource built into OS X since version 10.3) to handle print jobs.

The pr command formats pages before they are printed, adding a timestamp header to the top of each page. Option -l sets the number of lines per page, and option -F ensures that multi-page documents print correctly. Pipe the output from pr to lp to print the formatted document.

```
$ pr -l57 -F ~/Sites/deq/php-lib/db/Deq.php | lp
```

The less Pager

Type less followed by a filename to displays the file's contents one page at a time. The less command is not an editor; it will only display files.

```
$ less Sites/index.html
```

The less command provides a very quick way of flicking through a file. It doesn't wait for the entire file to load before displaying the first page, so it's faster than using an editor to view a file. You can page through the file by pressing the spacebar. Search for a specific pattern by typing /pattern and then pressing Return. Press n to move to the next occurrence of the pattern and N to move to the previous occurrence. Press q to quit less. Read the man page for less: It has many options and navigation keystrokes, and will take some reading. To save you time, the most useful features are summarized below.

Navigation

Use the following keystrokes to move forward and backward through the file:

▸   space and b to move forward and back a page at a time

▸   d and u to move down and up a half-page

- Down arrow and up arrow to move forward and back a line at a time

- Right arrow and left arrow to scroll horizontally

- n**g** to move to line number *n* (for example, type **11g** to go to line 11)

- g and G to move to the beginning and end of the file

- n% to move n% of the way through the file

- /pattern Return to search forward for lines containing a pattern

- ?pattern Return to search backward for lines containing a pattern

- n and N to search for the next and previous occurrences of a pattern

- :e filename to examine (view) another file

- :n and :p to view the next and previous file when less is given more than one file to view (like less *.txt)

- Control-g to display a status line

- R to repaint (handy if the file being viewed is changing)

- h to display a help screen

- q to quit less

Options

Here are some of the more useful options:

- -a causes a search to resume from the last line displayed, rather than from the last match—handy when a single page shows many matches.

- -i causes less to ignore case when searching for strings unless the search pattern contains uppercase characters. So /hello matches hello and Hello, but /Hello matches only Hello.

- -M says to display a long prompt on the last line. The prompt can be customized; see the man page for less and search for ^PROMPTS to find the relevant section.

⊺ TIP

The less *command can use regular expressions in search patterns. Project 77 shows you how to use regular expressions.*

▶ -N displays a line number preceding each line of the file.

▶ -Q says shhhh! and stops less from ever dinging that annoying terminal bell.

Specify options to less in one of three ways:

▶ On the command line as usual.

▶ Interactively while viewing a file. Simply type an option like -a to toggle it on and off.

▶ In the environment variable LESS. When less is invoked, it assumes that the options listed in the environment variable LESS were actually passed on the command line.

Use Bookmarks

Set a bookmark so you can flip to the marked point in the file at any time. To set a mark, type m followed immediately by any lowercase letter from a to z. (You can have as many as 26 bookmarks per file). To return to a mark from elsewhere in the file, type ' (the single-quote character) followed immediately by the bookmark letter. Type '' (two single quotes) to flip between the last two bookmarks.

more or less

A Unix pager called more was a forerunner of less. It doesn't have half the features of less and cannot move backward when viewing a file. Unix under Mac OS X recognizes command more, but all it does is invoke less. So remember, more is less, less is more than more, and more is less than less!

heads or tails

Command head displays the first 10 lines of a file. Specify option -n followed by a number to display a different number of lines. To display the first five lines of the file index.html, we would type

```
$ head -n5 ~/Sites/index.html
```

Command `tail` displays the *last* 10 lines of a file. Specify option -n followed by a number to display a different number of lines. To display the last few events in the system log file, we would type

```
$ tail -n5 /var/log/system.log
May 25 08:55:00 saruman CRON[14842]: (root) CMD (/usr/l...
May 25 09:00:00 saruman CRON[14844]: (root) CMD (/usr/l...
May 25 09:05:00 saruman CRON[14847]: (root) CMD (/usr/l...
May 25 09:05:04 saruman xinetd[323]: START: pop3s pid=1...
May 25 09:10:00 saruman CRON[14852]: (root) CMD (/usr/l...
```

View Live Files

The `tail` command has a few options, the most useful of which, -f and -F, let you monitor continual changes to a file's contents. Use option -f to track files that are continually *extended* by the addition of appended text. Use option -F to track files as they are *rewritten*—changed in a text editor or replaced with an updated file that takes its name.

A system log file is a good candidate for `tail`'s -f option. Whenever a line of text is appended to the file, `tail` displays the new line:

```
$ tail -f -n3 /var/log/system.log
May 25 09:10:00 saruman CRON[14852]: (root) CMD (/usr/l...
May 25 09:13:44 saruman xinetd[323]: START: pop3s pid=1...
May 25 09:15:00 saruman CRON[14871]: (root) CMD (/usr/l...
# then a little later
May 25 09:17:54 saruman sudo:   saruman : TTY=ttyp5 ;PWD...
```

Press Control-c to quit `tail`.

The Console Application

The Console application in `Applications:Utilities:Console.app` is the OS X-native equivalent of `tail -f`.

Changing or Rewriting?

When a file is changed, its *i-node* number remains the same. When a file is rewritten, a new file is created, and its i-node number changes; this is when `tail` requires option -F. Use the command `ls -i filename` to examine the i-node number of a file.

An i-node is an intermediary between the directory entry for a file and the file itself. The directory entry mentions the i-node number, and the i-node points to the location of the file on disk. A new file means a new i-node number.

The concept of i-nodes is explored in greater depth in Project 19.

⤤ LEARN MORE

Project 72 discusses Mac OS X
periodic maintenance.

⤤ LEARN MORE

Project 21 covers the
commands cat, more,
and less.

⤤ LEARN MORE

Project 27 shows you how
to compress and uncompress
files.

Project 22
Display Binary Files

"Can I view archived log files without uncompressing them first?"

This project focuses on compressed and binary files. It explains an easy way to view compressed text files, and shows you how to search binary files for text fragments. It covers the commands gzcat, zless, zmore, bzcat, bzless, bzmore, strings, hexdump, and xxd.

View Compressed Files

On occasions, you'll find it necessary to view the contents of a compressed file, such as an archived log file. The log files in /var/log are rotated by Mac OS X periodic maintenance, which means that the current files are compressed and renamed, and new ones are created. To view a compressed file, you *could* uncompress it and then view and delete the uncompressed file. A better way uses zless to view compressed-file content directly. The zless command is equivalent to less; there are also equivalents to cat and more, gzcat and zmore.

Let's view an old system log file. Type

```
$ zless /var/log/system.log.0.gz
```

Press the spacebar to view the next page and q to quit less. If you cannot find the example file, run daily maintenance, giving your administrator password when requested. This should rotate system.log and create system.log.0.gz. Type

```
$ sudo periodic daily
Password:
```

Unfortunately, zless isn't included in versions of Mac OS X older than 10.4, but you can simulate it by piping gzcat output to less.

```
$ gzcat /var/log/system.log.0.gz | less
```

The zless command works on files that have been compressed with command zip or gzip (GNU-Zip). You'll recognize such files by their extensions: .z for zipped files and .gz for g-zipped files.

A newer and better compression format is implemented by bzip2. A file compressed by bzip2 is given the extension .bz2 and must be displayed by a viewer that understands that particular compression format. Choose bzcat, bzmore, or bzless.

View Binary Files

Project 21 showed you how to view text files that contain some control characters by using the cat -v and vis commands. Other commands are better for working with *binary* files, such as those containing images and executable programs. Binary files contain large numbers of *nonprintable* characters.

Search for Strings

Search a binary file for sequences of printable characters by using the strings command. It can be used to extract version numbers, help text, error messages, and such like from executable files.

Let's search the executable file /usr/bin/du. We'll consider only strings of 16 or more printable characters (the default is four) by specifying option -16.

```
$ strings -16 /usr/bin/du
__dyld_mod_term_funcs
__dyld_make_delayed_module_initializer_calls
The kernel support for the dynamic linker is not presen...
@(#) Copyright (c) 1989, 1993, 1994
The Regents of the University of California.  All right...
$FreeBSD: src/usr.bin/du/du.c,v 1.28 2002/12/30 18:13:0...
invalid argument to option d: %s
can't allocate memory
usage: du [-H | -L | -P] [-a | -s | -d depth] [-c] [-h ...
cannot allocate memory
@(#)PROGRAM:du  PROJECT:file_cmds-82  DEVELOPER:root  B...
```

TIP

To be sure of a file's compression type, irrespective of its extension, employ the file *command. This trick is handy in a script, where* file *can be used to check the status of a file you expect to be compressed.*

```
$ file log.bz2
log.bz2: bzip2
compressed data, block
size = 900k
$ file /var/log/¬
    system.log.0.gz
/var/log/system.log.0.gz
: gzip compressed data,
was "system.log.0", from
Unix, max compression
```

Finder-Archived Files

An archive created by the Finder (choose File > Create Archive Of) cannot be uncompressed with gzip. Use the unzip command instead.

```
$ unzip archivename.zip
```

See Project 27.

View with hexdump and xxd

You'll probably never have to do this, but should you want to examine an executable file or explore how a file format such as JPEG is encoded, use the hexdump command. It displays a binary file by showing the hexadecimal value of each byte, rather than trying to display the equivalent (and probably nonprintable) ASCII character.

Let's view the executable file /bin/ls, specifying option -n32 to display the first 32 bytes of the file.

```
$ hexdump -n32 /bin/ls
0000000 feed face 0000 0012 0000 0000 0000 0002
0000010 0000 000f 0000 0778 0000 0095 0000 0001
```

Notice that the first four bytes of a Mac OS X executable file spell "feed face" in hexadecimal. ☺

File shows the type of file and is able to recognize different binary formats.

```
$ file  /bin/ls
/bin/ls: Mach-O executable ppc
```

To display the ASCII character equivalents too (where dot represents a nonprintable character), select option -C. (The output below has been squashed horizontally to fit on the page.)

```
$ hexdump -n64  -C /bin/ls
00000000 feed face 0000 0012 0000 0000 0000 0002 |................|
00000010 0000 000f 0000 0778 0000 0095 0000 0001 |.......x........|
00000020 0000 0038 5f5f 5041 4745 5a45 524f 0000 |...8__PAGEZERO..|
00000030 0000 0000 0000 0000 0000 1000 0000 0000 |................|
```

Similar to hexdump is the xxd command. In the next example, option -l64 says to display the first 64 bytes of the file.

```
$ xxd -l64 /bin/ls
0000000: feed face 0000 0012 0000 0000 0000 0002  ................
0000010: 0000 000f 0000 0778 0000 0095 0000 0001  .......x........
0000020: 0000 0038 5f5f 5041 4745 5a45 524f 0000  ...8__PAGEZERO..
0000030: 0000 0000 0000 0000 0000 1000 0000 0000  ................
```

The xxd command will display a file in binary instead of hexadecimal
if option -b is specified.

```
$ xxd -b -l24 /bin/ls
0000000: 11111110 11101101 11111010 11001110 00000000 00000000 ......
0000006: 00000000 00010010 00000000 00000000 00000000 00000000 ......
000000c: 00000000 00000000 00000000 00000010 00000000 00000000 ......
0000012: 00000000 00001111 00000000 00000000 00000111 01111000 .....x
```

Like commands vis and unvis, xxd can restore its own output into a
binary file—handy if you need to process or transmit a file in which
control characters may cause problems. As an example, we'll process
and then restore the ls command into the file new-ls.

```
$ xxd  /bin/ls > xxd-ls
$ xxd  -r xxd-ls > new-ls
```

To prove it has worked, we'll try to run our copy of the ls command.

```
$ chmod +x new-ls
$ ./new-ls
Documents       Library        Public         new-ls

...
```

↗ LEARN MORE

To unleash the full power
of `grep`, you must master
regular expressions. Read
Projects 77 and 78 to
become a black belt in
the art of `/re/`.

Project 23
Search File Content

"How do I find all files containing the text Dear Janet *before my wife does?"*

This project shows how to search a file, or many files, for particular
text. The search term can be straight text or a regular expression. The
project covers the commands `grep`, `wc`, `awk`, and `sed`.

Use grep

This chapter puts the spotlight on `grep` and friends. The `grep` command searches through files to find particular text that matches a
search pattern. A file is searched line by line, and a match occurs
when a line contains the search pattern. It's important to realize that
the search is done line by line and that to match, a line need only *contain* the search pattern, not be identical to it.

Let's search all text files (`*.txt`) in the current directory for the words
Dear Janet.

```
$ grep "Dear Janet" *.txt
hello.txt:Dear Janet,
lets-meet.txt:Dear Janet, sauciest of vixens
secret-liaison.txt:Dear Janet,
```

We see displayed all lines from all files that match, with the matching
line of text preceded by the filename.

grep Options

The `grep` command has many options, the most useful of which are
explained below.

To change the output format from *filename:text of matching line,* specify
the following:

▶ -l to display just filenames. Use this option when you are interested in which filenames match but not the matching lines—when generating a list of files to process, for example.

▶ -h to display just the matching line. Use this option when you want to process the lines of text and don't want filenames polluting the output.

▶ -n to display line numbers too. This option is handy when you wish to edit the file later, as you can jump straight to the line in question.

▶ -Cn to display n lines before and after the matching line. C is for context. This option is useful when you search text documents for information.

To change the pattern-matching rules, specify the following:

▶ -i to ignore case. Hello will match hello and Hello.

▶ -v to invert the sense of the match. Lines that *do not* contain the pattern will be displayed.

▶ -w to match complete words only. Jan will match Dear Jan, hello but not Dear Janet, hello.

▶ -x to match whole lines only. The line must *equal* the pattern, not just *contain* it. This option has the same effect as specifying start- and end-of-line anchors in the regular expression.

▶ -E to activate extended regular expressions. By default, grep matches against basic regular expressions. Invoking grep as the command egrep is the same as using grep -E.

▶ -F to match fixed strings only, not regular expressions. The grep command operates faster on fixed strings than on regular-expression patterns. Also, in this mode it's not necessary to escape characters like star that would otherwise be interpreted as pattern-matching operators. Invoking grep as the command fgrep is the same as using grep -F.

grep: It's an Odd Name!

The name grep comes from an ancient Unix text editor called ed, the forerunner of ex, which is the forerunner of vi, which is the forerunner of vim. To search for a regular expression from ed, you'd use the command sequence g/re/p. g is for global (the whole file), /re/ is the regular expression to search for delimited by /, and p says to print matching lines (for example, display onscreen). Back in the days of ed, CPU power and memory were expensive, so to avoid the overhead of running a general-purpose editor to perform what is a very common task, a new specialized command was written. It was called, as you have already guessed, grep.

And to prove it:

```
$ ed meeting.txt
110
g/Jan/p
Dear Janet,
Perhaps on Jan 31st?
q
```

↗ **LEARN MORE**

For an explanation of recursive processing, see "Recursion" in Project 2.

☼ **TIP**

Project 18 tells you all about find *with* xargs, *and Projects 15 and 17 show you how to use* find.

Use recursive mode:

▶ -r to recursively search directories listed on the command line. In the following example, grep searches all files and directories in the current directory.

```
$ grep -r "Janet" *
archive/old-letter.txt:Dear Janet,
hello.txt:Dear Janet,
lets-meet.txt:Dear Janet, sauciest of vixens
secret-liaison.txt:Dear Janet,
```

The next example of recursion doesn't work as expected. We intended to say, "Search the current directory recursively for all *.txt files." What actually happens is that the shell expands *.txt to include all matching filenames (which *does not* include the directory archive); grep then searches each filename in the expansion, and if it's a directory, grep does so recursively. We can't specify to grep both a directory to search recursively *and at the same time* which files to consider.

```
$ grep -r "Janet" *.txt
hello.txt:Dear Janet,
lets-meet.txt:Dear Janet, sauciest of vixens
secret-liaison.txt:Dear Janet,
```

The solution is to use find and xargs.

```
$ find . -iname "*.txt" -print0 | xargs -0 grep "Janet"
./archive/old-letter.txt:Dear Janet,
./hello.txt:Dear Janet,
lets-meet.txt:Dear Janet, sauciest of vixens
./secret-liaison.txt:Dear Janet,
```

Some grep Examples

Mac OS X has a handy dictionary (a list of words, but bereft of definitions) located at /usr/share/dict/web2. Let's use grep to count how many words contain the sequence xy. We use option -c to count the number of matches instead of displaying them.

```
$ grep -c "xy" /usr/share/dict/web2
579
```

How many words start with xy? This requires the use of a regular expression that says "a line that starts xy".

```
$ grep -c "^xy" /usr/share/dict/web2
75
```

Name two of them! (Xylophone is the easy one.)

The grep command is often combined with command ps to look for specific processes. In the next example, grep filters the output from ps to display only those lines containing safari. (The ps command does not require its options to be preceded by dash.)

```
$ ps axww | grep -i safari
27946  ??  S     31:08.79 /Applications/Safari.app/
Contents/MacOS/Safari -psn_0_1739980801
16705 std  R+     0:00.00 grep -i safari
```

If you want to use the results of this command to extract the process ID of Safari, for example, the second line of output is unwelcome. This can be eliminated in either of two ways.

Use grep −v.

```
$ ps axww | grep -i safari | grep -v grep
27946  ??  S     31:09.33 /Applications/Safari.app/
Contents/MacOS/Safari -psn_0_1739980801
```

Employ some clever regular-expression trickery.

```
$ ps axww | grep -i "safar[i]"
27946  ??  S     31:09.50 /Applications/Safari.app/
Contents/MacOS/Safari -psn_0_1739980801
```

How does this safar[i] trick work? It's a regular expression that's equivalent to "safari", so it still matches "Safari". The grep command line, however, does not match now because it contains "safar[i]" and not "safari". Think about it.

TIP

It's necessary to pass the option ww to ps; otherwise, long lines are truncated, possibly cutting off the command name we are searching for. Check the man page for ps for an explanation of all the options.

LEARN MORE

Read Project 39 to learn more about Unix processes and command ps.

LEARN MORE

Project 18 has examples of grep used in conjunction with find and xargs.

Escape and Double Escape

Remember to enclose a regular expression in single quotes to avoid interpretation by the shell. The regular-expression sequence `.*` matches any string of characters, for example, but it must be escaped from the shell to stop the shell from treating the star as a globbing character and potentially expanding it. To match `"line"` and then any character sequence and then `"1"`, we would type:

```
$ grep 'line.*1' *.txt
```

If we wish to search for the star character itself, star must also be escaped from regular-expression interpretation. To search for `"line *1"`, we would type:

```
$ grep 'line \*1' *.txt
```

The escape character ensures that star is matched literally rather than being interpreted as a regular-expression operator. Refer to Project 77 if you are unfamiliar with regular expressions.

The next line is equivalent.

```
$ grep line\ \\\* *.txt
```

Remember `fgrep`? It searches for fixed patterns and does not activate regular expressions, so we can type simply

```
$ fgrep 'line *' *.txt
```

Zipped Files

Use a `grep`-based command to examine the contents of a zip- or bzip2-compressed file directly by using these commands:

- ►   zgrep
- ►   bzegrep
- ►   bzfgrep
- ►   bzgrep

These `bz` variants correspond to the versions of `grep` discussed in the "grep Options" section above.

Count Words

The `wc` command counts the number of characters, words, and lines in a text file. It's often used to count the number of results returned by a command or pipeline. We can repeat the dictionary example from earlier by using `wc`.

```
$ grep "xy" /usr/share/dict/web2 | wc -l
    579
$ grep "^xy" /usr/share/dict/web2 | wc -l
     75
```

Option `-l` says to count lines only, and you can guess at options `-c` and `-w`.

Use awk to Isolate and Format Text

The `awk` command (named after its authors, Aho, Weinberger, and Kernighan) is a powerful pattern-processing language. It's explored in detail in Projects 60 and 62, but one (very simple) way it can be used is to isolate a particular portion of each line of text it receives as input.

More specifically, this use of `awk` involves printing a selected field from the input text—*field* in this instance meaning a sequence of characters separated by white space. We can use `awk` to isolate Safari's process ID (PID) from the results of our earlier `grep`/`ps` search, for example. This example extends the earlier command with a pipeline to `awk`. An `awk` script, enclosed in single quotes, tells `awk` to print the value of the first field (field #1) of each input line. Because the first text string in a line of `ps` output is always a PID, this yields the PID of process Safari.

```
$ ps axww | grep -i "safar[i]" | awk '{print $1}'
27946
```

The number 27946 is the PID of Safari, and this number can be given as an argument to the `kill` command to abort the running process. We'll enclose the pipeline sequence in `$()`, which tells Bash to execute it, write the result back to the command line, and then execute the new command line.

❚ NOTE

An `awk` *script takes* `print $0` *to mean "display the whole line" and* `print $n` *to mean "display field n."*

❚ NOTE

Other shells, such as Tcsh, use the syntax `` `command` `` *instead of* `$(command)`.

⬈ LEARN MORE

Consult Project 52 if you wish to learn more about Bash functions.

ⓘ TIP

To learn about `printf`, *type*

```
$ man 3 printf
```

The man page documents the library call `printf`, *which* awk *uses to implement its own* printf.

Before we do any actual killing, use echo to demonstrate that the expression enclosed by $() still outputs the Terminal PID.

```
$ echo $(ps axww | grep -i "safar[i]" | awk '{print $1}')
27946
```

Now run kill.

```
$ kill $(ps axww | grep -i "safar[i]" | awk '{print $1}')
```

For completeness, let's create a shell function killer to kill a given process by name.

```
$ killer () { kill $(ps axww | grep -i "$1" | ¬
    grep -v "grep -i $1" | awk '{print $1}'); }
$ killer safari
```

The awk statement printf prints a formatted, or embellished, version of each input line. Here's a quick example of what can be done.

```
$ ls -l | awk '{printf("Date: %s %s, File %s\n",$7,$6,$9)}'
Date: , File
Date: 13 Sep, File csv
Date: 13 Sep, File double-space
Date: 30 Aug, File script
```

The first line—Date: , File—results from the first line written by ls -l. This can easily be removed with grep.

Use sed

The sed command is a stream editor and, like awk, processes its input lines based on matching patterns. It's covered in detail in Projects 59 and 61, and we'll use it here simply to search text files for lines that match a given pattern (Jan). Here are a couple of examples equivalent to the grep examples shown earlier in this project.

Option -n stops sed from echoing *every* input line, which it usually does. The construct /re/p searches for a regular expression (re) and displays the lines that contain it.

```
$ sed -n '/Jan/p' *.txt
Dear Janet,
Dear Janet, sauciest of vixens
Dear Jan,
Dear Janet,
Perhaps on Jan 31st?
```

Next, we count the number of words starting with xy.

```
$ sed -n '/^xy/p' /usr/share/dict/web2 | wc -l
    75
```

To filter the output from ps:

```
$ ps axww | sed -n  "/Safar[i]/p"
  470  ??  S      0:15.71 /Applications/Safari.app/
Contents/MacOS/Safari -psn_0_3407873
```

Ignoring case is less elegant. One has to convert all uppercase letters to lowercase (or vice versa) by using the awk function y and then match the pattern.

```
$ ps axww | sed -n
"y/ABCDEFGHIJKLMNOPQRSTUVWXYZ/abcdefghijklmnopqrstuvwxyz/ ¬
   ;/safar[i]/p"
  470  ??  s      0:15.71 /applications/safari.app/
contents/macos/safari -psn_0_3407873
```

Project 24
View File Differences

"I recently made some changes to a file. Can I compare the new file with a copy of the original file to recall the changes I made?"

This project shows you how to compare two files and view their differences in several ways. It shows how to make a patch file to bring an older version of the file up to date and how to merge two sets of changes. It covers the commands `diff`, `sdiff`, and `patch`. On related themes: Project 25 employs the command `diff3` to compare two sets of changes against a common ancestor; and Project 26 shows how to sort text files and how to pick out commonalities and differences between sorted text files.

What's the difference?

We use the `diff` command to compare two files, or two versions of the same file, to discover the differences between them. It reports on lines that have been added, deleted, or changed. It works on text or binary files, but we'll stick to text files in this project; it's simpler to illustrate the principles involved by using files that can be displayed. Differences can be reported line by line or using a comparative side-by-side view. `diff` can also compare entire directory structures, reporting the differences between similar files and listing those files that appear in one directory but not the other.

The `diff` command can create a patch file describing the differences between a newer file and an older file. Applying the patch to the older file brings it up to date, which is useful to keep other people updated without needing to redistribute a potentially large original file.

We also look at the `sdiff` command, which interactively merges two files and allows the user to select lines from either file to create the new file.

diff Files

Let's use `diff` to compare two similar files. In the following example, file `index.php` (you might recognize it as a PHP script) was updated from an original saved as `index.old.php`. `diff` reports on lines that have been deleted, added, and changed in the new version compared with the old version. To view the changes, simply give the two file-names as arguments to `diff`, but make sure that the older file is the first argument; otherwise, the senses of *added* and *deleted* are reversed.

```
$ diff index.old.php index.php
22d21
< <img id="photo2" class="abs" src="/images/front/body....
52a52,53
>     <a id="box-contact" class="abs" href="tails/contact...
>     <a id="box-who" class="abs" href="tails/who.php"></a>
61c62
<     ("select who, quote from quotes where id = $quote;");
---
>     ("SELECT who, quote FROM quotes WHERE id = $quote;");
```

The first line, `22d21`, shows the line numbers of the old file (22) and new (21) where the first difference was detected. Letter `d` says that a line was deleted from the old version and so is not in the new version. The deleted text follows on the next line. Next, `52a52,53` shows that two lines were added (letter `a`) and displays the additions on the two subsequent lines. Finally, `61c62` indicates that line 61 was changed (letter `c`) and that it is now line 62 in the new file; the two lines that follow display the original line and its replacement.

Option `-i` tells `diff` to ignore changes that involve only case. Adding it to the previous example causes the changes detected in line 61 to be ignored.

⥿ TIP

For a list of the options understood by `diff`, *type*

`$ man diff`

For more information on `diff`, *type*

`$ info diff`

⥿ TIP

Specify option `-b` *to have* `diff` *ignore changes in the amount of white space (spaces and tabs), and option* `-B` *to ignore changes that just insert or delete blank lines. Specify* `-bB` *for both.*

```
$ diff -i index.old.php index.php
22d21
< <img id="photo2" class="abs" src="/images/front/body....
52a52,53
>     <a id="box-contact" class="abs" href="tails/contact...
>     <a id="box-who" class="abs" href="tails/who.php"></a>
```

Option -q (for *quiet*) causes diff to report whether the files differ but not show the differences.

```
$ diff -q index.old.php index.php
Files index.old.php and index.php differ
```

Differences Side by Side

Diff can report file differences by displaying the two files in two columns, side by side. This visual representation is easier to understand but demands a wider terminal screen. Specify option -y to activate side-by-side mode. You might find it prudent to specify wider columns than the default 64 characters each, using option -W, and to increase the width of the terminal window accordingly. Because a printed book is fixed width, I'm going to have to specify a somewhat-reduced width of 60 (30 for each column). The GNU-style multi-letter option --suppress-common-lines tells diff to display only changes, not common lines. That has the advantage of shortening output, but at the cost of context for the changes.

```
$ diff -yW60 --suppress-common-lines index.old.php index.php
  <img id="photo2" class="ab <
                           >     <a id="box-contact" class=
                           >     <a id="box-who" class="abs
            ("select who, q |              ("SELECT who, q
```

Compare Directories

If you wish to compare two sets of similar files, `diff` will scan two directories, comparing files of the same name and also reporting on files that have no counterparts in the other directory. First, we'll list the contents of directories, `old` and `new`, and then use `diff` to compare their contents.

```
$ ls new old
new:
index.php        new-file.php
old:
index.php        old-file.php
$ diff old/ new/
diff old/index.php new/index.php
22d21
< <img id="photo2" class="abs" src="/images/front/body....
52a52,53

...

Only in new/: new-file.php
Only in old/: old-file.php
```

To perform a full recursive search and compare directories within directories too, specify the option `-r`.

Make and Apply Patches

Suppose that your friend has an outdated version of a file that's several megabytes. Rather than send her an updated copy of the entire file, Unix lets you send her just the changes in the form of a *patch*, which she can apply to bring her old file up to date. Command `diff` is used to create a patch, and command `patch` applies it. Here's an example in which we patch `index.old.php` to bring it up to date.

First, we capture the output from `diff` in a file called `patchfile`. It's important to specify option `-C3`, which tells `diff` to provide context information around the changes. Context information is essential for `patch` to work correctly.

```
$ diff -C3 index.old.php index.php > patchfile
```

⬈ LEARN MORE

Refer to "Recursion" in Project 2 for a fuller explanation of recursion.

❧ NOTE

When creating the patch file, be sure that the filenames passed to `diff` *are in the correct order (name of outdated file followed by up-to-date version); otherwise, the patch will be applied in reverse. Fortunately,* `patch` *usually detects this error.*

ᵢ̈ TIP

For a list of the options understood by sdiff, *type*

```
$ man sdiff
```

For more information on sdiff, *type*

```
$ info diff
```

(That's diff, *not* sdiff.*)*

ᵢ̈ TIP

If you don't specify an output file, sdiff *will simply list the differences side by side, like* diff -y *does. The following are equivalent.*

```
$ sdiff -s -w60  ¬
    index.old.php ¬
    index.php
$ diff -y --suppress-¬
    common-lines  ¬
    -W60  index.old.¬
    php index.php
```

Next, send the (very small) patch to your friend, who updates her version of the file. (Her copy is probably called index.php, but we'll continue to use index.old.php to distinguish the two versions.)

```
$ patch index.old.php patchfile
patching file index.old.php
```

And to show that it worked:

```
$ diff index.old.php index.php
```

Merge with sdiff

If you are unsure which of two files contains your latest changes, or if you want to keep changes to both files in a pair, Unix provides two useful techniques. If both files are descended from a common ancestor, take a look at the diff3 command, demonstrated in Project 25. Otherwise, use sdiff to do an interactive *merge* of the files, in which you can choose to incorporate differences found in either file. The contents of both files are displayed in a two-column format like what we saw for diff -y.

In the next example, we merge two files into a new file called index.new.php, introduced by option -o. Option -s says to skip (not query or show) common lines, and option -w adjusts the column width. (Rather irritatingly, diff uses -W, whereas sdiff uses -w, so don't get mixed up!)

Pressing Return at sdiff's prompt (%) causes it to display a menu of options. In this simple case, we choose r in all cases to select the changes from index.php. Pressing l would select the changes from index.old.php. The output is written to index.new.php.

```
$ sdiff -s -w60 -o index.new.php index.old.php index.php
  <img id="photo2" class="ab <
%
l:     use the left version
r:     use the right version
e l:   edit then use the left version
e r:   edit then use the right version
e b:   edit then use the left and right versions concatenated
e:     edit a new version
s:     silently include common lines
v:     verbosely include common lines
q:     quit
%r
                              >    <a id="box-contact" class=
                              >    <a id="box-who" class="abs
%r
            ("select who, q |              ("SELECT who, q
%r
```

And to show that it worked:

```
$ diff index.new.php index.php
$
```

More diffs

Check out the man pages of some other diff variants:

diffpp to pretty-print diff outputs

diffstat to make a histogram from diff output

zdiff and bzdiff to compare zip and bzip2 compressed files

Project 25
View Three-Way Differences

"I've got two sets of edits to the same file. How do I merge the changes so I can see both sets of changes in one file?"

This project shows how to compare two files against a common ancestor file and view their differences relative to the common file. It shows how to merge the two sets of changes to create a single file that contains both sets and how to make patch files that bring either of the two files up to date. The project covers commands `diff3` and `patch`. It builds on concepts covered in Project 24, which uses commands `diff`, `sdiff`, and `patch` to compare and update pairs of files. Project 26 explores sorting of text files, and techniques for picking out commonalities and differences between sorted files.

Three-Way Comparison with diff3

We use the `diff3` command to compare two files against a common ancestor file. If two people copy and then change the same file independently, `diff3` can be used to merge both sets of changes into a new file. `diff3` can also create a patch file describing the additional changes in one file compared with the other. When the patch is applied to the other file, the result is a file that contains both sets of changes.

The `diff3` command reports on lines that have been added, deleted, and changed. It works on text or binary files, but we'll stick to text files in this project; it's simpler to illustrate the principles involved by using files that can be displayed.

The `diff3` command is useful when two (or more) people make independent changes to their own copies of the same original file. We have two (or more) new files, both of which are relevant, so we must merge both sets of changes. At first glance, two people editing their own copies of the same file, at the same time, may seem a silly thing to do, but it is done often in software development. Many software engineers work on the same project in parallel, each engineer copying the same base set of files and applying his particular updates. Mostly, the engineers will change different files from one another, but occasionally, changes overlap. When development is complete, all sets of changes must be merged. This principle is employed by concurrent version control systems such as CVS, which uses diff3 to merge the changes as each developer returns his set of files to the base set.

Let's look at an example that uses two independent sets of changes, made in files day1 and day2, to a common base file, orig. The three files are shown side by side. In day1, line 1 is edited, and line 5 is deleted. In day2, line 3 is edited, and line 7 is added. Our aim is to produce a merged file such that lines 1 and 3 are edited, line 5 is deleted, and line 7 is added, with respect to orig.

day1	orig	day2
line 11	line 1	line 1
line 2	line 2	line 2
line 3	line 3	line 33
line 4	line 4	line 4
line 6	line 5	line 5
	line 6	line 6
		line 7

We use diff3 to compare the changes made in day1 with those made in day2, relative to the base file orig.

You may be asking why the third file, orig, is required. It tells us that it was day1 that *deleted* line 5. Without comparing against orig, we couldn't be sure that it wasn't day2 that *added* line 5. Similarly, we know that day2 *added* line 7 and not that day1 *deleted* it. This information is important when the two files are merged, ensuring that diff knows to delete line 5 and add line 7 to produce the merged file.

TIP

For a list of the options understood by diff3, *type*

```
$ man diff3
```

For more information on diff3, *type*

```
$ info diff
```

(That's diff, *not* diff3.)

TIP

Specify one of the three files as a dash (-), and diff3 *will read from its standard input instead of a file. This is usually combined with pipelining to compare the actual results of a command against preprescribed results held in a file.*

↗ LEARN MORE

Refer to Project 6 to learn about redirection.

Merge Two Sets of Changes

Having determined that day1 and day2 both contain changes to the original file, we now merge both sets of changes into day3. Recall that our aim is to produce a file such that lines 1 and 3 are edited, line 5 is deleted, and line 7 is added. To do this, simply specify option -m (merge) and redirect output to day3.

```
$ diff3 -m day1 orig day2  > day3
$ cat day3
line 11
line 2
line 33
line 4
line 6
line 7
```

Patch the Differences

A more roundabout approach makes a patch file. First, use option -A and direct the output to the patch file.

```
$ diff3 -A day1 orig day2 > patchfile
```

Displaying patchfile, we see that it contains instructions on how to update day1 to incorporate the changes made to day2.

```
$ cat patchfile
5a
line 7
.
3c
line 33
.
```

Apply the patch to day1.

```
$ patch day1 patchfile
$ cat day1
line 11
line 2
line 33
line 4
line 6
line 7
```

Now day1 incorporates both sets of changes.

The patch could equally well be applied the other way around, as long as the diff is also done the other way around.

```
$ diff3 -A day2 orig day1 > patchfile
$ patch day2 patchfile
```

Resolve Conflicts

One final consideration: It's quite possible for the same line to be changed in both files, creating a *conflict* that must be resolved manually. (Computers are dumb.) This situation is illustrated below, where line 3 was changed in both files day1 and day2. You'll notice that diff produces a sequence of lines surrounded by <<<<<<< and >>>>>>> highlighting the area of conflict.

```
$ diff3 -m day1 orig day2
line 11
line 2
<<<<<<< day1
line 333
||||||| orig
line 3
=======
line 33
>>>>>>> day2
line 4
line 6
line 7
```

ᵢ TIP

Be careful that patch *is applied the correct way around. It does not warn you if it's applied the wrong way around.*

↗ LEARN MORE

Project 24 shows you how to use patch **with the command** diff**.**

↗ LEARN MORE

**Project 23 shows you how to
use** grep **and** wc.

Whenever you merge two files, check for conflicts. You can check the
return status of diff3 by examining the special shell variable $?. It's 0
for success and 1 for conflicts, and 2 means trouble (as the man page
puts it).

```
$ diff3 -m day1 orig day2 > day3
$ echo $?
1
```

Alternatively, dry-run the merge and count the number of conflicts.

```
$ diff3 -m day1 orig day2 | grep "<<<<" | wc -l
      1
```

If you get conflicts, complete the merge and then edit the new file
manually, choosing the appropriate line and removing the conflict
markers.

Project 26
Sort and Compare
Text Files

"How do I compare two files for common lines?"

This project shows you how to sort the contents of text files, pick out commonalities and differences between sorted files, and how to strip duplicate lines of content. It covers the commands sort, comm, and uniq.

Sort Files

First, we'll take a look at the sort command, which sorts the lines of a file into order and can also merge several sorted files. We'll demonstrate its most useful features by sorting a directory listing into file-size order.

Then, for our next trick, we'll demonstrate the use of sort, uniq, and comm in combination to detect identical image files that differ only in name. uniq removes duplicate lines from a sorted file. comm compares two sorted files, displaying lines that are common to both, and lines that occur in just one file or the other, in three columns.

The sort command sorts the lines of a text file into order. To demonstrate some of its features, let's sort a directory listing into file-size order. (This can be done by ls -lS, of course, but for the purpose of this exercise, we'll use ls merely to generate a file that's a suitable candidate for sort.)

We'll generate the file by piping a directory listing to awk and telling awk to print the ninth field (the filename) in a left-aligned 20-character column, followed by the fifth field (the file size in bytes).

↗ LEARN MORE

See Project 60 to learn more
about *awk*'s formatting
capabilities.

Project 6 explains
redirection and pipelining.

```
$ ls -l | awk '{printf "%-20s %s\n", $9, $5}'
GM-river-1.psd          34730919
GM-river-2.psd          35552718
Natacha-1.psd           26613850
Natacha-2.psd           21511927
ferdi-coll3.psd         16159247
ferdi-cool.psd          31266062
...
```

Next, we pipe the "file" directly to sort, which in the absence of a
filename accepts the output from awk as its standard input. The sort
command must be told, via option -k, which field is the *key* to sort
on. In this case, the key (file size) appears in field 2 of the input, so
the appropriate syntax is -k2.

```
$ ls -l | awk '{printf "%-20s %s\n", $9, $5}' | sort -k2
jj2.psd                 4645653
kids.jpg                11532
lips.psd                13333630
monsta.psd              1037986
jj12b8.psd              6102391
lor-sep.psd             20337917
...
```

That wasn't exactly as we expected. A gotcha with sort concerns the
field separator, which is a space or tab. Because our file has multiple
spaces between the fields, sort must be told to treat multiple spaces as
a *single* file separator, not many consecutive separators. To this end,
specify option -b.

```
$ ls -l | awk '{printf "%-20s %s\n", $9, $5}' | sort -k2 -b
monsta.psd              1037986
kids.jpg                11532
lor-stone2.psd          12178244
lips-red.psd            13333630
lips.psd                13333630
...
```

Better, but sort is treating the "number" as a sequence of characters and
not considering its numerical value. Another option, -n, is called for.

```
$ ls -l |awk '{printf "%-20s %s\n", $9, $5}' |sort -k2 -b -n
kids.jpg             11532
monsta.psd           1037986
ferdi-polish.psd     1676649
ferdi-gala.psd       1780828
gala-hair.psd        2616768
...
```

Perfect! That does what we want. Check out the man page for sort; it has many more options, one of the most useful being -t to specify a field separator other than space or tab.

Detect Duplicate Files

Now we'll look at uniq and comm and combine them with sort to detect duplicate image files. Suppose that we have a directory with many image files. Some files are identical to others, though their names do not necessarily indicate this. We want to detect the duplicates so we can delete them.

An image can be uniquely identified by a combination of its checksum and its size. Different images have different checksums; duplicate images have the same checksum. (There's a chance in a billion that two different images will have the same checksum.) We'll use command cksum (demonstrated below), which outputs a file's checksum in field 1, the file's size in field 2, and its filename in field 3:

```
$ cksum gala-hair.psd
1428733187 2616768 gala-hair.psd
```

Using cksum, we'll identify the nonduplicate files—quite the opposite of what is required, but we'll correct that later. We'll create a temporary file, /tmp/checksums, that contains the filename, checksum, and size of each image, sorted by checksum; then we'll use command uniq to filter out duplicate lines.

To create the checksum-sorted file, we'll use awk to rearrange the cksum output fields, placing the filename (field 3) first. (This will be required by uniq, as we shall see later on. The final stage of the pipeline uses sort to sort on field 2 (the checksum).

```
$ cksum * | awk '{print $3, $1, $2}' | sort -k2 > ¬
    /tmp/checksums
$ cat /tmp/checksums
gala-hair.psd 1428733187 2616768
gala-longhair.psd 1428733187 2616768
gala-longhairs.psd 1428733187 2616768
lor-sep.psd 1806568675 20337917
ferdi-polish.psd 1872815908 1676649
ferdi-cool.psd 2145153277 31266062
GM-river-2.psd 2170060896 35552718
GM-river-1.psd 2176652953 34730919
lor-stone.psd 2485586841 4266597
lor-stones.psd 2485586841 4266597
jj2.psd 2796515583 4645653
lips-red.psd 996895841 13333630
lips.psd 996895841 13333630
```

Next, we run the temporary file through the uniq command. If two or more adjacent lines are the same, uniq outputs only the first. We want to ignore filenames in this comparison, as we are interested only in the uniqueness of checksum and size, so we'll use uniq option -f n, which tells uniq to skip the first n fields before lines are compared. This is why we put the filename first earlier. (Note that the filename *is* needed; otherwise, we can't identify the file to delete later.)

To keep only unique files in the list, we use

```
$ uniq -f1 /tmp/checksums
gala-hair.psd 1428733187 2616768
lor-sep.psd 1806568675 20337917
ferdi-polish.psd 1872815908 1676649
ferdi-cool.psd 2145153277 31266062
GM-river-2.psd 2170060896 35552718
GM-river-1.psd 2176652953 34730919
lor-stone.psd 2485586841 4266597
jj2.psd 2796515583 4645653
lips-red.psd 996895841 13333630
```

Looking at the two listings above, it'd be easy to spot and delete the four duplicate files that are listed in /tmp/checksums but not in the uniq-filtered list. It wouldn't be quite so easy if we were working with 1,000-plus images, however! We need to compare the two lists automatically and pick out lines that appear in the first but not in the second. The comm command does exactly that. It compares two sorted files and outputs three columns: Column 1 contains lines found only in file1; column 2, lines found only in file2; and column 3, lines in both files. Options -1, -2, and -3 suppress printing of their respective columns.

Therefore, we pass to comm the full listing in /tmp/checksums as file1 and the uniq-filtered list as file2, *both sorted lexically as required by comm*, and suppress columns 2 and 3 from being output. We use a neat trick whereby we pipe the sorted list directly to comm's standard input instead of saving it to a temporary file. The second filename is given as dash, which tells comm to read its standard input.

Our final command displays just column 1—which is a list of those files that were filtered by uniq. Thus, we are left with the duplicate images.

The commands we have built up are

```
$ cksum * | awk '{print $3, $1, $2}' | sort -k2 > ¬
    /tmp/checksums
$ uniq -f1 /tmp/checksums | sort > /tmp/checksums-uniq
$ sort /tmp/checksums | comm -23 /tmp/checksums-uniq
gala-longhair.psd 1428733187 2616768
gala-longhairs.psd 1428733187 2616768
lor-stones.psd 2485586841 4266597
lips.psd 996895841 13333630
```

The output lists the duplicate files we can safely delete.

Finally, we want to remove each file—a goal easily achieved by adding a few more stages to the pipeline. Use awk to pass just the filename (field 1) on to the next stage in the pipeline and xargs to form a delete (rm) command from the list of filenames passed to it. The complete solution is shown below. Note that the rm command is preceded by echo. This causes the command line to *display* what would otherwise be *executed*—a sensible precaution until we are sure that the

TIP

Many commands take dash (-) as an input filename, which tells them to read standard input (which might be a pipeline) instead of a file.

❦ NOTE

This example will not work with filenames that contain spaces. Spaces in filenames are often problematic and require special treatment with regard to field separators.

A Shorter Version?

The eagle-eyed among you may have spotted that uniq has an option -d, which apparently does exactly what we needed here—it lists the non-unique files instead of the unique files. Unfortunately, it fails when a file has two or more duplicates.

```
$ cksum *.psd | awk ¬
    '{print $3, $1, ¬
    $2}' | sort -k2  ¬
    | uniq -f1 -d
gala-hair.psd 1428733187
2616768
lor-stone 2485586841
4266597
lips-red.psd 996895841
13333630
```

Only three duplicates have been detected instead of four.

pipeline is forming the correct command line. when we have verified that the command looks good, we can remove echo and commit to deleting the duplicate images.

The final command becomes

```
$ sort /tmp/checksums | comm -23 - /tmp/checksums-uniq ¬
    | awk '{print $1}' | xargs echo rm
rm gala-longhair.psd gala-longhairs.psd
lor-stones.psd lips.psd
```

Here's an alternative way to delete the files. We'll enclose the pipeline sequence in $(), which tells Bash to execute it, write the result back to the command line, and then execute the new command line.

```
$ echo rm $(sort /tmp/checksums | comm -23 - ¬
    /tmp/checksums-uniq | awk '{print $1}')
rm gala-longhair.psd gala-longhairs.psd
lor-stones.psd lips.psd
```

Project 27
Compress Files

"How do I compress and uncompress files?"

This project shows you how to compress (or zip) files. It covers the commands gzip, gunzip, bzip2, bunzip2, zip, and unzip.

Compress and Uncompress

Zipping is a cross-platform way to compress files. The compression is *lossless*, meaning that the original file can be reconstructed verbatim from the compressed file. Specialized compression techniques, such as the JPEG image compression format, are *lossy*, meaning that some information from the original image is lost in the compressed image.

Two compression formats are in widespread use:

▶ The original Lempel-Ziv coding (LZ77), implemented by the commands zip and unzip, and the GNU equivalents gzip and gunzip. We'll concentrate on the GNU equivalents in this project.

▶ The newer Burrows-Wheeler algorithm, implemented by the commands bzip2 and bunzip2. Compression generally is considerably better than that achieved by LZ77.

Many files can be compressed into a single archive file with command zip or the Unix "tape archiver" tar, which is covered in Project 28.

Let's simply compress and uncompress a file to demonstrate gzip and gunzip.

```
$ ls -lh
-rw-r--r-- 1 saruman saruman   1M ... list-all.txt
$ gzip list-all.txt
$ ls -lh
-rw-r--r-- 1 saruman saruman 282K ... list-all.txt.gz
```

ᵀ TIP

*To view information about a
compressed file, use*

```
$ gzip -l --verbose ¬
    list-all.txt.gz
```

ᵀ TIP

The gzcat *command is
equivalent to (and a few
characters shorter than)* gunzip
-c. *Also,* gzip -d *is
equivalent to* gunzip, *and*
gzip -dc *is equivalent to*
gunzip -c *and also* gzcat.

You'll notice three things: The compressed file is considerably smaller than the original, it has *replaced* the original, and it sports the extension .gz.

Now let's uncompress the file (extension .gz is assumed if not given).

```
$ gunzip list-all.txt
$ ls -lh
-rw-r--r-- 1 saruman saruman  1M ... list-all.txt
```

You may want to keep the original file when, for example, you compress a file to email it. Use option -c, which sends the compressed file to standard out, and redirect standard out to an appropriately named file.

```
$ gzip -c list-all.txt > list-all.txt.gz
$ ls -lh
-rw-r--r-- 1 saruman saruman   1M ... list-all.txt
-rw-r--r-- 1 saruman saruman 282K ... list-all.txt.gz
```

For the reverse case, in which you want to expand the compressed file and keep the original compressed copy, use gunzip with option -c. You must include the .gz extension in the filename when an uncompressed file with the same filename also exists.

```
$ gunzip -c list-all.txt > copy-of-list-all.txt

gunzip: list-all.txt: not in gzip format
$ gunzip -c list-all.txt.gz > copy-of-list-all.txt
$ ls -lh
-rw-r--r-- 1 saruman saruman   1M ... copy-of-list-all.txt
-rw-r--r-- 1 saruman saruman   1M ... list-all.txt
-rw-r--r-- 1 saruman saruman 282K ... list-all.txt.gz
```

Options -1 through -9 are used to set compression levels in gzip. Higher settings yield smaller compressed files but also increase compression times. The default setting is -6, so specify an option in the range -7 to -9 for better but slower compression, or use a setting from -5 to -1 for faster compression but larger compressed files.

```
$ gzip -9 -c list-all.txt >best.gz
$ gzip -1 -c list-all.txt >worst.gz
$ ls -lh
-rw-r--r-- 1 saruman saruman 271K ... best.gz
-rw-r--r-- 1 saruman saruman   1M ... list-all.txt
-rw-r--r-- 1 saruman saruman 345K ... worst.gz
```

Option --best is equivalent to -9, and --fast is equivalent to -1.

Create Compressed Archives

Many files can be compressed into a single file with a command like

```
$ gzip -c *.txt > all.gz
```

Be warned, however, that when all.gz is uncompressed, it will *not* be split back into its constituent files.

If you want to archive many files into a single compressed file and be able to recover them as individual files, either use zip and unzip, or archive them first by using the tar command (see Project 28).

Here's an example that uses zip to compress all the files in a directory called week1 into a single file. Command zip takes the name of the archive as its first argument, followed by a list of files to be *deflated* into the archive file. The wildcard pathname week1/* denotes every file in directory week1.

```
$ zip week1.zip week1/*
  adding: week1/friday.ws (deflated 48%)
  adding: week1/monday.ws (deflated 47%)
  adding: week1/thursday.ws (deflated 48%)
  adding: week1/tuesday.ws (deflated 46%)
  adding: week1/wednesday.ws (deflated 46%)
```

ṫ TIP

The commands cat, more, grep, *and* diff *have z-variants (*gzcat, zmore, zgrep, *and* zdiff*) that operate directly on zipped files.*

Other Formats

The *gunzip* command can uncompress files compressed with *gzip*, *zip*, and the older *compress*. The *zip* command appends the extension .z, and *compress* appends the extension .Z.

gunzip cannot handle files compressed with *zip* that have more than one member. If *gunzip* gives an error message complaining about more than one entry, use *unzip* instead. You'll get such an error message when trying to *gunzip* an archive created by the Mac OS X Finder.

```
$ gunzip week1.gz
```

gunzip: week1.gz has more than one entry -- unchanged

We can examine the contents of a zip file by giving option -l to unzip.

```
$ unzip -l week1.zip
Archive:  week1.zip
  Length    Date      Time     Name
  ------    ----      ----     ----
    1712   05-03-104  17:22    week1/friday.ws
    1593   05-03-104  17:22    week1/monday.ws
    1546   05-03-104  17:22    week1/thursday.ws
    1598   05-03-104  17:22    week1/tuesday.ws
    1545   05-03-104  17:22    week1/wednesday.ws
  ------                       -------
    7994                       5 files
```

(These files were apparently created in the year 104!)

To unzip the archive, use

```
$ unzip week1.zip
Archive:  week1.zip
  inflating: week1/friday.ws
  inflating: week1/monday.ws
  inflating: week1/thursday.ws
  inflating: week1/tuesday.ws
  inflating: week1/wednesday.ws
```

To find out more about zip and unzip, run them without any arguments. Versions of Mac OS X older than 10.4 do not have man pages for either of them.

Use bzip2

The `bzip2` and `bunzip2` commands are very similar to `gzip` and `gunzip` but use the newer Burrows–Wheeler algorithm to provide better compression. They use the extension `.bz2` or sometimes just `.bz`.

Here's a quick demonstration of `gzip` versus `bzip2`.

```
$ gzip -9 -c list-all.txt > list-all.txt.gz
$ bzip2 -9 -c list-all.txt > list-all.txt.bz2
$ ls -lh
-rw-r--r-- 1 saruman saruman   1M ... list-all.txt
-rw-r--r-- 1 saruman saruman 222K ... list-all.txt.bz2
-rw-r--r-- 1 saruman saruman 271K ... list-all.txt.gz
```

If you attempt to uncompress a damaged `bzip2` file, `bunzip2` will warn you of data corruption. There's a chance that you can recover the compressed file by using the `bzip2recover` command.

⚓ TIP

The commands `cat`, `more`, `less`, `grep`, `egrep`, `fgrep`, *and* `diff` *have* `bz`-*variants* *(*`bzcat`, `bzmore`, `bzless`, `bzgrep`, `bzegrep`, `bzfgrep`, *and* `bzdiff`*) that operate directly on b-zipped files, without requiring decompression.*

Project 28
Archive Files

"How do I squash a directory of files into a single compressed file?"

This project covers the tar command and shows you how to use it to combine a collection of files into a single archive file, how to retrieve those files from an archive, and how to use tar as a file-backup tool.

Make an Archive

Many files can be combined into an *archive* file for easy distribution or storage. An archive can contain anything from a few named files to a whole directory hierarchy. We'll take a look at creating *archives* by using the tar command and see how to compress the archive. Then we'll do the reverse; decompressing and extracting files from the archive.

Let's make an archive of the files in the directory week1 by using GNU tar, which is the version of tar supplied with Mac OS X. As arguments, tar requires a function followed by function modifiers. To create a new archive file, specify function c for *create* and modifier f directly followed by a filename for the archive. You may also include modifier v for *verbose*, which tells tar to list files and directories as they are added to the archive. (Preceding the function and its modifiers with a dash [-] is optional.)

```
$ tar cvf week1.tar week1
week1/
week1/friday.ws
week1/monday.ws
week1/thursday.ws
week1/tuesday.ws
week1/wednesday.ws
```

We retrieve files from the archive (*extract* files) and write them to the current directory by specifying function x. When an archive is extracted, tar automatically creates directories as needed to match each extracted file's pathname. If a file's target directory already exists, the file will be extracted into that directory and will overwrite any existing file that shares its name.

```
$ tar xvf week1.tar week1
week1/
week1/friday.ws
week1/monday.ws
week1/thursday.ws
week1/tuesday.ws
week1/wednesday.ws
```

To view archive contents, specify function t (for *table of contents*).

```
$ tar tf week1.tar
...
```

The tar command is inherently recursive. Applying it to a directory archives the directory's contents and those of all its subdirectories.

```
$ tar cvf Sites.tar ~/Sites
tar: Removing leading `/' from member names
...
Users/saruman/Sites/jan/
Users/saruman/Sites/jan/images/
Users/saruman/Sites/jan/images/background/
Users/saruman/Sites/jan/images/background/.DS_Store
Users/saruman/Sites/jan/images/background/shade-left-b.png
...
```

The strange comment Removing leading `/' from member names is explained in "Understand tar and Pathnames," later in this project.

Compress and Uncompress

To compress and uncompress tar archives, we could apply gzip and friends to the archive files manually, but built-in tar functions spare us that effort. Various modifiers instruct tar to pass archives to gzip, bzip2, or compress automatically:

ᵢ TIP

Extract just some of the files in an archive by naming the files to extract, possibly by using shell-style pattern matching operators, but escaping them from the shell. (Refer to Project 11 to learn about pattern matching.)

```
$ tar xvf week1.tar ¬
    'week1/t*'
week1/thursday.ws
week1/tuesday.ws
```

Tape Archive?

The tar command got its name from its original purpose, which was to archive onto magnetic tape. It's kept that name but nowadays is used mostly to create archive files—hence, the almost-universal application of modifier f followed by a filename.

➴ LEARN MORE

Refer to Project 27 to learn about compressing and uncompressing files.

▸ To gzip/gunzip a file, specify modifier z or --gzip. The standard extension for a tar-gzipped file is .tgz.

▸ To bzip2/bunzip2 a file, specify modifier j or --bzip2. The standard extension for a tar-bzipped file is .tbz2 or .tbz.

▸ To use the older compress, specify modifier Z or --compress. The standard extension for a tar-compressed file is .taZ.

When an archive is created, it will be compressed, and before files are extracted, the archive will be uncompressed.

We archive and compress with gzip, using either

```
$ tar czf week1.tgz week1
$ tar cf week1.tgz --gzip week1
```

Let's check that the archive is in fact compressed by using the file command.

```
$ file week1.tgz
week1.tgz: gzip compressed data, from Unix
```

To uncompress, use either

```
$ tar xzf week1.tgz
$ tar xf week1.tgz --gzip
```

We archive and compress with bzip2 by using either

```
$ tar cjf week1.tbz2 week1
$ tar cf week1.tbz2 --bzip2 week1
```

Let's check, again using file.

```
$ file week1.tbz2
week1.tbz: bzip2 compressed data, block size = 900k
```

To uncompress, use either

```
$ tar xjf week1.tbz2
$ tar xf week1.tbz2 --bzip2
```

Understand tar and Pathnames

It's important to understand the significance that pathnames have when an archive is extracted. It's also important to understand the different behaviors of tar toward relative and absolute pathnames.

Relative Pathnames

A tar archive includes the relative pathname of each file, from the current directory to the directory being archived. Previously, we archived the directory week1 from the directory that contained it (tips). This time, we'll move up one level, out of tips, and archive by specifying tips/week1. Compare this with the example at the start of the project.

```
$ cd ..
$ tar cf week1.tar tips/week1
$ tar tf week1.tar
tips/week1/
tips/week1/friday.ws
tips/week1/monday.ws
...
```

You'll notice that the pathname now includes tips/, and when the archive is extracted, it will be written back to tips/week1/ in the current directory, not directly to week1/. This ensures that when an archive is extracted, it will be written back to the same point in the directory hierarchy from which it was archived.

Note that if you were to extract this archive from within tips instead of the directory above from where it was archived, it would be written back to tips/week1 in the *current* directory—that is, tips/tips/week1.

Absolute Pathnames

If we specify an absolute pathname to tar, the leading slash character is dropped to make the pathname relative.

```
$ tar cf week1.tar /Users/saruman/Development/tips/week1
tar: Removing leading `/' from member names
$ tar tf week1.tar
Users/saruman/Development/tips/week1/
Users/saruman/Development/tips/week1/friday.ws
...
```

To extract the archive, you must change to the root directory.

```
$ cd /
$ tar xvf /path/to/week1.tar
```

If you do not move to the root directory, the entire pathname of Users/saruman/Development/tips/week1/ will be created below the current directory as the archive is extracted. If you really do want absolute pathnames in the archive, specify option -P or --absolute-names when creating the archive *and* when extracting from the archive.

Why is the leading / stripped? If it were not, the archive would *always* be written starting from the root directory, creating all other directories needed to match the archive pathname. At best, sending the absolute-pathname archive /Users/saruman to a friend would force him to create a directory called /Users/saruman that he doesn't need. At worst, if your friend lacks the permissions needed to create that directory, he will not be able to extract the archive.

Make Incremental Backups

We can use tar to make a backup of a directory and write the archive to CD or DVD. You might place the archive on an external drive or mounted server, and in this case, a neat trick uses the tar function update (u) to update the archive periodically. Updating an archive considers only those files that have changed, adding them to the end of the archive. It's obviously quicker and easier to update an existing archive than to create a new one.

In the following example, we create an archive of the directory `week1` and then change a couple of files with the `vim` text editor.

```
$ tar cf week1.tar week1
$ vim week1/tuesday.ws
$ vim week1/wednesday.ws
```

Next, we update the archive by using the function `u`. The modifier `v` gives reassurance that the changed files are detected and added to the archive.

```
$ tar uvf week1.tar week1
week1/
week1/tuesday.ws
week1/wednesday.ws
```

Editing and updating again:

```
$ vim week1/tuesday.ws
$ tar uvf week1.tar week1
week1/
week1/tuesday.ws
```

If we examine the archive, all the original files, plus the two sets of updates, will be shown.

```
$ tar tf week1.tar
week1/
week1/friday.ws
week1/monday.ws
week1/saturday.ws
week1/thursday.ws
week1/tuesday.ws
week1/wednesday.ws
week1/
week1/tuesday.ws
week1/wednesday.ws
week1/
week1/tuesday.ws
```

When the archive is extracted, earlier versions of `tuesday.ws` and `wednesday.ws` are replaced by the latest versions.

ℹ TIP

The `tar` *command has many more options; check its man page. Some of the most useful are*

`-A` *to add a new archive to an existing archive*

`-d` *to report differences between files in an archive and the original files*

`-r` *to append files to an archive*

`--delete` *to remove specific files from an archive*

⚓ TIP

If a file's content is human-readable, file *always includes the word* text *somewhere in the description. This fact can be used to filter a list of files (using* grep, *for example), leaving all and only those that are human readable.*

It's Magic

The file command determines the type of a file by examining its *magic number* stored near the beginning of the file, which is intended to identify the file type to the Unix operating system. If a file does not have a recognizable magic number, the content is scanned. Reference is made to the magic file in /usr/share/file/magic. This file maps magic numbers and content to file type.

In Mac OS X, Mach-O executables begin with the hexadecimal number feedface.

Can you find the file type that begins *cafebabe*? (cafe gives us a clue.)

Project 29
File-Content Tips

"Is there an easy way to format the contents of text files?"

This project gives you tips for detecting the type of content a file contains and introduces some handy text-processing utilities.

Determine File Content

Command file tells you the type of content a file contains.

```
$ file *
about-html.txt:  ASCII text
fake.html:       empty
index.html:      ASCII HTML document text
letter.doc:      ASCII English text
nodif:           a /bin/tcsh script text executable
smtp-auth-plain: a /usr/bin/perl script text executable
unix2mac:        a /bin/bash script text executable
week1:           directory
week1.tar:       POSIX tar archive
week1.tbz2:      bzip2 compressed data, block size = 900k
```

Specify option -i if you would like the file type displayed in *mime* format.

```
$ file -i *
about-html.txt:  text/plain; charset=us-ascii
fake.html:       application/x-empty
index.html:      text/html; charset=us-ascii
letter.doc:      text/plain, English; charset=us-ascii
nodif:           application/x-shellscript
smtp-auth-plain: application/x-perl
unix2mac:        application/x-shellscript
week1:           application/x-not-regular-file
week1.tar:       application/x-tar, POSIX
week1.tbz2:      application/octet-stream
```

Search for Files with a Specific Type of Content

We can pipe the results from `file` to `grep` to look for files with specific content.

```
$ file * | grep -i html
about-html.txt:  ASCII text
fake.html:       empty
index.html:      ASCII HTML document text
```

This simple approach suffers from a problem: If the filename contains the search term, it will match too, regardless of the content. We must add a little sophistication to the search term to absorb everything from the beginning of the line to the colon after the filename, using a regular expression such as "^.*:", and then search for html.

```
$ file * | grep -i "^.*:.*html"
index.html:      ASCII HTML document text
```

The regular expression searches from the start of a line (^) for anything (.*) followed by a colon and then anything followed by html.

Process Files with a Specific Content Type

It's easy to extend the pipeline example given above, making it pass the list of filenames to a command like Apple's `textedit`.

To realize this, we use `awk` to pass on just the filename, which is the first field of the line.

```
$ file * | grep -i "^.*:.*html" | awk '{print $1}'
index.html:
```

Then we use `sed` to chop off the colon.

```
$ file * | grep -i "^.*:.*html" | awk '{print $1}' ¬
    | sed 's/://'
index.html
```

Finally, we use `xargs` to form a command line from the list of files.

```
$ file * | grep -i "^.*:.*html" | awk '{print $1}' ¬
    | sed 's/://' | xargs open -a textedit
```

⤴ LEARN MORE

Refer to Project 23 to learn more about grep.

Project 77 covers regular expressions.

↗ LEARN MORE

Project 18 explains the use of xargs.

Projects 59 and 60 cover sed **and** awk.

In this example, the command line will be

```
open -a textedit index.html
```

The command `open -a` runs the specified GUI program, resulting in TextEdit's opening `index.html`.

An alternative approach uses option -F, telling `file` to separate the filename from the content type with space-colon instead of just colon. Consequently, the first field seen by `awk` will be the filename without the colon.

```
$ file -F " :" * | grep -i "^.*:.*html" ¬
  | awk '{print $1}' | xargs open -a textedit
```

Search Compressed Files

Option -z tells `file` to look inside compressed files. Compare the output of the next two examples.

```
$ file week1.tbz2
week1.tbz2: bzip2 compressed data, block size = 900k
$ file -z week1.tbz2
week1.tbz2: POSIX tar archive (bzip2 compressed data,
block size = 900k)
```

Expand and Unexpand Tabs

The `expand` command expands tab characters to the appropriate number of spaces, and `unexpand` does the reverse. Pass option -a to `unexpand` to ensure that all spaces are converted; otherwise, only leading spaces are converted.

Fold Long Lines

Long lines can be broken into shorter lines by the `fold` command. In this example, the output has lines of no more than 40 characters. Output is displayed on the terminal screen; to save the results, simply redirect output to a file by using > `name-of-output-file`.

```
$ cat longlines
```

```
this is a file with one very long line and no linefeeds in
it to demonstrate the use of fold to break long lines into
the specified width
```
```
$ fold -w40 longlines
```
```
this is a file with one very long line a
nd no linefeeds in it to demonstrate the
 use of fold to break long lines into th
e specified width
```

The fmt command is more sophisticated and breaks lines at spaces instead of midword.

```
$ fmt -40 longlines
```
```
this is a file with one very long line
and no linefeeds in it to demonstrate
the use of fold to break long lines into
the speficied width
```

Split Large Files

Use the split command to split a long file into many smaller files, each 1,000 lines long. Specify option -l to change the sizes of the smaller files.

ᵢ TIP

The fmt command does much more than break lines. Read its man page by typing

```
$ man fmt
```

Edit Files

4

This chapter is about creating and editing text files using the Unix text editors supplied with Mac OS X. It also takes a quick look at some graphical-based text editors. The seven projects cover the following topics:

nano: a simple text editor that's easy to use and sufficiently full featured to use as your everyday editor.

emacs: a big, fat, full-featured text editor that'll do all you want and more besides. It includes an extensive interactive help system and tutorials, making it easy to pick up the basics.

vim: a programmer's editor with syntax highlighting and a programmatic approach to forming edit commands. Like emacs, it has an extensive online help system. vim is upward-compatible with the older vi (pronounced *vee eye*) editor.

Graphical-based text editors such as Apple's TextEdit and the freeware editor TextWrangler, from Bare Bones Software.

These projects help you get up to speed using the three main Unix text editors supplied with Mac OS X: nano, emacs, and vim. The vim editor is covered in greatest detail because it's the toughest to learn—but also the most rewarding if you can learn to think in a vim-like way. Project 36 discusses OS X-native text editors. Chapter 7 offers some techniques for editing files programmatically by using commands such as sed and awk.

Project 30
Edit with nano

"What's the quickest route to take when I want to learn how to edit text files in Unix?"

This project introduces the nano text editor. It's very easy to learn and sufficiently powerful for you to use to write shell scripts and as your everyday text editor. Versions of OS X prior to 10.4 (Tiger) did not include nano. Earlier versions of OS X instead included an editor called pico, which lacked some basic features such as search and replace. See the sidebar "Get nano Info—and nano Itself" to learn how to install nano in pre-10.4 versions of Mac OS X.

Basics

Fire up nano, and we'll take a look at the basics. You should find a file called index.html in the directory Sites in your home directory. Make a copy of it to practice on, or use any other text file.

```
$ cd ~/Sites
$ cp index.html index-new.html
$ nano index-new.html
```

You'll see a terminal window similar to that shown in **Figure 4.1**. The top line shows the name of the file being edited; the version of nano is to the left; and to the right, you'll see the word Modified if you have modified the file. The bottom two lines are there to remind you of the basic commands, and the line above them is the *status bar,* showing important and informational messages. The caret symbol (^) means "press and hold Control," so to see the help screen, for example, press ^g or Control-g.

Optional nano *features* can be toggled on and off to change certain aspects of the editor. To enable a feature, press the Escape key and then press the single letter that represents that feature. (Don't hold down the Escape key, as you would the Control key.) Do the same to disable an enabled feature. The most useful features are covered in later sections.

Features in nano are disabled by default, but can also be enabled using the command line: Include a feature's option in a command line that invokes nano, and the feature will be activated when nano launches. Check nano's man page for full details.

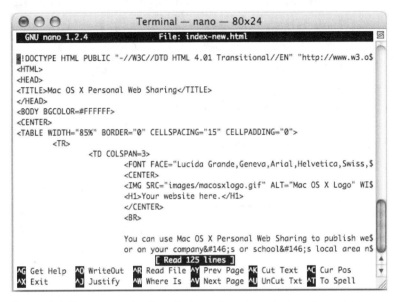

TIP

The Page Up and Page Down keys scroll Apple's Terminal. To get nano *to scroll the document, use Shift-Page Up and Shift-Page Down. Similarly, use Shift-Home and Shift-End to move to the start and end of the current line.*

If you use X11's xterm *as your terminal, Page Up and Page Down work without the Shift key, but Home and End do not work at all.*

Figure 4.1 The nano text editor displays relevant keystroke options at the bottom of its main window. The status bar just above the command menu provides user feedback.

Move Around

The cursor (arrow) keys work in the normal manner in nano and are the most common means of moving the text-insertion point. A nano feature also lets you position the cursor with your mouse, but unfortunately, it works in X11's xterm but not Apple's Terminal application. Even if it won't help you, activate it by typing Escape m; then type Escape m again to turn mouse support off. When you do either, note that the status line displays a message confirming that the setting has changed.

If you use Apple's Terminal, you can still get mouse support in nano (and other Unix programs as well). Launch the Terminal Inspector by choosing Terminal > Window Settings; select Emulation from the popup

ṫ TIP

The cursor can also be moved with Control sequences, as described in the nano *help screen.*

**Get nano Info—
and nano Itself**

The official site for nano, www.nano-editor.org, offers much useful information.

Most important for users of pre-10.4 releases of Mac OS X, which didn't include nano, the site provides free downloads of the program.

Download the source by clicking the "Get Nano" link at the bottom of the page, then clicking the file nano-[versionnumber].tar.gz. Type the following lines in the Terminal window (the version number may differ from the one shown here).

```
$ tar xzf nano-¬
    1.2.5.tar.gz
$ cd nano-1.2.5/
$ ./configure
  # ...much output
here....
$ make
$ sudo make install
Password:
  # ...output here...
```

menu, and check Option-Click to Position Cursor. Option-clicking in nano causes Terminal to send nano a series of cursor-movement keystrokes that move the cursor to the point where you clicked.

Press Control-c to display the cursor position in the status bar briefly. Type Escape c to toggle a continuous display of the cursor position in the status bar.

Get Help

Press Control-g to display a help screen. The help screen uses the caret symbol (^) to mean "press and hold the Control key" and M to mean "press the Escape key" (also referred to as the *Meta key*). Press Shift-Page Up and Shift-Page Down to move through the help screen, and press Control-x to exit it.

Edit File Contents

Basic text addition and removal are straightforward in nano. To insert text, place the cursor at the location where you want your addition to begin. The Delete key (often referred to as the *Backspace* key) deletes the character behind the cursor. Forward-Delete (the key above the left arrow on full-size Mac keyboards, emulated by pressing Fn-Delete on laptops) deletes the character under the cursor.

Cut and Paste

In nano, cut and paste work on whole lines only. Use

▶ Control-k to cut a line.

▶ Control-u to paste a line.

▶ Control-k Control-u to copy a line. (This, of course, cuts and repastes the line in question but also retains the cut text in a memory buffer so it can be pasted again.)

If you use Terminal, you can also employ the usual Mac method of selecting text and pressing Command-c to copy it and Command-v to paste it. It's not possible to cut text by using Command-x, however.

Save Your Edits

To save changes to the current file press Control-o and then Return. The status line displays the filename to save to; you may edit it before pressing Return, or type a name for a new file if you invoked nano with no filename.

Pressing Control-x exits nano, and if your document has unsaved modifications, you'll be prompted to save or discard the changes first.

Search and Replace

You can use nano to search and search and replace. In addition, switching on features can make the search case sensitive, enable regular-expression matching, and reverse the direction of the search.

To search the current file for some particular text, press Control-w. You'll see the prompt Search: displayed in the status bar. At the prompt, type the term to search for, press Return to find the first occurrence of the term. Press Control-w and then Return to find subsequent matches.

Type Escape c to switch case-sensitive matching on and off. (The feature is off by default when searching is activated.) You'll notice that the status-bar prompt changes to reflect that searches are now case sensitive. It's important to understand that this feature can be toggled only *after* pressing Control-w to enter search mode and that it remains active across searches until switched off. At other times, you'll recall, typing Escape c toggles the cursor-position display in the nano status bar.

Similarly, type Escape b to reverse the direction of the search.

Replace

To search and replace, press Control-\. This time, you'll see the prompt Search (to replace): displayed in the status bar. Type the search term and press Return. The prompt changes to Replace with: , at which point type the new string and press Return. The replacement is interactive, so you may accept or reject each occurrence as a candidate for replacement, or have all occurrences replaced. Just follow the instructions displayed on the bottom two lines.

ᵢ TIP

After pressing Control-w, *press Cursor Up to recall previous search terms and then Return to execute the search.*

ᵢ TIP

If you download nano *using the instructions in the "Get nano Info—and nano Itself" sidebar on page 190, the executable will be installed in* /usr/local/bin/nano *and the man pages in* /usr/local/man/. *If* /usr/local/bin *is not in your search path, you will either need to add it or else invoke* nano *by using its full pathname. See Project 50 to learn about search paths.*

↗ LEARN MORE

See projects 77 and 78 to learn more about extended regular expressions.

You can also activate the replace feature from within search mode (after you press Control-w) by pressing Control-r.

Use Regular Expressions

Normally, nano interprets search terms as simple text, not as patterns to match, but enabling its *regexp* feature lets you use regular expressions as search terms. Type Escape r from within search (or search-and-replace) mode. You'll notice that the status-bar prompt changes to reflect that the search term can now be a regular expression. This feature remains active across searches until switched off. Note that nano implements extended regular expressions, not just basic regular expressions.

Match Brackets

It's often useful, especially when writing code, to jump back and forth between pairs of *brackets*. Bracket-matching is built into nano. Place the cursor on any bracket character—([{ or <—and type Escape]. The cursor will move to the matching closing bracket. Type Escape] again, and the cursor returns to the matching open bracket. Try it on the mouth of a "smiley"—:-)—to see what happens when a bracket has no match.

Edit Multiple Files

Type Escape f to enable the multiple-buffers feature, which lets you open many files in a single nano session. You'll see a message in the status bar giving the current setting for this feature. Each file being edited is held in a separate buffer, and nano displays one buffer at a time. To load a second file, press Control-r; then type the name of the file to edit in the status bar and press Return. The old file will vanish, and the new file will be presented in the terminal window.

The old file is not lost; it's just no longer displayed. To display a hidden file type Escape > for the next buffer or Escape < for the previous buffer. You need not press the Shift key, so Escape , (comma) and Escape . (period) work too.

Note that if the multiple-buffers feature is not enabled, typing `Control-r` and then a filename reads the new file and inserts its contents into the current file.

Use Tabbed Completion

Use tabbed completion when entering a filename in the status bar, just as you would in the command line. Start typing a filename; then press Tab. If what you have typed is unambiguous, nano will complete the filename for you. If what you have typed is ambiguous, pressing Tab a second time will reveal a list of possible matches in the main window.

Use File Search

Whenever you enter a filename in the status bar, press `Control-t` to reveal a directory listing in the main window. You may now use the cursor keys to select a file to load and press Return to load it. Selecting a directory enters that directory and causes its contents to be displayed. To move to the parent directory, select the `..` (dot-dot) entry and press Return.

Format Text

Several nano features help you format code and text. Type

- Escape i to enable autoindenting. From now on, if you indent a line with spaces or tabs, subsequent lines will be indented automatically by the same amount.

- Escape w to enable autowrap. Long lines will be broken automatically before they exceed the width of the terminal screen. nano inserts a line break and always does so at white space or punctuation—never midword.

Pressing `Control-j` tells nano to wrap a series of long lines. All consecutive lines above and below the cursor are considered for wrapping. When a blank line is encountered, wrapping stops.

⚡ TIP

When using nano's tabbed completion feature, type `../` and then press Tab two times to list files in the parent directory.

nanorc Configuration File

When nano starts up, it reads a configuration file from your home directory. This file, which defines default settings for nano, must be named .nanorc and placed in your home directory. All the features that can be enabled on the command line or by escape sequences within nano can also be enabled in the configuration file.

To have multiple-buffers mode enabled by default, for example, add the line

set multibuffer

to ~/.nanorc

Other useful settings are

▶ set fill n to wrap lines at column n

▶ set tabsize n to set the width of each tab stop to n

▶ syntax and color to define syntax highlighting colors (see the next section)

For full details, see the nanorc man page by typing

$ man 5 nanorc

Syntax Highlighting

Like all good text editors, nano is capable of syntax highlighting. We can tell it to display HTML tags such as <head> in blue, for example, and escaped characters such as & in red. Enter the following in your nanorc file.

```
#HTML Syntax Highlighting
syntax "HTML" "\.html$"
color blue start="<" end=">"
color red "&[^;        ]*;"
```

Note: On the fourth line, the text between [and] includes a space character and a tab character.

The first line is a comment and is ignored by nano. The second line says that the HTML syntax is applied to all files whose names end with .html. The third line says that everything between < and > (possibly across multiple lines) is to be colored blue, and the fourth line says that everything between & and ; (when they are not separated by white space or semicolons) is to be colored red.

You may specify any of the colors white, black, red, blue, green, yellow, magenta, and cyan, and prefix any color name with the word bright. The string to match-and-color is specified with an extended regular expression. See projects 77 and 78 to learn more about extended regular expressions.

Try loading an HTML file, such as ~/Sites/index.html, into nano, and you should see the syntax highlighting described above in action.

Download the nano source files (see the sidebar "Get nano Info—and nano Itself"), and you'll find a file called nanorc.sample. This file gives examples of what can be placed in the configuration file and how to write syntax highlighting instructions.

Project 31
Edit with emacs

"What do I do once I've outgrown the nano *text editor?"*

This project introduces the emacs text editor, a full-featured text editor that'll do all you want and more, with an extensive interactive help system and tutorials to help you get started. Projects 32 through 35 cover the vim text editor, and Project 30 covers the simpler nano text editor.

Basics

Fire up emacs, and we'll take a look at what it can do. You should find a file called index.html in the directory Sites in your home directory. We'll work on a copy of it, which we'll call index-new.html, but you can use any other text file instead.

```
$ cd ~/Sites
$ cp index.html index-new.html
$ emacs index-new.html
```

You'll see a terminal window similar to that shown in **Figure 4.2**. The top line shows a menu bar. The bottom line is the *minibuffer,* in which you type command arguments such as the name of a file to load. The line above that, with white text on a black background, is the *mode line;* it shows status and important and informational messages such as the name of the file you are editing.

Commands in emacs are introduced with either the Control key or the Escape key (termed the *meta key*). Control sequences are shown in the emacs documentation as, for example, C-a, which means press Control-a. Meta-key sequences are shown as, for example, M-a, which means press Escape and then the letter a. (Don't hold the Escape key down, as you would the Control key.)

Move Around

Use the cursor (arrow) keys in the normal manner to select an editing position in a file. To position the cursor by clicking, you must first

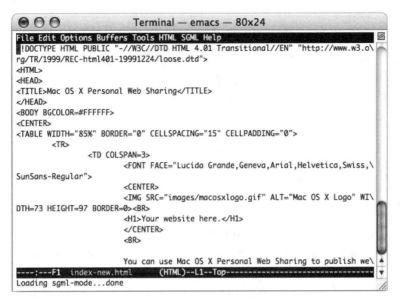

Figure 4.2 The emacs text editor provides more tools and greater sophistication than the simpler nano editor.

TIP

The Page Up and Page Down keys scroll Apple's Terminal. Use Shift-Page Up and Shift-Page Down to get emacs to scroll the document.

If you use X11's xterm as your terminal, the Page Up and Page Down work without the Shift key.

enable Terminal's Option-Click to Position Cursor feature. Launch the Terminal Inspector by choosing Terminal > Window Settings; select Emulation from the pop-up menu, and check Option-Click to Position Cursor. (If you did this already to enable mouse clicks in nano, you don't need to do it again for emacs.) Option-clicking tells Terminal to send a series of cursor-movement keystrokes to emacs, thereby moving the cursor to the point where you clicked.

Other useful sequences are

▸ Control-a to move to the start of the line

▸ Control-e to move to the end of the line

▸ Escape a to move to the start of the sentence

▸ Escape e to move to the end of the sentence

▸ Escape < to move to the start of the document

▸ Escape > to move to the end of the document

▸ Control-l (letter ell) to center the document on the current cursor position

ⓘ TIP

*The cursor keys have control-
sequence equivalents. Try*
Control- *and* p, n, f, b. *Also,*
Control-v *is equivalent to
Page Down, and Escape* v *is
equivalent to Page Up.*

ⓘ TIP

To undo changes, press
Control-_ *(underscore) or
type* Control-x u.

Note that control sequences move the cursor by characters and lines, whereas the corresponding escape sequences move the cursor by syntactic elements such as words and sentences.

Get Help

Press Control-h to enter the help system and then

▶ ? to display the help screen

▶ t to enter the tutorial

▶ k and then a Control or Escape sequence on which to get help

If you enter the help system while editing another file, return to the file by typing Control-x b. See "Multiple Files (Buffers) and Windows" later in this project.

Type Control-x Control-c to exit emacs.

Edit File Contents

Inserting and removing text is straightforward in emacs. To add text, place the cursor at the location where you want your addition to begin. The Delete key (also referred to as the *Backspace* key) deletes the character behind the cursor. Forward-Delete (the key above the left arrow on full-size Mac keyboards, emulated by pressing Fn-Delete on laptops) removes the character under the cursor.

Other useful delete sequences are

▶ Control-k to delete (kill) from the cursor to the end of the current line

▶ Escape k to delete (kill) from the cursor to the end of the current paragraph

Cut and Paste

Cut text: In emacs lingo, you don't cut text, you *kill* it. Press Control-@ (or Control-space, if that key combination is not already used as a hot key elsewhere), to mark the start of a section to be killed. Move the cursor to just after the end of the section to be killed, and press Control-w. This kills (cuts) the text and saves it in a buffer.

Paste text: The emacs term for "paste" is *yank*. Position the cursor where you want some previously cut text to be inserted, and press Control-y. Any operation that *kills* text also makes that text available to be yanked back with Control-y. This applies to the deletion sequences described in "Edit File Contents" earlier in this project.

As with nano, if you use Apple's Terminal application for Unix sessions (instead of the X11 xterm), you can also copy text by pressing Command-c and paste it by pressing Command-v. It is not possible to cut text by using Command-x.

Save Your Edits

To save changes to the current file, type Control-x Control-s. You'll see confirmation of the save on the bottom line. The first time the changes are saved, the original file is renamed to end with a tilde (~). If you later decide you want the original file back, it'll be there ready and waiting for you.

To discard changes, type Control-x Control-c. You'll see a prompt on the bottom line, to which you should answer "no" by typing n; then answer yes to the next prompt to confirm that you do indeed intend to discard all changes made to the current document.

Search and Replace

emacs has search, and search-and-replace, capabilities. In addition, you may search in a case-sensitive manner, employ regular-expression matching, and search in the reverse direction.

To search for a term such as *web*, press Control-s. In the minibuffer at the foot of the window you'll see the prompt I-search:. Type the search term, and if you type slowly, you'll notice the search happening as you type with all matches highlighted. As you type more letters, the search becomes more selective. (Known as an *incremental* search, this method will be familiar to users of Mac OS X 10.4's Spotlight search tool.)

TIP

When you do several kills, each kill is saved in a separate buffer. Yanking pastes the most recent kill. When you follow Control-y *with Escape* y, *previous kills are recalled, overwriting the text that was just pasted. Type Escape* y *several times to choose which kill to paste.*

Official emacs Information

The official home site for emacs is www.gnu.org/software/emacs. It provides lots of useful information, including a comprehensive manual.

If many matches are found, press `Control-s` repeatedly until the desired match is highlighted. If you overshoot, press the Delete (Backspace) key to return to the previous match. When you have found what you are looking for (which is more than U2 ever did), press Return to end the search.

To repeat the last search, type `Control-s Control-s` and then press Return. To search backward, use `Control-r` instead of `Control-s`.

To perform a nonincremental search, press `Control-s` and then Return. The prompt in the minibuffer changes from `I-search:` to `Search:`. Continue as before, typing the search term and then pressing Return.

If the search term you enter is in all lowercase, the search is made in a case-insensitive manner, so `hello` matches `hello` and `Hello`. Entering an uppercase character anywhere in the search term makes the search case sensitive, so `Hello` matches `Hello` but not `hello` or `HellO`.

Replace

To perform a search and replace, type Escape `x` `replace-string` and then press Return (type literally `replace-string`). At the minibuffer prompt `Replace string:` , type the string to be replaced and press Return. The prompt will change to `Replace string with:` . Type the new string and press Return. All occurrences of the search string will be replaced by the new string.

To perform an interactive search and replace, in which you get to choose which matches are replaced and which are not, type `query-replace` instead of `replace-string`. At each match, emacs will prompt for confirmation. Reply with one of the following:

▶ y for yes, to replace the string

▶ n for no, to not replace the string

▶ q for quit, to quit without replacing any more strings

▶ ! for replace, to replace all occurrences without further prompting

Use Regular Expressions

emacs is capable of searching for, and replacing, regular expressions. To search for a regular expression, prefix a normal search (as described above) with Control-u and then continue by pressing Control-s as usual. To perform a search and replace when matching a regular expression, proceed as for a standard search and replace, but type replace-regexp instead of replace-string.

More

There is much more to searching and replacing in emacs than is presented here. Refer to the online documentation (see the sidebar "Official emacs Information") for full details.

Multiple Files (Buffers) and Windows

emacs lets you open many files in a single session. Each open file is held in a separate buffer, and emacs displays one buffer at a time. To load a second file, type Control-x Control-f. The minibuffer on the bottom line will show the prompt Find file: followed by the name of the current working directory. Type a name for the new file in the minibuffer, and press Return. The old file will vanish, and the new file will be presented in the terminal window. The old file is still loaded in emacs and can be recalled for editing later.

To switch between open files (or buffers) to continue editing a previous file, type Control-x b. At the prompt, type the name of the file to edit and press Return. You may notice that emacs shows a default filename in the prompt; if this is the one you want, you need only press Return.

If you wish to create a new file, type Control-x Control-f. The minibuffer on the bottom line will show the prompt Find file: followed by the name of the current working directory. Type a name for the new file in the minibuffer and press Return.

Type Control-x Control-b to display a list of buffers. This operation opens a second window. To close it, see the next section, "Open Multiple Windows."

⬈ LEARN MORE

See projects 77 and 78 to learn more about regular expressions.

⚡ TIP

Use the Cursor Up and Cursor Down keys to recall filenames you've typed previously.

⚡ TIP

Split a window vertically by typing Control-x 3.

To save or discard all modified buffers interactively, type Control-x s. For each buffer, emacs will ask for confirmation. Reply with one of the following:

▶   y for yes, to save the buffer

▶   n for no, to skip the buffer

▶   q for quit, to skip all remaining buffers

▶   ! for save all, to save all remaining buffers without further prompting

Open Multiple Windows

To open a second window, type Control-x 2. The new window will initially contain a copy of the current buffer, but you can read another file into it by typing Control-x Control-f, as described above. To flip between windows, type Control-x o.

If you have two windows open and wish to close the other window, type Control-x 1. You may open a third window by typing Control-x 2.

Use Tabbed Completion

When entering a filename in the minibuffer, use tabbed completion just as you would on the command line. Start typing a filename; then press Tab. If what you have typed so far is unambiguous, emacs will complete the filename; you need only press Return to load that file. If what you have typed is ambiguous, press Tab a second time to reveal a list of possible completions in a new window. Continue typing until what you have typed is unambiguous; then press Tab again to complete the filename and press Return to load the file.

Alternatively, when the completions are showing, type Escape v or Page Up (Shift-Page Up in Apple's Terminal) to move the cursor into the *completions buffer.* From here, use the cursor keys to make a selection from the list of possible completions. Press Return to load the selected filename. Select a directory and press Return to enter the directory, listing its contents in the completions buffer. To move to the parent directory, select the .. (dot-dot) entry and press Return.

Repetition

Most commands can be repeated any number of times with `Control-u`. To move the cursor down 30 lines, for example, type `Control-u 30` and then the command or keystroke to repeat—in this case, the Cursor Down key. To insert a line of 80 stars, type `Control-u 80 *`.

To kill the next 20 lines, type `Control-u 20 Control-k`. This operation is actually slightly different from pressing `Control-k` 20 times, as the first `Control-k` of a pair kills the contents of the line, and the second kills the line itself, so only 10 lines will be killed. Try it. All the killed lines are added to the yank buffer, so pressing `Control-y` will reinsert all the lines at the current cursor position.

Much More

The `emacs` text editor has many, many more features. This project presents enough for you to start using `emacs` for your day-to-day editing needs. Refer to the help system, or the tutorial, for more information. Alternatively, visit the `emacs` home page listed in the sidebar "Official `emacs` Information."

Try one of the following:

▶ Escape x `life`

▶ Escape x `dunnet`

▶ Escape x `tetris`

▶ Escape x `pong`

When you get bored, type Escape x `quit`.

ⓘ TIP

You may use filename-completion tricks when switching buffers with `Control-x b`. *Press Tab to complete a buffer name, and press Tab twice to open the completions buffer. You may move the cursor to the completions buffer to select a buffer.*

ĭ TIP

Most people who don't like vim *have never seriously tried it.*

Project 32
Edit with vim

"What do I do once I've outgrown the nano *text editor?"*

This project introduces the powerful, highly configurable vim text editor. Ideal for writing code and maintaining configuration files, vim is highly efficient, enabling you to edit with the minimum number of keystrokes. The vim text editor is an improved version of the standard vi (pronounced vee eye) text editor traditionally distributed with Unix systems. The three projects following this one—33, 34, and 35—cover some of the more advanced features of vim. Project 31 introduces the emacs text editor, and Project 30 introduces the simpler nano text editor.

Basics

Fire up vim, and we'll take a look at what it can do. Use any text file; we'll once again work on a copy of ~/Sites/index.html.

```
$ cd ~/Sites
$ cp index.html index-new.html
$ vim index-new.html
```

You'll see a terminal window similar to that shown in **Figure 4.3**. The bottom line (the vim *command line*) shows important and informational messages such as the current mode, and is also where you type vim commands. **In this project and the others covering vim (Projects 33–35), the term *command line* refers to vim's command line, not that of the shell unless specifically stated.**

Before we continue, there's something you should understand. To reap the benefits of vim, you must invest a little time in learning the basics. If you are prepared to do so, you'll be rewarded with a powerful and very productive editing tool. If not, take a look at nano.

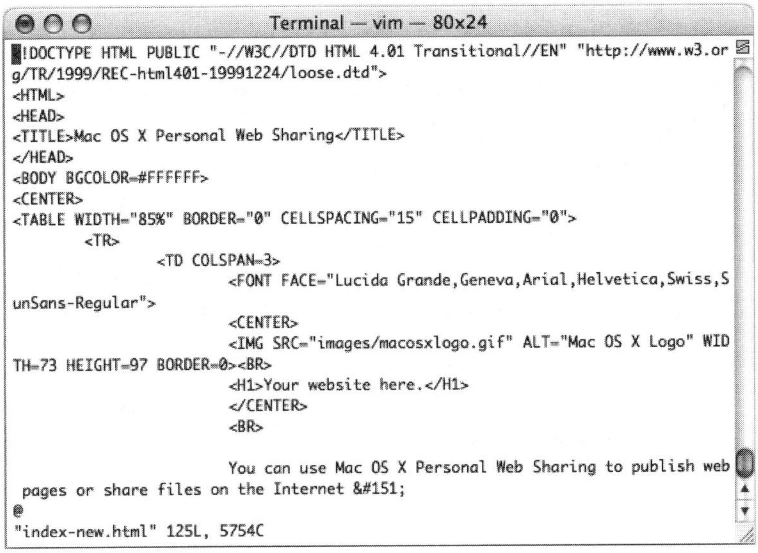

```
Terminal — vim — 80x24
<!DOCTYPE HTML PUBLIC "-//W3C//DTD HTML 4.01 Transitional//EN" "http://www.w3.or
g/TR/1999/REC-html401-19991224/loose.dtd">
<HTML>
<HEAD>
<TITLE>Mac OS X Personal Web Sharing</TITLE>
</HEAD>
<BODY BGCOLOR=#FFFFFF>
<CENTER>
<TABLE WIDTH="85%" BORDER="0" CELLSPACING="15" CELLPADDING="0">
        <TR>
                <TD COLSPAN=3>
                        <FONT FACE="Lucida Grande,Geneva,Arial,Helvetica,Swiss,S
unSans-Regular">
                        <CENTER>
                        <IMG SRC="images/macosxlogo.gif" ALT="Mac OS X Logo" WID
TH=73 HEIGHT=97 BORDER=0><BR>
                        <H1>Your website here.</H1>
                        </CENTER>
                        <BR>

                        You can use Mac OS X Personal Web Sharing to publish web
 pages or share files on the Internet &#151;
@
"index-new.html" 125L, 5754C
```

Figure 4.3 The vim text editor takes a little getting used to, but it's incredibly flexible, powerful, and even fun after you become familiar with it.

Override vi Compatibility

Because it's based on the old `vi` editor, `vim` runs by default in `vi`-compatibility mode, which doesn't expose all its features. We'll want to run in full `vim` mode, and the easiest way to activate it is to create an empty `vim` configuration file in your home directory.

```
$ touch ~/.vimrc
```

You can edit this file later to change `vim`'s default settings.

Understand vim Modes

You can't just plunge straight into `vim` and start typing; weird things will happen. `vim` operates in one of two modes:

- Normal mode. `vim` starts up in normal mode. In this mode, characters you type are interpreted as commands, not additions to file content. There's no need to use the Escape and Control keys to prefix each command. To enter normal mode from insert mode (see below), press Escape.

Official vim Information

The official home page for `vim` (called vim online) is at www.vim.org. You'll find lots of useful information, including a hyperlinked version of the `vim` help system, FAQs, tips including an RSS feed, and an online version of Steve Oualline's book about `vim`.

Mac OS X includes the Terminal version of `vim`, which is the one we'll be using in this project. There's also an Aqua (OS X-native) version that's essentially the same, but with the addition of menus and mouse clicks. It can be downloaded from http://macvim.org.

To quote vim online:

"`vim` is charityware. Its license is GPL-compatible, so it's distributed freely, but we ask that if you find it useful you make a donation to help children in Uganda through the ICCF."

LEARN MORE

Project 35 covers `vim` **configuration.**

ⓘ TIP

When in command-line mode (after having typed : *), use the up and down arrow (cursor) keys to recall previous commands.*

Why Two Modes?

vim's modal operation can scare people away, but it needn't. In normal mode, you are able to issue commands simply by typing letters. Compare this with the more traditional approach taken by emacs. Because emacs does not have separate modes, every command must be a control sequence or must be preceded by the Escape key. You effectively have to enter normal mode for almost every command keystroke, and in return, you benefit from being automatically thrown back into insert mode. You'll no doubt make up you own mind as to which of the two you prefer.

Some vim commands require arguments, and these are entered on the vim command line. Such commands are introduced by typing a colon (:). Type a colon now, and you'll see it echoed on the command line, followed by the cursor. This is known as vim *command-line mode*. Now type help and then press Return. A new vim window will open (the Terminal window will split into two horizontal sections) showing the vim help pages in the top window. Type :q (colon followed immediately by q) to quit help, closing the new window and returning to the main document.

▸ Insert mode. You must change from normal mode to insert mode to insert text. The most common way to do this is simply to type i (other ways are described later). In this mode, typed characters are added to file content in the usual manner. When in insert mode, you'll notice the text -- INSERT -- on the left end of vim's command line. Press Escape when you wish to return to normal mode.

Move Around

The arrow (cursor) keys work as expected and, most important, do so in both normal and insert modes, so there's no need to switch modes just to cursor around the file. In X11's xterm, but *not* Apple's Terminal, you can enable positioning of the cursor via mouse clicks by entering normal mode, typing

`:set mouse=a`

and pressing Return. You'll see this echoed on the vim command line, as in the help example earlier.

To enable mouse-click positioning of the vim cursor within Terminal, turn on Terminal's Option-Click to Position Cursor feature. Launch the Terminal Inspector by choosing Terminal > Window Settings; select Emulation from the pop-up menu, and check Option-Click to Position Cursor. (If you did this already to enable mouse clicks in nano or emacs, you don't need to do it again for vim.) Option-clicking tells Terminal to send a series of cursor-movement keystrokes to vim, thereby moving the cursor to the point where you clicked.

In normal mode, vim supplements the arrow keys with several cursor-movement shortcut keystrokes. Following are some of the most useful, listed in an order that will become apparent as you read them:

- gg   Move back to the start of the file

- {   Move back one paragraph

- (Move back one sentence

- -   Move up (back) one line

- ^   Move back to the start of the current line

- b   Move back one word

- h j k l   Equivalent to left, down, up, right

- w   Move forward one word

- $ Move forward to the end of the current line

- +   Move down (forward) one line

-)   Move forward one sentence

- }   Move forward one paragraph

- G   Move forward to the end of the file

The difference between minus (-) and k is that minus moves to the first nonblank character on the line, whereas k will happily move the cursor to leading white space. Plus (+) and j are similarly different.

Jump to a Line

You may jump straight to line number *n* within a file by using either of the following command syntaxes within vim normal mode. Type

- nG (for example, 24G to move to line 24).

- :n (for example, :100 to move to line 100).

To jump halfway into a file, type 50%. I'll leave you to figure out how to jump one-third of the way into a file (but integer numbers only, please!).

ⓘ TIP

If you forget which vim *mode you're in, check the command line at the foot of the window for the text* --INSERT--*, or press Escape to go to normal mode. You can also press Escape to abandon a command that you're midway through typing.*

ⓘ TIP

The Page Up and Page Down keys scroll Apple's Terminal. Use Shift-Page Up and Shift-Page Down to get vim *to scroll the document.*

If you use X11's xterm *as your terminal, the Page Up and Page Down work without the Shift key.*

ⓘ TIP

Press Control-G *in normal mode to display the current filename and cursor position on the* vim *command line.*

If a command is preceded by a colon when issued, you must precede it with a colon when getting help on it. Typing `:help :s` *gives help on a different command from the one you get help on by typing* `:help s`.

Read the 30-minute vim *tutor by invoking* vim *from the shell prompt as (all one word)*

`$ vimtutor`

Get Help

To enter the vim help system, press Escape if you are not in normal mode, and type

`:help`

and then press Return. (Remember that typing a colon positions the cursor on the vim command line, where you then type `help`.) The vim help pages will appear in the top half of a split screen. Use the arrow keys to move around the help pages. In fact, the help pages are simply a non-modifiable document.

Cursor down a few lines until you reach the section labeled "BASIC:". Below it, you'll find sections labeled with vertical bars on either side, such as "|quickref|" and "|tutor|". Position the cursor on one of these *tags,* and press Control-] (hold down the Control key while pressing the] key). A tag is like a hyperlink and takes you to the appropriate point in the help system. Press Control-t to move back from the linked page to the original page.

To get help on a specific command, type

`:help`

in normal mode, followed by the keystroke(s) for the command you want to learn about. For example:

`:help j`
`:help ctrl-]`
`:help :s`

To get help on a particular topic, type

`:help the-topic-here`

To exit the help system and return to the main document, type

`:q`

Add and Remove Text

When you wish to insert text, type i for *insert*. From then on, editing is pretty much as you would expect. To add text, place the cursor at the location where you want your addition to begin. The Delete key (also referred to as the *Backspace* key) deletes the character behind the cursor. Forward-Delete (the key above the left arrow on full-size Mac keyboards, emulated by pressing Fn-Delete on laptops) removes the character under the cursor.

Different keystrokes for switching from normal to insert mode determine where text insertion begins after the mode switch. From normal mode, enter insert mode by typing one of the following:

▶ I to start inserting at the beginning of the line

▶ i to start inserting at the cursor

▶ a to start inserting just after the cursor

▶ A to start inserting after the end of the line

▶ O to open a new line above the current line

▶ o to open a new line below the current line

If you want to replace (overwrite) existing text instead of inserting new text, type the following in normal mode:

▶ r to replace a single character. Typing rT, for example, replaces the character under the cursor with T, and you remain in normal mode.

▶ R to replace continually. Every character you type overwrites a character in the file. You'll notice that vim's command line now displays the message -- REPLACE --.

▶ C to delete to the end of the line and enter insert mode.

▶ S to delete the entire line and enter insert mode.

❦ NOTE

From here on, I won't continually remind you to enter normal mode or to press Return after typing a command on vim's command line.

↗ LEARN MORE

See Project 33 to learn more about cut, copy, and paste in vim.

Undo Changes

To undo changes, enter normal mode and type one of the following:

▶ u to undo the last change. vim has multi-level undo, so you can repeat this many times to go farther back in the editing history.

▶ U to undo all changes applied to the last line that was edited. If you inserted, deleted, and inserted some more, all on the same line, U undoes all three sets of changes and in this example is equivalent to uuu.

▶ Control-r to redo changes that have just been undone. Like undo, redo is multi-level and can redo many undos.

Simple Cut, Copy, and Paste

Here are the most basic cut, copy, and paste commands for vim. Remember to enter normal mode when you issue these commands.

▶ Cut text. Type dd to cut *(delete)* the current line, and type x to delete the character under the cursor.

▶ Copy text. Type yy to copy *(yank)* the current line.

▶ Paste text. Type p to paste *(put)* a cut or copied line *below* the current line, and type P to paste it *above* the current line. Similarly, cut characters are pasted after or before the cursor position.

To cut or copy a specific number of lines, precede the command with a count. To copy 20 lines and then paste them back elsewhere, for example, type 20yy, move the cursor, and then type p.

If you use Apple's Terminal application, you may also use the standard Mac methods of pressing Command-c to copy selected text and Command-v to paste it (in vim insert mode). It's not possible to cut text by using Command-x.

Save Your Edits

Here are some of the most useful commands. Type

▶ :w to save changes to the current file.

- `:w new-file-name` to save the changes to a new file.

- `:q` to quit `vim`. If you have unsaved changes you wish to save first, type `:wq`.

- `:q!` to quit `vim` and abandon all changes since the last save.

Edit as Root

System configuration files are writable only by root. To modify them, you must run `vim` as user root, using the `sudo` command, and type your administrator password when prompted.

```
$ sudo vim filename
Password:
```

Search and Replace

The `vim` text editor has search, and search-and-replace, capabilities. In addition, the search can be case sensitive, employ regular-expression matching, and be performed in the reverse direction.

To search for a term like *web* in `vim`, type / (forward slash) in normal mode. The cursor will be placed on the `vim` command line. Now type the search term `web` and press Return. The cursor will be placed on the first match. To move to the next match, type `n`; and to move backward to the previous match, type `N`. If a search reaches the end of the file, it will wrap back to the beginning, displaying the message `Search hit BOTTOM, continuing at TOP` on vim's command line.

To repeat the last search, type / and press Return. To search backward, use ? instead of / and then proceed as before.

Search Options

If you wish to change the way searches behave, `vim` has several options that you can enable (or *set*), either interactively on vim's command line or in the configuration file (see Project 35). When these

⊺ TIP

Follow a command with pling (!) to tell `vim` *to proceed with the command where normally it might balk and issue a warning instead.*

⌁ LEARN MORE

See "How to Become the Root User" in Project 2 for more details on the sudo **command.**

⊺ TIP

After typing /, you can use the Cursor Up and Cursor Down keys to recall previous search terms.

⚓ TIP

The substitute command takes several flags that modify its behavior (making it interactive or case insensitive, for example). To learn more about substitute, consult the vim *help pages by typing*

`:help :s`
`:help :s_flags`

❦ NOTE

Because vim *treats all search terms as regular expressions, search characters that have special meaning within regular expressions—such as dot, star, question mark (query), and square brackets—must be escaped within search terms, using the backslash character. For example:* \. * \? \[\].

⚓ LEARN MORE

See projects 77 and 78 to learn more about regular expressions.

options have been set, they affect all searches, not just the next search made. Here are some of the most useful. Type

- `:set ignorecase` to make searches case insensitive. `apple` will match `apple`, `Apple`, and `APPLE`.

- `:set smartcase` in conjunction with `ignorecase`. If the search term contains any uppercase characters, the search becomes case sensitive. If the search term is entirely lowercase, the search remains case insensitive.

- `:set hlsearch` to tell `vim` to highlight all matches. (Typing `:nohl` switches off the highlighting resulting from the last search but won't switch off `hlsearch` for subsequent searches.)

- `:set incsearch` to active *incremental* search mode. If you type slowly, you'll notice the search happening as you type, with the next match highlighted. As you type more letters, the search becomes more selective.

Switch off any of the above options by preceding the option name with `no`. For example:

`:set noignorecase`

Replace

To perform a search and replace *(substitute)*, type

`:%s/search-text/replace-text/g`

Let's analyze this command. The initial percent (%) symbol means "all lines in the file." Without it, the search operates on the current line only. The next part says to search for and then substitute (s) search-text with replace-text. The forward-slash characters delimit the text. The final g says do this globally across each line, as without it, only the first match on each line is substituted.

Use Regular Expressions

`vim` is capable of searching for, and replacing, regular expressions. No special commands are necessary; simply use a regular expression as the search term.

Project 33
Learn Advanced vim

"I like vim. What more can I do with it?"

This project covers some of the more advanced features of the vim text editor, such as global editing, bookmarks, compound commands, macros, and filtering text through external commands. Project 32 introduces vim, and Projects 34 and 35 cover vim windows, buffers, and advanced configuration.

Quick Matching

Project 32 showed you how to search a file for specific text. Sometimes, and especially when writing code, you may want to match the word under the cursor or to locate matching bracket pairs.

If the cursor is sitting on a function name, for example, type star (*) to move to the point in the file where that function is mentioned next. If you have enabled search highlighting (refer to Project 32), all occurrences are highlighted. To move to the next occurrence of the function name, type n. In fact, all the features and options applicable to searching apply to quick matching, too (again, refer to Project 32). To initiate a backward search, type hash (#) instead of star.

Match Bracket Pairs

Place the cursor on an open bracket, and type % to locate the corresponding close bracket and % again to move back to the open bracket. vim understands the (), [], and {} bracket pairs. Rather oddly, vim does not match <> bracket pairs, but this is easily corrected with the matchpairs option. Its default setting is

```
matchpairs=(:),{:},[:]
```

Add angle brackets to the list using the command

```
:set matchpairs+=<:>
```

↗ **LEARN MORE**

See projects 77 and 78 to learn more about regular expressions.

ℹ **TIP**

When entering commands or filenames on the vim *command line, you can use tabbed completion. Simply press Tab, and the command or filename is completed. If what you have typed so far is ambiguous, either type some more and press Tab again, or continue pressing Tab, and* vim *will cycle through all possible completions.*

Notice that we use += instead of = to *add to* the existing definition instead of *overwriting* it.

Find a Character

Sometimes, it's handy to jump forward on a line to a particular character, such as a bracket or quote. To find the next quote, for example, simply type f' (*f* immediately followed by a single quote). To find subsequent occurrences of the quote, type ; (semicolon); to find previous occurrences, type , (comma).

Perform Global Edits

Try this vim command.

`:g/.*/m0`

The command reverses the order of the lines in the file. Not in itself useful, it nevertheless illustrates the global command quite nicely. The global command (g) searches every line of the file for the pattern enclosed in //. In this example, we have specified a regular expression (.*) that matches everything. For each line that matches (every line in the file, in this example), the function immediately following the pattern is applied. In this example, m0 *moves* the current line to a position of line 0 (the top of the file). Each subsequent line becomes the top line, thereby reversing the order of the lines.

We can delete specific lines by using function d. To delete all lines starting with NOTE, for example, we use the regular expression ^NOTE followed by d. A caret at the start of a regular expression says "at the start of the line." The global command is

`:g/^NOTE/d`

Line Ranges

You are able to limit the scope of the global command by specifying a range of lines to consider, by using either line numbers or pattern matching, and separating the start and end of the range with a comma.

If we wish to delete all lines starting with NOTE (using regular expression ^NOTE), but *only* within the range line 10 to line 100, we type

`:10,100g/^NOTE/d`

Alternatively, to consider a range of lines delimited by patterns, we type

`/START/,/END/g/^NOTE/d`

This example searches for a line that contains START and then a subsequent line that contains END. This defines the range of lines to which the global function is applied. Then the function further searches the range for lines that start with NOTE and deletes each one.

The special line range % means all lines in the file.

Use vim Commands as Functions

The global command has a limited number of functions of its own (called *ex functions* because they descend from the old ex editor upon which vi and vim are based). Standard vim functions and commands can also be used as functions to the global command if they are preceded with the special function normal. To insert -- at the start of each line beginning with NOTE, for example, we apply the vim command I-- to each matched line. Type

`:g/^NOTE/normal I--`

It may be easier to understand global commands by trying a few examples yourself on a test file. Also, have a look at the vim help pages for global by typing

`:help :g`

Set Bookmarks

The vim text editor lets you set up to 26 simultaneous bookmarks, labeled a to z. To assign bookmark a to the point under the cursor, type ma (mb for bookmark b, and so on). If you move elsewhere in the file and wish to return to a bookmarked line, simply type a single quote (') followed by the bookmark label ('a, for example).

⚓ TIP

The most useful of vim's *special bookmarks is quote. Typing quote-quote (* `''` *) flips you between the current cursor position and the last mark set. Check out the mark (m) command by typing*

`:help m`

An alternative method precedes the bookmark label with the back-quote character (`` ` ``). This returns the cursor to the *character* that was bookmarked, whereas the single-quote method places the cursor at the start of the marked *line*. Try setting a few books marks and whizzing back and forth by using both quote and back-quote.

Jumping to a bookmark is classified as a *motion command*. You can use motion commands in combination with other commands, such as delete (d) to delete a marked block of text. See "Build Command Sequences" later in this project, which tells you how to use motion commands as part of a command sequence.

Another 26 vim bookmarks, labeled A to Z, work across files. Set a mark, for example, by typing mA and then quit vim. Restart vim, but editing a different file, and type `'A`. You will be transported to the original file and placed right on the marked line (or the marked character, if you recalled the mark by typing `` `A ``).

At this point, you get into the realm of multiple files and buffers. See Project 34 to learn more. If you wish to flip between two loaded files, the easiest method is to press `Control-^`. You may also type:

`:ls!`

to list the current files. To return to a particular file, note its buffer number in the listing, and type

`:bu`<buffer number>

Build Command Sequences

Many of vim's commands can be combined to build more complex command sequences, rather like you combine executables and shell statements to build more complex command lines. In the following sections, we'll take a look at a few useful techniques: repetition counts, motion commands, and macros.

Repetition Counts

Recall from Project 32 that dd deletes the current line. Preceding it with a repetition count lets us delete any number of lines. To delete four lines, type 4dd.

To insert 80 stars, we could type 80 stars, or we could use repetition and the i command, typing 80i* and then pressing Escape. Similarly, to move the cursor forward 20 characters, type 20 and then press the right arrow key, or type 20l. (Project 32 explains the cursor-movement keys, noting that h, j, k, and l are equivalent to the left, down, up, and right arrow keys.) Visit Project 32 if necessary, as it'll help later if you are familiar with the basic cursor-movement commands.

More Motion Commands

The concept of *motion commands* is fundamental to vim and can be used to great effect when combined with other commands. The command w , for example, is a motion command that moves the cursor forward one word. We can apply a repetition count to a motion command. To move the cursor forward by four words, use 4w.

A motion command can be given as the argument to a function, such as d for delete. So far, we have considered only dd, which is a special case of function d to perform a very common task: delete the current line. The d function usually takes as its argument a motion command that defines the region of text to delete. Motion commands use the current cursor position as the start point for defining a region and designate the end of the region as point to where the cursor would move if the motion command were applied. Hence, dw deletes the word following the cursor; d$ deletes from the cursor to the end of the line; and dG deletes from the cursor to the end of the document.

Combine Them All

Much of vim's power lies in the ability to combine repetition counts, motion commands, and functions. d4w, for example, means "Delete the next four words," and 4dw means "Repeat four times 'delete the next word'." The former applies a repetition count to the motion command, and the latter applies it to the delete function. As long as 2 x 2 = 4, of course, we could also write 2d2w.

Motion commands defined by bookmarks are especially useful. To delete a section of text, we mark one end of the section with ma and then move the cursor to the other end. The motion command 'a now defines a region of text from the cursor to the mark, so the command `d'a` deletes all lines from the cursor line to the book-marked line.

To delete a specific portion of text, say from X to Y in the example below,

```
This will remain X and all
of this text will be
deleted Y and this will also remain.
```

we must use back-quote instead of quote in recalling the bookmark. You'll remember that back-quote honors the position within a line, whereas quote simply honors the line. Position the cursor on X and type `ma`; then move to just after Y and type `d`a`.

Cut, Copy, and Paste

Project 32 touched on cut, copy, and paste. Now it's time to revisit this subject and apply our new knowledge. Remember that `vim` uses `d` to cut (delete) text, `y` to copy (yank) text, and `p` to paste text.

Registers

First, let's discuss *registers*. When you cut text, `vim` places the text in a register, and when you paste text, it is copied from a register. (`vim` uses the term *register* in this context and *buffer* to denote the area of memory used to store the file currently being edited.) There are 26 registers for copy and paste in `vim`, labeled `a` to `z`. You can use them to store text for reuse. You may cut or copy selected text into a specific buffer by typing a double-quote character (") followed by the register label ("a , for example). To cut the next three lines of text into register a, we precede the cut (delete) command with the named register.

`"a3dd`

This translates as "Into register a, place the results of: 3 x delete the current line."

To copy text from the cursor to the end of the line into register b, we type

`"by$`

This translates as "Into register b, place the results of: copy (yank) from the cursor position to the end of the line."

To paste the contents of a register, precede the paste command (p) with a register name (a double quote followed by the label letter). The following pastes the contents of register b.

```
"bp
```

To copy (or cut) a specific region of text, we'll combine what we have learned about bookmarks, registers, and yanking (or deleting). Place the cursor at the start of the region to be copied and type ma; move the cursor to the end of the region and type

```
"ay`c
```

This translates as "Into register a, copy the results of: copy text from the current cursor position to bookmark c, honoring the position within the line."

At first glance, these commands look like hieroglyphics. But if you understand the concepts discussed in this project, it's easy to decipher them. Similarly, it's very easy to build such commands: A lot can be achieved with just a few keystrokes.

More Registers

The last copy or cut in vim is always placed in the special register named dot. Its contents can be recalled in the usual manner: by typing its name (the period character) after a double-quote character.

```
".
```

If you wish to *append* text to the contents of a register, rather than *overwrite* the contents, use a capital letter to name the register. To collect three dispersed lines into register a and paste them elsewhere, for example, we use (omitting the necessary cursor-movement commands)

```
"ayy
"Ayy
"Ayy
"ap
```

> **ⵣ TIP**
>
> *Type* `:registers` *to view the contents all the registers and* `:help registers` *to read the* vim *help pages on registers and black holes.*

☝ TIP

Add new keystrokes to an existing macro by using a capital letter to name the macro. qA, for example, adds keystrokes to the existing macro a.

Repeat Commands with Macros

Very often, you need to repeat the last command a number of times. Suppose that you wish to comment out a number of lines in your PHP code by preceding them with //. To do this, you insert the text // at the start of a line by typing I// followed by Escape. Now press Cursor Down and then dot (.). The previous insert sequence will be repeated. Dot repeats the last simple command, such as an insert or delete sequence.

The dot command can save a lot of typing with repetitive tasks, but we can often reduce effort even more by using a *macro,* defined by recording a series of keystrokes. We might improve on the example above by recording the keystrokes

I// Escape Cursor-Down

You can store up to 36 macros in vim, named 0 to 9 and a to z. To record a macro, type q followed by the label you want to assign to the macro (qa, for example). Start typing, and when you're done recording, type q again. Replay the macro by typing @ followed by the macro label (@a, for example).

Comparing our macro a with the dot example above, the inclusion of a cursor-down keystroke makes the macro easier to use than the dot command, and the macro is also better suited to the use of a repeat count, as in 10@a.

If you find yourself using a macro frequently, you can assign it to a keystroke command—a technique termed *key mapping.* That's covered in Project 35.

Filter through External Commands

vim lets you pop into the shell temporarily to run a command without ever leaving the editor. Type

:!ls

to list the contents of the current directory using the Unix command ls; then press Return to return control of the Terminal screen to vim.

The pling (!) command says to interpret whatever follows as a shell command and pass it to the shell.

If you wish to capture the output from a command into the file you are editing, rather than have it written to the Terminal, type `!!` followed by that command. Try `!!date`. Neat!

The cursor should be positioned on a blank line to prevent the contents of that line from being replaced by the output of the external command. In fact, there's more happening than is at first apparent. The current line is being *filtered* through the external program. Here's how.

The pling (!) command can take a motion command as an argument, in much the same way as commands y and d (as you saw in "Cut, Copy, and Paste" earlier in this project). The lines encompassed by the motion command are cut from the file and presented to the external command as its standard input. The external command executes, and its output (standard out) is written back to the file.

This is best illustrated with an example. Type

`!5j sort`

You'll notice that after you type `!5j`, the cursor moves to the vim command line so you can see what you type next. Analyzing this command, `5j` says to move the cursor down five lines, thereby defining six lines—from the current cursor position down—as the lines to filter. The Unix command `sort` sorts its input lines into order, so the six lines encompassed by the command are sorted in alphabetic order and written back to the file.

An alternative method of specifying the lines to filter uses a range of lines. In this case, start by typing a `:` to move to vim's command line and then type a range like `1,10` (for the first 10 lines of the file) or `%` for the entire file. (See "Line Ranges" earlier in this project.) Follow the range with the name of the command through which to filter the range of lines. The following example sorts the entire file.

`:%!sort`

⬉ LEARN MORE

Filter commands can be bound to keystrokes; see Project 35 to learn how to define key mappings.

Filtering can be used to great effect. Experiment with it, and you'll no doubt find your own favorite uses. I have a program called HTML Tidy that verifies and tidies HTML text. Running all lines through this program provides me a neat way to verify HTML code without leaving the vim text editor. HTML Tidy can be downloaded from SourceForge at http://sourceforge.net/projects/tidy/

Project 34
Use vim Windows

"How do I edit multiple files in one vim session?"

This project introduces windows and buffers, and shows you how to edit many files is a single vim session. Project 32 introduces vim, and Projects 33 and 35 cover advanced vim features and configuration.

Edit Multiple Files

You may list any number of files on the vim command line. vim reads all the files, loading each in its own *buffer* and presenting the first-named file in the main window. You might edit all HTML files in the current directory, for example, by typing

```
$ vim *.html
```

When you finish editing the first file, save the edits and move to the next file by typing

```
:wn
```

Omit the w if you've already written the changes back to the first file. To discard changes to the current file and move to the next, type

```
:n!
```

To move back to a previous file, type

```
:wprev
```

Other methods of moving between buffers (open files) include

▶ :ls! to list all the buffers. Each buffer is numbered.

▶ :bn to move to buffer number n.

▶ n Control-^ also moves to buffer number n.

To quit vim before all buffers have been visited, type

```
:qa
```

ᵢ TIP

vim supports tabbed completion when you enter a command or filename on its command line. Simply press Tab, and the command or filename is completed. If what you have typed so far is ambiguous, either type some more or continue pressing Tab, and vim will cycle through all possible completions.

To also discard all changes not currently saved, type

`:qa!`

Read Files

From within vim, you may load additional files for editing by typing

▸ `:e filename` to read a file into a new buffer

▸ `:r filename` to include a file within the text of the current file, just below the cursor

Browse Directories

You need not type the full pathname of a file you wish to load. Instead, browse the current directory by typing

`:edit .`

This tells vim to open a new window, from which you choose a file to edit. Use the cursor keys to select a file, and press Return. If you choose a directory, vim will list all the files in that directory. To move to the parent directory choose the `..` (dot-dot) entry.

Open Many Windows

To view several files at once, you could start several Terminal sessions and invoke vim in each of them. It's not necessary to do this, however. Sometimes, it's easier to use vim's multi-window feature, whereby the main window is split into two or more subwindows. You saw this in action before, when you typed `:help`. Recall that vim split the current window and loaded the help pages into the top split.

In vim terminology, a *window* is a portion of the Terminal screen where a file is displayed. A *buffer,* you'll recall, is a copy of a file being edited. There's no hard limit to the number of windows and buffers you can use at any time.

Split the Screen

To open a new window, thus splitting the Terminal screen into two parts, type

`:split`

The cursor is placed in the new window (the top split), as shown in **Figure 4.4**. You'll notice that each window now sports a status bar showing a filename. Both windows are editing the same file, enabling you to view one part of the file while editing another. If you wish to edit a different file in the new window, either use `:e` as described above or give a filename argument to `split`.

`:split filename`

To flip between two (or more) windows, type one of the following:

▸ `Control-w Control-w` to rotate through the windows

▸ `Control-w j` to move to the bottom window

▸ `Control-w k` to move to the top window

Figure 4.4 There's no limit to the number of windows vim can keep open at any time, and its split-window option is great for comparing files.

ᵢ̇ TIP

Type :only *to close all but the active window. Other windows must not contain unsaved modifications. Type* :only! *to override this. The other buffers are still loaded but not displayed in any window.*

ᵢ̇ TIP

If you use X11 and xterm, enable the mouse in vim *by typing*

:set mouse=a

Now you are able to change windows by clicking in the desired window and to adjust the size of windows by dragging the status bar. Very GUI-like!

vim does not limit you to two windows. You may split any number of times to create more windows.

Close a window by typing

:close

The buffer that was displayed in the window is not lost; you can view it again by loading it into this or another window by using the techniques discussed in "Edit Multiple Files" earlier in this project.

To open a new, blank window, type

:new

Change Window Sizes

When you open a new window, vim adjusts the new and existing windows to be of equal size. To override this feature, you may specify a size in lines for the new window. To create a 20-line window, for example, type

:20 split new-filename

It's also possible to adjust the size of existing windows up or down by typing, for example, 7 Control-w + to increase the window size by seven lines and 3 Control-w − (that's a minus sign) to decrease the window size by three lines.

Compare Files

If you wish to compare two files side by side, create a vertical split by typing

:vsplit file2

Alternatively, get vim to do the all the hard work of comparing files and marking the differences. Type either of the following:

▶   :diffsplit file2 to compare files one of top of the other

▶   :vert diffsplit file2 to compare files vertically, side by side

A similar effect can be achieved by invoking `vim` as `vimdiff` and giving it the names of two files to compare.

```
$ vimdiff file1 file2
```

More

There's a lot more to windows in `vim`. Type

```
:help windows
```

for a detailed description of all the available features and commands.

➤ **LEARN MORE**

Refer to Project 32 to learn more about search and replace, and the options that are available.

Official vim Information

The official home page for vim (called vim online) is at www.vim.org. You'll find lots of useful information, including a hyperlinked version of the vim help system, FAQs, tips including an RSS feed, and an online version of Steve Oualline's book about vim.

🛈 **TIP**

Read about each setting in the vim *help pages by typing*

`:help setting-name`

To read all about all the settings, make a gallon of coffee and type

`:help option-summary`

Project 35
Configure vim

"How do I make my vim *settings stick, and how do I define my own features?"*

This project takes a brief look at configuring vim. The topic is too large to cover in this book, so the project simply suggests some useful settings and shows you where to place them. It also describes how to set up a configuration directory. Project 32 introduces vim, and Projects 33 and 34 cover advanced vim features, as well as vim windows and buffers.

Create a Configuration File

Other vim projects have suggested settings that can be applied from the vim command line. To enable case-insensitive searching, for example, we used

`:set ignorecase`

To make these settings stick across vim sessions, we must write them to a configuration file. Your personal settings are written to a file named .vimrc in your home directory. Edit this file now (perhaps using vim ☺) and add some of the settings listed below. Put each setting on its own line. Blank lines are allowed anywhere, and comments are introduced by double quotes.

A sample .vimrc is available at the official home site for vim. See the sidebar "Official vim Information."

The following settings configure vim search, and search-and-replace functions. Refer to Project 32 for more details on these options.

```
" These settings configure searching
"
set ignorecase   " make searching case insensitive
set smartcase    " make searching case sensitive when the
                 " search term has one or more capitals
set hlsearch     " highlight text matching the search term
                 "  type :nohl to remove current highlights
set incsearch    " search as the search term is being typed
set matchpairs+=<:>  " add angle brackets to the %
                     " function bracket matching list
```

The settings in the next batch configure the way vim wraps text and how it treats tab characters. The comment text next to each sample setting explains what it does pretty clearly, but a couple of them bear some extra explanation: The nowrap (no wrap) setting turns off soft wrap. *Soft wrapping* is the default vim behavior of displaying long lines of text across multiple lines within a window, but without inserting hard line breaks. The wrapmargin setting, by contrast, tells vim to insert line-feed characters at the end of wrapped lines so that their line returns become permanent within a file. This feature should not be used when writing code.

```
" These settings configure auto-formatting features
"
set nowrap       " wrap long lines (on by default)
set linebreak    " wrap long lines on one of these
                 "  characters: "space ^I!@*-+;:,./?"
set wrapmargin=2 " insert linefeed to wrap text 2 chars
                 "  before right-hand side of window
set expandtab    " expand Tab characters to spaces
set softtabstop=3 " expand Tab characters as 3 spaces
```

The sample settings below switch on and tweak the look of the vim status bar, which is not usually displayed unless the Terminal screen is split into two or more vim windows.

```
" Switch on display of status line and tweak the settings
"
set laststatus=2  " always show the status line
set ruler         " show the cursor position
set showcmd       " display incomplete commands
```

We can tweak the vim command line, too.

```
" Tweak the setting of Vim's command line
"
set showmode      " show the current Vim mode
set history=50    " keep 50 lines of command line history
set report=0      " report # lines changed by each command
```

Shown below are just a few of the many vim settings designed to help programmers. Sometimes, it's easier to hide inner details when reading a complex piece of code, and the vim folding technique does so by collapsing (or *folding*) sections into single placeholder lines within the vim window.

The foldmethod setting is most often indent, meaning that code sections that reach a specified level of indentation are folded. The foldlevel setting specifies the level of indent at which text is folded. The shiftwidth setting specifies how many columns are equivalent to one level of indent. Typing zr and zm reduces and increases the amount of folding. In the sample below, folding would occur after 8 levels of indent or the equivalent 24 leading-space characters.

```
" Some settings that are useful when coding
"
set number        " display line numbers
set showmatch     " after typing a bracket, briefly show
                  "   the matching bracket
set autoindent    " automatically indent new lines
set foldmethod=indent  " fold by indent level
```

```
set foldlevel=8     " initially fold levels beyond 8
                    " changed by the zr and zm commands
set shiftwidth=3   " this is the size of an indent and must
                    " match the setting softtabstop above
```

The next settings turn on color display and syntax highlighting. Setting `vim` variable `term` overrides Terminal's native setting. When this is set to `xterm`, rather than `xterm-color`, `vim` cannot display in color. (This seems to be the case with X11's `xterm`.)

```
" Turn on color display and syntax highlighting
"
set term=xterm-color  " incase Terminal is set incorrectly
set t_Co=16         " enable 16 color display over 8
syntax enable       " enable syntax coloring
" here is a good point to load your own color scheme
let colors_name = "cool"  " enable cool color scheme
```

Finally, here are some miscellaneous settings.

```
" Miscellaneous settings
"
set autowrite       " autosave on commands such a :next
set nocompatible   " not vi compatible
set backup          " write a backkeep a backup file
set modeline        " Vim will check for setting embedded in
                    " text file, see :help modeline
set modelines=8     " # lines checked for embedded settings
set vb t_vb=        " Switch off the annoying bell
```

Create Key Shortcuts

vim has a few features that can save you typing and make light work of repetitive tasks. These are

▶ Macros. Define up to 36 macros by assigning macro names—*a* to *z* or *0* to *9*—to a series of keystrokes. The keystroke sequences can be replayed at any time. Macros are covered in Project 33.

▶ Abbreviations. Define short sequences of characters that automatically expand into longer sequences when you type them.

⚡ TIP

To view the current state of a setting from within vim, *type*

`:set setting-name?`

That is, append the query (?) character to the end of the setting name.

◣ NOTE

When defining abbreviations and macros in vim, *you must first type a colon to move onto* vim's *command line; if you write settings into a* .vimrc *configuration file, no colon prefix is necessary.*

ᵢ̆ TIP

Use abbreviations for autocorrecting common typos, such as

ab teh the

▶   Key mappings. Assign sequences of keystrokes to a single key or sequence of keystrokes.

Abbreviations

You define an abbreviation as follows: Type ab and then the abbreviation, followed by the text to which the abbreviation should expand. For example:

ab PP Peachpit Press

From now on, each time you type PP, vim will replace it with Peach-pit Press. Naturally, PP has to stand alone to be replaced, so APPLE won't mutate into APeachpit PressLE.

Key Mappings

With vim, you can map a sequence of keystrokes to a given key, such as Function-2 (denoted by <F2>), or a few keystrokes, such as \h1. There's an important difference between abbreviations and key mappings. An *abbreviation* replaces text for text, whereas a *key mapping* replaces keystrokes with keystrokes. Therefore, a key mapping can comprise sequences of vim commands that insert text, delete text, move the cursor, or even perform a search-and-replace or global command.

Let's look at an example. Suppose that you often write HTML code and want a key mapping that encloses text between the HTML heading tags <h1> and </h1>. More specifically, you'd like to be able to place the vim cursor on the untagged heading line below and trigger your macro keystroke sequence \h1 . . .

This is a Heading One

Text...

. . . so that you finish with your cursor on the text line Text... and the heading tagged, like so.

<h1>This is Heading One</h1>

Text...

To pull this off, we must first determine the keystrokes that will insert the tags at the start and end of the heading and then assign those keystrokes to \h1. When preparing any macro, we must also consider the mode vim will be in when the key mapping is applied. If a macro that needs the command line is to be run in insert mode, for example, its first recorded keystroke should be Escape. Fortunately, vim allows you to assign two mode-specific variants of a macro to the same keymap, so you can have identical keymap behavior in either mode.

Keymaps for vim normal mode are defined with command map, and their insert-mode counterparts are defined with map!. (Actually, we'll use noremap and noremap!—variants that are most often the best ones to choose; type :help map for full details.)

Let's start by defining a key mapping for normal mode. We must insert at the start of the line (I) the text <h1> and then press Escape (denoted by typing literally <ESC>).

I<h1><ESC>

Next, move to the end of the line, using A, and add text </h1>. Then press <ESC>.

A</h1><ESC>

Finally, for convenience, we move down two lines (jj) to leave the cursor on the first line of text after the heading and move to the start of that line (^).

jj^

Putting this all together, and using noremap to define the normal-mode sequence, we have

noremap \h1 I<h1><ESC>A</h1><ESC>jj^

The version applied in insert mode is the same, plus an initial <ESC> and a final I, and is assigned with noremap! (with a pling at the end).

noremap! \h1 <ESC>I<h1><ESC>A</h1><ESC>jj^I

You may want to insert two linefeeds instead of moving the cursor down, which you can do with <CR><CR>.

vim Configuration Directories

Many default vim configurations—such as those for file-type mapping, syntax coloring, key mappings, and autoindentation—are defined in a global configuration directory. You may override global settings and add your own by setting up a local configuration directory. The next two sections discuss this topic very briefly, just to make you aware of the further potential of vim configuration.

Global

Explore this directory, which contains all the global vim configuration files: /usr/share/vim/vim62. (vim62 may be vimnn, where nn is the version of vim you have installed.)

Local

The key mappings we defined above are applicable only to HTML files, so we might want to define \h1 differently for other file types—and, of course, with vim we can. For vim to load custom keymap definitions for different file types, the definitions must be stored in special configuration files, or *plugins,* rather than in the file ~/.vimrc.

Create a directory called .vim in your home directory. Within this directory, you might create the following subdirectories.

```
$ ls -lR ~/.vim
drwxr-xr-x  6 saruman saruman  264 Apr 16 16:36 colors
drwxr-xr-x  4 saruman saruman  264 Oct  6  2003 ftplugin
~/.vim/colors:
-rw-r--r--  1 saruman saruman 3569 Dec 24 16:02 cool.vim
-rw-r--r--  1 saruman saruman 3206 Apr 19  2003 html.vim
~/.vim/ftplugin:
drwxr-xr-x  5 saruman saruman  264 Jun 20 23:35 html
drwxr-xr-x  3 saruman saruman  264 Oct  6  2003 php
~/.vim/ftplugin/html:
-rw-r--r--  1 saruman saruman  628 Jan  4 14:19 colors.vim
-rw-r--r--  1 saruman saruman 2521 Dec 19  2004 tags.vim
~/.vim/ftplugin/php:
-rw-r--r--  1 saruman saruman 874  Oct  6  2003 tags.vim
```

Within colors, you can place custom color schemes.

Within ftplugin, you can place plugins for different file types. Create a subdirectory for each file type you want to customize, and use the file type's extension as the name of the subdirectory. Here, we have subdirectories for HTML and PHP files.

Whenever vim loads a file of one of those types, it will execute all the .vim configuration files in the corresponding directory.

So we'll place the HTML-heading key mapping we defined earlier in a file called tags.vim (the file can have any name, as long as it ends with .vim), and place it in the HTML plugin directory.

ℹ **TIP**

Try the following vim *help topics:*

`:help ftplugin`
`:help syntax`
`:help :color`

Project 36
Edit with GUI-Based Editors

"Can I use 'normal' editors, with mouse clicks and menus, to edit configuration files and write shell scripts?"

This project takes a brief look at using graphical editors that run in the Mac OS X Aqua environment. It touches on Apple's TextEdit and on TextWrangler—a free editor from Bare Bones Software.

Configure Your Editor

It's perfectly acceptable to use a graphical-based text editor to write code and shell scripts, and to edit Unix configuration files. There's one drawback, though: Your Unix colleagues may mock you for not "doing it the Unix way" ☺.

Keep It Plain

If you use an OS X text editor, there is one golden rule you must follow: Make sure your files are saved as plain text. Word processors and Rich Text editors embed unwanted font and formatting information in files. Also, choose a fixed-width font so that columns align correctly, and choose a face in which the letters l and O (ell and oh) are clearly distinguishable from the digits 1 and 0.

Line Breaks

Watch out for line-break characters. Traditional Macintosh editors use a carriage return (*CR*, ASCII character code 13) to break lines. Unix requires a line feed (*LF*, ASCII character code 10). If your editor has an appropriate option or preference, make sure it is set to write Unix line feeds.

If you find yourself with text files that contain Mac-style line breaks, the contents of those files will appear to Unix commands to be one long line. A simple way to fix this is to use the command `tr`, which translates a file containing CR breaks into one with LF breaks.

```
$ tr '\r' '\n' < mac-file > unix-file
```

Edit as Root

System configuration files are writable only by root. You'll find it more difficult to edit such files in a graphical editor. Some editors, such as TextWrangler (discussed later in this project), recognize this situation and will ask you to authenticate to modify the file.

TextEdit

Apple's TextEdit application can be used to edit Unix files. If you ensure that the file is plain text (**Figure 4.5**), TextEdit will write Unix LF characters automatically when the file is saved.

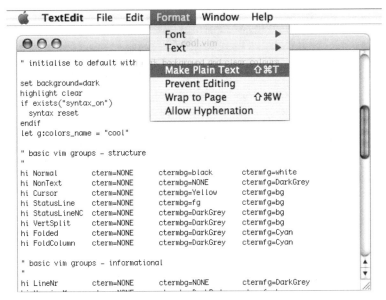

Figure 4.5 Choose Format > Make Plain Text in TextEdit if you're working on Unix files.

❚ NOTE

Old mechanical typewriters required both a carriage return, which moved the carriage back to its start position on completion of a line, and a line feed to move the paper up. Microsoft Windows requires both, too.

↗ LEARN MORE

Project 6 gives some more examples of using the `tr` command.

↗ LEARN MORE

See "How to Become the Root User" in Project 2.

If you try to edit an HTML file with TextEdit, you'll find the program suffering an identity crisis: It suddenly becomes a browser. It will let you edit displayed text, but it won't show you the HTML tags in the file. As a clunky workaround, open the file you want to edit in Safari, and choose Source > View Source. Copy the HTML text that's displayed, and paste it in to a new plain-text TextEdit file.

TextWrangler

TextWrangler (**Figure 4.6**) is an excellent programmer's editor, available as a free download from the Bare Bones Software web site, (www.barebones.com).

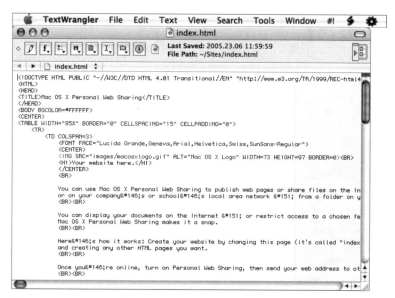

Figure 4.6 TextWrangler, the free text editor from Bare Bones Software, is a Mac OS X application that's outstanding for editing Unix files.

As a programmer's editor, TextWrangler has some powerful features, such as:

▶ Support for Unix and Mac end-of-line formatting.

▶ Syntax coloring for a variety of programming languages, including Unix shell scripts, Perl, HTML, and PHP.

▶ Autoindenting.

▶ Multi-file search and replace with regular-expression matching. (Projects 77 and 78 cover regular expressions.)

▶ Multiple clipboards.

▶ File difference and merging. (Projects 24 and 25 feature Unix file-difference and merging tools.)

▶ Remote file access via FTP (File Transfer Protocol) and SFTP (Secure File Transfer Protocol), enabling you to edit files on a remote machine.

Keep an Eye on Your Mac

5

This chapter is about hardware, software, *processes* (currently executing system and user programs), and log files. It shows you how to profile and monitor many aspects of your Mac—from processes to power management, SMARTies to statistics. The seven projects cover the following topics:

Hardware. Check the system hardware configuration, and change power management settings.

Software. Check and update the system software, and change Open Firmware settings.

Processes. Learn how to list running processes, stop those you'd rather weren't running, and restart daemons.

Log files. View system log files, and configure the system logging daemon to change what's logged and where it's logged to.

These projects help you monitor your Mac, using command-line alternatives to some of Apple's graphical, OS X–based monitoring tools. Command-line tools are essential for writing shell scripts that perform administrative functions and for administering a remote server.

The projects in Chapter 8 cover system administration tasks such as maintaining user accounts, mounting and repairing disk drives, scheduling commands, and managing local network settings.

⬈ LEARN MORE

Refer to Project 21 to learn more about less.

⬈ LEARN MORE

Refer to Project 23 if you are unfamiliar with grep and its variants.

Project 37
Profile the Hardware

"How do I view the hardware and power management settings of my Mac?"

This project shows you how to run Apple's System Profiler from the command line and how to extract specific details from its output. Then it looks at utilities for viewing and configuring the power management hardware (Energy Saver settings). It covers the commands system_profiler, pmset, arch, machine, and hostinfo.

Profile from the Command Line

You may be familiar with Apple's System Profiler. If not, choose Apple > About This Mac and click the More Info button to launch System Profiler. You'll see a window where you may browse for information about hardware, software, and network settings.

The same information is delivered by system_profiler, the command-line version of the tool. It returns a lot of information, so pipe the output to the less command, or redirect it to a file, for easy viewing.

```
$ system_profiler | less
```

The tool presents information as plain text. As such, it makes a suitable grepping victim when you need to filter for specific details. The next section shows how we might use this information to monitor disk drives for impending failure.

Be Smart

A heavily used drive like your system disk may start developing faults after just 3 years of use. It's prudent to replace the drive *before* it fails, but how do you know when a drive is about to fail? Get SMART. Most modern hard-disk drives use a technology called SMART (Self-Monitoring, Analysis, and Reporting Technology) to detect and predict impending problems. We'll use system_profiler to check drives' SMART status.

Almost all the configuration data you could want is lurking some-where in the output from system_profiler. To use it, we extract just those fragments that interest us. Before attempting this, examine the output from system_profiler to determine how the relevant data can be consistently and uniquely identified; then choose the appro-priate text-filtering utilities to grab it.

Perusal of system_profiler output reveals that the best search term for our target data is S.M.A.R.T. (humans dropped dots from the acronym, system_profiler hasn't). Output from a Mac with multiple drives also tells us we should capture the two lines that follow each match, to be sure which drive's status is reported in the matched line.

To check the SMART status of all mounted drives, then, we'll filter system_profiler output with fgrep, using option -A2 to capture two lines of context in addition to each matching line.

```
$ system_profiler | fgrep -A2 "S.M.A.R.T."
                S.M.A.R.T. status: Not Supported
                Volumes:
                    Backup:
--

        S.M.A.R.T. status: Verified
        Volumes:
            Macintosh HD:
```

The output reports on two drives: one that does not support SMART, and the main system drive, which does. The system drive's status is Verified, which is good, and the drive is healthy; if it reported About to Fail, it'd be time to back up the disk and replace it.

Ironically, we chose to search for S.M.A.R.T. with fgrep because that command is *less* smart than grep: Because fgrep does not support regular expressions, it doesn't require us to escape the five periods grep would have treated as special characters.

Adding this SMART-status command to a bash startup file (such as /etc/profile) lets you keep regular tabs on your disk drives. If you don't want drive status displayed every time you start bash, change the search term to "About to Fail", and you'll see nothing unless SMART issues that report: No news is good news.

NOTE

I've never seen a SMART status indicating that a drive was about to fail, but Apple's help tells me the relevant message would be About to Fail.

LEARN MORE

Project 67 gives more advice on taking care of disk drives.

✒ LEARN MORE

Project 6 explains the principles of pipelining.

✒ LEARN MORE

Project 26 covers the commands sort **and** uniq. **See Project 60 to learn more about the** awk **text processing language.**

Profiler Tips

Suppose we're writing a Bash script that acts on the IP address of every router mentioned in the network configuration (as shown in the Network section of System Preferences). Here's how we might do so, using the now-familiar grep filtering technique on the output from system_profiler.

```
$ system_profiler | grep "Router:"
        Router: 217.155.168.150
        Router: 10.0.2.1
            Router: 217.155.168.150
            Router: 10.0.2.1
```

Next, we refine the search by employing the awk utility to print just the second field of each line—the field that contains the IP address.

```
$ system_profiler | grep "Router:" | awk '{print $2}'
217.155.168.150
10.0.2.1
217.155.168.150
10.0.2.1
```

Finally, to skip duplicate IP addresses, we sort the lines into order with sort and drop consecutive duplicate lines with uniq.

```
$ system_profiler | grep "Router:" | awk '{print $2}' ¬
    | sort | uniq
10.0.2.1
217.155.168.150
```

Profiler Options

The system_profiler command uses options that specify which hardware to profile and how much information to return. The default setting for the detail-level option, -detaillevel, is basic. It reports personal information. To omit that information, request a detail level of mini instead.

```
$ system_profiler -detaillevel mini
```

A detail level of `full` reports lots more information than `basic`, including a list of all installed applications.

You can limit a profiler report to specific hardware subsystems or software categories by specifying *datatypes* as arguments to `system_profiler`. Discover the possibilities by typing

```
$ system_profiler -listdatatypes
Available Datatypes:

...
```

We could rewrite our SMART example from earlier in this project to be a little more selective (and to run quicker) by confining it to internal serial ATA drives.

```
$ system_profiler -detaillevel mini SPSerialATADataType ¬
    | fgrep "S.M.A.R.T."
            S.M.A.R.T. status: Verified
```

Finally, specify the option `-xml`, and `system_profiler` will produce reports written in XML format. XML (eXtensible Markup Language) is used extensively in Mac OS X for configuration and preference files. Write the report to a file with the extension `.spx`, and you'll get a double-clickable document that opens in the graphical System Profiler.

```
$ system_profiler -xml > profile.spx
```

Display Processor and RAM Information

A couple of standard Unix commands are available to report on the architecture (processor family) and machine (processor type).

```
$ arch
ppc
$ machine
ppc970
```

NOTE

The settings available to `-detaillevel` *are different in versions of Mac OS X before 10.4 (Tiger). Consult the appropriate man pages by typing*

```
$ man system_profiler
```

TIP

Employ the `-xml` *option when gathering a profile on a remote machine and then view the profile on the local machine with System Profiler.*

ᵢ̈ TIP

Apple is getting much better at providing Unix man pages for its command-line utilities. Type

`$ man pmset`

for full, if rather terse, information about pmset.

ᵢ̈ TIP

Not all options listed on the pmset *man page are available on every Mac. The following script tests whether a feature such as* halfdim *is supported on your Mac.*

```
if [ $(pmset -g cap | ¬
    grep "halfdim") ]
then echo "Supported"
else echo "Not ¬
    Supported"
fi
```

Briefly, we use the option -g cap *to return a list of all supported capabilities, then* grep *the output for the capability of interest. We tell Bash to write the* grep *output to the command line by enclosing the command in* $(...).

↗ LEARN MORE

Projects 9 and 10 introduce shell scripting, and Chapter 9 covers it in greater detail.

Control Power Management

Apple provides a command-line tool, `pmset`, for viewing and setting Energy Saver preferences. It's useful when you need to change such settings from the command line or a script. You'll see the same settings in the System Preferences Energy Saver pane.

View the current setting by typing

```
$ pmset -g
Active Profiles:
AC Power                -1*
Currently in use:
 womp           1
...
 displaysleep   22
 dps            1
```

Power management settings (or *profiles*) are maintained individually for AC (mains), battery, and UPS (Uninterruptible Power Supply) power sources. The example above shows the current (live) profile for AC power.

To display profiles for all power sources, type

```
$ pmset -g disk
```

(Settings are saved on disk.) You'll see only those profiles that are relevant to your hardware. Desktop Macs won't list battery settings, for example.

To change settings, you must run `pmset` as the root user, just as you must authenticate when changing Energy Saver settings in System Preferences. To set the Display Sleep time to 22 minutes, type the following, and give your administrator password at the prompt.

```
$ sudo pmset displaysleep 22
Password:
```

Project 38
Profile the System Software

"What version of Darwin am I running, and how do I update Mac OS X from the command line?"

This project illustrates a few Unix commands that return information about system software and shows you how to run Software Update from the command line. Then it looks at utilities for viewing and configuring Open Firmware settings in NV-RAM (Non-Volatile RAM). It covers the commands softwareupdate, nvram, and uname.

Display Darwin Information

To discover details such as the processor type and operating-system version, use the Unix command uname. We display all this information in one go by typing

```
$ uname -a
Darwin sauron.mayo-family.com 8.1.0 Darwin Kernel Version
8.1.0: Tue May 10 18:16:08 PDT 2005; root:xnu-792.1.5.obj
~4/RELEASE_PPC Power Macintosh powerpc
```

Alternatively, select individual system characteristics by specifying the appropriate option. Here are a few examples displaying the machine (processor) name, the operating system (OS), the OS version (revision), and the machine's *node name* (Internet host name).

```
$ uname -m
Power Macintosh
$ uname -s
Darwin
$ uname -r
8.1.0
$ uname -n
sauron.mayo-family.com
```

TIP

Use system_profiler, *covered in Project 37, to discover more OS details. Select detail level* full *to see information on all installed software.*

Update Mac OS X

Apple has provided a command-line version of the Software Update application—useful for updating a machine remotely. The features of softwareupdate are similar to those in the graphical application: They allow you to view available updates, install them, download them without installing, or ignore them.

List all available updates by typing

```
$ softwareupdate --list
Software Update Tool
Copyright 2002-2005 Apple

Software Update found following new or updated software:
   * SecUpd2005-006Ti
        Security Update 2005-006 (1.0), 6600K...
```

Apply all updates by typing the following command, giving your administrator password when prompted.

```
$ sudo softwareupdate --install --all
Password:

...
```

Option --all says to install all available updates. Alternatively, you may specify which updates to install by naming them on the command line, exactly as shown by the --list option.

Manage Open Firmware

When your Mac powers up, and before the kernel is loaded and Unix springs into life, it executes Open Firmware (OF) commands. OF initializes the hardware, selects a startup disk, and initiates the boot process. OF configuration parameters are held in NV-RAM. You may view and set then by using the *nvram* command. To view the current setting of all NV-RAM variables, type

```
$ nvram -p
```

A discussion of Open Firmware is beyond the scope of this book. We'll look at just one example to show how OF variables may be set.

Suppose you wish to boot into *verbose mode,* whereby the Unix underbelly is revealed as the boot process proceeds. To enable verbose mode, set the NV-RAM variable boot-args to -v, using the following command, and give your administrator password when prompted. (Check the output from *nvram -p* first, and if boot-args is already set to some value, don't try this example.)

```
$ sudo nvram boot-args="-v"
Password:
```

Setting boot-args to -v has the same effect as holding down the key sequence Command-v while your Mac boots.

Restore boot-args to its default null value by typing

```
$ sudo nvram boot-args=""
```

Threads vs. Processes

A *process* is a separately schedulable unit of software executing under the auspices of the kernel. A process has its own environment and its own protected area of memory, and is guaranteed a *slice* (a share) of processor time. When you launch Safari, for example, it runs as a single process.

A *thread,* often called a *lightweight process,* shares its environment and memory with other threads, all of which belong to the same parent process. Threads are closely cooperating parts of a single application that run independently. Safari, for example, might create a new thread for each browser window that's opened, allowing all the windows to load in parallel.

Project 39
View Processes

"What's running on my Mac, and who's running it?"

This project introduces commands and techniques for discovering what processes are executing on your Mac; it shows you how to list all processes and how to monitor processes continually in a "league table." It covers the commands top and ps. Project 40 shows you how to manage a process (by terminating or restarting it, for example).

View Process Information

A *process* (or task) is a program that's actively executing on your Mac. Every Unix command you issue, such as bash or ls, creates a new process. So does each daemon, such as httpd, and each application, such as Safari. The kernel assigns a unique process identification number (PID) to each process when it's created.

The top command lets us view continually updated information about each process. It sorts processes by PID and displays one process per line. To view basic information on all processes, simply type

```
$ top
Processes: 125 total, 3 running, 122 sleeping, 391 threads
Load Avg:  0.93, 0.62, 0.46    CPU usage:  24.7% user,...
SharedLibs: num =  232, resident = 49.3M code, 5.51M da...
MemRegions: num = 22758, resident =  492M + 28.7M priva...
PhysMem:   147M wired,  550M active,  306M inactive, 10...
VM: 13.0G +  150M   239329(0) pageins, 113394(0) pageouts


    PID COMMAND      %CPU    TIME   #TH #PRTS #MREGS RPRVT...
  15591 top          20.5% 0:04.18   1    18     22  1.04M...
  15519 mdimport      0.0% 0:00.33   3    64    127  1.04M...
  15191 writeconfi    0.0% 0:00.05   1    22     26   372K...
  15188 System Pre    0.0% 0:07.04   2   136    372  12.7M...
  14934 iChat         0.0% 0:13.81  10   337    331  12.3M...
  ...
```

The `top` command takes a sample every second, and you'll see the screen updated by each new sample. The first block shows global information; the top line tells us there are currently 125 processes and 391 threads. This may sound like a lot, but most are background processes, idle (sleeping) and awaiting an event to spark them back into life. In fact, of the 125 processes shown above, 122 are sleeping.

Load average reflects the number of processes ready to run and waiting to be given CPU time. The three figures show this averaged over the last minute, 5 minutes, and 15 minutes. When the load is less than 1, the CPU has time to spare.

The last two lines of global information give a breakdown of physical and virtual memory usage. Don't worry if there appears to be very little free physical memory. The kernel makes good use of what's available by keeping processes in memory and caching data read from disk. When an active process requires more memory, the kernel flushes caches or swaps out an inactive process to virtual memory.

Below the global-information block, processes themselves are listed, complete with statistics on CPU and memory usage. The `top` man page tells you what each field represents.

Type q to quit top.

Find the Top Hogs

Suppose you find your Mac running slowly and want to discover what process is hogging the processor. To do this, invoke `top` with option -o to order processes, and follow it with `cpu` to specify descending order by CPU usage. (Older versions of `top` expect -u instead of -o `cpu`.)

```
$ top -o cpu
...
PID COMMAND       %CPU   TIME     #TH #PRTS #MREGS RPRVT  ...
15931 top         26.4%  0:29.98   1    18     22  1.04M...
14631 Microsoft   20.5%  6:00:56   4    96    368  23.2M...
10898 Terminal     7.3% 20:17.01   8   105    193  3.37M...
14140 Safari       1.3% 38:12.23   7   291    412  24.0M...
   69 WindowServ   1.3%  4:29:47   2   882   2914  34.8M...
...
```

Grab a Snapshot

The top command executes in either of two modes: *interactive*, which is the default, or *logging*, where it writes to the screen in the normal manner instead of redrawing it. If you wish to grab a single sample for later processing, invoke top in logging mode by typing a command such as

```
$ top -o th -l1 > top.txt
```

This tells top to write one sample (-l1) before exiting, and to list processes in descending order by thread count (-o th). Our command writes the top output to a text file for processing later, but we could just as easily have piped it to another command for immediate processing.

Log Activity

If you wish to monitor processes over an extended period and write the results to a log file, use a command such as

```
$ top -s60 -l120 > top.log &
```

Here, we tell top to sample at a rate different from its once-per-second default. Option -s60 says to sample every 60 seconds, and option -l120 tells top to exit after taking 120 samples (at the set rate). All output is redirected to the file top.log; the ampersand sends the command into the background so it won't monopolize the command line for two hours.

Process the Output from top

In our final example, we wish to display the five longest-running processes. Let's construct a pipeline to perform this. We'll start with

```
top -o time -l1
```

This displays one sample, sorted in order of total execution time (-o time).

Next, we use `grep` to extract lines that display process information, searching for those that start with optional leading space and then a digit (look at the output from `top` to confirm that).

```
grep "^[[:space:]]*[[:digit:]]"
```

We use `awk` to display fields 2 and 4 of each matched line, which correspond to the process name and its execution time, in columns 10 characters wide. (The `awk` stage won't work with process names that contain spaces. Use a command such as `cut -c 7-32` instead.)

```
awk '{printf "%10s %10s\n", $2, $4}'
```

Finally, `head` is employed to display the first five lines only.

Putting this together, we get (typed all on one line)

```
$ top -o time -l1  | grep "^[[:space:]]*[[:digit:]]" ¬
    | awk '{printf "%10s %10s\n", $2, $4}' | head -n5
    Safari     7:06:24
 Microsoft     6:40:31
    Safari    94:10.98
    Safari    41:19.00
    iTunes    24:20.88
```

The results show three Safari processes because three users are running Safari.

View Process Status

Similar to `top` is the `ps` command. It lists processes but does not display samples continually. The `ps` command is most often used to discover the PID of a named process. By default, it displays only processes you own that have *controlling terminals* (that is, that are running in terminal windows), typically including at least a few Bash shells. Specify option `-x` to display all processes you own. Option `-c` tells `ps` to display just the name of a process instead of the whole command line used to invoke it.

↗ LEARN MORE

See Project 55 to learn about background jobs.

ⓘ TIP

If you wish to take a snapshot and are interested in CPU percentage, you must take two snapshots and ignore the first; such statistics are calculated for the period between samples.

↗ LEARN MORE

Project 6 explains the principles of pipelines.

↗ LEARN MORE

Refer to Project 23 to learn more about the `grep` command, and see Project 60 to learn more about the `awk` text processing language.

↗ LEARN MORE

Project 77 covers regular expressions.

🏹 LEARN MORE

Project 40 looks at how to use ps **in conjunction with** kill **to abort or restart a process.**

Let's list all our processes by command name.

```
$ ps -cx
  PID  TT  STAT      TIME COMMAND
  196  ??  Ss     3:02.28 WindowServer
  198  ??  Ss     0:03.68 ATSServer
  202  ??  Ss     0:01.21 loginwindow
  ...
  389 std  Ss     0:00.16 -bash
  478  p2  S      0:00.12 -bash
```

You'll notice that each line begins with a PID, just as we saw in output from top. Column TT shows the terminal to which a process is attached. It will be ?? for all processes except those with controlling terminals. Column STAT represents the *state* of a process as a sequence of one or more characters. See the ps man page for status-sequence definitions and details about many more ps options.

To display all processes, not just those you own (that is, running with you as user), specify option -a. Use option –u to increase the amount of information displayed for each process. Applying both options together reveals extended information for all processes. Note that the first column now lists the user who owns each process.

```
$ ps -acux
USER       PID   %CPU %MEM  ... TIME       COMMAND
saruman    16255 18.4 3.9   ... 9:15.60    Microsoft Word
root       18670 11.0 0.1   ... 0:00.29    sshd
saruman    10898 8.5  1.5   ... 22:58.57   Terminal
ferdinan   14254 3.3  4.4   ... 95:36.61   Safari
```

Suppose you are interested in specific processes only. Let's display all running copies of iChat by piping the output of ps to grep and searching for iChat. Try the following command.

```
$ ps -acux | grep  "iChat"
loraine    14171 0.0  1.8   ... 0:02.89    iChat
loraine    14172 0.0  0.7   ... 0:00.82    iChatAgent
galadrie   14190 0.0  1.9   ... 0:04.46    iChat
```

```
galadrie 14191    0.0   0.7  ... 0:00.85     iChatAgent
saruman  14933    0.0   0.8  ... 0:01.75     iChatAgent
saruman  14934    0.0   3.1  ... 0:58.23     iChat
```

The results include unwanted data because the name of process iChatAgent matches the search term given to grep. Telling grep to return only whole-word matches (option –w) corrects this problem; it returns only the exact process name iChat.

Define a ps Function

If you find yourself employing the ps–to–grep trick on a regular basis, consider writing a simple bash function such as the one defined below. This command defines function psx and equates it to the command shown in braces. The command pipes the output from ps to grep, which is set up to perform a case-insensitive search for whole-word matches. Arguments passed to our new psx function are inserted at the pointed marked by $*.

To define function psx, type

```
$ psx () { ps -acux | grep -iw $*; }
```

To discover all instances of iChat, type

```
$ psx ichat
loraine  14171    0.0 1.9  ...  0:03.18     iChat
galadrie 14190    0.0 2.0  ...  0:04.98     iChat
saruman  14934    0.0 3.6  ...  2:34.80     iChat
```

Here's an alternative version that does not employ option -c. I'll leave it as an exercise for you to figure out why the second grep is required.

```
$ psx2 () { ps -auwwx | grep -iw $* | grep -v "grep -iw";}
```

TIP

By default, ps limits the length of output lines to the width of your terminal window. Sometimes, especially when ps option -c isn't used, this causes process names to be cut off—an undesirable effect if you want to search output for process names or use them in other operations. Avoid this by using option -ww to stop ps from truncating long lines.

LEARN MORE

Project 4 touches on Bash functions, and Project 52 covers them in greater depth.

ᵢ̆ TIP

To get more detailed information on all the signals and what they mean, type

`$ man 2 sigaction`

Project 40
Manage Processes

"How do I abort an errant process?"

This project shows you how to send a signal to a process to ask it to finish, tell it to finish, or ask it to restart. It uses the `ps` command, covered in Project 39, to find a process and the `kill` command to send the appropriate signal. The project also covers techniques for changing process priority by using `renice` and `nice`.

Understand Signals

Signals are a feature built into Unix. A signal is like an interrupt: Sending a signal to a process causes the process to stop what it's doing and to respond to the signal. Signals give us a way of tapping a process on the shoulder and asking it to take specific action, such as restarting, terminating, or temporarily halting. The most useful signals are

‣ TERM (terminate). A process will finish upon receipt of this signal.

‣ KILL (abort). This signal cannot be ignored by a process and forces the process to finish. Use KILL if a process does not respect TERM.

‣ HUP (hang up). This signal is interpreted by many daemons as a request to restart.

There are many more signals, and individual processes can elect to respond to some signals and ignore others. Each process may respond to a signal in its own particular way.

Stop Interactive Processes

Interactive processes (those that run in Terminal and read from the keyboard) usually respond to the signals INT and QUIT by terminating and to the signal SUSP by suspending and becoming a background job. For convenience, these signals are mapped to the following key sequences.

▸ INT (terminate). Mapped to `Control-c`.

▸ QUIT. A more forceful request to terminate. Mapped to `Control-\`.

▸ SUSP (suspend). Mapped to `Control-z`.

To have `bash` list current key mappings, type

```
$ stty -e
```

You may change the key mappings—for example, setting INT to `Control-x` by typing

```
$ stty intr ^x
```

(Type the caret [^] symbol followed by x.) See the `stty` man page for more information.

Kill Errant Processes

Suppose that we wish to abort a process. It might be a Unix daemon, a Bash script, or an application like Calculator. To do so, we send a TERM signal from `kill`. The `kill` command identifies a process by its process identification number (PID), whereas we humans usually refer to a process by its name. We'll use the `ps–grep` combination, covered in Project 39, to translate from process name to PID.

```
$ ps -xc | grep "Calculator"
24815 ??  S     0:00.63 Calculator
```

↗ **LEARN MORE**

Project 55 explains background and foreground jobs.

↗ **LEARN MORE**

Bash scripts can be written to respond to signals. See Project 86 for more information.

⫯ **TIP**

To find out which signals a command or daemon respects, check its man page and search for the section "SIGNALS."

TIP

To list the signals recognized by kill, *issue the command*

```
$ kill -l
    1) SIGHUP
    2) SIGINT
    3) SIGQUIT
    . . .
```

LEARN MORE

Project 4 touches on Bash functions, and Project 52 covers them in more depth.

LEARN MORE

Project 6 explains the principles of pipelines.

LEARN MORE

Refer to Project 23 to lean more about the grep **command, and see Project 60 to learn more about the** awk **text processing language.**

The PID is shown as the first item on the line—in this case, 24815. To terminate Calculator, we need only issue the command

```
$ kill 24815
```

and it silently dies. Unless instructed otherwise, kill sends a TERM signal.

Force Quit

Suppose that Calculator has crashed and is not responding to the TERM signal. This situation calls for a KILL (force-quit) signal. To send a specific signal from kill, apply option –s, followed by the name of the desired signal.

```
$ kill -s KILL 24815
```

Define a Killer Function

We can easily write a Bash function to kill a process by name. Here's the definition for a function called killx.

```
killx () { kill $(ps -xc | grep -w $* | awk '{print $1}');}
```

We'd use it to terminate a process—Calculator, for example—by typing

```
$ killx Calculator
```

Let's build killx stage by stage to see how it works. First, to isolate the PID of the target process, we employ the usual ps-to-grep trick.

```
$ ps -xc | grep -w Calculator
```

Adding a third stage to the command, we pipe the grep output to awk and tell it to display only the PID (field 1 of each line).

```
$ ps -xc | grep -w Calculator | awk '{print $1}'
$ 24815
```

Now let's kill (abort) the process by using kill. We'll enclose the pipeline we just built inside $(), which tells bash to execute it; write the result back to the command line; and then execute the remainder of the command line. (Other shells, such as tcsh, use the syntax `command` instead of $(command).)

Before we do any actual killing, use echo to demonstrate that the expression enclosed by $() still outputs the PID.

```
$ echo $(ps -xc | grep -w Calculator | awk '{print $1}')
24815
```

All that remains now is to pass the PID to kill instead of echoing it.

```
$ kill $(ps -xc | grep -w Calculator | awk '{print $1}')
```

To make a function of this command, we enclose it in braces and assign it to killx (). Obviously, we don't want to kill Calculator every time—we want to pass an argument to killx—so we'll replace Calculator with the marker $*. When the function is executed, the argument passed to killx replaces $*.

```
$ killx() { kill $(ps -xc | grep -w $* | awk '{print $1}');}
```

Restart

Many system services, like the Apache Web server, are daemons—processes that sit in the background until they are needed. If you ever have to restart such a process (after changing a configuration file, for example), check its man page to see whether it understands the HUP signal. Many daemons do, and they interpret it as a request to reload their configuration settings.

We tell process 12345 to reload its configuration by typing

```
$ sudo kill -HUP 12345
```

Restarting a daemon is more elegant than terminating and restarting it.

Change Process Priority

Unix dynamically assigns a *priority* to each process, based on how much processor time the process has been using. A process that has had little CPU time is given a higher priority and moved toward the front of the CPU queue. A process that has hogged the CPU is given a lower priority and moved backward in the queue. When the CPU is busy, higher-priority processes are favored.

⚓ TIP

Many daemons leave a calling card in directory /var/run. *It's usually a file named after the daemon, with the extension* .pid. *This file contains the PID of the daemon on the first line and is especially useful when a daemon like Apache creates multiple instances of itself (to cope with multiple connections). When that occurs, one process is the master of all the incidences: That's the one to HUP, and that's the one that's listed in* /var/run. *HUP Apache by typing*

```
$ sudo kill -HUP ¬
    $(head -n1 ¬
    /var/run/httpd.pid)
```

Many daemons, httpd *included, have their own control programs to effect starting, stopping, and reloading. When available, those programs are preferable to* kill. *Apache responds to the command* apachectl.

✎ NOTE

Don't try to make sense of changes in priority (PRI) reported by ps. *Remember that priority changes dynamically depending on system load and the demands a process is making on the CPU.*

Make a Process Play Nice

Suppose that a background process is hogging a lot of CPU time, slowing your word processor. You can use the command renice to reduce the background process's priority so that it'll be treated less favorably.

In the following example, iPhoto is rearranging its library, slowing the applications I'm working on. I'm going to make it *nicer*—less likely to hog the CPU— by giving it a nice value of 15. Values can range from 0 (the default) to 20 (the nicest and least likely to hog the CPU).

First, run ps with option -O (letter oh) to tell ps to report the priority of a process (pri) and its nice value (nice).

```
$ ps -xc -O pri,nice | grep iPhoto
  PID PRI NI  TT  STAT     TIME COMMAND
25132 38  0  ??  R      0:02.70 iPhoto
```

Next, make iPhoto nicer by typing the renice command, followed by the new nice value and the target PID.

```
$ renice 15 25132
```

Examine the status of iPhoto again, and we see that it reflects the new nice value of 15.

```
$ ps -xc -O pri,nice | grep iPhoto
  PID PRI NI  TT  STAT     TIME COMMAND
25132 30 15  ??  SN     0:04.71 iPhoto
```

It's possible to influence a process's priority in the other direction, giving it more CPU time, by specifying a nice value between 0 (the default) and –20 (the nastiest and most likely to hog the CPU). Because this sort of thing can mess up the system, only the root user is allowed to be nasty.

```
$ sudo renice -15 25132
Password:
$ ps -xc -O pri,nice | grep iPhoto
  PID PRI  NI  TT  STAT     TIME COMMAND
25132 18 -15  ??  S<     0:04.72 iPhoto
```

Launch a nice Process

You can alter commands' nice values as you launch them by invoking them through the command nice. To launch command number-cruncher, assign it a low priority, and send it to the background, type

```
$ nice -n 20 ./number-cruncher &
```

The allowable range of nice values is the same as those for renice, with negative values increasing priority and positive values decreasing it. Also, as with renice, only the root user may launch a process with increased priority (a negative nice value).

Project 41
View System Log Files

"How do I check whether Mac OS X is running smoothly behind the scenes and discover who's been hitting my Web site?"

This project considers log files, showing you where they are kept and how to use the `tail` command to view them in real time. It also discusses rotation, which stops log files from growing too big. Project 42 shows you how to view log files by using Apple's system log utility and how to control the system log daemon.

Know Your Log Files

Behind the scenes, your Mac runs many *faceless* applications. A faceless application runs in the background and has no direct user interface. Examples include many of the system components of OS X itself, the Apache Web server, and the firewall. Quite frequently, these applications have something to tell you, such as who's just hit your home page or that someone has tried to hack past the firewall. The applications have no way of presenting this information directly, and usually, the information is not of immediate concern anyway, so they write a report to a *log file*.

Take a look in directory /var/log, and you'll see several log files.

```
$ ls /var/log/*.log
/var/log/asl.log    /var/log/lpr.log    /var/log/system.log
...
/var/log/ipfw.log   /var/log/secure.log
```

All log files are written to /var/log/ or a subdirectory within it. Here's a list of the most useful ones and what they report.

▸ system.log. This is a general log file used by many system components. You'll see reports about network status, idiosyncratic behavior of applications, and indications of minor problems. This is a good place to look when you experience system hiccups.

▸ secure.log. This log file tracks all attempts at authentication, both successful and unsuccessful.

▸ ipfw.log. All attempts to access ports blocked by the firewall are logged here.

▸ httpd/access_log. This log file records every page served by Apache.

▸ httpd/error_log. This log file records Apache startup, shutdown, and error events.

▸ mail.log. If you run the Postix mail server, it'll keep you informed from here.

Let's take a look at Apache's log files, which are in the httpd subdirectory.

```
$ ls /var/log/httpd/*_log
/var/log/httpd/access_log    /var/log/httpd/error_log
```

If you don't have these files, start Personal Web Sharing from System Preferences: Click Sharing, then click the Services tab, and check Personal Web Sharing. Launch Safari, and type the URL http://local-host/. You should see a page saying "Seeing this instead of the website you expected?". We're not interested in the Web page—just the log files Apache will have created.

View Log Files

Let's view some log files. They can get very big, so you may want to use an editor such as nano or browse them by using less. In this example, we'll use tail, which displays just the *last* ten lines of a file. Specify option -n followed by a number to display that number of lines instead of ten.

↗ LEARN MORE

Project 21 shows you many ways to view text files, covering cat, less, **and** tail. **Project 30 covers the** nano **text editor.**

‚Ï TIP

*Define a Bash function to
tail a log file. Type*

$ **tlog () { tail ¬
    -n${2:-15} ¬
    /var/log/$1; }**

Now you can simply type
tlog system.log *to view the
last 15 lines of the system log
or* tlog system.log 30 *to
view the last 30 lines. Type*
tlog httpd/access_log
*to view the last 15 lines of
Apache's access log.*

*The odd-looking variable
expansion* ${2:-15} *says
take the value of the second
argument* $2 *if given; other-
wise, use the value 15.*

‚Ï TIP

Use grep, *covered in Project
23, or* sed, *covered in Project
59, to search log files for specific
information.*

View the Apache log files by typing

```
$ tail /var/log/httpd/access_log
...
127.0.0.1 - - [07/Jul/2005:17:25:38 +0100] "GET / HTTP/...
127.0.0.1 - - [07/Jul/2005:17:25:39 +0100] "GET /apache...
127.0.0.1 - - [07/Jul/2005:17:25:40 +0100] "GET /favico...
$ tail /var/log/httpd/error_log
Processing config directory: /private/etc/httpd/users/*...
...
 [Thu Jul  7 17:21:14 2005] [notice] Apache/1.3.33 (Dar...
 [Thu Jul  7 17:21:14 2005] [notice] Accept mutex: floc...
 [Thu Jul  7 17:25:40 2005] [error] [client 127.0.0.1] ...
```

You should see something like the lines above, including a record of
your recent attempt to view the URL http://localhost/. This project won't decipher specific log files; its purpose is to make you aware
of them and give you some tips on viewing them.

Mac OS X also maintains a console log. It is written per user to
/Library/Logs, not to the more usual /var/log directory. View your
own by typing

```
$ tail /Library/Logs/Console/501/console.log
```

Replace 501 with your own UID (refer to Project 7 to learn about
UIDs). To discover your own UID, type

```
$ id
```

View Log Files in Real Time

Sometimes, we are interested in watching reports as they are written.
Let's view a continually changing log file by using tail. Specify
option -f, and tail won't exit after displaying the last few lines but
will continue monitoring the log file, displaying each new line as it's
appended.

```
$ tail -f -n3 /var/log/httpd/access_log
127.0.0.1 - - [07/Jul/2005:17:25:38 +0100] "GET / HTTP/...
127.0.0.1 - - [07/Jul/2005:17:25:39 +0100] "GET /apache...
127.0.0.1 - - [07/Jul/2005:17:25:40 +0100] "GET /favico...
```

If you still have the page http://localhost/ open, click the link "The Apache documentation has been included with this distribution," and watch the output from tail. You should see something like this.

```
127.0.0.1 - - [07/Jul/...] "GET /manual/ HTTP/1.1" 200 ...
127.0.0.1 - - [07/Jul/...] "GET /manual/images/apache_h...
127.0.0.1 - - [07/Jul/...] "GET /manual/images/pixel.gi...
127.0.0.1 - - [07/Jul/...] "GET /manual/images/index.gi...
```

Press Control-c to quit tail.

The Console Application

The Console application in Applications:Utilities:Console.app is the OS X-native equivalent of tail -f. Click Logs at the left end of the toolbar to reveal a list of log files.

Log File Rotation

Log files can get very big. To stop them from becoming excessively so, they are *rotated* and archived each week. The log file is zipped (compressed), and a new one is created. The zipped file is given the extension .0.gz. A previously zipped file is kept and renamed .1.gz. In fact, the last four log files are kept, as shown in the listing below. Each week, a new log file is created, and the old ones are shuffled down.

Let's confirm this by looking at the Apache access_log files for a server that's been running for more than a month.

```
$ cd /var/log/httpd/
$ ls access_log*
access_log        access_log.1.gz access_log.3.gz
access_log.0.gz access_log.2.gz access_log.4.gz
```

You may need to view a compressed log file. To avoid the uncompress–view–delete cycle, use gzcat or zless, both of which display compressed files directly. Functionally, gzcat is equivalent to cat, and zless is equivalent to less.

Let's view last week's Apache access_log file.

```
$ zless /var/log/httpd/access_log.0.gz
```

Log File Analyzers

Log files can be difficult to read and do not provide information in a statistical manner. They are, however, amenable to analysis by third-party applications. One such application is awstats, which generates Web, FTP, and mail statistics.

Find out more at http://awstats.sourceforge.net/.

❧ NOTE

The system log file is rotated every day, and the last eight log files are archived.

🏹 LEARN MORE

Project 27 shows you how to compress and uncompress files.

🎇 TIP

When the periodic maintenance scripts run, they add an audit trail to daily.out, weekly.out, *and* monthly.out, *as appropriate. These files are in* /var/log.

🏹 LEARN MORE

Project 72 discusses periodic maintenance in more depth.

Press the spacebar to view the next page and q to quit zless.

Unfortunately, OS X doesn't include ztail, and pre-10.4 versions didn't include zless. You can simulate either of them by typing

```
$ gzcat /var/log/httpd/access_log.0.gz | tail -f
$ gzcat /var/log/httpd/access_log.0.gz | less
```

Periodic Maintenance

Log files are rotated during periodic maintenance, which is run in the early hours of the morning and initiated by Apple's launchd (or by crontab in OS X versions before 10.4). If necessary, run the files manually, giving your administrator password when prompted. The following example will, among other things, rotate system.log, creating system.log.0.gz.

```
$ sudo periodic daily
Password:
```

Rotation of the other log files occurs weekly, so run

```
$ sudo periodic weekly
```

Project 42
Manage the System
Log Daemon

"How do I control what system messages are logged, and to which file they are logged?"

This project looks at the system log server (or system log daemon) to which log messages are sent. It shows how the default configuration for this daemon might be changed, how to send log messages manually, and how to view log messages. Project 41 looks at viewing log files by using more traditional Unix tools, such as `tail`.

Understand Logging

As we saw in Project 41, your Mac runs many background processes, such as the system components of OS X itself, the Apache Web server, and the firewall. When these components have something to report, they write to a log file. Major servers such as the Apache Web server control their own logging. Others, such as mail and FTP (File Transfer Protocol), and system components such as `crontab` and the kernel log messages through the *system log* daemon (`syslogd`).

The System Log Daemon

The `syslogd` daemon is the central point to which log messages may be sent. A process using `syslogd` need not take responsibility for *contention* (more than one process writing to the same log file at the same time) or configuration issues such as what messages should be logged and to where.

A message sent to `syslogd` generally includes a *facility,* which is an indication of the originating system, and a *level,* which is an indication of the urgency. The `syslogd` daemon filters and channels messages based on these two parameters.

Eight levels are defined. In decreasing order of severity, they are

▪ Error levels: emergency, alert, critical, error

▪ Warning and information levels: warning, notice, informational, and debugging

Facilities include

▪ Daemons for system components: authorization, `cron`, FTP, kernel, and mail

▪ General-purpose facilities: user and locally defined `local0` to `local7`

The `syslogd` daemon directs messages by considering their associated level and facility. For example:

▪ All messages with facility ftp, whatever their level, go to `/var/log/ftp.log`.

▪ All messages with a level of notice and above, whatever their facility, go to `/var/log/system.log`.

▪ Messages from `netinfo` with a level of error and above go to `/var/log/netinfo.log`.

The three examples above can be expressed in the form `facility.level log-file`. A star (*) in place of a facility or level name denotes "all."

▪ `ftp.* /var/log/ftp.log`

▪ `*.notice /var/log/system.log`

▪ `netinfo.err /var/log/netinfo.log`

The configuration file for `syslogd` is in `/etc/syslog.conf`. Display it, and you'll see how the examples above fit in. A semicolon-separated list of `facility.level` pairs, or *selectors,* is permissible to channel several categories to the same log file.

Here's an extract of the file:

```
$ cat /etc/syslog.conf
...
*.notice;authpriv,remoteauth,ftp,install.none;
  kern.debug;mail.crit  /var/log/system.log
...
mail.*                  /var/log/mail.log
ftp.*                   /var/log/ftp.log
netinfo.err             /var/log/netinfo.log
install.*               /var/log/install.log
install.*               @127.0.0.1:32376
local0.*                /var/log/ipfw.log
*.emerg                 *
```

Configure syslogd

We change configuration settings by editing the file /etc/syslog.conf and restarting the daemon. Suppose that we wish to log errors (or, more precisely, all messages with a level of error or more severe) to the file /var/log/my.log. First, we edit the configuration file /etc/syslog.conf, giving an administrator password when prompted.

```
$ sudo nano /etc/syslog.conf
$ Password:
```

Add this line to the end of the file (making sure to terminate it by pressing Return).

```
*.err                   /var/log/my.log
```

Next, create an empty log file, and restart syslogd by typing

```
$ sudo touch /var/log/my.log
$ sudo kill -HUP $(head -1 /var/run/syslog.pid)
```

Naturally, you'll want to test this new logging configuration. You can use the wait-and-see approach, waiting for an error message to be logged and then viewing my.log. Alternatively, send an appropriate message to syslogd directly (see the next section, "Send Log Messages").

TIP

Type

```
$ man 5 syslog.conf
```

for more information about the syslog *configuration file.*

NOTE

Other shells, such as Tcsh, use the syntax `command` *instead of* $(command).

NOTE

It's necessary to create the log file before restarting syslogd. *This is not necessary when* syslogd *is stopped and started from scratch.*

LEARN MORE

Refer to "How to Become the Root User" in Project 2 for more information on the sudo **command.**

LEARN MORE

Project 30 covers the nano **text editor, and Project 40 explains how to restart daemons by using** kill -HUP**.**

ᵢ̆ TIP

*Send an urgent message to all
users and all terminal sessions
by typing*

```
$ logger -p user.emerg ¬
    Urgent message to ¬
    all users ...
```

syslogd in Tiger

In OS X 10.4 (Tiger), Apple
replaced the BSD syslogd
with its own compatible, but
extended, daemon of the same
name. Apple's variant holds
messages in an internal
database as well as sending
them to the traditional log
files. It's this database that
syslog queries, watches, and
prunes.

The syslog utility is also new
in Tiger. In earlier versions,
you have to use logger.

Send Log Messages

Suppose that we wish to test our new `syslogd` configuration. To this
end, we have two utilities at our disposal:

▶   Unix's `logger` utility

▶   Apple's own `syslog` utility

Let's use `logger` to send a log message. We specify option -p followed
by the selector `facility.level`. To test our new selector `*.err`, we
send a log message with a level of error (or above) and with any facility. Let's send an error message purporting to come from the mail system. Type

```
$ logger -p mail.err This is an error message
```

Now view the log file.

```
$ tail /var/log/my.log
Jul 10 20:14:22 saruman saruman: This is an error message
```

Alternatively, we might send a critical message by using the local1
facility.

```
$ logger -p local1.crit This is a critical message
$ tail /var/log/my.log
Jul 10 20:14:22 saruman saruman: This is an error message
Jul 10 20:15:37 saruman saruman: This is a critical message
```

Apple's syslog

The `syslog` command is an Apple utility written to perform a variety
of tasks relating to the system logging facility. It lets you send messages
(just like `logger`, described in the preceding section), view messages, and
prune (remove) unwanted messages.

Let's use `syslog` to send a log message to `syslogd`. We specify option -s
to send and option -k followed by any number of keyword–value pairs
to describe the selector and the message. We might send a mail system
(`Facility mail`) error (`Level error`) message (`Message "message
text..."`) by using the following command.

```
$ syslog -s -k Facility mail Level error Message ¬
    "Mail system error."
```

The default `syslogd` configuration has this message sent to both the system and mail log files, as we can see by `tail`ing both files.

```
$ tail -n1 /var/log/system.log
Jul 11 13:50:39 localhost syslog[4450]: Mail system error.
$ tail -n1 /var/log/mail.log
Jul 11 13:50:39 localhost syslog[4450]: Mail system error.
```

The `syslog` command can read and filter the message database. Let's search for the message we just sent and all others from facility mail at level error. (Note that -k is required before every keyword–value pair, unlike the send-message example above, which allows a list of pairs to follow a single -k switch.)

```
$ syslog -k Facility mail -k Level error
...
Jul 11 13:50:39 syslog[4450] <Error>: Mail system error.
```

As a final example, let's display all critical error messages from the secure shell server (`sshd`). We specify that Sender must be `sshd` and Level must be `critical`.

```
$ syslog -k Sender sshd -k Level critical
Jul  9 03:31:58 Sauron sshd[27172] <Critical>: fatal:
Timeout before authentication for 216.138.221.246
```

The `syslog` command is capable of quite complex message sending and retrieval. We display all mail logs for which the level is error *or less severe* (has a greater numerical value than) by typing

```
$ syslog -k Facility mail -k Level ge error
```

Read the `syslog` man page for full details.

It can also prune the message database to remove unwanted messages and stop the database from getting too big. Check out the Unix man page for more information.

❝ NOTE

A log message that is sent to two or more log files will nevertheless appear just once in the syslog *message database.*

⏻ TIP

The syslog *command has a* tail -f *mode of operation enabled by the option* -w.

Send Messages to Another Host

You'll need admin access to two Macs to follow this example.

Sometimes, you may wish to employ a logging policy whereby all machines log to a central server. Let's do this, logging all error messages to the host 217.155.168.146. (In "Configure syslogd," earlier in this project, we sent the same set of log messages to the file /var/log/my.log.)

First, we must configure the server to accept log messages from the network. To do this, we relaunch syslogd, specifying option -u. The syslogd daemon is one of the services launched by Apple's launch daemon launchd (but not in versions before Mac OS X 10.4). Edit launchd's configuration settings for syslogd by using a text editor such as nano, adding the line "<string>-u</string>".

```
$ sudo nano ¬
    /System/Library/LaunchDaemons/com.apple.syslogd.plist
$ Password:
```

After this

```
<string>/usr/sbin/syslogd</string>
```

Add this

```
<string>-u</string>
```

Then tell launchd to reload (stop and restart) syslogd.

```
$ sudo launchctl unload ¬
    /System/Library/LaunchDaemons/com.apple.syslogd.plist
$ sudo launchctl load ¬
    /System/Library/LaunchDaemons/com.apple.syslogd.plist
```

Finally, check that syslogd has indeed been launched with the -u option specified by typing

```
$ ps ax | grep syslogd
29287  ??  Ss     0:03.73 /usr/sbin/syslogd -u
```

Make sure UDP traffic isn't blocked by your firewall (System Preferences, Sharing, Firewall tab, Advanced... button).

On the client machine(s), we edit `/etc/syslog.conf` so that all error message are logged to the server. Follow the instructions given in "Configure syslogd" earlier in this project, but add the following line instead (specifying the IP address of one of your servers, not mine, please!).

`*.err @217.155.168.146:514`

Now restart `syslogd`.

```
$ sudo kill -HUP $(head -n1 /var/run/syslog.pid)
```

We'll use `logger` to send an error-level log message, which should appear in `system.log` on the local machine *and* on the server if our changes have worked correctly.

```
$ logger -p local0.err This is a cross-host test message
```

! WARNING

Your machine is vulnerable to attack when UDP port 514 is open. A malicious remote server could flood you with bogus log messages. Although my server has this port open, the firewall facing the Internet does not—so don't even think about it. ☺

ṫ TIP

To send all log messages to a central server and have none accepted locally, configure the clients with a `syslog.conf` *file containing just*

`*.* @Server-IP-address`

Project 43
System Voyeur Tips

"How do I check on the activity of system components such as the file system and the network?"

This project gives tips for viewing system activity and statistics, such as system calls and virtual-memory statistics, file system activity, network activity, and kernel information. It presents some quick tips, each of which introduces a useful voyeur command. It covers the commands sc_usage, latency, uptime, vm_stat, dmesg, fs_usage, lsof, netstat, tcpdump, ktrace, and sysctl.

Glimpsing Possibilities

Many of the commands suggested in this project have extensive capabilities and would take a project or two to cover fully. The purpose of this project is merely to introduce several useful commands, describe briefly what each command does, and give examples of how the commands might be used. As ever, the Unix man pages will furnish you with further, if rather terse, details.

System Activity

This section presents commands that display system activity such as system calls, virtual-memory statistics, system messages, and open files.

Display Live System Calls

Use the command sc_usage to display live statistics of system-call and virtual-memory usage. Invoke sc_uage as root, giving the name of a process to monitor. We might monitor the *nano* text editor by using the command

```
$ sudo sc_usage nano
Password:
```

You'll see a screen presenting statistics and updating in real time. It shows information such as the number and type of system calls, CPU time consumed, current scheduling priority, and so on. You'll see the "read" and "write" counts increase for every character you type into the editor.

Monitor Scheduling and Interrupt Latency

The command `latency` measures the time your system takes to switch between processes *(scheduling latency)* and to respond to *interrupts* (external events from the network and peripherals). It records the number of such events that fall within a range of delays. To monitor in real time (option `-rt`), use

```
$ sudo latency -rt
```

How Long Has Your Mac Been Up and Running?

The command `uptime` reports on the length of time your Mac has been running since it was last rebooted. It also shows the load average over the past 1, 5, and 15 minutes. The load measures the number of processes queuing for CPU time; a value of less than 1 means that the CPU has time to spare.

```
$ uptime
10:20  up 49 mins, 3 users, load averages: 0.64 0.63 0.48
```

The rather pathetic uptime (49 minutes) shown above reflects a recent power cut. (And why does Microsoft Word never recover a document in a satisfactory manner?)

Display Virtual-Memory Statistics

Use the `vm_stat` command to display statistics on usage of virtual memory (VM), showing how much is free, used, and *wired* (can never be swapped out and usually is reserved by the kernel). It also counts *pageins* and *pageouts*. The pageouts statistic is particularly interesting, as it shows how much *swapping* is occurring. If this value is continually increasing by hundreds every few seconds, your system is running out of physical memory and is having to swap executing processes in and out. It's time to invest in some additional memory.

To view VM statistics accumulated since the last restart, type

```
$ vm_stat
Mach Virtual Memory Statistics: (page size of 4096 bytes)
Pages free:                     155884.
Pages active:                    35132.
...
Pageouts:                            0.
```

To monitor continually what is happening every five seconds, type

```
$ vm_stat 5
Mach Virtual Memory Statistics:(page size 4096 bytes, ca...
free   active  inac wire   faults ...reactive pageins pageout
155880 35132 50299 20833 653414 ...      0    22302       0
155880 35522 50299 20443     60 ...      0        0       0
156736 31521 49558 24329     89 ...      0        0       0
...
```

Display the System Message Buffer

The command dmesg displays kernel messages. These messages are written to the system message buffer, not to the log files. When the kernel boots, it reports ongoing progress and problems, such as device drivers not loading, to the system message buffer. It's a good source of debugging information if you experience startup and device-driver problems.

```
$ dmesg
standard timeslicing quantum is 10000 us
vm_page_bootstrap: 252593 free pages
mig_table_max_displ = 70
97 prelinked modules
Copyright (c) 1982, 1986, 1989, 1991, 1993 The Regents of
...
MacRISC4CPU: publishing BootCPU
FireWire (OHCI) Apple ID 52 built-in now active, GUID
001124ff fe3c5c76; max speed s400.
...
AFP_VFS afpfs_mount: /Volumes/saruman, pid 218
```

Show Live File System Calls

Use the `fs_stat` command to trace file system calls in real time. Trace file system calls made by the Mac OS X Finder by typing

```
$ sudo fs_usage Finder
```

List Open Files

Discover all the files (and directories) that are open and being read from or written to. To view a complete list, type

```
$ lsof
```

You might want to filter the output lines by command—for example, using `grep` to search for lines that start with `iTunes`.

```
$ lsof | grep "^iTunes "
```

If you are interested in a particular file, specify the filename as an argument to `lsof`.

```
$ lsof /Users/saruman/Music/iTunes/iTunes\ Library
COMMAND PID    USER   FD    TYPE DEVICE SIZE/OFF   NODE NAME
iTunes  483 saruman  15r  VREG    14,2    13097 613145
  /Users/saruman/Music/iTunes/iTunes Library
```

Network Activity

To display active Internet connections, use the `netstat` command. Include option `-I` to specify a particular network interface. To display statistics for AirPort (usually the second Ethernet port, or `en1`), we could type the command

```
$ netstat -I en1
Name Mtu  Network        Address        Ipkts Ierrs ...
en1  1500 <Link#5>       00:11:24:ba:a1:ce 667890      0 ...
en1  1500 sauron.loca fe80::211:24ff:fe 667890      - ...
en1  1500 10.0.2/24      sauron.wless      667890      - ...
```

The `netstat` command has many options and is capable of much more than is suggested by this simple example.

ⓘ TIP

Pipe the output from `fs_usage` *to* `grep` *to filter results by call type. (Project 23 covers the* `grep` *command.)*

```
$ sudo fs_usage Finder ¬
  | grep " open "
```

The tcpdump command is used to trace network packets, displaying the headers of all packets captured. As a simple example, let's trace all packets involved in communication with the host osxfaq.com. The option -vvv specifies a high degree of verbosity in displaying packet-header details.

```
$ sudo tcpdump -vvv host osxfaq.com
tcpdump: listening on en0, link-type EN10MB (Ethernet),
capture size 96 bytes 12:06:03.223924 IP (tos 0x0, ttl
64, id 10127, offset 0, flags [DF], length: 60) sauron.
mayo-family.com.49295 > arthur.hostwizard.com.http:
...
```

Kernel Information

Trace all kernel operations (such as system calls and input–output) performed during execution of a given command. The trace information is written to a trace file named ./ktrace.out. To trace the execution of ls and view the results, type

```
$ ktrace ls
Desktop    Library    Music     Public     ktrace.out
Documents  Movies     Pictures  Sites
$ kdump -f ktrace.out | less
...
```

The sysctl command will view and change kernel settings. This command does not make much sense unless you understand kernel state, which is beyond the scope of this project.

Here are a few examples. We display the current kernel state and all settings by using the following command. In this example, we also filter the output looking for state information relating to the firewall (.fw.).

```
$ sysctl -a | grep "\.fw\."
net.inet.ip.fw.enable: 1
net.inet.ip.fw.debug: 1
net.inet.ip.fw.verbose: 0
...
```

This brief extract shows that the firewall is enabled (`net.inet.ip.fw.enable: 1`).

Change kernel settings by specifying option -w and running `sysctl` as user root.

Other kernel-related commands include

▶ `zprint` to display information on kernel zones

▶ `kextload` to load a kernel extension

▶ `kextunload` to unload a kernel extension

▶ `kextstat` to display kernel-extension statistics

❦ NOTE

Even though the firewall is enabled, it might show as "off" when viewed in System Preferences. Even when switched off, the firewall is running but is not blocking any ports.

Make the Most of the Shell

6

This chapter shows how you can customize your command-line environment. The 13 projects focus on shell features that make entering commands quicker and easier. They cover the following topics:

Customizing Apple's Terminal application

Customizing the shell, configuring features such as command line completion and history

Enhancing command entry by taking advantage of command line recall and editing

Defining shell aliases and functions, employing them as short cuts to entering commands

Job control and background processes

Although written mainly for the Bash shell, additional sections give Tcsh shell equivalents.

↗ LEARN MORE

Refer to Project 9 if you are new to writing shell scripts.

Project 44
Customize the Terminal

"How do I make a clickable shell script?"

This project uses a few tricks to customize the look of Apple's Terminal application, saving settings and shell scripts in clickable documents. Other projects in the chapter look at customizing the shell.

Create a Clickable Shell Script

You might find yourself having to write a shell script for colleagues who refuse to be separated from their mice. To help you in this task, Terminal recognizes when a file contains a shell script. Double-clicking such a file launches a new Terminal window in which the script is automatically executed.

Let's write a simple script to illustrate this. A file that contains a script must be associated with Terminal; by using the extension .command we make the association automatic. The example script that follows displays the names of files in your Documents folder that were modified less than a day ago.

```
$ cat mod.command
#!/bin/bash
echo "All Documents modified less than a day ago"
find ~/Documents  -mtime -1
```

The script must be made executable before it can be run.

```
$ chmod +x mod.command
```

To run the script, select the file mod.command in the Finder, and double-click it. A new Terminal window will open and immediately start executing the script. The window will remain open so you can view the results, which will be followed by logout and [Process completed].

Save Custom Window Settings

Terminal allows you to define and save custom settings, such as the window size and its position onscreen, font and background colors, and the scrollback buffer size. You may wish to define several different looks—a large black-on-white window for editing, for example, and a smaller green-on-black window for issuing commands—selecting the appropriate look when opening a new Terminal window.

To accomplish this, make a custom window by choosing Terminal > Window Settings. Set up the window as you wish; then save the settings in a dot-term file by choosing File > Save As. Ensure that the filename you give has the extension `.term`. After the file is saved, double-clicking the file in the Finder will open a new Terminal window sporting the preset look.

By default, Terminal should apply the correct extension and save to the directory `~/Library/Application Support/Terminal/`. All dot-term files saved to this directory will appear when you choose File > Library, enabling you to open a new custom window easily from Terminal itself.

Run a Script in a Custom Window

You *can* have your Unix cake and eat it, should you wish to create a clickable shell script that *also* opens in a custom window. To do so, use the dot-term file you created in the section above. Open it in a text editor such as nano, and search for the following lines.

```
<key>ExecutionString</key>
<string></string>
```

When Terminal opens a custom window from a dot-term file, it automatically executes the commands it finds in the Execution String. Therefore, we might add the little script from "Create a Clickable Shell Script" earlier in this project by changing the Execution String to read

```
<key>ExecutionString</key>
<string>
    echo "All Documents modified less than a day ago"
    find ~/Documents -mtime -1
</string>
```

ॐ TIP

When saving a custom look, you may set up several windows and select All Windows from the What to Save pop-up menu in the Save As dialog box. Subsequently opening such a custom window actually opens all the windows exactly as they were when the settings were saved.

↗ LEARN MORE

Chapter 4 covers the Unix text editors, including nano.

☫ TIP

If the Execution String contains many commands, write the commands to a shell script and call the script instead. The effect is the same, but we put the commands in a more accessible script file, rather than embedding them in the middle of a dot-term file. Use an absolute pathname in the Execution String to refer to the shell script file.

When we use the edited dot-term file to open a new Terminal window, not only will it sport a custom look, but it will also display the names of all files in ~/Documents that were modified less than a day ago.

If you wish the window to close afterward, simply add an exit statement to the end of the Execution String and make sure Terminal is configured to close windows on exit: Choose Terminal > Window Settings to open the Terminal Inspector palette; choose Shell from its pop-up menu, and click the "close the window" button.

Change the Title Bar

Terminal lets you customize what's displayed in its title bar. Choose Terminal > Window Settings to open the Terminal Inspector palette; then choose Window from its pop-up menu.

Of course, that's not a very Unix-like way of doing things: We can instead employ a neat trick from the command line that affords much more flexibility in what's displayed. Let's reflect the current username and hostname in the title bar. Issue the command

```
$ echo -e  "\033]0;$USER@$HOSTNAME\007"
```

and check the title bar. You should see *yourusername@yourhostname* and perhaps some additional details displayed by Terminal itself (which can be removed by changing Terminal's Window Settings).

You'll no doubt want to know how this works! Option -e applied to the command echo tells it to interpret backslash sequences such as \033, which translates to Escape. The sequence Escape] 0 ; tells Terminal to write the text that follows on its title bar (instead of onscreen), up to the sequence \007. The real flexibility lies with the Bash shell's expanding the text before it is echoed and sent to the title bar. In this example, Bash expands the variables $USER and $HOSTNAME.

Instead of echo, you may use printf to achieve the same effect.

```
$ printf "\033]0;$USER@$HOSTNAME\007"
```

Dynamic Title Bars

A static title bar is no good when the information being displayed changes from time to time; we want the title bar to reflect the changes. To this end, Bash has a useful trick up its sleeve: the *prompt command*. Set the shell variable PROMPT_COMMAND to any command sequence, and Bash will execute the commands immediately before it issues a prompt. This gives us the hook needed to implement a dynamic title bar; we set the prompt command to be exactly the command used in the previous section.

```
$ PROMPT_COMMAND='echo -n -e "\033]0;$USER@$HOSTNAME\007" '
```

If you're in the habit of logging into other machines, glancing at the title bar will remind you of where, and who, you currently are. If you're not, perhaps an alternative may be of more use. Try this.

```
$ PROMPT_COMMAND='echo -n -e "\033]0;$PWD - $(date)\007" '
```

This information could be displayed in the prompt rather than the title bar (see "Think Different" in Project 45), but on the title bar it's less in your face and prevents an excessively long prompt.

You may want to make such changes permanent by adding the appropriate commands to a Bash configuration file (see Project 47).

❚ NOTE

To rename the title bar in the Tcsh shell, use the same printf *command as for Bash, but replace* $HOSTNAME *with* $HOST.

❚ NOTE

The Tcsh shell uses an alias called precmd *to achieve the same effect as Bash's* PROMPT_COMMAND *shell variable. Try this.*

```
% alias precmd 'printf ¬
    "\033]0;$PWD - ¬
    `date`\007" '
```

⌑ TIP

You may use PROMPT_COMMAND *for any purpose, not just setting the title bar.*

ᵢ̆ TIP

Settings shown in this project can be made permanent by writing them to a Bash configuration file. See Project 47.

ᵢ̆ TIP

Read the Bash man page to learn about the available shell options. Type

`$ man bash`

and then /`shopt \[` and press Return to jump straight to the relevant section.

Learn how to use shell options by reading this chapter.

Project 45
Customize the Bash Shell

"What tricks can I employ to customize the look and feel of Bash?"

This project looks at shell options and attributes, both of which affect the behavior of Bash. Although attributes change existing behavior, options switch on and off additional (or optional) behavior. The project also shows you how to change the default Bash prompt. It introduces the commands `shopt` and `set`.

Use Shell Options

Bash is touched on in many other projects throughout the book and particularly in this chapter. Because the book is task focused rather than theoretical, particular aspects of Bash are dealt with when they coincide with a specific task, such as managing the command-line history in Project 48. Consequently, you'll find that options and attributes appear in other projects, too. This project sweeps up the most useful of the "other miscellaneous" Bash features that don't fit into any other project.

Shell options are viewed and set with the command `shopt`, whereas shell attributes require the command `set`. This division can be confusing. The following sections divide options and attributes by functionality.

Use the `shopt` command with no arguments to display the current setting of each shell option, shown as either on or off.

`$ shopt`

To display just those shell options that are on, specify option -s (for set); and to display just those that are off, specify option -u (for unset).

Switch on a shell option by typing a command such as

`$ shopt -s nameofoption`

Switch off a shell option by typing

```
$ shopt -u nameofoption
```

Now let's look at some useful shell options.

The cdspell Option

Bash is able to correct minor typos in directory names given to the `cd` command. It recognizes misspelled names in which you have added or omitted one letter, or transposed a pair of letters. Let's try an example in which we incorrectly type `Destop` instead of `Desktop`.

```
$ cd Destop
-bash: cd: Destop: No such file or directory
```

Now switch on shell option `cdspell`, and Bash will correct minor typos from now on. Type

```
$ shopt -s cdspell
$ cd Destop
Desktop
```

To switch the option back off, type

```
$ shopt -u cdspell
```

Globbing

The shell options `dotglob`, `extglob`, `nocaseglob`, and `nullglob` change the way Bash performs globbing, and as such are covered in Project 12.

History

Project 48 covers `histappend`, and Project 49 covers `histverify`, two shell options that add features to Bash's history mechanism.

Use Shell Attributes

Obtain information on all the shell attributes by typing

```
$ help set
```

ⓘ TIP

Read the Bash man page to learn about the available shell attributes. Type

$ **man bash**

and then /set \[*and press Return to jump straight to the relevant man section.*

You'll notice that each attribute is represented by both a single-letter flag, such as -f, and an option name introduced by -o, such as -o noglob. Use either form to switch an attribute on or off. (In fact, a few option names don't have a single-letter equivalent.) Before we look at particular attributes, let's display the current settings. To display those attributes that are currently on, and in single-letter-flag format, type

$ **echo $-**

To display attribute status by option name, use either of the following.

$ **set -o**
$ **set +o**

To switch on an attribute—for example, -f or noglob—type either of the following.

$ **set -f**
$ **set -o noglob**

To switch off an attribute, type either of the following.

$ **set +f**
$ **set +o noglob**

Useful Attributes

Here are some useful attributes described by option name, none of which is switched on by default.

▶   Attribute allexport tells Bash to mark automatically all shell variables and functions for export. This attribute causes all new and modified variables to become environment variables and all new and modified functions to be exported.

▶   Attribute noclobber stops redirection from overwriting existing files. As an example, assume that we have a file called letter, which we'll create for this example by using the command touch, and then accidentally overwrite it.

   $ **touch letter**
   $ **ls > letter**

If you wish to prevent this from happening, set the `noclobber` attribute.

```
$ set -o noclobber
```

Now when we attempt to redirect to an existing file, Bash prevents us from doing so.

```
$ ls > letter
-bash: file: cannot overwrite existing file
```

If at any time you really do want to overwrite `letter`, override `noclobber` by using `>|` (arrow-pipe) as the redirection symbol.

```
$ ls >| letter
```

▶ Attributes `emacs` and `vi` affect command-line editing, changing the mode to either `emacs` style or `vi` style. See Project 53 for further information.

▶ Attribute `xtrace` tells Bash to echo each command line *before* it's executed but *after* the shell has parsed it and applied all expansions. This attribute is useful as a debugging aid when you're setting up shell variables and aliases.

Useful Attributes for Shell Scripts

The following attributes are useful for debugging a shell script and are covered in more detail in Chapter 9.

▶ Attribute `noexec` dry-runs a script. The script won't be executed, but it will be parsed for syntax errors.

▶ Attribute `nounset` (no unset) tells Bash to raise an error if an unset variable is read.

▶ Attribute `verbose` echoes each command line before it's executed. `verbose` is like `xtrace` except that the line is echoed *before* it's expanded.

⟋ LEARN MORE

Refer to Project 6 to learn about redirection.

⫸ TIP

Change the default trace prompt by setting the shell variable PS4.

ⓘ TIP

Read the Bash man page to learn about readline. *Type*

$ man bash

and then /^READLINE *and press Return to jump straight to the relevant section.*

Enhance Command-Line Completion

The basics of command-line completion—such as pressing Tab to complete a filename—are covered in Project 4. This section shows you how to change the default behavior.

The readline Library

Bash uses the readline library of functions to receive keyboard input, and readline manages command-line completion on behalf of Bash. To customize completion, we must write the appropriate configuration commands to readline's configuration file, called .inputrc, in your home directory (~/.inputrc).

Here are some of the most useful configuration settings. To try them out, write the lines shown below to ~/.inputrc, and start a new shell.

Bell Style

If you object to the annoying Terminal beep generated whenever filename completion fails, change the bell style to none (be quiet).

```
set bell-style none
```

Add the configuration line either by editing .inputrc with one of the Unix text editors covered in Chapter 4, or by appending it directly to the file with the echo command.

```
$ echo "set bell-style none" >> ~/.inputrc
```

Other possible arguments to bell-style are visible, to flash the screen, and audible, to ring the Terminal bell. (Terminal's own Window Settings may override readline's settings.)

Case-Insensitive Completion

The HFS+ file system used in Mac OS X is not case sensitive, so it makes sense to ignore case during completion. This allows Documents to be recognized as a completion match when you type lowercase do and press Tab, for example. To do so, type

```
set completion-ignore-case on
```

This setting is different from that given in Project 12, where we enabled the shell option nocaseglob. That setting affects how wildcard expansion (which is done by the shell) reacts to case. It does not affect readline's handling of normal completion.

Completion Query Threshold

If the number of matches found for an ambiguous completion attempt exceeds 100, you are prompted with

```
$ ls /usr/bin/
Display all 717 possibilities? (y or n)
...
```

To change the threshold value from 100 to, say, 200, use

```
set completion-query-items 200
```

Show If Ambiguous

After you press Tab to complete, a second press is required to list possible matches when the completion is ambiguous. Switch on the show-all option to cause completions to be shown immediately after the first Tab press by using

```
set show-all-if-ambiguous on
```

Set Visible File Type Indication

If you'd like ambiguous completion to give an indication of file type after each filename displayed, use

```
set visible-stats on
```

We now see / after directories and @ after links.

```
$ ls <Tab>
directory-name/  file.txt       link-name@
```

⫯ TIP

Use command expansion in the prompt. For example, we could display the current date and time by setting PS1 *to*

```
$ PS1='$(date) \$ '
Wed Jul 13 13:40:24
BST 2005 $
```

ANSI Codes

ANSI codes are escape sequences that control output to the Terminal screen. They can move the cursor or change the current foreground and background colors.

Do a "Google" (http://google.com/) for "ANSI Codes" to learn more.

Think Different

Tired of seeing the same old prompt 1,000 times a day? Would you like to put some color into your life? Then you need a new, improved PS1.

Bash displays the value of shell variable PS1 as the main prompt. To change it, simply change PS1. Type the following for a more subservient prompt.

```
$ PS1='What now, master? '
What now, master?
```

More usefully, Bash defines several special-character sequences that insert specific information into the prompt. Naturally, we can take advantage of variable expansion in the prompt, too. Here's a more complex example using ANSI codes (see sidebar) to control the color of the text written to the screen. Try this for a blue prompt.

```
What now, master? PS1='\e[34m\u@\h \w\e[0m\n\$ '
saruman@sauron ~
```

The sequence \e represents Escape and is followed by the ANSI code [34m to set the Terminal foreground color to blue. At the end, we set the color back to black by using Escape [0m. The special characters \u, \h, \w, \n, and \$ are documented in the Bash man page. Search for "PROMPTING" at the start of the line by typing /^PROMPTING within the Bash man page.

Project 46
Customize the Tcsh Shell

"I liked Project 45, but what if I'm using the Tcsh shell?"

This project gives Tcsh shell alternatives to some of the Bash customization techniques shown in Project 45.

Tcsh customization is effected by setting special shell variables. Simply type a command at the shell prompt or add it to a Tcsh configuration file (see Project 47).

Enhance Command-Line Completion

Tabbed completion in Tcsh works in a similar manner to the way it works in Bash. By default, this feature is enabled, but when faced with an ambiguous completion, it doesn't display possible matches. We can change this behavior by typing (directly in a shell prompt)

```
% set autolist
```

From now on, when you type a partial filename and press Tab to complete, Tsch will display possible completions when the filename is ambiguous. You need to press Tab only once.

```
% ls D<Tab>
Desktop/    Documents/
% ls D
```

To see completion in color, so that different file types appear in different colors, type

```
% set color
```

If you object to the annoying Terminal beep generated whenever completion fails, switch off match beeping by typing

```
% set matchbeep = never
```

(Terminal's own Window Settings may override Tcsh settings.)

The HFS+ file system used in Mac OS X is not case sensitive, so it makes sense to ignore case during completion. To make do complete to Documents, for example, type

```
% set complete = enhance
```

This setting also considers hyphens and underscores to be equivalent.

Tcsh can spot typos in command names and attempt to correct them. Here's an example in which we enable autocorrect and tell Tcsh to correct command names.

```
% set autocorrect
% set correct = cmd
```

Invoke nano as nuno to see autocorrect in action.

```
% nuno
CORRECT>nano (y|n|e|a)? yes
```

Type y to accept the correction and launch nano.

Specify argument all instead of cmd, and Tcsh will attempt to correct everything on the command line—commands and filenames too. This feature sounds tempting, but I've found that more often than not, it does something I'd rather it didn't. For example, editing a new file whose name is close to that of an existing file causes Tcsh to attempt filename correction. D'oh!

Change Your Prompt

Tcsh displays the value of shell variable prompt as the main prompt. To change it, simply change prompt.

```
% set prompt = "Next? "
```

Tcsh defines several special characters that insert specific information into the prompt. Naturally, we can take advantage of variable expansion in a prompt, too.

Here's a more complex example that uses ANSI codes to control the color of the text written to the screen. You should see a red prompt showing the current directory.

Next? **set prompt = "%{\033[31m%}%c3%{\033[0m%} %# "**
~/Documents %

The sequence %{...%} marks an ANSI code—in this case,\033
(Escape) [31m to set the text color to red and Escape [0m to set it back
to black. In the middle, %c3 displays the current working directory up
to a maximum of three levels. %# displays the first character listed in
shell variable promptchars or the second character when the user is
root. The default value of promptchars is

% **echo $promptchars**
%#

Special-character sequences like %c3 are documented in the Tcsh man
page. Search for %/ by typing /%/ in the Tcsh man page, and you
should be taken to the start of a section called "prompt."

⚓ TIP

*Use command expansion in the
prompt. For example, we could
display the current date and
time by using*

% **set prompt = "`date` ¬
    %# "**
Wed Jul 13 13:49:29 BST
2005 $

↗ LEARN MORE

Project 2 covers the sudo **command, and the projects in Chapter 4 show you how to create and edit files by using several Unix text editors.**

Project 47
Customize Shell Startup

"How do I get my Bash customization commands to be executed automatically whenever I launch a new shell?"

This project explores Bash configuration files. Configuration files are simply Bash shell scripts that Bash automatically executes during its startup phase. We learn where to place customization commands—both global commands that apply to all users and private commands that apply to an individual user. We also learn about the difference between login and non-login shells, and how this affects the configuration files. The last section covers Tcsh shell equivalents.

Configure Login Shells

When we start a new Terminal window, Terminal launches a new instance of the Bash shell. During its startup phase, the Bash shell executes commands from a configuration file called `/etc/profile`. It is to this file that we write customization commands to do any, or all, of the following:

▶ Set environment variables such as PATH (Project 50)

▶ Define and export functions (Project 52)

▶ Define local functions (Project 52) and aliases (Project 51)

▶ Set shell variables such as the prompt (Project 45) and history settings (Project 48)

▶ Set shell options and attributes (Project 45)

The `/etc/profile` script file is executed no matter which user opens a new Terminal window and must be edited as root with the **sudo** command.

Should you wish to apply personal customization settings on top of those set in /etc/profile, place them in the configuration file .bash_profile in your home directory (~/.bash_profile). You may add to or change these settings without affecting other users.

Configure Non-Login Shells

Terminal performs a full Unix login whenever you open a new Terminal window and always launches what's called a *login shell*. A login shell starts in a clean environment, setting environment variables such as HOME and USER. A command (such as ls) launched from the shell does not go through the login process but runs within the parent shell process, inheriting its environment.

When you launch a new instance of Bash from the command line by typing

```
$ bash
```

this, too, runs within the current shell, inheriting its environment. Bash launched in such a manner is called a *non-login shell* and starts up differently from a login shell. It does not need to execute customization commands that affect its environment, because it's already inherited the environment. A non-login shell, therefore, does not execute the login configuration scripts in /etc/profile and ~/.bash_profile; instead, it executes two equivalent non-login configuration scripts, the files /etc/bashrc and ~/.bashrc.

You should use the non-login configuration scripts only for the following customizations, with the same global/personal split we saw for login shells:

▶ Define local functions and aliases

▶ Set shell variables

▶ Set shell options and attributes

Avoid the duplication of having to include the same configuration commands in both sets of configuration files by adopting the following policy.

⵱ TIP

To start Bash from the command line and make it act as though it had been invoked as a login shell, specify the option -l *or* --login.

❦ NOTE

*It's important to ensure that commands that **add to** an existing environment variable are executed once only—that is, they must be run by login shells only. For example, this extension to the* PATH *environment variable must be executed just once.*

```
$ PATH=$PATH:~/bin
```

⬧ **LEARN MORE**

Project 9 tells you more about writing simple shell scripts.

☙ NOTE

Remember that the tilde (~) symbol is used as shorthand for the absolute pathname of your home directory. ~/.bashrc *means the file* .bashrc *in your home directory.*

X11 and xterm

If you use X11 and xterm, be warned that xterm, unlike Apple's Terminal, does not start a login shell. To force a login shell, either invoke xterm with the option -ls or add this line to the file ~/.Xdefaults.

XTerm*.LoginShell: True

In the login scripts /etc/profile and ~/.bash_profile, we write commands to:

▸   Set environment variables

▸   Define and export functions

In the non-login scripts /etc/bashrc and ~/.bashrc, we write commands to:

▸   Define local functions and aliases

▸   Set shell variables

▸   Set shell options and attributes

Finally, we add commands to execute the corresponding non-login script from each login script. Then we simply have the login scripts fetch the appropriate settings from the non-login scripts. (The default /etc/profile supplied with Mac OS X already does this.) Here's what to do:

▸   Add this line to the end of /etc/profile:

    source /etc/bashrc

▸   Add this line to the end of ~/.bash_profile:

    source ~/.bashrc

Noninteractive Shells

Login and non-login shells are also *interactive* shells, meaning that they are launched to service the command line. A shell launched to run a shell script, which exits when the script completes, is termed a *noninteractive* shell. It does not execute any configuration scripts and, therefore, will inherit its parent's environment but won't set up any of configuration of its own.

The Tcsh Shell

The Tcsh shell has a similar global/local and login/non-login split. A login shell executes the following script files, and in this order.

```
/etc/csh.cshrc
/etc/csh.login
~/.tcshrc
~/.login
```

A non-login shell executes following script files, and in this order.

```
/etc/csh.cshrc
~/.tcshrc
```

A noninteractive Tcsh shell executes /etc/csh.cshrc and ~/.tcshrc, unlike a Bash noninteractive shell, which does not execute any configuration scripts.

Many commands in ~/.tcshrc are not necessary for noninteractive shells, such as setting shell variables and aliases. We filter these commands for noninteractive shells like this. Include this statement near the top of ~/.tcshrc

```
if ($?prompt) set interactive
```

and surround all interactive-only commands with

```
if ($?interactive) then
    ... interactive only commands are here...
endif
```

↗ LEARN MORE

Project 49 gives you more ways to recall information from the command-line history.

ℹ TIP

Should you ever wish to save the history under a different filename, change the value of the shell variable HISTFILE.

Project 48
Customize Command History

"How do I prevent sensitive commands from being recorded in Bash history?"

This project looks at the Bash history mechanism and how to customize its behavior. Examples show you how to increase history size, merge histories from simultaneous Terminal sessions, and control what's recorded in the history books. It introduces the history command.

Recall History

Bash saves every command you type in its *command-line history.* Press the up arrow (Cursor-Up) key to recall previous command lines, and the down arrow (Cursor-Down) key to move in the opposite direction.

View the history by using Bash's built-in history command. To limit what's displayed to the last n commands, pass an argument n.

```
$ history 5
  514  cat ~/.bash_history
  515  echo $HISTFILE
  516  shopt
  517  help history
  518  history 7
```

To discover more about the history command, type

```
$ help history
```

When you exit a shell, all the commands you entered during the session (up to a configurable maximum number) are saved to a file called .bash_history in your home directory. When you start a new shell session, those commands are read back into the command-line history.

The last 500 commands issued in the current shell session are remembered and saved to the history file. Should you wish to change this value, change the shell variable HISTSIZE. Here, we increase the value to 5,000.

```
$ HISTSIZE=5000
```

The maximum size of the history *file* is defined separately by the shell variable HISTFILESIZE. Change it from the default value of 500 to 5,000 by typing

```
$ HISTFILESIZE=5000
```

Change History

Be the envy of politicians and rewrite the history books.

Disable History

Should you have something to hide, you can switch off the history mechanism by unsetting the shell attribute history.

```
$ set +o history
```

To switch it back on again, type

```
$ set -o history
```

Hide History

When you issue the same command two or more times in succession, the duplicate lines are added to the history. This is pointless, so fix it by typing

```
$ HISTCONTROL="ignoredups"
```

Of particular use is the ability to prevent certain commands from being written to the history. We have two options: prevent all commands that start with a space character and/or prevent consecutive duplicate commands.

TIP

The settings shown here can be made permanent by writing them to a Bash configuration file. See Project 47.

LEARN MORE

Project 45 covers Bash shell options and attributes in general, showing you how to display them and switch them on and off.

To hide commands that start with a space, we set `HISTCONTROL` to `ignorespace`. To enable both this feature and ignore duplicates, type

```
$ HISTCONTROL="ignoreboth"
```

Here's an example in which we mount an AFP (Apple File Sharing) volume. The command line to do so includes a password, `mypass`. To prevent this password from appearing in the command-line history and from being written to the history file, we must issue the command by typing a space character as the first character on the command line.

```
$ mkdir s-on-c
$  mount_afp afp://saruman:mypass@carcharoth/saruman ~/s-on-c
mount_afp: the mount flags are 0000 the altflags are 0020
$ umount s-on-c/
```

When we view the history, we do not see the `mount_afp` command.

```
$ history
...
   22  HISTCONTROL="ignoreboth"
   23  mkdir s-on-c
   24  umount s-on-c/
   26  history
```

We can also tell Bash to prevent a whole class of commands from being recorded. To do this, we set the `HISTIGNORE` shell variable to a colon-separated list of commands to ignore. For example, to prevent all command lines that start with `sudo` or `mount` from being recorded, type

```
$ HISTIGNORE="sudo*:mount*"
```

Each pattern must either match the entire command line or finish with a star character.

Merge History

If you're in the habit of running many shell sessions at the same time, you'll want to ensure that as each shell is closed, it merges its history into the history file. Normally, a shell overwrites the existing file, thus losing the most recent commands from any shells closed earlier. To enable merging, we switch on shell option histappend *(history append)* by typing

```
$ shopt -s histappend
```

Tcsh Shell History

The Tcsh shell has history-size and history-merge features similar to those in Bash. To increase history size, type

```
% set history = 2000
```

To enable history merging and change the history file size too, type

```
% set savehist = (2000 merge)
```

Project 49
Use Command-Line Recall

"How can I quickly reissue a command I issued a while back?"

This project shows you several ways to recall a previously issued command from the command-line history and how you might edit that command after it has been recalled. Project 48 covers the history mechanism itself.

Search History

Project 4 showed you how to recall previously issued commands by pressing the up arrow (Cursor-Up) key to move back through the command-line history. By typing Escape <, we can move straight to the first line in the history and press the down arrow (Cursor-Down) key to move forward through the history. Typing Escape > moves us straight to the end of the history.

Bash also provides several mechanisms to recall previous commands by searching the history. The first mechanism is called an *incremental search*. To instigate such a search, press Control-r and then start typing a command. As you type, the history will be reverse-searched for the first line that matches what you have typed so far. For example, press Control-r and then type ls followed by a space. Assuming that you have issued such a command within recorded history, Bash will complete the command line for you.

```
$ Control-r
(reverse-i-search)`':
(reverse-i-search)`ls ~/D': ls ~/Documents/
```

If the command shown is not the one you are looking for, either type more characters to identify it uniquely or press Control-r repeatedly until the desired command is found. Each press of Control-r causes Bash to search farther back in history for a matching command.

```
(reverse-i-search)`ls ~/De': ls ~/Desktop/
```

Press Return to execute the command. Alternatively, press Escape to edit the command, from where you could also press `Control-k` to delete the line.

You initiate a *nonincremental* search by typing Escape `p`. Unlike an incremental search, it does not happen as you type, but when you press Return. Suppose that we wish to recall the `tail -f` command line shown in the history listing below.

```
$ history
...
502   tail -f /var/log/system.log
503   ls -al
504   tab2space ~/Documents/letter.txt
505   history
```

Let's recall it by pressing Escape `p` and then typing `ta`.

```
$ <Escape>p
$ :ta<Return>
```

Pressing Return initiates the search.

```
$ tab2space ~/Documents/letter.txt
```

If the recalled line is not the one we wanted, we type Escape `p` and then press Return again.

History Expansion

History expansion uses the exclamation mark (!) to recall a previous line. Here's an example of what history expansion offers. Suppose that we have the following command-line history.

```
$ history
...
6   du
7   echo "Hello"
8   exit
9   history
```

ℹ TIP

It's not necessary to type the first letters of the command you wish to search for. Pressing `Control-r` *and typing* `Doc` *will search for any command that contains* `Doc`*, not just those that begin with* `Doc`*.*

↗ LEARN MORE

Project 45 covers Bash shell options and attributes in general, showing you how to display them and switch them on and off.

To recall the last line (history), type

```
$ !!
```

To recall line 7 (echo "Hello") type

```
$ !7
```

To recall three lines back, type

```
$ !-3
```

To search backward for the first line that starts with "ec", type

```
$ !ec
```

Verify First

A command that has been recalled via history substitution is immediately executed. If we enable the shell option histverify, Bash will display the recalled line first, waiting for Return to be pressed before executing it.

Let's enable history verify and search backward for the first command containing the string "He".

```
$ shopt -s histverify
$ !?He?
$ echo "Hello"<Return>
```

Notice that in this example, we typed !?He? to search for a command that *contains* the string "He", whereas previously, we typed !ec to search for a command that *starts* with the string "ec".

Recall Arguments

Should you wish to reuse an argument from a previously issued command, placing it in situ on the current command line, employ the following technique. Suppose that we issued the command

```
$ cat a-big-filename-one a-big-filename-two
I am big file one
I am big file two
```

Now we wish to edit with nano the file a-big-filename-two. We note that it was the second argument, which we denote with :2, of the last-issued command, which is recalled with !!, as shown earlier in this project. Putting this together, we type

```
$ nano !!:2
```

Bash echoes the expanded command line, which we can edit, or we can simply press Return to execute it as is.

```
$ nano a-big-filename-two<Return>
...
```

Sometime later, we might want to edit the file a-big-filename-one. To recall the filename to the current command line, we search back for the command that mentioned it and then recall argument one. The most recent command was cat, which we recall by typing !cat, and we recall argument one by typing :1. The command to type, therefore, is

```
$ nano !cat:1
```

Again, Bash echoes the expanded command line, and we press Return to accept it.

```
$ nano a-big-filename-one<Return>
```

Edit the Last Command Line

Bash gives us a way of making a quick substitution-style change to the last command line entered. Suppose that we misspell a-big-file-name-one.

```
$ cat a-bug-filename-one
cat: a-bug-filename-one: No such file or directory
```

We correct bug to big by typing

```
$ ^bug^big
cat a-big-filename-one<Return>
I am big filename one
```

TIP

Type !! to recall all arguments.*

TIP

There's lots more to history expansion than mentioned here. Read the Bash man page and search for HISTORY EXPANSION by typing /^HISTORY EXP within the man page.

Project 50
Change the Command Path

"What do I do when Bash claims it cannot find a Unix command that I know is installed?"

This project explains the environment variable PATH and shows you how Bash knows where in the file system to look for a Unix command. It shows you how to change PATH and how such changes affect the Unix manual. Project 16 shows you how to locate Unix commands manually within the file system.

Know the PATH

You may have wondered where Bash looks to find Unix commands and why sometimes, it cannot find them. First, let's explain the file-system structure as it applies to commands.

You'll find commands at the following standard locations:

▶ /bin/—essential core commands.

▶ /sbin/—essential, core system commands.

▶ /usr/bin/—the rest of the vendor-supplied commands.

▶ /usr/sbin/—the rest of the vendor-supplied system commands.

▶ /usr/local/bin/—commands installed locally. That is, the commands that you have installed, as opposed to those that are part of the standard (vendor-supplied) Mac OS X install.

▶ /usr/local/sbin/—system commands installed locally.

You usually expect to issue a command by typing the bare command name, such as ls, not by typing a full pathname, such as /bin/ls. Consequently, Bash requires a list of pathnames to search when given a bare command name. That's where the environment variable PATH comes in; display it, and you'll see a list of colon-separated pathnames.

```
$ echo $PATH
/bin:/sbin:/usr/bin:/usr/sbin
```

Check this against the list above, and you'll notice that only the local paths are missing. An executable in any directory listed in the pathname list can be referenced by typing the bare command name. An executable outside the pathname list will not be found, unless you reference it by typing a full pathname (or change PATH, as described below).

If a command of the same name exists in several of the directories listed in the pathname list, Bash will invoke the first one it encounters, searching the paths in the order in which they are listed. To invoke a different variant, use that variant's full pathname.

The default value of PATH is set in the systemwide Bash configuration file.

```
$ cat /etc/profile
# System-wide .profile for sh(1)
...
PATH="/bin:/sbin:/usr/bin:/usr/sbin"
export PATH
```

Change the PATH

You might want to set up a custom path for all users by changing the default PATH setting in /etc/profile. Alternatively, change just your own settings by defining a new path in ~/.profile.

Try this command; it'll fail if you are using the default pathname list.

```
$ xterm &
-bash: xterm: command not found
```

A useful addition to the pathname list is the directory /usr/X11R6/bin, which would give easy access to X11 commands. You also might want to add /usr/local/bin, /usr/local/sbin and, if you have installed the developer tools, /Developer/Tools.

Edit either the global or local Bash configuration file stated above, setting the environment variable PATH to

```
PATH="/usr/local/bin:/usr/local/sbin:/Developer/Tools:
/bin:/sbin:/usr/bin:/usr/sbin:/usr/X11R6/bin"
```

⚡ TIP

The command type *tells you where Bash will find a specific command. It's covered in detail in Project 16.*

Recommended Search Order

The order in which pathnames are listed in PATH defines the order in which Bash conducts its search. You'll want to place the pathnames for locally installed commands (like those in /usr/local/...) toward the start of the list. In this way, if you install an alternative version of a standard Unix command, Bash will find your version first. You might also install your own private commands in ~/bin, and would place this pathname first in the list.

↗ LEARN MORE

Project 47 covers Bash configuration files.

↗ LEARN MORE

Refer to Chapter 4 for information on Unix text editors, and see Project 55 to learn more about background jobs.

✎ NOTE

X11 is an optional install. You must select the X11 package when you first install Mac OS X or add it later by performing an additional install. In either case, opt for a custom install, and select the X11 package. Also, you must be running X11, located in Applications: Utilities on the system disk, before you can execute xterm.

Start a new Terminal session, and try to launch xterm. This time, the executable should be found.

```
$ declare -x  DISPLAY=":0.0"
$ xterm &
[1] 18040
```

The first line is necessary to define the display device. In the second, we launch xterm, but in the background to regain immediate control of the original Terminal window.

We should also be able to refer to developer tools without the need for a full pathname.

```
$ cpmac
usage: cpmac [-r] [-p] <source-path> <dest-path>
       cpmac [-r] [-p] <source-path>... <dest-dir>
```

Add to the PATH

You might want to include your own personal Unix executables directory, such as ~/.bin, in the pathname list. This is best done by *adding* to the standard path rather than redefining it. Let's write such a command to your personal Bash configuration file ~/.bash_profile. Add the line shown below.

```
$ cat .bash_profile
PATH=~/bin:$PATH:.
```

Now start a new Terminal session or simply source the configuration file by typing

```
$ source ~/.bash_profile
```

If we examine the new value of PATH, we should see that the directory bin in our home directory now appears at the start of the pathname list.

```
$ echo $PATH
/Users/saruman/bin:/bin:/sbin:/usr/bin:/usr/sbin:.
```

Dotty PATHs

You'll notice that we also added dot to the end of the path. This trick ensures that the current directory, no matter what it is, is always in the path, affording us the luxury of typing simply

```
$ scriptname
```

to execute a script in the current directory, instead of

```
$ ./scriptname
```

Tcsh Shell Paths

Setting an environment variable in the Tcsh shell uses a different syntax. We might define PATH by typing

```
% setenv PATH "list/of/pathnames/here..."
```

We might add to the start and end of PATH by typing

```
% setenv PATH ~/bin:${PATH}:.
```

Know the MANPATH

The Unix manual uses PATH to search for "nearby" directories that may contain man pages. The search for man pages is made in the same order as for executables. This ensures that all commands in the pathname list have accessible man pages and that in the case of duplicate commands in different paths, the correct man page will be found.

Check the Unix manual page of the man command itself for a full explanation. The man command reads a configuration file called /usr/share/misc/man.conf.

In versions of Mac OS X before 10.4 (Tiger), the Unix manual relied on the manpath command, or the MANPATH variable, to determine the locations and search order for man pages. Its configuration settings are stored in the file /etc/manpath.config.

Dotty PATHs and Security

Placing dot in your path has security implications.

If you were to mistype cat as car, you'd get a command not found error. However, if the current directory happened to contain an executable or script called car, you'd execute it accidentally.

There are those who rate this as a significant security risk, arguing that a malicious user might plant a harmful executable such as car, or some other common misspelling of a standard command, in a public directory that you might have set as your current working directory. Make your own judgment as to the risk versus the benefits of dotty paths.

Note that a dot at the beginning is a more serious risk. A malicious user need only plant a fake command such as ls to have you to execute it instead of the real ls.

❧ NOTE

There's no need to set the MANPATH variable.

Project 51
Define Shell Aliases

"How do I define a shortcut for a commonly used command line?"

This project explores Bash aliases—how to define them, list them,
and undefined them—and shows you a few neat alias tricks. The last
section covers Tcsh shell equivalents. It introduces the commands
alias and unalias. Project 52 covers Bash functions.

Define an Alias

Bash supports the definition of aliases. An alias can be defined to be a
complete or partial command line. When an alias is used as the first
word on a command line, Bash *expands* the alias by replacing it with
its definition. Note that the alias *must* be the first word on the command line; otherwise, it will not be recognized as an alias and will not
be expanded.

Here's an alias that creates a shortcut, called ll, for the command line
ls -lt. Although doing so is not necessary in this example, it's cus-
tomary to enclose the definition of an alias in single quotes to ensure
that the shell doesn't interpret it before it's assigned.

```
$ alias ll='ls -lt'
```

Typing ll on the command line issues the command ls -lt.

```
$ ll
drwx------   36 saruman saruman 1224 Jul 15 18:50 Library
drwx------    4 saruman saruman  136 Jul 15 08:44 Desktop
drwxr-xr-x    5 saruman saruman  170 Jul  2 15:03 Public
...
```

An alias need not form the complete command line. For example, it
will accept arguments and option settings that work with the command it's based upon. We specify arguments after the alias name, and
they are added to the end of the expanded command line.

```
$ ll Sites
total 16
drwxr-xr-x   5 saruman saruman  170 Jul 16 11:54 images
-rw-r--r--   1 saruman saruman 5754 Jun 23 11:59 index.html
```

Aliases in Aliases

Bash allows you to use an existing alias in the definition of a new one so long as it's the first word in the definition. To define a shortcut to "long list" your home directory with the previously defined alias ll, type

```
$ alias lh='ll ~'
```

When the command line is interpreted by Bash, lh expands to ll ~, which in turn expands to ls -lt ~ and ultimately, through tilde expansion, to ls -lt /Users/yourhomedir.

List and Remove

To recall the definition of an alias, use its name as an argument to alias.

```
$ alias ll
alias ll='ls -lt'
```

Used without options or arguments, the alias command displays the definitions of all aliases. To remove an alias you've created, use the unalias command.

Alias Expansion Quirks

Bash expands aliases when a command line is read, not when it is executed. In the example below, in which we have two commands on the same line (separated by a semicolon), the alias d becomes defined only upon execution of the command and, therefore, is not available for expansion when the second command on the line—the supposed expansion of alias d—is parsed.

```
$ alias d="cd ~/Documents"; d
-bash: d: command not found
```

❗ NOTE

Bash expands aliases before it expands most other syntax elements, such as tilde (~) and $VARIABLE. *This means that aliases' definitions may rely on most shell expansions.*

💡 TIP

Make an alias permanent by writing it to a Bash configuration file. See Project 47.

Issuing the command d *will* work immediately after the defining line has executed.

```
$ d
$ pwd
/Users/saruman/Documents
```

The Double-Alias Trick

Earlier in this project, we learned that an alias *must* be the first word on the command line; otherwise, it won't be recognized as an alias and won't be expanded. Let's illustrate this by typing the following sequence of commands.

```
$ alias ls='ls -l'
$ alias d='~/Documents'
$ ls d
ls: d: No such file or directory
```

We can employ a trick to make Bash expand d even though it's not the first word on the command line. An alias definition that ends with a space character signals Bash to consider the next word for expansion, too. Let's redefine the alias but add a space to the end.

```
$ alias ls='ls -l '
```

This time, both the aliases ls and d will be expanded.

```
$ ls d
drwxr-xr-x  4 saruman saruman  136 Jun 15 12:39 AppleW...
drwxr-xr-x 11 saruman saruman  374 Jun 24 16:45 Downloads
drwx------ 95 saruman saruman 3230 Jul 14 19:48 iChats
...
```

We could also define an alias for the cd command to take advantage of our directory shortcut.

```
$ alias cd="cd "
```

Aliases in Scripts

Here's a gotcha that might catch you out one day: You can define and use an alias in a shell script, but it won't be expanded. We can change this behavior, however, by changing the shell option expand_aliases. In an interactive shell, the option is on by default, as we can see by typing

```
$ shopt | grep alias
expand_aliases  on
```

For a noninteractive shell (as launched to run a shell script), alias expansion is off by default.

```
$ cat script
shopt | grep alias
$ ./script
expand_aliases  off
```

To switch on alias expansion, simply include the following command in the script file.

```
shopt -s expand_aliases
```

Arguments to Aliases

Aliases do not take arguments, although you can include arguments on the command line after the alias name. A chief difference between aliases and functions (covered in Project 52) is that a function followed by arguments can expand as a command sequence with the arguments inserted into the middle of the sequence.

Tcsh Shell Aliases

The Tcsh shell supports aliases but uses a slightly different syntax. We define an alias by typing a command such as

```
% alias ls 'ls -l'
```

The Tcsh shell does not support functions, but its aliases can take arguments and have them inserted into the middle of the expanded sequence.

❧ NOTE

Shell scripts usually do not employ aliases. Functions are the preferred choice.

➐ LEARN MORE

Project 45 covers Bash shell options and attributes in general, showing you how to display them and switch them on and off. Project 47 briefly explains the difference between interactive and noninteractive shells.

316 MAKE THE MOST OF THE SHELL

✎ NOTE

In the Tcsh shell, you must escape the ! character, even when it is placed inside single quotes.

Let's define an alias e to demonstrate this. For illustrative purposes, our alias simply echoes its arguments in the reverse order to which they are given and then echoes all arguments. The sequence !:n expands to argument number *n*, and the sequence !:* expands to all arguments.

```
% alias e 'echo arg2=\!:2 arg1=\!:1 all=\!:*'
% e one two
arg2=two arg1=one all=one two
```

Project 52
Define Shell Functions

"How do I define a shortcut for a commonly used command line, to which I can pass arguments?"

This project explores Bash functions: how to define them; how to handle arguments; and how to list, export, and undefine them. Project 51 covers aliases.

Functions are similar to aliases. Bash philosophy sees functions replacing aliases in almost all circumstances. The declarative syntax of a function lends itself to a more complex definition than would ever be assigned to an alias. Functions are closer to mini shell scripts but execute in the environment of the current shell. (Scripts are executed by new shell instances.)

Define a Function

Let's illustrate functions by defining one. A good candidate for a simple function is this command line.

```
$ grep -riw "dear janet" .
./text/jan.txt:Dear Janet
```

The command performs a recursive, case-insensitive search for whole-word matches, rooted in the current directory. We'll make this into a function and parameterize the search text, thereby encapsulating this useful sequence as a custom command.

To define a function, we must use the correct syntax. Start the definition with the function name followed by (), and enclose the body of the function in braces. Each command in the body, including the last, must be terminated by a semicolon. Be aware that the space after the opening brace must be present.

```
$ function-name () { command; command; ...;}
```

↗ LEARN MORE

Projects 9 and 10 get you started with shell scripting, and the projects in Chapter 9 cover the subject in greater depth.

↗ LEARN MORE

Project 23 covers the grep command.

ᵢ̈ TIP

*The more-please prompt > is
held in shell variable PS2 and
can be changed by typing*

```
$ PS2="more please> "
```

ᵢ̈ TIP

*Make a function permanent by
writing it to a Bash configuration
file. See Project 47.*

A function definition may be split across lines, making entry easier when the body of the function contains many commands. Equivalent to the above example, we could have typed

```
$ function-name () {
> command
> command
> ...
> }
$
```

You'll notice that when Bash expects more input to complete the command, it'll prompt with > instead of $.

Our new function, which we'll call grepx, can be defined by typing

```
$ grepx () {
> grep -riw $* .
> }
```

The sequence $* expands to the text of all arguments passed to the function.

To use our new function, we simply type its name followed by a list of arguments (just as you would for any Unix command or shell script).

```
$ grepx janet
Binary file ./iChats/Janet Forbes on ....ichat matches
Binary file ./iChats/Janet Forbes on ....ichat matches
./text/jan.txt:Dear Janet
```

Debug a Function

There's a problem with this function, which illustrates a common and easy mistake to make. Type the following command.

```
$ grepx "dear janet"
grep: janet: No such file or directory
Binary file ./iChats/Janet Forbes on ....ichat matches
./text/jan.txt:Dear Janet
```

The error `grep: janet: No such file or directory` was perhaps not something you expected to see. The function as defined has `grep` searching for the word `dear` in the files `janet` and the current directory (.). It's equivalent to the command line

```
$ grep -riw dear janet .
```

The problem arises because quoting is lost when `$*` is expanded. To solve the problem, we must quote `$*` itself. Redefine the function by typing

```
$ grepx () {
> grep -riw "$*" .
> }
```

Now try again.

```
$ grepx "dear janet"
./text/jan.txt:Dear Janet
```

Function Arguments

So far, we've expanded "all arguments" by using `$*`. Argument (or, more strictly, parameter) expansion within a function is very similar to that in a shell script, and Bash functions support the following parameter expansions:

▪ `$*` expands to all arguments.

▪ `$#` expands to the number of argument passed.

▪ `$n` expands to argument number n.

▪ `$0` expands to the name of the current shell or shell script.

▪ `$FUNCNAME` expands to the function's name.

⊥ TIP

Export a function. Exporting a function is like exporting a shell variable to make it into an environment variable. (Project 4 explains the difference between shell and environment variables.) Type

```
$ export -f grepx
```

Enter and run this example function, which illustrates parameter expansion.

```
$ params () {
> echo "$# parameters given"
> echo "the second is $2 and the first is $1"
> echo "my name is $FUNCNAME and I was called from $0."
> }
$ params number-one "number two"
2 parameters given
the second is number two and the first is number-one
my name is params and I was called from -bash.
```

Let's extend our simple grepx function to take additional arguments, which will be options we pass through to grep. A naïve attempt such as that shown next will not work.

```
$ grepx -l "dear janet"
grep: invalid option --
Usage: grep [OPTION]... PATTERN [FILE]...
Try `grep --help' for more information.
```

Our attempt forms the following command line.

```
$ grep -ir "-l dear janet" .
```

We must change grepx to expand its parameters in the form $1 "$2", not "$*". Additionally, the passing of extra options to grep must be made optional, so we have two situations:

▶   If $1 starts with a dash (-) character (that is, if it's an option), expand parameters in the form $1 "$2".

▶   Otherwise, expand parameters in the form "$1" (or "$*").

Here's our new function, which employs an if-else statement. Remember that the body of a Bash function is just like a shell script.

```
$ grepx () {
> if [ "${1:0:1}" = "-" ]
> then
>   grep -riw $1 "$2" .
> else
>   grep -riw "$1" .
> fi
> }
```

⏻ LEARN MORE

Project 76 covers Bash
parameter expansion in
more detail.

We'll test the new function by specifying option -l to grep, which says to list the names of matching files but not display the matching line of text.

```
$ grepx -l "dear janet"
./text/jan.txt
```

We used a neat trick to test the *first character* of parameter 1 instead of the whole string. The special expansion ${1:0:1} expands $1 but considers only a partial string from character 0 (the first character) of length 1.

⏻ LEARN MORE

Refer to Project 16 for more
on command.

Recursive Functions

A function can be *recursive*—that is, it can call itself. I'll not teach recursive programming here but will point out a gotcha that is a side effect of the recursive nature of functions.

We define a function ls to be shorthand for ls -al argument-list. The following attempt doesn't work but gets stuck in a loop.

```
$ ls () { ls -al $*; }
```

Function ls attempts to call the Unix *command* ls, but because recursion is allowed, the function ends up calling itself instead. Futile attempts to call command ls continue forever—or until we interrupt the process by pressing Control-c.

The next version works. We use Bash's built-in command command to make function ls call the Unix command ls instead of itself.

```
$ ls () { command ls -al $*; }
```

List All Functions

To list all currently defined functions, type

```
$ declare -F
declare -f grepx
declare -f params
```

Alternatively, specify option -f (lowercase) to list function names *and* their definitions.

Delete a Function

Delete a function (or two) by using the unset command.

```
$ unset grepx params
```

Tcsh Shell Functions

The Tcsh shell does not support functions. However, Tcsh aliases support arguments (see Project 51).

Project 53
Edit Command Lines

"What features does the Bash shell offer when I wish to edit a command line?"

This project shows how to edit a command line while typing it from scratch or after recalling it from the command-line history. It discusses key bindings and demonstrates how to change them by using the command bind. The last section covers Tcsh shell equivalents. Project 49 shows the many ways in which you may recall a previously typed command line.

Know the Key Keystrokes

Bash provides extensive command-line-editing capabilities, but we'll consider just a subset of those. Command-line editing, like history and recall, is implemented by the readline library. For full details, refer to the Bash man page, and search for section "READLINE" by typing /^READLINE within the man page.

Here are the most useful editing keystrokes.

For general editing tasks, press

- Left and right arrow to move the cursor left and right
- Delete (Backspace) to delete the character behind the cursor
- Control-d to delete the character ahead of the cursor
- Control-a to move to the start of the line
- Control-e to move to the end of the line

To cut (kill) text and place it in the yank buffer, press

- Escape-Backspace to cut the word behind the cursor
- Escape-d to cut the word ahead of the cursor
- Control-k to cut from the cursor to the end of the line
- Control-u to cut from the cursor to the start of the line

To paste text from the yank buffer, press

▶ Control-y to paste (yank) cut text

▶ Escape-y after Control-y to cycle through the yank buffer. A cut keystroke adds the cut text to the yank buffer but does not over-write previous cuts; they are still available for pasting.

To insert text from previous command lines, press

▶ Escape Control-y to insert the first argument from the previous command line

▶ Escape . (period) to insert the last argument given on the last command line

To insert special characters, press

▶ Control-v to insert a character literally. To insert the escape char-acter, for example, press Control-v and then press the Escape key.

Expand the Command Line

You may want to expand a command line to check that it expands as expected or to edit the command line after expansion. To do so, press Escape followed by Control-e to tell the shell to expand variables and aliases, and then present the new command line. Here's an example. First, define an alias and a shell variable.

```
$ alias ls='ls -lF'
$ d='~/Documents'
```

Now type a command line that uses the alias and shell variable. Don't press Return, but press Escape followed by Control-e.

```
$ ls $d<Escape><Control-e>
```

You'll see the command line expanded to

```
$ ls -lF ~/Documents
```

Note: After you have defined d='~/Documents', typing ls $d and pressing Return will not work as expected. Try it. This is because the shell expands the tilde character (~) to the pathname of your home directory and does so before shell variable expansion. As the shell takes only one sweep at the command line, tilde will not be expanded.

Expand Completions

You may expand shell completions directly onto the command line by pressing Escape followed by star (*). Expand the star pattern-matching character by typing

```
$ ls *<Escape>*
```

Change readline's Key Bindings

Suppose you wish to assign a macro to a keystroke or change the default key bindings because you prefer different editing keystrokes. You can do so, and can in fact completely reconfigure the default key bindings, by taking advantage of Bash's built-in command `bind`.

Display the current key bindings by typing

```
$ bind -p
```

In the output that follows, you'll see the current key bindings, shown like this.

```
"\C-k": kill-line
```

`"\C-k"` means `Control-k`. `kill-line` is a `readline` function, and we can see that it is bound to `Control-k`. The form shown here is suitable for use as an argument to `bind`. You'll also notice that some lines show `"\M-"`, which means press Escape. The `readline` functions are documented in the Bash man page; search the page for the section called "READLINE" by typing `/^READLINE` within the man page.

Let's have a bash at defining our own keystrokes. First, we'll bind a macro to `Control-p`, being the text `ps auxc\r`. (The sequence `\r` represents Return and is a way of pressing Return from within the macro.) Type the following, noting that the entire sequence is enclosed in single quotes.

```
$ bind '"\C-p": "ps auxc\r"'
```

⬈ LEARN MORE

"Check Completion" in Project 12 shows other ways in which you can complete wildcard expansion directly onto the current command line.

The readline Library

Bash uses the `readline` library to receive keyboard input, and `readline` manages key bindings on behalf of Bash. To configure key bindings permanently, we would add settings to the `readline` configuration file, which is `.inputrc` in your home directory (`~/.inputrc`). Type `bind -p` to list the current bindings in a form that can be written to `.inputrc`.

These binding examples generally can be written to the configuration file in the same form shown here. Thus, we, we set the `kill-whole-line` binding.

```
$ cat ~/.inputrc
"\C-k": kill-whole-line
```

Now press `Control-p`, and you'll see that the command `ps auxc` is executed.

Next, let's bind the `readline` function `kill-whole-line` to `Control-k`. The default bindings have `Control-k` and `Control-u` deleting opposing halves of the command line. After you type the following command, `Control-k` will delete the whole line, even when the cursor is placed midline.

Let's just check that `kill-whole-line` is not already bound.

```
$ bind -p | grep kill-whole
# kill-whole-line (not bound)
```

Now let's bind it to `Control-k`.

```
$ bind '"\C-k": kill-whole-line'
```

emacs or vi

If you are familiar with the `emacs` text editor (covered in Chapter 4), you'll recognize that Bash editing keystrokes mirror those used by `emacs`. If you are a user of the `vi` text editor, you might hanker after vi-style editing. If so, all you need do is type

```
$ set -o vi
```

To switch back to `emacs`, type

```
$ set -o emacs
```

Tcsh Shell Bindings

The Tcsh shell offers equivalent functionality to Bash's `bind` via its `bindkey` command.

To list all editing functions, type

```
% bindkey
```

To assign a macro to `Control-p`, type

```
% bindkey -c ^P "ps auxc"
```

Option -c specifies a command and issues the macro followed by Return. If you do not want an automatic Return, use option -s (string) instead.

```
% bindkey -s ^P "ps auxc"
```

To make Control-k kill the whole line, type

```
% bindkey ^K kill-whole-line
```

To switch command-line binding to a more vi-like style, type

```
% bindkey -v
```

To switch back to emacs style, type

```
% bindkey -e
```

↗ LEARN MORE

Project 80 explains the intricacies of shell quoting.

Project 54 Understand Bash Internals

"How does Bash's internal processing affect my command lines?"

This project explores the workings of the Bash shell and shows you how to avoid writing command lines that expand and process incorrectly. It highlights shell special characters that must be escaped on the command line and shows the order in which a command line is parsed and executed.

Shell Special Characters

Particular characters have a special meaning to the Bash shell. If you wish to use them literally, they must be *escaped* (hidden from the shell) to prevent interpretation. We can do this in any of three ways:

▶ Enclose in double quotes

▶ Enclose in single quotes

▶ Precede with a backslash

Let's illustrate this with an example. We'll set up two shell variables and echo Jan owes me $20. We'll use double quotes, which escape all special characters except variable expansion, and then use backslash to escape the dollar symbol that should be taken literally.

```
$ name="Jan"; amount=20
$ echo "*** $name owes me \$$amount"
*** Jan owes me $20
```

Table 6.1 lists the shell special characters and their meaning.

Table 6.1 Shell Special Characters

Character Sequence	Meaning
#	Introduces a comment
;	Command separator
{...}	Signifies a command block
(...)	Forces execution in a subshell
&& ||	Logical AND/OR placed between commands
~	Expands to current user's home directory
~user	Expands to user's home directory
/	Directory and filename separator
$var	Expands the shell or environment variable var
`...`	Executes a command, writing output back to the command line
$(...)	Bash's preferred syntax for `...`
$((...))	Evaluates an integer arithmetic expression
((...))	Evaluates integer arithmetic in a condition
'	Strong quote to prevent interpretation of shell special characters
"	Weak quote within which $variable is expanded
\	Take the next character literally (cancels any special meaning)
*	Wildcard pattern-matching operator
[...]	Character-set wildcard
?	Single-character wildcard
&	Forces a command to be executed in the background
< >	Redirects stdin/stdout
|	Constructs a pipeline
!	Pipeline logical NOT

Command Search Order

When Bash parses a command line, it interprets the first word as a command. That command may be an external Unix command, an alias, or perhaps both. Bash considers each possibility and picks the first that fits. The order in which Bash considers possible interpretations affects the meaning of the command line. The order is:

‣ Aliases.

‣ Bash keywords (such as `if`, to start a conditional statement).

‣ Functions.

‣ Bash built-in commands. Type `help` to obtain a list of Bash's built-in commands.

‣ External Unix commands like `ls` and `nano`.

Three Bash built-in commands are available to override the natural order in which commands are considered. They are:

‣ `command`, which forces a command to be considered as either a built-in or a Unix executable, ignoring aliases and functions.

‣ `builtin`, which forces a command to be considered as a built-in only.

‣ `enable`, which enables and disables built-in commands.

Command-Line Processing

You'll find it handy to know the order in which Bash evaluates and expands a command line, if only to understand why a particular command line might fail and how to correct it.

Bash first reads a command line and *tokenizes* it, dividing it into elements like commands, variables, aliases, and strings. Processing then occurs in the following order:

‣ Expand aliases and then reparse the command line to expand aliases within aliases.

‣ Expand braces. Braces signify a command block.

▶ Expand tilde to the full pathname of your home directory and
   ~user to the full pathname of the user's home directory.

▶ Expand $variables, both shell and environment variables.

▶ Perform command substitution, such as $(date), which executes
   the date command, and then write the output from the command back to the command line.

▶ Evaluate $((...)) integer arithmetic expressions.

▶ Split words. After variable and parameter expansion has taken
   place, the expanded text is split into words.

▶ Expand pathnames.

Here are some examples that illustrate the significance of the command-line processing order.

Tokenization and alias expansion are repeated until no more aliases
are found. Take advantage of this by defining an alias within an alias.
In the example that follows, we define the alias lf, which includes in
its definition the alias dir.

```
$ alias lf=dir
$ alias dir='ls -F'
```

Alias lf will be expanded to dir and then alias dir will be expanded
to ls -F.

```
$ lf
Desktop/    Library/    Music/      Public/     backup/
Documents/  Movies/     Pictures/   Sites/
```

Next, we demonstrate that aliases are expanded before tilde by virtue
of the fact that the following example works.

```
$ alias ld="ls ~/Documents"
$ ld
AppleWorks User Data    Microsoft User Data    iChats
Downloads               Sophie.ichat           text
```

↗ **LEARN MORE**

**Refer to Project 16 for more
information on Bash's
command search order.**

ᵢ̈ TIP

Type Escape Control-e *to expand a command line in situ.*

```
$ lf<Escape>Control-e
$ dir<Escape>Control-e
$ ls -F
```

However, tilde is expanded before variables, which is why the next example fails.

```
$ doc="~/Documents"
$ ls $doc
ls: ~/Documents: No such file or directory
```

The next two examples demonstrate that variables are expanded after aliases, and show what tricks will and will not work. (Aliases lf and dir from the example above must be defined.)

```
$ alias hi='$Hello'
$ Hello='echo "Hello there!"'
$ hi
"Hello there!"
$ command='lf'
$ $command
-bash: lf: command not found
```

Finally, we take advantage of the fact that variables are expanded before command substitution takes place.

```
$ command="date"
$ echo $($command)
Thu Jul 28 11:03:03 BST 2005
```

Project 55
Run Background Jobs

"How do I regain control of the shell session after launching a command such as xterm, *which opens its own window?"*

This project takes advantage of Bash's job-control features, placing jobs in the background and swapping jobs in and out of the foreground. It gives some hints on how to manage background jobs, covering the commands fg, bg, and jobs. The Tcsh shell also supports job control and works in a more-or-less identical manner to Bash. This project is good for both Bash and Tcsh.

Start a Background Job

Most modern shells, including Bash and the Tcsh shell, implement *job control.* Essentially, what this means is that a command can be launched and then *detached* from Terminal. When a process becomes detached, the job is said to be a *background job.* A background job continues executing as though it were in the foreground, but with the exception that it will be suspended if it tries to read input from the keyboard.

Putting a job into the background releases its hold on Terminal, and the shell becomes the *foreground job.* This lets the current shell session continue, and you are free to issue more commands at the prompt while the background job continues to execute.

We would use a background job for a command that either takes a long time to complete and does not perform input or starts its own window, like the xterm command that comes as part of X11.

We'll illustrate background jobs by launching the top command. We tell top to report on running processes every 60 seconds (option -s60) and make 120 reports in total (option -l120). Such a command will take 2 hours to complete and does not require any input. Therefore, it's a good candidate to be backgrounded, with one caveat: It writes to the Terminal screen. This is not a problem, however, as we can redirect the command's output to a file for viewing later.

Type the following command line, noting the ampersand (&) character at the end of the line. Ampersand says to launch the command and run it in the background.

```
$ top -s60 -l120 > top.log &
 [1] 22885
```

You'll notice two things. First, we regain the prompt immediately. The `top` command is still executing, but in the background.

Second, the line `[1] 22885` is displayed. `[1]` is the job number and can be passed to the `fg` command to bring the job back into the foreground (which we do later). `22885` is the PID (process ID) of the running task, as would be reported by the `ps` command.

```
$ ps axc | grep top
22885  p0  S      0:05.20 top
```

To confirm that `top` is running, check the size or contents of the output file `top.log`, or watch it growing by using the `tail` command.

```
$ tail -f top.log
```

To display a list of all background jobs, and their job numbers and PIDs, use the `jobs` command.

```
$ jobs -l
[1]+ 22885 Running        top -s60 -l120 >top.log &
```

Note that each instance of Bash launches and controls its own list of jobs. Typing `jobs -l` in another Terminal window will not show the job with PID 22885. It might show another job number [1], but that will be a different job, which was launched by the other Bash session and will have a different PID.

Control Background Jobs

We can bring a background job into the foreground by using the `fg` command, passing the job number preceded by %. It's also possible to specify a PID by omitting the %.

```
$ fg %1
top -s60 -l120 >top.log
```

You'll see that Bash reflects the command we originally issued, but without the & to indicate that it's now a foreground job. You'll also notice the lack of a prompt.

How would we send the job back into the background, given that we cannot type in Terminal? Simple—issue an interrupt, which is sent directly to the running job. Control-c tells the job to abort, and Control-z tells it to stop and suspend. Let's suspend the job.

```
^Z
[1]+  Stopped              top -s60 -l120 >top.log
```

The job is now stopped. It's not aborted, but suspended. We have the Terminal prompt back and can continue issuing commands.

To put job [1] into the background, simply type

```
$ bg %1
[1]+ top -s60 -l120 >top.log &
```

The job is now running in the background, as signified by the & symbol at the end of the echoed command line and by the fact that we are immediately presented with the Bash shell prompt.

Use the same technique of issuing Control-z and then bg if you launch a command you intended to run in the background but accidentally left off the trailing & (by typing xterm instead of xterm &, for example).

Supply Input to a Background Job

Scripts that require input usually aren't good candidates for background jobs, but once in a while it makes sense to run one in the background. On those rare occasions, you can use some redirection tricks to send a background job the input it needs.

↗ LEARN MORE

Project 39 explores the top **and** ps **commands, and Project 6 covers redirection.**

ṫ TIP

Press Control-y *instead of* Control-z *to stop the foreground job only after it next tries to read input from Terminal.*

◣ NOTE

It's perfectly OK to put a job that writes to the Terminal screen into the background. Its output will be interspersed with the regular output from your shell session, and eventually, it'll irritate you.

ᵢ TIP

Bash notifies you of any change in the status of a background job not immediately, but when the next prompt is issued, to prevent the notification from being lost among regular output. To change this so that notifications are displayed immediately, type

$ **set -o notify**

Specify option +o instead of -o to switch off notify.

Here's a simple script that reads a single line of input and echoes a response.

```
$ cat script
#!/bin/bash
read -p "Name: " name
echo You claim to be $name.
```

Let's construct an input file to be read by the script.

```
$ echo "Adrian" > in
```

Now make the script executable, and run it, redirecting both input and output.

```
$ chmod +x script
$ ./script <in >out &
[1] 23014
```

To prove that it worked, examine file out.

```
$ cat out
You claim to be Adrian.
[1]+  Done            ./script <in >&out
```

You may also supply Terminal input to a background job that has stopped, awaiting input. In the following example, we launch the same script with no redirection. When the script requires input, it tries to read from Terminal but gets suspended.

```
$ ./script &
[1] 23016
$ Name:
```

Let's assume that the script requires input at some time in the future, rather than immediately. When it eventually stops, we'll see this line printed before the prompt.

```
[1]+  Stopped         ./script
```

To find out why the job has stopped, type

```
$ jobs -l
[1]+ 23016 Stopped (tty input)   ./script
```

The expression `(tty input)` confirms that the script requires input from Terminal. To enter input, we bring the job into the foreground and supply the necessary input.

```
$ fg %1
./script
Adrian  <<we type our input here
You claim to be Adrian.
```

At this point, the script completes, but if it were to continue, you might want to put it back into the background, as we did in the `top` example above.

Avoid Orphaned Jobs

If a shell exits while background jobs that it controls are still running, those jobs become *orphaned*. They can be stopped only by issuing a force-kill command like

```
$ kill -KILL <PID>
```

To prevent a shell script from creating orphaned jobs in the first place, use the `wait` command. Issuing `wait` prevents the shell from exiting until all background jobs under its control have completed.

To be more selective about which jobs we wait for, type

```
$ wait %n
```

to wait only for job number `n`. You may specify a PID instead of a job number if you omit the preceding `%`.

TIP

Kill a background process by giving its PID to the `kill` *command.*

```
$ kill -KILL 22885
```

Project 56
Cool Shell Tips

"How do I override the shell's command-line processing order?"

This project gives some miscellaneous tips for the Bash and Tcsh shells.

Create Your Own Message of the Day

The message (of the day) you see at the top of every new Terminal window—Welcome to Darwin!—is read from the file /etc/motd. It's easy to change this message; simply edit the file. Because of the permissions set on the file, you must edit it as the root user, using the sudo command. Type the following.

```
$ sudo nano /etc/motd
Password:
...
```

If you want the message to truly be a Message of the Day, you'll have to change it every day!

Format Output with printf

The printf command is much more powerful than echo. It takes a format string and a set of arguments to print within the context of the format string.

Let's define a function that takes two arguments and displays them in aligned columns, with the first number in red. The function is written purely to illustrate some tricks we can employ in printf.

Type the following.

```
$ function display () {
> norm="\033[00m"
> red="\033[31m"
> indent=${3:-4}
> spacer=$((20-$indent))
> printf "%${indent}s%-${spacer}s${red}%7s,${norm}%7s\n" ¬
    " " "Values:" $1 $2
> }
```

Let's examine the function line by line.

First, we define two variables called norm and red. They each hold an ANSI code that changes the color of the text written to Terminal. The sequence \033 is interpreted by printf to be an escape character. We didn't have to define variables; instead, we embedded the sequences in the printf statement. The variable route is neater, especially in real-world scenarios where a function or script contains numerous printf statements.

Variable indent is set to the value of the third parameter unless it is undefined, in which case a default value of 4 is assigned. Variable spacer is set to 20-$indent. The sequence $((...)) tells Bash to perform integer arithmetic when evaluating the expression.

Finally, we form a printf statement. The first argument is a format string, which, for a default value of 4 for indent, evaluates to

```
printf "%4s%-16s\033[31m%7s,\033[00m%7s\n" "" "Values:"
aaa bbb
```

The format string is a sequence of characters that will be displayed onscreen, with special placeholder sequences like %ns and %-ns interspersed. The sequence %ns says to display a string right aligned in an n-character field, and %-ns says to display a string left aligned in an n-character field. After the format string, we must provide a value for each placeholder sequence. In this example, the values are "", "Values:", "aaa", and "bbb".

↗ LEARN MORE

The projects in Chapter 4 look at several Unix text editors, including nano.

⟋ LEARN MORE

**Project 52 covers Bash
functions in detail.**

⟋ LEARN MORE

To learn more about `printf`,
refer to its man page.

`$ man 3 printf`

Try the function, and play with some examples yourself to understand what is happening.

```
$ display 3141 2178 6
    Values:            3141,   2178
```

Prevent Execution of Initialization Scripts

To launch a login shell from the command line, specify the option `--login`.

```
$ bash --login
```

To prevent Bash from running /etc/profile and ~/.bash_profile when it is invoked as a login shell, specify the option `--noprofile`.

```
$ bash --login --noprofile
```

To prevent a non-login shell from running /etc/bashrc and ~/.bashrc, specify option `--norc`.

```
$ bash --norc
```

Script vs. source vs. .

When you execute a script from the command line by typing

```
$ ./name-of-script
```

a new shell instance is launched to execute the script. If you want the script to be executed by the current shell—when it changes the shell environment, for example—you must *source* it by typing

```
$ source name-of-script
```

or

```
$ . name-of-script
```

Argument Recall

Recall the last argument of the last command by typing Escape period (.).

Auto Options

If you always use a particular command with a specific set of its options turned on, an alias can save typing: Just make the generic command name an alias for the option-enabled version. An alias can include its own name in the definition, and Bash understands not to attempt expansion during the definition.

```
$ alias ls='ls -lt'
```

Override Command-Line Processing Order

A very handy trick, should you fall afoul of Bash's command-line processing order, uses the eval command to tell the shell to take a second sweep at processing and expanding a command line.

Here's an example in which we are tripped up by the fact that the shell evaluates tilde expansion before variable expansion.

```
$ d="~/Documents"
$ ls $d
ls: ~/Documents: No such file or directory
```

We solve this problem by telling the shell to evaluate the command line a second time. Now, after the first sweep has expanded $d to ~/Documents, the second sweep will expand tilde to be your home directory.

```
$ eval ls $d
AppleWorks User Data    Microsoft User Data    iChats
Downloads               Sophie.ichat           text
```

↗ LEARN MORE

Refer to Project 47 for more information on Bash initialization scripts.

↗ **LEARN MORE**

**Project 51 covers Bash
aliases in detail.**

↗ **LEARN MORE**

**Project 54 covers Bash
command-line parsing.**

Tcsh

Try the following Tcsh built-in command. (There's no space around the dash.)

```
% ls-F
```

If you never want to hear another beep from Tcsh, ever, simply type

```
% set nobeep
```

Programmatically Change Files   7

This chapter is about editing text files with Unix text-processing utilities. These utilities work from scripts or simple editing instructions and automatically edit files by following those instructions. The seven projects cover the following topics:

Utilities to filter files. Apply simple transformations such as stripping blank lines and converting to lowercase.

Batch-editing files. Search for files to process and apply the same set of edits to each file.

The sed stream editor. Make complex modifications to a file by writing a script of editing commands.

The awk pattern-scanning and processing language. Like sed, awk works from a script, but its scripting language is more powerful.

By using the techniques described in this chapter, you can apply the same set of edits quickly and easily to many files, either as a one-off job, or as part of a periodic routine.

↗ LEARN MORE

Project 6 explains the concept of input/output redirection.

Project 57
Edit Text Files

"How do I quickly strip blank lines from hundreds of files?"

This project introduces utilities that apply simple transformations to text files, such as translating case, removing excessive white space, stripping blank lines, folding long lines, and converting between space and tab characters. It covers the commands tr, expand, unexpand, fold, and fmt. When you need to modify a file in a more complex manner, consider using either sed, covered in Projects 59 and 61, or awk, covered in Projects 60 and 62.

Change File Content

The tr command searches a file for specific characters and translates them into other characters. It takes as its arguments two strings, translating characters found in the first string into the corresponding characters from the second string. Rather oddly, tr does not take filename arguments but always reads its standard input and writes to its standard output. We'll get 'round this by using input/output redirection.

Let's convert the contents of the file jill.txt to be all uppercase, reading jill.txt as standard input and writing to loud.txt as standard output.

```
$ cat jill.txt
She likes black. I'm not sure if she has ambitions to be a
Goth, or an undertaker. Just a passing phase I suspect -
hearse today, gone tomorrow.
$ tr 'abcdefghijklmnopqrstuvwxyz' ¬
    'ABCDEFGHIJKLMNOPQRSTUVWXYZ' <jill.txt >loud.txt
$ cat loud.txt
SHE LIKES BLACK. I'M NOT SURE IF SHE HAS AMBITIONS TO BE A
GOTH, OR AN UNDERTAKER. JUST A PASSING PHASE I SUSPECT -
HEARSE TODAY, GONE TOMORROW.
```

The tr command understands character classes such as "all lowercase characters" or "all printable characters." Therefore, we can shorten our command to

```
$ tr '[:lower:]' '[:upper:]' <jill.txt >loud.txt
```

Read the man page for tr for a list of the classes it recognizes.

Convert from Mac to Unix

A typical use for tr is to convert an old-style Mac file to a Unix-compliant file. Mac OS 9 used a Return character (ASCII code 13) to mark the end of a line, whereas Unix uses a Newline character (ASCII code 10). A Mac-style text file appears to consist of one very long line when viewed by a Unix text-processing utility and editor.

Suppose that we have files imported from Mac OS 9 and wish to make them play nice in a Unix environment. We use tr to translate Return, represented by the special sequence \r, into Newline, represented by \n.

```
$ tr '\r' '\n' < mac-file > unix-file
```

Write Back to the Original File

It's not possible to write output back to the file being read because of the way input/output redirection works. However, the following trick, which uses a semicolon to separate two commands on a single line, will produce that effect. The command before the semicolon redirects translated output from mac-file to a new file called tmp. When that command completes, the mv command renames tmp to mac-file, overwriting the original file with a translated replacement.

```
$ tr '\r' '\n' < mac-file > tmp; mv tmp mac-file
```

Strip Lines and Characters

In this section, we look at ways to tidy up files. You might want to strip out nonprinting characters, for example, or remove excessive white space.

TIP

If you wish to know exactly which characters are included in a particular class, check out the Section 3 man page for the corresponding library function. A library function is named like its class but starts is. *To read about character class* [:space:], *for example, look at the man page for* isspace *by typing*

```
$ man 3 isspace
```

ᵢᵗ TIP

Employ commands such as grep *to edit files. Here, we search for lines that are empty, using the regular expression* ^$*, and report on all lines that do not match (are not empty). The results are written back to the original file via the temporary-file trick shown in the main text.*

```
$ grep -v '^$' space > ¬
    tmp; mv tmp space
```

Project 23 covers grep*, and Projects 77 and 78 explain regular expressions.*

Let's start by removing excessive white space—which we define as being two or more consecutive spaces, tabs (\t), or Newlines (\n)—from file spaced. We employ the tr command again, with option -s to squeeze repeated occurrences of selected characters into a single occurrence, and direct the translated output to file squashed.

```
$ tr -s ' \t\n' <spaced >squashed
```

Alternatively, if we accept the definition of white space given by man 3 isspace, we can achieve the same effect by typing

```
$ tr -s '[:space:]' <spaced >squashed
```

Next, suppose that you have a file containing control and other non-printing characters that you wish to remove. Let's view the file by using cat and option -v to display nonprinting characters visibly (for example, Control-a is displayed by ^A).

```
$ cat -v control
abc^A^B^C    def^D^E^F    ghi^G^H jkl
uvw^U^V^W    xyz
```

To remove all nonprinting characters, use tr. As a first attempt, try applying it with option -d, which deletes specified characters. Use the class [:print:], which specifies all printing characters (the ones you want to preserve), but then use option -c to specify the inverse of the class (everything that isn't in the class):

```
$ tr -cd '[:print:]' <control
abc    def    ghijkluvw    xyz$
```

This deletes all *non*printing characters, all right, but unfortunately, those characters include some, such as Tab and Newline, that are essential to text formatting. We can get around this problem by adding the class [:space:] to the selected characters. Our next attempt deletes all characters that are not printable but leaves behind "white space" that provides formatting.

```
$ tr -cd '[:print:][:space:]' <control
abc    def    ghi jkl
uvw    xyz
```

Expand and Unexpand

The command expand expands tab characters into the appropriate number of spaces; the command unexpand does the reverse. Pass option -a to unexpand to ensure that all spaces are converted; otherwise, only leading spaces are converted.

Files containing long lines, such as those often found in HTML source code, can have their contents broken into shorter lines with the fold command. Here's the original file (which is one long line, but shown split across four lines in the book).

```
$ cat count
He puzzled at my counting. Did I exceed his range?
Apparently, there is an African tribe who count one, two,
many. So perhaps he's related. More likely he's related to
the African tribe who have "one too many".
```

We specify that the output should be lines exactly 50 characters in length by using the option -w50. The output is shown displayed on the Terminal screen, but we could redirect it to a file or back to the original file by using the technique described in "Write Back to the Original File" earlier in this project.

```
$ fold -w50 count
He puzzled at my counting. Did I exceed his range?
 Apparently, there is an African tribe who count o
ne, two, many. So perhaps he's related. More likel
y he's related to the African tribe who have "one
too many".
```

Alternatively, we might use the command fmt, which breaks lines at spaces instead of midword.

```
$ fmt -50 count
He puzzled at my counting. Did I exceed his range?
Apparently, there is an African tribe who count
one, two, many. So perhaps he's related. More
likely he's related to the African tribe who have
"one too many".
```

Just for Fun

Here's a command that parses file.txt and produces a count of the ten most-used words. See Project 26 for examples of how to use the sort and uniq commands.

```
$ tr -cs "[:alpha:]\'" ¬
    '\n' < file.txt | ¬
    sort | uniq -c | ¬
    sort -nr | head -10
   75 the
   46 and
   45 to
...
```

ᴛ TIP

The fmt *command does much more than just break lines. Check its man page by typing*

```
$ man fmt
```

⚡ TIP

When you write your own shell scripts, by falling back on the techniques discussed in this project, you can avoid having to code your script to accept a list of files.

↗ LEARN MORE

Project 11 explains wildcard expansion.

Project 58
Batch-Edit Files

"How do I find and edit potentially hundreds of files by using a single command line?"

This project gives some techniques for batch-editing files—that is, selecting many files and passing them one at a time to an editing utility. The solutions explored here are discussed in the context of the tr and sed commands but apply equally well to other commands. Project 57 covers the tr command, and projects 59 and 61 cover the sed command.

Add Utility to the tr Command

Because the tr command doesn't accept a list of filenames and cannot write back to the file being processed, it makes a good subject around which we can build some batch-processing utilities. (It would be no challenge if tr simply took a list of files to edit.) We'll develop some techniques for editing batches of files that use tr and overcome its limitations.

Use a for Loop

A simple trick uses a shell for loop that selects each file to be processed and forms a command line to process it. In the following example, we take advantage of shell wildcard expansion, using the expression *.txt to select all text files in the current directory.

In our command, the shell variable file assumes the value of each filename in turn, and the tr command processes the file. The editing operation tr performs here—changing every a character it finds in a file to z—is frivolous, but it illustrates the technique.

```
$ for file in *.txt; do
>     echo "Processing $file..."; tr 'a' 'z' <"$file"
> done
Processing car.txt...
Sophie poured me into the czr, stzrted the engine, zbused
some cogs, znd grzted her wzy out from the czr pzrk.

Processing jill black.txt...
Jillezn likes blzck. I'm not sure if she hzs zmbitions to
be z Goth, or zn undertzker. Just z pzssing phzse I suspect
- hezrse todzy, gone tomorrow.
```

For each new value of variable `file`, the `echo` expression displays a filename (within the phrase `Processing [filename]`…). For this solution to cope with filenames that contain spaces (such as `jill black.txt`), the use of double quotes around `"$file"` is essential.

We could extend the `tr` command to write back to the original file, using what we learned in Project 57.

```
$ tr 'z' 'a' <"$file" >tmp; mv tmp "$file"
```

Make It a Function

We can encapsulate the `for` loop in a function, which we'll call `each`, thereby saving a little typing whenever we wish to process a batch of files. Function `each` will allow us to issue a command such as

```
$ each txt tr 'a' 'z'
```

The `each` function is written to use its first argument as a filename extension and form the wildcard pattern `*.extension`. All other arguments are assumed to be part of the command to execute. Here's the function:

```
$ each () {
> filetype="$1"; shift
> for file in *.$filetype; do
>     echo "Processing $file..."; $* <"$file"
> done
> }
```

⬐ LEARN MORE

Projects 9 and 10 introduce shell scripting. Refer to Project 10 if you are unfamiliar with for loops.

↗ **LEARN MORE**

Project 52 covers bash functions.

Examining the code: We save the extension (argument 1) in variable filetype and then shift down all other arguments so that 3 becomes 2, 2 becomes 1, and the original argument 1 drops off the end. (This enables the tr command to process subsequent arguments as it would normally.)

The for loop assigns each filename that matches the *.extension pattern to variable file, writes the Processing [filename]... notice onscreen, and passes the contents of the matching file as standard input, ready for tr to process. Recall that $* expands to tr 'a' 'z'.

Issue the command

```
$ each txt tr 'a' 'z'
```

and our each function will form the following command line for each filename.

```
tr 'a' 'z' <"filename.txt"
```

Here's an alternate version, each2, that takes a filename specification, rather than an extension, as its direct argument. This gives us the option of using an individual filename or expressions that contain one or more wildcard characters, rather than just a file extension, to specify files to be processed by tr.

This time, we pass *.txt as the first argument, remembering to escape the star so that it won't be interpreted by the shell.

```
$ each2 () {
> filetype="$1"; shift
> for file in $filetype; do
>     echo "Processing $file..."; $* <"$file"
> done
> }
$ each2 \*.txt tr 'a' 'z'
```

Write a Generic each Function

The function examples so far have been very specific to the tr utility they serve. The main processing command in function each

```
$* <"$file"
```

specifically uses the input redirection required by tr. A more versatile technique uses a generic *each* function that expects the utility being called to sort out its own idiosyncrasies. Here's one possible solution.

```
$ geach () {
> command=$1; shift
> for file in "$@"; do
>     $command "$file"
> done
> }
```

We pass the whole command line to geach, which simply expands its first argument as the command to run and takes subsequent argument(s) as filename(s) to process one at a time.

This technique works nicely in this instance, but it's seldom so easy to specify a whole command as a simple parameter. Weaving "$file" into this command line works because the variable is used to place an argument at the end of the command line. If this required insertion of arguments into the middle of the command line, as many other commands and functions do, it wouldn't work.

A better solution is to write the command to be executed as function, or as a mini shell script within its own file. Let's define a function called trx that does the usual *a*-to-*z* translation on the contents of a filename specified as argument 1 and writes back to the original file:

```
$ trx () { tr 'a' 'z' <"$1" >tmp; mv tmp "$1"; }
```

Function trx takes one argument, which is the filename to process. We combine this with the generic *each* function, geach, by typing

```
$ geach trx *.txt
```

For each file it finds, the geach function forms the command line

```
trx filename.txt
```

and the trx function in turn executes

```
tr 'a' 'z' <"filename.txt" >tmp; mv tmp "filename.txt"
```

(You'll notice that this lets us place "$file" in the middle of our command line, as well as at the end.)

Note that we must write a new trx function for each different editing task, but doing so does not involve much more than typing the raw command. When the generic reach function is defined, we have an easy way of sending a batch of files, *one at a time*, to any function or shell script.

It's possible to make a generic trx too and to incorporate its functionality into geach, but it involves more serious scripting. See Project 83.

Search with find

The examples in the previous section made use of shell wildcard expansion (or globbing) to drive a for loop. Sometimes, you might want to search a complete directory hierarchy, recursively, for files to process. To this end, we employ the find command (see Projects 15, 17, and 18 for detailed examples of using find). We can either take advantage of its primary -exec or pipe the output to xargs -n1, both of which will hand off matching files, one at a time, to the target command for editing or other processing.

Here's a recursive file search similar to the geach function we wrote earlier, which we'll call rgeach.

```
$ rgeach () {
> command=$1; shift
> find . -iname "$*" -print0 | xargs -0 -t -n1 $command
> }
```

This time, we'll make trx a shell script instead of a function, partly to show an alternative approach to the previous examples, but mostly because the xargs command that we use here to invoke trx does not recognize Bash functions.

```
$ cat trx
tr 'z' 'a' <"$1" >tmp; mv tmp "$1"
$ chmod +x trx
$ rgeach trx "*.txt"
trx ./backup/jan.txt
trx ./car.txt
trx ./jill black.txt
```

Project 59
Learn the sed Stream Editor

"How do I write a script to perform the same sequence of editing commands on a number of text files?"

This project shows you how to use the sed stream editor, which changes text files by reading editing commands from a script. Project 58 shows how to apply such commands to a batch of files. Project 61 covers more advanced use of sed, and Projects 60 and 62 cover the awk command.

The sed Basics

The sed stream editor was written to edit text files, but it's not an interactive editor like nano, vim, or emacs. Instead of following commands entered "live" by a user, sed executes edits according to instructions provided in a command script. The most common use of sed is to apply the same set of edits to many files, either as a one-time transformation or at regular intervals—to make a small change across hundreds of HTML files, for example, or to process Apache log files once a day.

The sed command writes its output to standard out, so it can easily create new files as it edits existing ones. As of Mac OS X 10.4 (Tiger), sed also accepts the option -i, which directs it to write changes back to the original source file.

A sed script consists of editing commands; each command describes a *line range* and a *function*. When sed receives files as input, it reads each line by line. When an input line falls in a command's line range, sed applies the corresponding function to that input line. An input line may fall in the line range of many commands and, therefore, will have many functions applied to it.

ⓘ TIP

*Specify option -i and a
filename extension to make
sed write the edits back to the
input file instead of to standard
out. The original file is saved
in a backup file named as the
original file plus the specified
extension. The following
command changes* fuse.txt
and writes the original file to
fuse.txt.bak.

```
$ sed -i .bak  ¬
    's/Jill/Jillean/g' ¬
    fuse.txt
```

You can write a sed script directly to the command line or to a file.
This project considers simple scripts of just a few lines, which we'll
write directly to the command line. Scripts that are more complex
are usually written to files and are the subject of Project 61.

Next, we'll look at a few examples to clarify what we've just learned.

Let's Edit

Substituting one pattern for another is a common use for sed. Should
you wish to be formal and replace Jill with Jillean, for example,
you could employ the following command.

First, let's view the original file.

```
$ cat fuse.txt
Jill has a short fuse - light it and stand well back. So
who lit Jill's fuse, and did he stand well back? Read on
```

Next, invoke sed to perform the edit by typing

```
$ sed 's/Jill/Jillean/g' fuse.txt
Jillean has a short fuse - light it and stand well back. So
who lit Jillean's fuse, and did he stand well back? Read on
```

We invoked sed, passing the quoted script 's/Jill/Jillean/g' and
the name of the file to process. Although not necessary in this example, it's wise always to quote the script to prevent the shell from
expanding special characters before passing them to sed.

Our script consists of one command, which does not define a line
range; therefore, its function is applied to every line of the file. The
function is s for *substitute,* which has the syntax s/match-
text/replace-text/flags. The flag g is for *global replace;* see "sed
Functions" later in this project.

Our next example deletes all blank lines from a file. The sed command to do this specifies a line range "every blank line" and the function delete. "Every blank line" is defined by the regular expression ^$,
delimited by forward slash characters (/). The function d deletes the
matched line.

```
$ sed '/^$/d' blanks.txt
```

Line ranges are usually given as plain text or regular expressions, and all lines that contain a match for the text or regular expression fall in the line range.

Make sed grep

Make sed behave like grep by combining function p, to print matching lines, and option -n, to suppress the automatic echoing of every input line. We'll search the file biff.txt for all lines that contain the text Biff.

```
$ sed -n '/Biff/p' biff.txt
*I forget the name — let's assume Biff for want of a single
syllable, grunt-able word).
*'Biff' grinned, and I swear that I could hear a few
synaptic connections sparking the thought 'threesome'
(had he been able to count to three).
*I declined the unspoken suggestion, confusing Biff somewhat
```

(I've added a star [*] to mark each line because lines in the original text occupy several lines when printed in this book.)

In this example, the line range is described by the plain-text expression /Biff/; every line that contains the text Biff will fall in the range and be printed by the function p.

Encode a File

Have some fun encoding text files. In this example, we apply function y, which transforms input lines by replacing characters listed in the first set with those listed in the second set. Our example shifts all letters in the input text one place to the right. No filenames are specified, so sed reads and writes standard input and output. Press Control-d (end of input) when you get bored.

```
$ sed 'y/abcdefghijklmnopqrstuvwxyz/¬
    bcedfghijklmnopqrstuvwxyza/'
this is just a bit of fun
uijt jt kvtu b cju pg gvo
<Control-d>
```

↗ LEARN MORE

Projects 77 and 78 explain regular expressions.

ǐ TIP

In older versions of sed *that do not have the* -i *option, you can write back to the original file as follows.*

```
$ sed 's/witch/which/' ¬
    input > tmp; ¬
    mv tmp input
```

Project 6 covers input/output redirection.

ⓘ TIP

Specify option -E *should the expression be an extended regular expression; otherwise,* sed *will recognize only basic regular expressions.*

ⓘ TIP

You can specify line addresses to sed *with a line number instead of a pattern. To make* sed *act like the* head *command and print the first three lines of a file, for example, we could type*

```
$ sed -n '1,3p' ¬
    index.php
```

Line Ranges in sed Scripts

Let's examine line ranges in more detail. The most basic line range is the empty one that matches all lines in the input file. When not empty, a line range may be a single address, which usually consists of a regular expression (such as /^$/ to select all empty lines) or plain text (such as /Jill/ to select all lines containing the text Jill).

Two addresses separated by a comma select all lines from the first line that matches the first address to the first subsequent line that matches the second address. To select just the lines in Chapter One, for example, we might specify the line range /Chapter One/,/Chapter Two/ (assuming that Chapter One starts with the text "Chapter One," and similarly for Chapter Two).

sed Functions

Immediately following a line range, sed expects to see an editing function to be applied to each line in the range. Here are some of the most useful sed functions:

▸ s substitutes one pattern for another pattern. For example, s/witch/which/ replaces all occurrences of witch by which. Only the first occurrence on each line is replaced. If you wish to replace all occurrences on a line, specify the flag g (global) s/witch/which/g. The pattern to match against may be a regular expression.

▸ d deletes the line.

▸ p prints the line to standard out.

▸ w writes the line to a file.

▸ y replaces characters like the tr command, covered in Project 57. To convert a line to all capitals, we would specify the function y/abcdefghijklmnopqrstuvwxyz/ABCDEFGHIJKLMNOPQRSTUVWXYZ/.

Multiple sed Commands

Suppose that we have a couple of replacements to make to a text file and that we also want to delete lines that contain the author's notes. We could apply sed several times, once for each edit, but instead, let's take advantage of the fact that a sed script, like any script, can include multiple commands.

With sed, there are three methods available for writing multiple-command scripts:

▸ Separate the commands with semicolons.

▸ Present several commands by specifying sed option -e.

▸ Write multiple commands to a script file.

The following examples have Jan drinking gin instead of vodka, make Sophie 5 years younger (she'll love me for that), and remove the author's notes. Here's the original text.

```
$ cat sophie.txt
Note Move this section down
I returned to planet earth when a lady sat down beside me
and announced: "Hi, I'm Sophie".
"Hello, I'm... (thinking through a Vodka haze) Jan".
Note Check the grammar here
She smiled and we chatted for a while.
Sophie was about 30, bleached-blonde, good-looking, and
just a shade overweight.
```

Now let's apply a three-command sed script in which we separate the lines of the script with semicolons.

```
$ sed 's/Vodka/Gin/g;s/30/25/g;/^[N|n]ote/d' sophie.txt
I returned to planet earth when a lady sat down beside me
and announced: "Hi, I'm Sophie".
"Hello, I'm... (thinking through a Gin haze) Jan".
She smiled and we chatted for a while.
Sophie was about 25, bleached-blonde, good-looking, and
just a shade overweight.
```

Alternatively, we could specify three separate commands by typing

```
$ sed -e 's/Vodka/Gin/g' -e 's/30/25/g' -e '/^[N|n]ote/d' ¬
    sophie.txt
```

For the third alternative, we'll create a script file called 3edits and pass the name of that file to sed. A sed script is a regular text file with each edit command on a separate line.

```
$ cat 3edits
s/Vodka/Gin/g
s/30/25/g
/^[N|n]ote/d
$ sed -f 3edits sophie.txt
```

All three alternatives yield the same results.

Complex Line Ranges

In previous examples, we used a single address (in the form of a regular expression) to match the lines we wanted to edit. Tell sed to select a *range* of lines to edit by specifying two addresses. The first line to match the first address marks the start of the range. The first line after that to match the second address marks the end of the range.

As an example, suppose that we want to remove all of many paragraphs within an HTML file that have been assigned the class tail. Each begins with the HTML tag <p class="tail">, and each ends with a closing tag </p>, like this abbreviated example.

```
<p class="tail">
<b>Six Vodkas: </b>A tale of Vodka, misunderstanding, an...
</p>
```

To delete all such paragraphs, we use the following command.

```
$ sed '/<p class="tail">/,/<\/p>/d' tails.html
```

Having matched and deleted the first such paragraph, sed continues to search the file for subsequent ranges and deletes all those it finds.

To print the paragraphs instead of deleting them, type

```
$ sed -n '/<p class="tail">/,/<\/p>/p' index.php
...
<p class="tail">
<b>The Immovable Object: </b>A tale of pain, pursed lips...
</p>
```

Suppose you wish to edit only in paragraphs that meet certain criteria —changing `tale` to `tail` only within paragraphs of class `tail`, for example. To do so, we again use a range to specify the matching criteria and apply a `sed` substitute function to the range.

```
$ sed  '/<p class="tail">/,/<\/p>/s/tale/tail/' index.php
<p class="tail">
<b>The Immovable Object: </b>A tail of pain, pursed lips...
</p>
```

✎ NOTE

In these examples, we allowed sed *to write to standard output to better illustrate what's happening. Normally, we would write back to the original file by specifying option* -i.

Tails

If you are wondering why tales is spelled `tails`, visit the home page of Jan's Web site (http://jan.1dot1.com); it's an HTML joke.

Project 60
Learn the awk
Text Processor

"How do I write a script to perform the same sequence of editing and process-ing commands on multiple text files?"

This project shows you how to use the awk text processing language to change text files by reading edit commands from a script. Project 58 shows how to apply such commands to a batch of files. Project 62 covers more advanced use of awk, and Projects 59 and 61 cover the sed command.

An Editing Language

The awk text processor was written to scan text files for matching patterns of text. Each pattern can have an associated action that prints or edits the text, or perhaps increments a counter or calls a function. It's not an interactive editor like nano; instead, it reads editing com-mands from a script. It's most often used to apply the same set of edits to many files—sometimes as a one-time operation, sometimes at reg-ular intervals. You might want to reformat hundreds of files of source code or generate daily statistics by reading log files. The awk com-mand is similar to the sed command (discussed in Project 59) but has a more powerful, and C-language-like, processing language.

Because awk is like a programming language, it's not as easy to master as sed. If you've had no experience writing code, you'll probably find it difficult to pick up without a more in-depth tutorial. You might want to skip the theoretical treatment until you've tried some of the examples in "Scripts for awk" later in this project.

The awk Basics

The awk command writes its output to standard out, so it can easily create new files as it processes existing ones. An awk script consists of editing commands; each command describes a *pattern* and an *action*. awk reads its input file line by line. If a line matches one (or more) of the patterns, awk applies the corresponding action(s) to that line. An input line may match many patterns and, therefore, will have many actions applied to it.

You may write the script directly to the command line or to a file. This project considers simple scripts of just a few lines. Scripts that are more complex are usually written to files and are the subject of Project 62.

The awk command sees each line of input it reads as a series of *fields* separated by white space. Command awk defines its own special variables, $1 to $n, to represent field numbers 1 to n; $0 represents the entire line. These *field variables* are used just like any other variables: You can compare them; examine their contents by using string functions; or, as is the most usual, print them by using the print and printf statements.

Patterns

The most basic pattern is an empty one that matches all lines in the input file. When not empty, a pattern may be a regular expression (such as /^$/ to select all empty lines) or plain text (such as /Sophie/ to select all lines containing the text Sophie).

More-complex patterns involve many regular expressions connected by the Boolean operators && (AND), || (OR), and ! (NOT). As an example, the pattern /Sophie/&&/rescue/ matches all lines that contain both Sophie *and* rescue, whereas the pattern /Sophie/&&!/rescue/ matches all lines that contain Sophie *but not* rescue.

A pattern need not involve matching text against the input line but may be any expression allowed in the awk language. The pattern rand() < 0.5, for example, has a 50–50 chance of matching each line, and (jumping ahead a little) the pattern length ($0) > 59 matches input lines longer than 59 characters.

The awk Command is Comprehensive

The awk command provides a powerful C-like processing language that includes features such as conditional statements, loops, variables, and functions. It would take a whole book to teach awk, and certainly more than two projects. To give you the most benefit from limited coverage, the two awk projects here illustrate the most useful awk techniques. Think of them as a sampling that reflects the potential of awk.

ᵢ̆ TIP

You can instruct awk to recognize field separators other than white space by using special awk variable FS. To see how this works when commas are used as separators, see "Process a CSV File" in Project 62.

Two patterns separated by a comma select all lines from the first line that matches the first pattern to the first subsequent line that matches the second pattern. To select just those lines in Chapter One, for example, we might specify the pattern /Chapter One/,/Chapter Two/ (assuming that Chapter One starts with the text "Chapter One," and similarly for Chapter Two).

Actions

Immediately following a pattern, awk expects to see an action delimited by braces. An *action* is a sequence of statements executed against each line that matches the pattern. Here are some of the most useful awk statements:

▶ if(expression) statement [else statement]

▶ while(expression) statement

▶ for(expression ; expression ; expression) statement

▶ for(var in array) statement

▶ variable assignment

▶ print [expression-list] [> expression]

▶ printf format [, expression-list] [> expression]

Scripts for awk

An awk script consists of a list of pattern–action pairs. An action is a list of statements in braces to be applied to input lines that match its pattern. The following sections present some simple awk scripts.

Delete Blank Lines

Suppose that you wish to remove blank lines from a file. We construct a pattern matched by a nonblank line and an action that prints the line. Let's make our pattern the regular expression .+, which is matched by lines that consist of one or more characters, and let's make our action the statement print $0, which prints the line. Putting these together, we get

```
$ awk '/.+/{print $0}' sophie.txt > sophie2.txt
```

We read `sophie.txt`, detect nonblank lines, and print them to `sophie2.txt` by redirecting standard out.

It's not possible to write output back to the file being read because of the way input/output redirection works. The following trick produces that effect. The command before the semicolon redirects translated output from `sophie.txt` to a new file, `tmp`. When that command completes, the `mv` command renames `tmp` to `sophie.txt`, overwriting the original file with a translated replacement.

```
$ awk '/.+/{print $0}' sophie.txt > tmp; mv tmp sophie.txt
```

Make awk grep

The example above has `awk` behave like `grep` (see Project 23 for information on `grep`). Here's another example that searches the file `vodkas.txt` for `six`.

```
$ awk '/six/{print}' vodka.txt
```

Print Fields

A very common use for `awk` is to scan an input file, perhaps matching specific lines, and print just certain fields of each line. Suppose that we wish to filter a long listing produced by typing

```
$ ls -l *.txt
-rw-r--r-- 1 saruman saruman   468 Aug 3 21:19 biff.txt
-rw-r--r-- 1 saruman saruman 37080 Aug 5 15:42 big-file.txt
...
```

We wish to display just the filename followed by the file size. We note that the filename is field 9, which `awk` recognizes as `$9`, and that the size is field 5, which `awk` recognizes as `$5`.

To realize this, type the following command.

```
$ ls -l *.txt | awk '$5>400 {print $9, $5}'
biff.txt 468
big-file.txt 37080
mark.txt 402
```

↗ LEARN MORE

Project 6 covers input/output redirection.

◦ TIP

If you don't specify $0, it's often assumed. The statement print $0 *is equivalent to* print. *In fact, if no action is specified, the default action is to print the input line. Therefore, the command* awk '/.+/{print $0}' sophie.txt *is equivalent to* awk '/.+/' sophie.txt.

◦ TIP

You'll often see a command combining grep *and* awk, *such as*

```
$ ps | grep 'bash' | ¬
    awk '{print $1'}
```

With our newfound awk *powers, we can eliminate* grep *from the pipe by typing*

```
$ ps | awk ¬
    '/bash/{print $1'}
```

☵ TIP

The printf *statement implemented by* awk *uses the* printf *library documented in Section 3 of the Unix manual. To read all about what* printf *can do for you, type*

```
$ man 3 printf
```

We've thrown in a pattern, too.

$5>400

This says to match a line if the value of field 5 is more than 400. Our filtered list, therefore, displays the names and sizes of files whose size is more than 400 bytes.

An alternative to print is the printf command, which formats and embellishes its output according to a format string. The format string is a sequence of characters to be displayed onscreen, interspersed by special placeholder sequences. One such placeholder sequence is %ns, which displays a value space-padded so that it's n characters wide. Following the format string, we must provide the value required by each placeholder sequence.

We'll illustrate printf by repeating the example above but making the output more informative.

```
$ ls -l *.txt | awk 'BEGIN {print "Formatted Listing"}; ¬
    $5>400 {printf "File: %-15s Size= %10s bytes\n", $9, $5}'
Formatted Listing
File: biff.txt       Size=          468 bytes
File: big-file.txt   Size=        37080 bytes
File: mark.txt       Size=          402 bytes
```

We threw in another trick, to generate the "Formatted Listing" header. The special pattern BEGIN matches the start of the input file, and we used it to perform a one-off action that is executed before any lines of input are read.

Print and Skip Blocks

We can build a pattern to specify a range of lines, should we wish to process a block of text. Suppose that we wish to display just those lines between clearly attempting... and helped me up..., inclusive, from the text file sophie.txt. Here's the original file.

```
$ cat sophie.txt
I hopped out of the car and promptly ate gravel. The
non-retracting seat belt had wrapped itself around my ankle
clearly attempting to do what Sophie failed to do during
```

```
the drive home - kill me. :-) Sophie rushed to my rescue,
helped me up, and brushed off the stones from my dress.
There are better ways to get "stoned"!
```

The pattern we use consists of two regular expressions separated by a comma, and we print the matched range of lines with a command such as

```
$ awk '/^clearly/,/^helped/' sophie.txt
clearly attempting to do what Sophie failed to do during
the drive home - kill me. :-) Sophie rushed to my rescue,
helped me up, and brushed off the stones from my dress.
```

Next, let's employ a trick to skip the selected range of lines and print the rest of the file instead. To the previous pattern, we apply the action next, which says to skip to the next input line without further processing. We also specify a second pattern–action combination (with an empty pattern), separated from the first by a semicolon, whose action is print.

Normally, every pattern–action pair would be applied to every input line. The action next, however, specifically skips the rest of the script for input lines that match. The net result is that matching lines are skipped and nonmatching lines are printed.

```
$ awk '/^clearly/,/^helped/{next}; {print}' sophie.txt
I hopped out of the car and promptly ate gravel. The
non-retracting seat belt had wrapped itself around my ankle
There are better ways to get "stoned"!
```

Substitute with awk

Here's an example demonstrating text replacement (or substitution) in awk. Similar to the s function of sed is the awk substitute function sub. Let's substitute breakfast for lunch in the file wakes.txt. Here's the original file.

```
$ cat wakes.txt
Sorry, breakfast is cancelled.
Nobody wakes Janet Forbes at 7 am
and lives long enough to see breakfast.
```

⚓ TIP

All awk functions are documented in the awk man pages.

We call the function sub and pass two parameters; the first is a regular expression to match against, and the second is the substitute text. All text that matches the regular expression is replaced with the substitute text, as in this example.

```
$ awk '{sub("breakfast", "lunch"); print}' wakes.txt
Sorry, lunch is cancelled.
Nobody wakes Janet Forbes at 7 am
and lives long enough to see lunch.
```

Because awk is essentially a programming language, you'll find that all features are exposed as traditional functions that take parameters enclosed in parentheses. Contrast this with the sed command, in which substitution uses the syntax s/breakfast/lunch/.

Like all awk scripts, this one has a pattern (empty) followed by an action. To be more selective which lines we execute sub on, specify a nonempty pattern:

```
$ awk '/cancelled/{sub("breakfast", "lunch"); print}' ¬
    wakes.txt
Sorry, lunch is cancelled.
```

Finally, if you also wish to print all lines in the file, move the print statement into its own action, preceded by a blank pattern.

```
$ awk '/cancelled/{sub("breakfast", "lunch")} {print}' ¬
    wakes.txt
Sorry, lunch is cancelled.
Nobody wakes Janet Forbes at 7 am
and lives long enough to see breakfast.
```

Project 61
Learn Advanced sed

"What functionality does the **sed** *command offer for the more advanced editing tasks?"*

This project presents a couple of tasks that illustrate some of the more advanced editing capabilities of the **sed** stream editor. Project 58 shows how to apply such commands to a batch of files. Project 59 covers basic use of **sed**, and Projects 60 and 62 cover the **awk** command.

Highlight a Block of Text

We'll illustrate some of the advanced feature of **sed** through a couple of tasks that highlight first a block of text and then individual lines of text.

For task one, we'll write a **sed** script that highlights a block of text by placing >>> at the start of each line in the block. Let's assume that the region to be highlighted has previously been marked by **mark-start** and **mark-end**.

The (abridged) text looks like this. (In reality we might have hundreds of lines to mark, justifying the use of **sed**.)

```
$ cat sophie.txt
I hopped out of the car and promptly ate gravel. The
non-retracting seat belt had wrapped itself around my ankle
mark-start
clearly attempting to do what Sophie failed to do during
the drive home - kill me. :-) Sophie rushed to my rescue,
mark-end
helped me up, and brushed off the stones from my dress.
There are better ways to get "stoned"!
```

The **sed** script must specify the line range as /mark-start/,/mark-end/, and within this range, add the text >>> to the start of each matching line. ("Start of line" is denoted by the regular expression ^.)

↗ LEARN MORE

**See Project 77 if you are
unfamiliar with regular
expressions.**

To highlight the marked block from file `sophie.txt`, type the following command.

```
$ sed '/mark-start/,/mark-end/s/^/>>>/' sophie.txt
I hopped out of the car and promptly ate gravel. The
non-retracting seat belt had wrapped itself around my ankle
>>>mark-start
>>>clearly attempting to do what Sophie failed to do during
>>>the drive home - kill me. :-) Sophie rushed to my rescue
>>>mark-end
helped me up, and brushed off the stones from my dress.
There are better ways to get "stoned"!
```

(For illustrative purposes, we've let output go to the Terminal screen. Normally, you'd write it back to the file by specifying option -i or—before Mac OS X 10.4—by redirecting output to a new file.)

When you wish to remove the highlights we just added, write a `sed` script to delete >>> from the line range; then delete the marker lines too (we probably don't want them there). The following command does just this, using three edit commands: one to remove >>> and one each to remove the two marker lines.

```
$ sed '/mark-start/,/mark-end/s/^>>>//;/mark-start/d;¬
   /mark-end/d' sophie.txt
```

If you'd like to remove the highlight characters from the text but leave the marker lines in, *including the highlight*, you need to be a bit cleverer. We could either remove >>> and then add them back to lines starting with `mark-`, or we could be more specific in selecting the range of lines to modify. The latter alternative shows off more `sed` tricks, so we'll choose that one.

Type the following command line.

```
$ sed '/mark-start/,/mark-end/{/^>>>mark-/!s/^>>>//;}' ¬
    sophie.txt
I hopped out of the car and promptly ate gravel. The
non-retracting seat belt had wrapped itself around my ankle
>>>mark-start
clearly attempting to do what Sophie failed to do during
the drive home - kill me. :-) Sophie rushed to my rescue,
>>>mark-end
helped me up, and brushed off the stones from my dress.
There are better ways to get "stoned"!
```

This does the trick but requires some explanation. The pattern should be familiar. The action employs braces {...} to introduce a function list. A *function list* lets us apply more than one function to a line range, where normally only one is allowed, and also allows us to apply a further line range within the existing one.

The example selects lines within the marked block that *also* start with >>>mark- by specifying /^>>>mark-/ within the braces. The exclamation point that follows inverts the sense of the match, thereby selecting only lines that *do not* start with >>>mark- (within the marked block). To the selected lines, we apply a substitute function s/^>>>// to remove the text >>> from the start of the line. The function list is terminated by ;}.

Highlight Lines

For our second task, we'll search a text file for a pattern, sophie, and mark each line that contains the pattern by inserting a line containing vvvvvvvvvvvv before it and another containing ^^^^^^^^^^^^ after it. To make things more interesting, we'll make our search case insensitive.

TIP

If a pattern contains the delimiter character /, escape it by using a backslash. For example, we can specify the pattern http:// *using* /http:\/\//. *Alternatively, for the substitute function (but not for specifying a line range), we can choose a different delimiter, such as* %. *We would type* %http://%.

↗ LEARN MORE

Project 59 covers basic sed
**use and has an example of
using the** y **function.**

Here's the sed script, which we've written to a script file called mark.script.

```
$ cat mark.script
# convert input to lower case, making a copy in hold space
h; y/ABCDEFGHIJKLMNOPQRSTUVWXYZ/abcdefghijklmnopqrstuvwxyz/
# match lines that contain the search term 'sophie'
/sophie/ {
i\
vvvvvvvvvvvv
a\
^^^^^^^^^^^^
}
# restore original input from the hold space, and print it
x
```

Let's examine the script. First, lines starting with the hash (#) symbol are treated as comments and ignored by sed.

The sed command does not provide a case-insensitive pattern match, so we employ the y function to convert the input line to lowercase, and later, we specify the search term in lowercase. Before we corrupt the input line, we must preserve it by copying it to the *hold space,* using function h. Note that neither function has a line range and, therefore, is applied to every line of input.

Next, we operate on all lines containing the text sophie. The line range is followed by a function list in {...}, meaning that every function inside the braces is applied to a matching line. The function i\ writes the text vvvvvvvvvvvv before the current line, and the function a\ writes the text ^^^^^^^^^^^^ after the current line. The text to be written must be on a new script line, as shown.

Finally, the function x exchanges the contents of the hold space with the current input line, effectively restoring our input to its original mixed-case form before sed writes it to the Terminal screen.

The text passage we'll be marking is in file `sophie.txt`.

```
$ cat sophie.txt
I hopped out of the car and promptly ate gravel. The
non-retracting seat belt had wrapped itself around my ankle
clearly attempting to do what Sophie failed to do during
the drive home - kill me. :-) Sophie rushed to my rescue,
helped me up, and brushed off the stones from my dress.
There are better ways to get "stoned"!
```

To mark the text, we invoke `sed`, and pass it the name of our script and the input file as arguments.

```
$ sed -f mark.script sophie.txt
I hopped out of the car and promptly ate gravel. The
non-retracting seat belt had wrapped itself around my ankle
vvvvvvvvvvv
clearly attempting to do what Sophie failed to do during
^^^^^^^^^^^
vvvvvvvvvvv
the drive home - kill me. :-) Sophie rushed to my rescue,
^^^^^^^^^^^
helped me up, and brushed off the stones from my dress.
There are better ways to get "stoned"!
```

Project 62
Learn Advanced awk

"What other advanced editing tasks can I accomplish with the awk command?"

This project covers three tasks that illustrate some of the more advanced editing capabilities of the awk text-processing language. Project 58 shows you how to apply such commands to a batch of files. Project 60 covers basic use of awk, and Projects 59 and 61 cover the sed command.

Process, Count and Report with awk

We'll illustrate some of the more advanced feature of awk through three tasks: processing a *CSV* (comma-separated-value) file, counting lines in a file, and analyzing and reporting on a file.

The awk processing language is a full-fledged programming language, providing variables, conditional statements, loops, and functions. It follows very closely the syntax of the C programming language (which has been adopted by other languages, such as PHP). The aim of this project is not to teach the language but simply to give a few examples of awk's capabilities.

Process a CSV File

A CSV file is a plain-text representation of a data table or spreadsheet, and most spreadsheet programs can write and read CSV files. A CSV file contains a table of values in which columns are separated by commas and rows are separated by line breaks. Because awk expects white space to be used as a field (or column) separator, we must tell it to expect a comma instead. Here's a simple example that extracts the field 2 (surname) and field 4 (position) from a CSV file. We specify the field separator by using option -F.

```
$ cat people.csv
scott,sheppard,mr,editor in chief,01
adrian,mayo,mr,editor,02
jan,forbes,miss,goddess,68
$ awk -F "," '{printf ("%-15s %s\n", $2,$4)}' people.csv
sheppard        editor in chief
mayo            editor
forbes          goddess
```

Internally to awk, the variable FS holds the field separator, and we could have set it directly within the script as an action to the BEGIN pattern (which matches the start of the file).

```
$ awk  'BEGIN {FS=","}; {printf ("%-15s %s\n", $2,$4)}' ¬
    people.csv
```

The field separator is actually a regular expression. Here's an example in which we specify a regular expression containing a list of possible separators.

```
$ cat people2.csv
scott:sheppard,mr,editor in chief-01
adrian:mayo,mr,editor-02
jan:forbes,miss,goddess-68
$ awk  'BEGIN {FS=",|:|-"}; {printf ¬
    ("%-15s %-15s Code %s\n", $2,$4, $5)}' people.csv
sheppard        editor in chief Code 01
mayo            editor          Code 02
forbes          goddess         Code 68
```

↗ LEARN MORE

See Project 77 if you are unfamiliar with regular expressions.

ⓘ TIP

The technique of setting the awk variable FS is handy when you wish to swap the field separator midway through a script. Identify a pattern that corresponds to the point in the text where the separator changes, and attach an action to it that resets the FS variable.

Count Lines

Take a look at this awk script, which counts the number of lines in a file and reports on which lines contain the text Sophie.

```
$ cat sophie.txt
I hopped out of the car and promptly ate gravel. The
non-retracting seat belt had wrapped itself around my ankle
clearly attempting to do what Sophie failed to do during
the drive home - kill me. :-) Sophie rushed to my rescue,
helped me up, and brushed off the stones from my dress.
There are better ways to get "stoned"!
$ awk 'BEGIN {n=0}
> {n=n+1}
> /Sophie/{printf("Line %d\n", n)}
> END {printf ("Total lines in file %d\n", n)}' sophie.txt
Line 3
Line 4
Total lines in file 6
```

This example demonstrates the use of awk variables. We set variable n to be 0 at the start of the script, using the BEGIN pattern. For each line read, we increment n and print the current line number if the line contains Sophie. Finally, at the end of the file, matched by the special pattern END, we print the total number of lines in the file.

Use Conditionals

Our final example shows the use of conditional statements in an awk script. Suppose that we have a file, posts.txt, that lists the members of a bulletin board and the number of posts each member has made to the board. Let's process this file to find who has made the most posts and print the names of all members who have made 50 or more posts. We'll write our awk script to a script file instead of typing it on the command line. Here's our test input file.

```
$ cat posts.txt
Mayo 50 posts
Forbes 35 posts
Sheppard 12 posts
Trevor 345678 posts
Hollis 17 posts
```

And here's our awk script, arbitrarily called script.awk.

```
$ cat script.awk
BEGIN { print "Fifty or more posts"; max = 0; name = ""}
{if ($2 >= 50) print $0}
{if ($2 > max) {max = $2; name = $1}}
END { printf ("Max posts %d by %s\n", max, name); print "---
"}
```

Lines 2 and 3 are if statements. Line 2 tests whether the number of posts (the value of field 2) is greater than or equal to (using the *relational operator* >=) our threshold value of 50, and if so, the code prints the input line. Line 3 tests whether the number of posts is greater than the maximum so far (set to 0 at the beginning), and if so, the code saves this value and the poster's name to the variables max and name.

```
$ awk -f script.awk posts.txt
Fifty or more posts
Mayo 50 posts
Trevor 345678 posts
Max posts 345678 by Trevor

---
```

⚓ TIP

The awk language has constructs that mirror those of the C programming language. Check the man page for more details.

➦ LEARN MORE

**Project 6 explains
redirection.**

Project 63
Editing Tips

"How do I format and embellish the output from my scripts?"

This project gives you some handy tips for editing files with commands not covered elsewhere in this chapter.

Edit with echo

The echo command provides a quick and easy way of adding a line of text to the end of an existing text file, or creating a new one-line file, without having to use a text editor. For example, to stop Terminal from beeping (see Project 45), add the appropriate line to ~/.inputrc as follows.

```
$ echo "set bell-style none" >> ~/.inputrc
```

It's important to use a double redirect symbol (>>), not a single one (>), when redirecting output to an existing file. The double redirect *appends* to the target file, whereas the single redirect creates a new file that overwrites any existing file of the same name.

Edit with cat

Using echo is fine for creating single-line files, but if you need to create a few-line file quickly, try the cat command instead. In the absence of an input filename, cat reads from the keyboard. Type the following, and finish by pressing Control-d to create a small file called jan.txt.

```
$ cat > jan.txt
Dear Janet,
Just a quickie to let you know
I'll be free...
Adrian<Control-d>
```

Edit with printf

Take advantage of the formatting capabilities of the `printf` command to create a file with consistently formatted lines.

The `printf` command uses a format string, which is a sequence of characters that will be displayed onscreen, interspersed with special placeholder sequences like `%s`. Following the format string, we must provide a value for each placeholder sequence.

We can take advantage of a neat feature of `printf`. If the number of arguments exceeds the number of placeholders, `printf` takes another sweep at the format string. Let's illustrate this by using `printf` to create an HTML table. We'll write a format string that expects two values and surround the `%s` placeholders with appropriate HTML tags.

Type the following command, providing six values, and you'll see that `printf` takes three sweeps at the format string.

```
$ printf "<tr>\n    <td>%s</td>\n    <td>%s</td>\n</tr>\n" ¬
    one 1 two 2 three 3
<tr>
    <td>one</td>
    <td>1</td>
</tr>
<tr>
    <td>two</td>
    <td>2</td>
</tr>
<tr>
    <td>three</td>
    <td>3</td>
</tr>
```

The character sequence \n tells `printf` to print a Newline.

We'll extend the example, employing a barrel-load of tricks to convert the output from the `ls` command to an HTML table. The table shows the filenames and sizes of all text files in the current directory.

First, instead of typing values on the command line, we generate them automatically by executing the command

```
$(ls -l *.txt | awk '{print $9, $5}')
```

This generates a long directory listing, using the awk command to filter fields 9 (the filename) and 5 (the file size). Surrounding the command with $(...) tells Bash to execute it and write the output back to the command line. The output from this command becomes the arguments to the main printf command. Additional printf commands before and after print HTML table tags. All output is redirected to the file list.html. Note that the entire sequence is encapsulated within (...) before the output is redirected. This is necessary; otherwise, the redirection is applied to only the last command.

```
$ ( printf "<table border='1'>\n";
> printf "<tr>\n    <th>Filename</th>\n    <th>¬
    Size</th>\n</tr>\n"
> printf "<tr>\n    <td>%s</td>\n    <td>%s</td>\n</tr>\n" ¬
    $(ls -l *.txt | awk '{print $9, $5}')
> printf "</table>\n") >list.html
```

Let's examine the file that this command generates.

```
$ cat list.html
<table border='1'>
<tr>
    <th>Filename</th>
    <th>Size</th>
</tr>

...

<tr>
    <td>jan.txt</td>
    <td>66</td>
</tr>
<tr>
    <td>sophie.txt</td>
    <td>348</td>
</tr>
</table>
```

That's a pretty nifty way to generate an HTML table from a directory listing, but let's take it further.

Here's a Bash function that creates HTML tables. It builds on what we have already done, additionally assigning the command sequence to a function that takes three parameters (in this order): our output filename, the first table header, and the second table header. If you are familiar with Bash functions and simple scripting, check it out.

```
$ htmltable () {
> filename="$1"; shift;
> h1=$1; h2=$2; shift; shift
> ( printf "<table border='1'>\n"
> printf "<tr>\n  <th>$h1</th>\n    <th>$h2</th>\n</tr>\n"
> printf "<tr>\n    <td>%s</td>\n    <td>%s</td>\n</tr>\n" $*
> printf "</table>\n") > $filename
> }
```

Let's use the function to build a table of ages, which are read from the file ages.

```
$ cat ages
Jan 27
Sophie 31
Jill 32
$ htmltable ages.html Name Age $(cat ages)
$ cat ages.html
<table border='1'>
<tr>
    <th>Name</th>
    <th>Age</th>
</tr>
<tr>
    <td>Jan</td>
    <td>27</td>
</tr>
<tr>
    <td>Sophie</td>
    <td>31</td>
```

code continues on next page

↗ LEARN MORE

Refer to Project 52 to learn more about Bash functions, and to Projects 9 and 10 for basic shell-scripting advice.

```
</tr>
<tr>
    <td>Jill</td>
    <td>32</td>
</tr>
</table>
$
```

Figure 7.1 shows how the table may look in a browser.

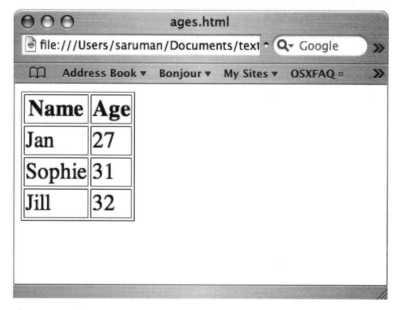

Figure 7.1 A function built around the `printf` command generated this HTML table, displayed here in Safari.

Edit with split

The `split` command breaks a large file into multiple smaller ones. To split `big-file.txt` into multiple files, each no bigger than 5KB, type

```
$ split -b5k big-file.txt
```

The resulting small files are named like this.

```
$ ls x*
xaa     xab     xac     xad     xae     xaf     xag     xah
```

To split a file limiting size by lines instead of bytes, type

```
$ split -l200 big-file.txt split_
```

The final argument, `split_`, tells `split` to replace the `x` prefix assumed in the previous example with `split_` when naming the output files.

Edit with paste

The `paste` command merges two files line by line. Here's an example to illustrate it.

```
$ cat f1
Line 1
Line 2
...
$ cat f2
rest of line 1
rest of line 2
...
$ paste f1 f2
Line 1 rest of line 1
Line 2 rest of line 2
...
```

↗ LEARN MORE

Check out some of the projects in Chapter 3. They show you how to view, search, sort, and compare text files.

Administer the System

8

This chapter introduces utilities, tricks, and tips for administering your Mac. Although Apple-supplied graphical utilities such as System Preferences and Disk Utility maintain Mac OS X, the relevant subsystems are also accessible via command-line tools. The 11 projects cover the following topics:

User accounts. Query and maintain user accounts through the Directory Services command-line tool.

Disks and discs. Use a combination of Unix and Apple tools to query, mount, unmount, and repair disk drives.

Scheduling. Schedule tasks to run at periodic intervals, and maintain the daily, weekly, and monthly periodic maintenance scripts.

Network. Query and change the network settings, and change the active network location, from the command line.

Project 64
Get Information about Users

"What's my name?"

This project covers standard Unix commands that report on user account information and active users. It covers the commands who, w, last, id, and groups. Project 65 covers Apple-supplied tools that manage user accounts. Project 7 explains the concepts behind users and groups, as well as user and group identification numbers (UIDs and GIDs).

Who's There?

To access a computer running Unix, you must have an account on that computer, identified by a username and password. When you boot your Mac and type your username and password at the login window, you are *logging in*. (If you don't type a username and password at startup, your Mac is set to log in automatically in System Preferences.)

There are other ways to log in, such as starting a new Terminal window or using Remote Login (ssh) on another Mac, or *host*. Unix allows each user many simultaneous logins, and many different users can be logged in concurrently. It provides several ways to discover who is currently logged in and who logged in previously.

Use the who and w commands to display who is currently logged in. The two commands are similar; w provides more information.

```
$ w
11:07 up 4 days, 2:13, 2 users, load averages:1.44 1.47 1.32
USER     TTY     FROM              LOGIN@  IDLE WHAT
saruman  console -                 15Jul05 24days -
saruman  p0      -                 10:55       - w
$ who
saruman  console Jul 15 12:56
saruman  ttyp0   Aug  9 10:55
```

The first line displayed by w is equivalent to results obtained from the uptime command. It reports how long your Mac has been running since the last restart, giving the load average over the past 1, 5, and 15 minutes. *Load average* is the average number of tasks queuing for processor time; a value of 1.00 indicates a well-used but not over-loaded system.

Both who and w list users who are logged in, and each indicates the TTY (TeleTYpe, or terminal) to which each login is attached. You'll always see the first two entries shown in the example above; console is the master terminal or, in the case of Mac OS X, the main log in under which the Finder, the Dock, and all other applications run.

The second line displayed by who, and the fourth displayed by w, shows the open terminal window used to issue the command itself. Start a new terminal window, and if you are able, log in from a remote machine too. You'll see an extra couple of lines displayed.

```
$ who
saruman   console   Jul 15 12:56
saruman   ttyp0     Aug  9 10:55
saruman   ttyp1     Aug  9 11:34
saruman   ttyp3     Aug  9 11:35 (saruman.wless)
```

The third line shows the login started by the new Terminal window; the fourth line shows the remote login and the IP address or host-name of the remote host.

Amnesia

A variant of who reminds you who you are and to which Terminal window the current login is attached. It's useful when you operate several user accounts or need to determine the current user from a shell script.

```
$ who am i
saruman   ttyp0     Aug  8 20:54
```

ⓘ TIP

To view a login history that has been archived, issue a command such as

```
$ (gzcat ¬
    /var/log/wtmp.0.gz ¬
    > tmp; last -f tmp; ¬
    rm tmp) | less
```

List Login History

Use the `last` command to list a history of logins, both closed and current.

```
$ last
loraine ttyp4                      Tue Aug 9 12:57    still logged in
saruman ttyp3 saruman.wlessTue Aug 9 12:11 - 12:57  (00:46)
saruman ttyp1                      Tue Aug 9 11:34    still logged in
saruman ttyp1                      Tue Aug 9 11:34 - 11:34  (00:00)
saruman ttyp0                      Tue Aug 9 10:55    still logged in
...
```

This information is held in the file /var/log/wtmp. The file is archived every month by periodic maintenance, as we discover by typing

```
$ grep -R  "wtmp" /etc/periodic/
/etc/periodic/monthly/500.monthly:for i in wtmp install...
```

(See Project 72 to learn about periodic maintenance.)

Report on Users and Groups

Project 7 explains that every user is identified by a username and a numeric user identity (UID). Every user belongs to at least one group (his self-named primary group) and may belong to any number of other groups. Like a user, a group has a name and a numeric group identity (GID).

The commands `id` and `groups` show this information about the current user or any other specified user. Let's check my (saruman's) credentials.

```
$ id
uid=501(saruman) gid=501(saruman) groups=501(saruman),
81(appserveradm), 79(appserverusr), 80(admin)
$ groups
saruman appserveradm appserverusr admin
```

This shows that my UID is 501 (username **saruman**) and my primary group is 501 (group name **saruman**). As an administrator user, I also belong to three other groups called appserveradm, appserverusr, and admin.

View the same information for other users, too—for example, the normal (nonadministrator) user loraine.

```
$ id loraine
uid=504(loraine) gid=504(loraine) groups=504(loraine)
$ groups loraine
loraine
```

If you wish to use this information in a shell script, try the following variations, which yield results more amenable to automatic processing.

Use option -u with id to display the UID of the specified user.

```
$ id -u saruman
501
```

Option -g displays the designated user's primary-group GID.

```
$ id -g loraine
504
```

Option -G displays all GIDs, in no particular order. Like the other id options, it assumes that the current user is intended if no username is given as an argument.

```
$ id -G
501 81 79 80
```

Add n to any of the id option codes above to display names instead of numbers. Can you see that command id -Gn is equivalent to command groups?

Project 65
Manage User Accounts

"How do I create a new Unix user or group from the command line?"

This project focuses on Apple's Directory Services Command Line (dscl) tool. This general-purpose utility is used to view and change Directory Services, where information regarding Unix user accounts and groups is held. The project covers the commands dscl, nifind, and nireport. Project 7 explains users, groups, and user and group identification numbers (UIDs and GIDs).

DIY UIDs and GIDs

The tools Apple includes with OS X for managing user accounts are adequate for many tasks, but they lack flexibility. The Accounts pane in System Preferences lets you create a new user account but does not give you the tools to create a user account with a specific UID, create a new group, or add a user to a new group. Similarly, the NetInfo Manager utility lets you view and change local user information but offers no easy method for creating and maintaining accounts. For those tasks, you need the power of Unix.

Account details are held in a local NetInfo database unless you are part of a network with centrally maintained user accounts. The examples in this project assume that account information is held on the local machine, not on a central server.

To let you view and change account information from the command line, and perhaps write your own shell scripts to create new users and groups, Apple provides the dscl tool and a few other commands, such as nifind and nireport. It would take a chapter or two to cover dscl in detail, so this project aims only to present some ideas and tips to get you started. As usual, man pages for the utilities provide additional information.

First, let's take a look at how we might view account information.

View Account Information

Type the following command to discover what information is maintained by dscl.

```
$ dscl . list /
AFPUserAliases
Aliases
Groups
...
Users
```

The first argument to dscl is the Directory Services *datasource*, which we'll always specify as dot (.) to mean the default NetInfo directory on the local machine. The second, list, is a dscl command to list information; the path / says to start at the root, or top level, of the information hierarchy. The results reveal that information is maintained on, among others, groups and users. Specify the paths /Users and /Groups to list all users and groups. (Paths used by dscl refer to the NetInfo database and have nothing to do with Unix filename paths.)

```
$ dscl . list /Users
amavisd
appowner
saruman
...
$ dscl . list /Groups
accessibility
admin
...
```

If we try to list /Users/saruman, we'll find that it contains no further paths.

```
$ dscl . list /Users/saruman
```

What it does contain is information about the user account saruman in the form of *property* and *values* pairs. We view this with the read command of dscl. To view the for user saruman, for example, type

```
$ dscl . read /Users/saruman
_shadow_passwd:

...

PrimaryGroupID: 501
RealName: Adrian Mayo

...
```

Similarly, to view comparable information for group admin, type

```
$ dscl . read /Groups/admin

...

PrimaryGroupID: 80
RealName: Administrators
RecordName: admin

...
```

This information, which corresponds to what you see in NetInfo Manager, is presented in the form

```
Property Name: Property Value
```

Report and Find

Two useful utilities, nireport and nifind, display account information.

The nireport command searches for specific properties across many paths. Display the UID, username, and shell for all users (path /users) by typing

```
$ nireport . /users uid name shell
-2      nobody   /usr/bin/false
0       root     /bin/sh
501     saruman  /bin/bash

...
```

The nifind utility reports on whether a particular path exists. We test whether user saruman exists by checking the path /users/saruman.

```
$ nifind  /users/saruman .
/users/saruman found in ., id = 92
```

When a path does not exist, nifind reports nothing.

```
$ nifind  /users/xxx .
$
```

(Note that users must be in lowercase, and nifind requires the data-source, dot, to be the last argument, not the first.)

Here's how we might employ nireport and nifind in a script. Let's assume that we are writing a script to create a new account with username testuser and UID 511. Every user's primary-group name and short username should be identical, as should their UID and primary GID, so our script must first check that no user or group already has been assigned our intended name or ID number.

The script extract below assumes that the shell variable user is set to the user's intended short name/primary-group name and that the shell variable uid is set to the UID/GID. (Script lines beginning with the hash mark [#] are *comments*, provided for the benefit of human readers and ignored by Unix.)

```
...
# search NetInfo for the given user - it should not exist
str="$(nifind /users/$user .)"
if [ ! -z "$str" ]; then
  echo "Error: User $user already exists"; exit
fi
# search NetInfo for the given uid - it should not exist
str="$(nireport . /users uid | grep -w $uid)"
if [ ! -z "$str" ]; then
  echo "Error: User ID $uid already exists"; exit
fi
# search NetInfo for the given group - it should not exist
str="$(nifind /groups/$user .)"
```

code continues on next page

❧ NOTE

Assign "500" UID numbers to new user accounts. Numbers below 500 are not recognized as user accounts by Apple's graphical interface and won't, for example, appear in the login window or the Accounts pane in System Preferences.

↗ LEARN MORE

Projects 9 and 10 introduce
shell scripts, and the
projects in Chapter 9 cover
the subject in more detail.

```
if [ ! -z "$str" ]; then
 echo "Error: Group $user already exists"; exit
fi
# search NetInfo for the given gid - it should not exist
str="$(nireport . /groups gid | grep -w $uid)"
if [ ! -z "$str" ]; then
 echo "Error: Group ID $uid already exists"; exit
fi
...
```

Change Account Information

To add or modify account information, we use `dscl` and its `create` command: Run `dscl` as user `root`, either via the `sudo` command or from a root shell gained by typing `sudo -s`. (See "How to Become the Root User" in Project 2.) The hash prompt, shown in place of a dollar sign in the examples below, signifies a root shell.

To create a new path, type a command such as

`# dscl . create /Path/name`

To add properties and values to the new path, type a command such as

`# dscl . create /Path/name property-name value`

Check that what you've done has worked correctly: Invoke `dscl` with the `list` and `read` commands described earlier, or view from NetInfo Manager.

We'll clarify this with some examples.

Create a New Group

Here's how we might create a new group called `testgroup`. First, we create the path `/Groups/testgroup` by typing (as root)

`# dscl . create /Groups/testgroup`

Then we add the necessary properties and their values. We've chosen a GID of 600.

```
# dscl . create /Groups/testgroup name testgroup
# dscl . create /groups/testgroup passwd "*"
# dscl . create /groups/testgroup gid 600
```

Naturally, we must first ensure that the group and its GID do not already exist. Check by hand or as part of a script, as in the examples given earlier.

Verify that our new group was created by typing

```
# dscl . read /Groups/testgroup
AppleMetaNodeLocation: /NetInfo/DefaultLocalNode
GeneratedUID: 3D5386BA-EBBA-4777-9211-A4842CE0BCEA
Password: *
PrimaryGroupID: 600
RecordName: testgroup
RecordType: dsRecTypeStandard:Groups
```

Add a User to a Group

To add information to an existing entry, we use the `dscl` command `merge`. To add a user to a group, for example, we merge the user's name into the `users` property of the group entry. If the `users` property does not already exist, it will be created; if it does exist, the new value will be added to the list of values already assigned to the property.

Let's add the users `saruman` and `loraine` to our new group.

```
# dscl . merge /Groups/testgroup users saruman
# dscl . merge /Groups/testgroup users loraine
```

Now check the group membership (it may take a few seconds for the newly added information to register).

```
$ groups
saruman appserveradm testgroup appserverusr admin
$ groups loraine
loraine testgroup
```

ⓘ TIP

Password fields contain a one-way hash encoding of the password (not the actual password, for obvious security reasons). A very short hash, like star (*), has no corresponding password and, therefore, can be assigned to "locked" accounts that should never be used as login accounts. A star hash is used for groups and for users such as www that exist only to run daemons.

↗ LEARN MORE

Project 64 covers the groups **command.**

ⓘ TIP

Add a user to the groups admin, appserveradm, *and* appserverusr *to make that user an administrator.*

Remove a User from a Group

To remove a user from a group, we delete the user's name from the users property. Select the delete command, and specify the path, property, and value to delete. To delete loraine from our new group, testgroup, type

```
# dscl . delete /Groups/testgroup users loraine
$ groups loraine
loraine
```

Change a User's Shell

To change information such as a user's shell, we use the dscl command change, and specify the path, property, and value to change. Because a path may contain a list of properties, it's necessary to specify the old value too. To change Loraine's shell from tcsh to bash, type

```
# dscl . change /Users/loraine shell /bin/tcsh /bin/bash
```

Create a New User

Creating a new user is more involved. We do the following:

- Verify that none of the steps we are about to perform will overwrite an existing user, group, UID, GID, or home directory.

- Create a new user by using dscl and its create command.

- Create a primary group with the same name as the user.

- If the new user is an administrator, add her to the groups admin, appserveradm, and appserverusr.

- Create a new home directory from the template home directory.

- Set a password for the new user.

Here's an example in which we create the user jan with a UID of 520.

```
$ sudo -s
Password:
```

First, we create the user.

```
# dscl . create /users/jan
# dscl . create /users/jan name jan
# dscl . create /users/jan passwd "*"
# dscl . create /users/jan uid 520
# dscl . create /users/jan gid 520
# dscl . create /users/jan home /Users/jan
# dscl . create /users/jan shell /bin/bash
# dscl . create /users/jan realname "Jan Forbes"
```

Then we create the group.

```
# dscl . create /groups/jan
# dscl . create /groups/jan name jan
# dscl . create /groups/jan passwd "*"
# dscl . create /groups/jan gid 520
```

Next, we create Jan's home directory by copying the English-language template home directory.

```
# mkdir /Users/jan
# ditto -rsrc /System/Library/User\ Template/¬
    English.lproj/ /Users/jan
```

We make the new directory owned by user jan and group jan.

```
# chown -R jan:jan /Users/jan
```

Finally, we set a password for the new account.

```
# passwd jan
Changing password for jan.
New password:
Retype new password:
```

If you examine entries for users created from System Preferences, you'll notice other (nonessential) properties that we haven't set here, such as picture and _shadow_passwd. They may be set in exactly the same manner.

You should be able to login as the new user from the login window. It may take a while for the new user to appear in the Fast User Switching menu.

Delete a Group or User

To delete a user or group, we use the `dscl` command `delete`, just as we did when removing a user from a group. It's not necessary to specify a property and value—just the path to the user or group to be deleted. The following command deletes all information associated with the group `testgroup`.

```
# dscl . delete /Groups/testgroup
```

Project 66
Manage File Systems

"How do I find out what local disks and remote volumes are mounted?"

This project explains what a file system is and then shows you how to list and obtain information about currently mounted file systems. It covers the commands lsvfs, df, and du. Projects 67 and 68 show what you can do with Apple's diskutil command.

Systems and Sharing

We think of a disk in terms of the files and directories it contains and perhaps other properties, such as owners, permissions, and file metadata. The way this information is represented on the disk is a consequence of the system software that creates, reads, and writes files on the disk. This software defines the type of *file system* employed on the disk. The native file system in Mac OS X is Apple's HFS+ (Hierarchical File System); in other Unix systems, it's UFS (Unix File System).

File systems are not limited to local drives. If we mount a *share* from another Mac by using AppleShare, another file system is needed to manage the remote volume in accordance with the protocol by which the local and remote machines communicate. In the case of AppleShare, the file system and the protocol are called AFP (Apple File Protocol).

List File Systems

Use the lsvfs command to list all file systems currently loaded (but not necessarily in use). For example:

```
$ lsvfs
Filesystem              Refs Flags
----------------------- ----- ---------------
ufs                     0 local
nfs                     5
fdesc                   1
cd9660                  0 local
union                   0
hfs                     3 local, dovolfs
volfs                   1
devfs                   1
afpfs                   2
webdav                  1
udf                     1 local
```

The Refs column refers to the number of currently mounted volumes (disks, partitions, and shares) of that file-system type. When a file system is flagged as local, it means that the device is attached to the local machine and not a remotely mounted share from another machine.

Reading the output from lsvfs, we see that the local file systems comprise no UFS volumes, no CD-ROMs (file system cd9660), three HFS+ volumes, and one DVD (file system udf). We also see three remote shares: two AppleShare (afpfs) mounts and a WebDAV mount. WebDAV is the protocol used by dot-Mac to mount your iDisk. The supposed five NFS (Network File System) shares reflect (I think) four NFS IO daemons launched at system startup and an FTP (File Transfer Protocol) server mounted by the Finder.

Note: The remainder (fdesc, union, volfs, and devfs) are special file systems that map device names to the device drivers in /dev and also manage the mysterious /.vol directory.

Discover Mounted Drives

The lsvfs command shows the active file systems and how many mounted volumes each of them services. Use df to discover what is actually mounted, displaying the device and its path, or *mount point*. The df command also displays the size and available capacity of each mounted volume. (Option -h displays the capacity data in human-readable form, with size-unit abbreviations; omit the flag to see how nonhumans read the data.)

```
$ df -h
Filesystem                  Size  ... Mounted on
/dev/disk0s3                234G  ... /
devfs                       100K  ... /dev
fdesc                       1.0K  ... /dev
<volfs>                     512K  ... /.vol
automount -nsl [188]          0B  ... /Network
automount -fstab [192]        0B  ... /automount/Servers
automount -static [192]       0B  ... /automount/static
/dev/disk1s3                 20G  ... /Volumes/Macintosh HD
/dev/disk1s5                129G  ... /Volumes/Backup-sauron
afp_0TQCUU0QrZsg00vJDV...    12G  ... /Volumes/saruman
afp_0TQCUU0QrZsg00vJDV...    12G  ... /Volumes/OSX-saruman
/dev/disk2                  4.9G  ... /Volumes/MONTY_PYTHON
https://secure/webdav/    -512.0B ... /Volumes/share
ftp://carcharoth           1.0G  ... /Volumes/carcharoth
```

The Mounted on column shows the Unix pathname of the mounted volume. The automount volumes control remote volumes that you'll observe below the Network icon in the top-left pane of the Mac OS X Finder.

↗ **LEARN MORE**

Projects 67 and 68 use the diskutil command to manage local drives and to manually mount and unmount them.

Mount Points

In Unix, a volume (disk, partition, or remote mount) does not have a name by which you reference it. This is at odds with the Mac OS X Finder, which gives all volumes names. In the Finder, mounted volumes such as CD-ROMs, external drives, and file servers are represented on a peer level with the system disk. In Unix, nothing is on a peer level with the system disk; all other volumes are mounted within it, and their pathnames are listed under its root.

When a disk is mounted, it mounts into a directory. This can be any directory anywhere on the file system but generally is one created specifically for the mount and named appropriately. Darwin automatically mounts all volumes at /Volumes/name-of-vol-in-Finder. A mounted volume named Backup-sauron, then, appears to the Unix command line as /Volumes/Backup-sauron.

ᵢ̆ TIP

To view information on just local drives, type

`$ df -lh`

ᵢ̆ TIP

To total the size of all files in a particular directory hierarchy, use the du command. To find the total size of all files in your home directory, for example, type

`$ du -hs ~`

To get a breakdown by directory, type

`$ du -hs ~/*`

You may use Apple's `diskutil` command to list mounted volumes, but it shows only local disk drives.

```
$ diskutil list
/dev/disk0
   #:                       type name           size    identifier
   0: Apple_partition_scheme                   *233.8 GB disk0
   1:       Apple_partition_map                 31.5 KB disk0s1
   2:                 Apple_HFS OSX-sauron     233.6 GB disk0s3
/dev/disk1
   #:                       type name           size    identifier
   0: Apple_partition_scheme                   *149.1 GB disk1
   1:       Apple_partition_map                 31.5 KB disk1s1
   2:                 Apple_HFS Macintosh HD    19.8 GB disk1s3
   3:                 Apple_HFS Backup-sauron  129.0 GB disk1s5
```

Project 67
Look after Your Disks

"Is there a command-line alternative to Apple's Disk Utility application?"

This project looks at the `diskutil` command. It's a command-line interface to Apple's Disk Management framework, providing the same functionality as the Disk Utility application. The project considers disk maintenance and presents examples verifying and repairing disks. Project 68 uses `diskutil` to mount and unmount local drives.

Take Command of Disks

We saw in Project 65 that there are Unix command-line equivalents to Apple's NetInfo Manager and the Accounts panel in System Preferences. There's also a Unix equivalent to the OS X Disk Utility tool: the `diskutil` command. In this case, the command-line tool can't claim more features than in its graphical counterpart, but its extra value lies in its capability to work within extended Unix commands and scripts.

The `diskutil` command can partition, format, mount and unmount drives, and verify and repair file systems. It can be used to manage any locally mounted drive, including internal drives, USB and FireWire drives, as well as removable media, such as CDs and DVDs. Where the Disk Utility application (in Applications:Utilities) is a graphical interface to Apple's Disk Management framework, `diskutil` is the command-line equivalent.

Get information on `diskutil` by typing either of the following.

```
$ man diskutil
$ diskutil
```

↗ **LEARN MORE**

Project 66 discusses file systems and includes a sidebar, "Mount Points," that compares Unix mount points with mounted volumes as seen by the OS X Finder.

For information on a specific diskutil command (or *verb*)—verifyVolume, for example—type

```
$ diskutil verifyVolume
```

You'll notice that most verbs operate on a volume. A volume may be identified by its mount point, disk identifier, or device node. We get this information by applying the verb list. Type

```
$ diskutil list
/dev/disk0
   #:                      type name         size   identifier
   0: Apple_partition_scheme             *233.8 GB disk0
   1:     Apple_partition_map             31.5 KB disk0s1
   2:              Apple_HFS OSX-sauron  233.6 GB disk0s3
/dev/disk1
   #:                      type name         size   identifier
   0: Apple_partition_scheme             *149.1 GB disk1
   1:     Apple_partition_map             31.5 KB disk1s1
   2:              Apple_HFS Macintosh HD  19.8 GB disk1s3
   3:              Apple_HFS Backup-sauron 129.0 GB disk1s5
```

Let's examine this output.

Information is displayed for every disk drive that's attached (even if it's not mounted); each listed disk is followed by an indented list of the disk's slices.

A disk is identified by its entry in the device directory /dev in the form /dev/diskn, where n is the disk number. Here, we see the main system disk (/dev/disk0) and an external FireWire drive (/dev/disk1).

If a disk is partitioned (*sliced*), each slice also has an entry in the device directory, identified by /dev/disknsm, where n is (still) the disk number, m is the slice number, and the s in between is just shorthand for "slice." The diskutil command does not show the full /dev entry, or *device node*, for each slice; instead, it uses a (slightly) shorter *device identifier* of the form disknsm (without the leading /dev/).

We see that the system drive has one partition named OSX-sauron. Its device node is /dev/disk0s3; its device identifier (shown in the identifier column on the right) is disk0s3. The FireWire drive has two partitions—Macintosh HD and Backup-sauron—at slices 3 and 5, respectively.

We obtain more information about a disk or a partition with the diskutil verb info. Here's how we might get information on the system partition (disk 0, slice 3).

```
$ diskutil info disk0s3
  Device Node:        /dev/disk0s3
  Device Identifier:  disk0s3
  Mount Point:        /
  Volume Name:        OSX-sauron

  File System:        Journaled HFS+
                      Journal size 8192k at offset 0xa701000
  ...
  Ejectable:          No
```

We could also have typed:

```
$ diskutil info /
$ diskutil info /dev/disk0s3
```

Verify and Repair a Volume

If you need to perform preventative disk maintenance, or report on the status of your disk drives, the diskutil command makes an ideal tool to incorporate into a shell script. Let's look at some examples that verify and repair a file system, and verify the OS X Unix permissions on the system volume.

Continuing on the system cited in the preceding examples, let's verify the file system on "Backup-sauron", which is disk1s5, using diskutil verb verifyVolume. The argument following the verb specifies the target volume, in this case by its mount point (/Volumes/Backup-sauron). We also could have used its device node, /dev/disk1s5, or

TIP

The commands df -l and mount also list information on local drives, including device-to-mount point mappings. They consider only mounted drives, not drives that are attached but unmounted.

NOTE

Every disk partition occupies one slice, but not every slice is a partition. A slice may contain device drivers or the partition map. The terms partition *and* volume *are interchangeable.*

☂ TIP

If a volume is not mounted, it can still be verified and repaired, but you must identify it by its disk identifier or device node.

device identifier, disk1s5. (You cannot specify an entire disk such as disk1; you must specify a particular volume.)

```
$ diskutil verifyVolume /Volumes/Backup-sauron/
Started verify/repair on volume disk1s5 Backup-sauron
Checking HFS Plus volume.
Checking Extents Overflow file.
Checking Catalog file.
Checking multi-linked files.
Checking Catalog hierarchy.
Checking volume bitmap.
Checking volume information.
The volume Backup-sauron appears to be OK.
Mounting Disk
Verify/repair finished on volume disk1s5 Backup-sauron
```

If diskutil reports errors, you should attempt to repair the volume by typing:

```
$ sudo diskutil repairVolume disk1s5
Password:
...
```

If you try to repair a mounted volume, diskutil will first attempt to un-mount the volume, which will fail if the volume is in use (a file is open or your current working directory lies within the volume). The system volume is *always* in use: To verify it, you must boot from an alternative system on another partition or drive, boot from a Mac OS X install disk, or use a third party disk repair program. (Note that prior to Mac OS X 10.4.3, it was not possible to verify the system volume.)

Verify Permissions

Verify the permissions on the system volume or on any volume that contains a Mac OS X system.

```
$ diskutil verifyPermissions /
Started verify/repair permissions on disk disk0s3 OSX-sauron
Determining correct file permissions.
We are using special permissions for the file or directory
./Library/Widgets.   New permissions are 16877
Permissions differ on ./Library, should be drwxrwxr-t , they
are drwxrwxr-x
Permissions differ on ./private/var/log/secure.log, should
be -rw------- , they are -rw-r-----
We are using special permissions for the file or directory
./usr/lib/php/build/acinclude.m4.  New permissions are 33060
The privileges have been verified or repaired on the
Verify/repair finished permissions on disk disk0s3 OSX-sa...
```

If problems are reported, reissue the command as `repairPermissions`.

Be Smart with diskutil

You can use `diskutil` to check any mounted drive's SMART status (described in the "Be Smart" section of Project 37). Let's do so, by employing the `grep` command to filter the relevant information from `diskutil` output. We are interested in lines that contain the text SMART—so that's the text we'll match with `grep`.

```
$ diskutil info disk0 | grep SMART
    SMART Status:          Verified
$ diskutil info disk1 | grep SMART
    SMART Status:          Not Supported
```

We check both drives and find that the external FireWire drive does not support SMART, but the main system drive does. The system drive's status is `Verified`, which is good, and the drive is healthy. If it reported `About to Fail`, it would be time to back up the disk and replace it.

⚓ TIP

A disk that is badly damaged may be beyond the repair capabilities of diskutil. *It's not lost forever, however: Third-party disk-repair utilities try much harder to fix disks and save data. The cost of such a program is usually less than the value of the recovered data.*

⚓ TIP

To manage disk images or burn them to optical media, look at Apple's hdiutil *tool. Use the* drutil *tool to burn CDs and DVDs.*

Project 68
Mount and Unmount
Local Disks

"How do I manually mount and unmount local file systems?"

This project presents examples that mount and unmount volumes on locally attached disk drives, including removable media. It employs both the traditional Unix commands `mount` and `umount`, as well as Apple's `diskutil` command. The `diskutil` command is a command-line interface to Apple's Disk Management framework, providing the same functionality as its Disk Utility application. Project 67 uses `diskutil` to verify and repair the integrity of file systems.

Manage Volumes Manually

Mac OS X automatically mounts disk drives and removable media such as CDs as they become available, and unmounts them at the click of a mouse. Mounted volumes are accessible from the command line in a directory named `/Volumes/name-of-drive`.

You'll rarely want to mount a volume manually, but occasionally, the situation arises. You may need to remount an external drive after unmounting (ejecting) it. I have a backup disk that's permanently attached for nightly backups, but I want it mounted only during the backup process. At other times, I prefer that it remain hidden and out of harm's way.

We'll look at two methods to mount and unmount volumes manually: the Unix `mount` and `umount` commands, which let you choose where in the file system a volume is mounted, and Apple's `diskutil`, which requires less work but gives you no choice in where a volume is mounted.

Use the Unix mount Command

Before we can mount a disk, we must discover its device node. The easiest method is to use `diskutil` to list all attached devices. Fortunately, `diskutil` lists *all* attached devices, not just those that are mounted.

To mount the volume labeled `Backup-sauron`, invoke `diskutil`, and filter its output by using the `grep` command.

```
$ diskutil list | grep "Backup-sauron"
   3:        Apple_HFS Backup-sauron   129.0 GB   disk1s5
```

From this (and from reading Project 67), we conclude that the device node is `/dev/disk1s5`. We mount the volume by typing

```
$ mount /dev/disk1s5 /Backup
/dev/disk1s5 on /Backup: No such file or directory
```

... but fail to do so! Because `mount` lets you choose the mount point, you are left to your own devices (pun intended) to create the mount point. You may mount at any point in the file system; choose a suitable one, and create an appropriately named *directory*. We choose to mount the drive at the root of the file system in a directory called `/Backup`.

```
$ mkdir /Backup
$ mount /dev/disk1s5 /Backup
/dev/disk1s5 on /Backup: Incorrect super block.
```

Foiled again! The `mount` command assumes that a volume is formatted as UFS (Unix File System), whereas Mac OS X uses Apple's HFS+. Let's try again, specifying the appropriate file system. Type either of the following.

```
$ mount -t hfs /dev/disk1s5 /Backup
$ mount_hfs /dev/disk1s5 /Backup
```

Check that the mount was successful. The mount-point directory is replaced by the mounted volume and takes on the permissions assigned to the top level of that volume.

```
$ ls -ld /Backup
drwxrwxr-t  31 root  admin  1156 Jun 24 13:21 /Backup
$ ls /Backup
Applications    Users       mach.sym
Desktop DB      Volumes     mach_kernel
Desktop DF      automount   private
...
```

↗ LEARN MORE

Project 67 shows how to use `diskutil` **to list attached drives and identify a drive or partition by its mount point, its device identifier, or its device node.**

ℹ **TIP**

After you mount a volume, you'll notice that the mount *command reports various options as disabled, such as* nodev *and* nosuid. *That's a security measure. To enable those options, you must mount the volume as the root user with the* sudo *command. Check the man page for* mount *to learn more about these options. The SUID bit is explained in "The s-bit" in Project 8.*

To view all currently mounted file systems, invoke the mount command with no arguments. We should see our new mount at the end of the list.

```
$ mount
/dev/disk0s3 on / (local, journaled)
...
/dev/disk1s5 on /Backup (local, nodev, nosuid, journaled,
mounted by saruman)
```

Unmount Drives

To unmount a volume, specify either the device node or the mount point to the umount command.

```
$ umount /dev/disk1s5
$ umount /Backup
```

Don't forget to remove the directory too (although there's no harm in leaving it for the next time you mount the volume).

```
$ rmdir /Backup/
```

Show in the Finder

Mounting a volume from the Unix mount command does so behind the Finder's back. If you wish the mounted volume to show up in the Finder, tell it to refresh its list of mounted volumes by typing

```
$ disktool -r
Refreshing Disk Arbitration ...
```

(The disktool command is supposedly obsolete, but I don't know of any other way to refresh the Finder.) One problem you may encounter after letting the Finder know about a mount: When you unmount the volume, it might be busy.

```
$ umount /Backup
umount: unmount(/Backup): Resource busy
```

If this is the case, you'll have to unmount it by using either the Finder or diskutil (examples of which are given later in this project).

Mount a CD or DVD

Mounting a CD or DVD is similar to mounting any other volume. Here's an example that mounts an audio CD.

First, pop in a CD, which will be mounted automatically by Mac OS X. Before we mount the CD, we have to unmount it manually, but without ejecting it. To do this, use the `df` command to determine its device node, which in this example is /dev/disk2, and unmount it. Also, tell the Finder to refresh its list of mounted volumes.

```
$ df
Filesystem      512-blocks ... Capacity   Mounted on
/dev/disk0s3    489972528 ...       22%   /
...
/dev/disk1         965307 ...      100%   /Volumes/Hot Fuss
$ sudo umount /dev/disk1
Password:
$ disktool -r
Refreshing Disk Arbitration ...
```

To mount the CD, we note that the file system on audio CDs is CD-DA, and we choose the mount command mount_cddafs (or mount -t cddafs).

```
$ mkdir /Audio_CD
$ mount_cddafs /dev/disk1 /Audio_CD
$ ls /Audio_CD
1 Jenny Was A Friend Of Mine.aiff   5 All These Things ...
10 Midnight Show.aiff               6 Andy, You're A St...
11 Everything Will Be Alright.aiff  7 On Top.aiff
2 Mr. Brightside.aiff               8 Glamourous Indie ...
3 Smile Like You Mean It.aiff       9 Believe Me Natali...
4 Somebody Told Me.aiff
```

Unmount the CD in the normal manner, and use `diskutil` to eject it.

```
$ umount /Audio_CD
$ ls /Audio_CD
$
$ diskutil eject /dev/disk1
Disk /dev/disk1 ejected
$ rmdir /Audio_CD/
```

CD Formats

A CD can be formatted for any of several file systems: audio, enhanced audio with multiple partitions, CD-ROM, data CDs formatted as Apple's HFS+ file system, and so on. You'll use different mount types for the different file systems.

Type

`$ ls /sbin/mount*`

to display a list of the mount variants.

To mount a DVD, we perform the same steps as those for mounting a CD, except that we specify the file system as cd9660.

```
$ sudo umount /dev/disk1
Password:
$ disktool -r
Refreshing Disk Arbitration ...
$ mkdir /DVD
$ mount_cd9660 /dev/disk1 /DVD
$ ls /DVD
VIDEO_TS
$ umount /DVD
$ ls /DVD
$ diskutil eject /dev/disk1
```

Manage On-Disk Permissions

After mounting a volume, it's wise to ensure that Unix permissions are enabled. They are not necessarily enabled on a non-system volume, especially on an external drive. Select a volume in the Finder, and press Command-i (or choose File > Get Info). At the bottom of the info window, you'll see a check box labeled Ignore Ownership on This Volume. There's a command-line alternative to checking and unchecking this box, called vsdbutil. For instructions on using this (badly documented) command, specify option -h.

```
$ vsdbutil -h
Usage: vsdbutil [-a path] | [-c path ] [-d path] [-i]
  -a adopts (activates) on-disk permissions on the spec...
  -c checks the status of the permissions usage on the ...
  -d disowns (deactivates) the on-disk permissions on t...
  -i initializes the permissions database to include al...
```

Switch on *(adopt)* permissions by typing

```
$ sudo vsdbutil -a /The-mount-point-here
```

Use the diskutil Tool

Using `diskutil` to mount and unmount volumes is easier than using the Unix `mount` and `umount` commands. It takes care of creating and deleting the mount-point directory. You do not have the flexibility to choose where a particular volume is mounted, however. It will always be mounted at /Volumes/name-of-volume.

Here's an example in which we use `diskutil` to mount and unmount the volume *Backup-sauron*. First, we determine the device identifier. (We could also specify the device node.)

```
$ diskutil list | grep "Backup-sauron"
   3:       Apple_HFS Backup-sauron   129.0 GB   disk1s5
```

Mount the volume by typing

```
$ diskutil mount disk1s5
Volume disk1s5 mounted
$ ls /Volumes
Backup-sauron OSX-sauron
```

To unmount the volume, type

```
$ diskutil unmount /Volumes/Backup-sauron
Volume /Volumes/Backup-sauron unmounted
```

The `diskutil` command can mount and unmount entire disks in a single command, in which every volume (partition) on the disk is mounted or unmounted. Here's an example in which we mount and then unmount both partitions on `disk1`.

```
$ diskutil mountDisk /dev/disk1
$ diskutil unmountDisk /dev/disk1
Disk /dev/disk1 unmounted
```

This technique is also applicable to CDs and DVDs. Additionally, to eject a CD or DVD, type a command such as

```
$ diskutil eject disk2
Disk disk2 ejected
```

TIP

Manually mounting and unmounting volumes can confuse the Finder. Issue the command `disktool -r`*, or relaunch the Finder (force quit) to unconfuse it.*

NOTE

The older `disktool` *command is depreciated in favor of* `diskutil`*.*

➹ LEARN MORE

Refer to Project 8 to learn about Unix permissions and Project 7 to learn about users and groups.

Project 69
Delete Immutable Files

"Why can't I delete a particular file, even as the root user?"

This project gives some tips on how you might delete a file that appears to be indestructible, and covers the chflags command. It explains permissions in terms of the Unix flags, which supplement the normal permissions covered in Projects 7 and 8.

Immutable Files

You're probably familiar with the concepts of Unix users, groups, and permissions, but you're less likely to have encountered Unix *flags:* settings that can give files special attributes. Flag attributes include *immutable,* which prevents deleting or changing a file in any way, and *append only,* which allows content to be added to a file but forbids changing information that the file already contains. Each of these attributes comes in two flavors: user level and system level. *User-level* attributes govern how normal users may access the file; *system-level* attributes apply to the root user too.

To switch attribute flags on and off, use the chflags command. (Read the man page for chflags to see a list of all the supported flags.) Let's look at an example in which we lock a file so that it cannot be written to or deleted by any user other than root.

As an example, create the file immutable, and set the *user immutable* (uchg) flag.

```
$ touch immutable
$ chflags uchg immutable
```

To see which flags are set on a file, use the ls command with options -o and the usual -l. You'll notice the text uchg just after the file owner and associated group saruman.

```
$ ls -ol immutable
-rw-r--r-- 1 saruman saruman uchg 0 Aug 13 12:36 immutable
```

Despite the owner's having write permission for the file `immutable`, it cannot be written to or deleted, by the owner or by any user other than root. Let's attempt to write to the file and remove it.

```
$ echo "Change me" >> change
-bash: change: Operation not permitted
$ rm immutable
override rw-r--r--  saruman/saruman uchg for immutable? y
rm: immutable: Operation not permitted
```

Attempting to edit the file with a text editor such as `nano` will also fail.

To unset the immutable flag, use `chflags`, but add `no` to the name of the flag we previously set.

```
$ chflags nouchg immutable
$ ls -lo immutable
-rw-r--r--  1 saruman saruman  - 0 Aug 13 12:36 immutable
```

We may now change the file and delete it.

```
$ echo "Change me" >> immutable
$ rm immutable
```

The undeletable flag (`uunlnk`) is not supported by the HFS+ file system used by Mac OS X.

```
$ chflags uunlnk delete
chflags: invalid flag: uunlnk
```

System Immutable

Here's an example in which we set the *system immutable* flag.

! WARNING

BE WARNED—read the whole of this section before deciding to try out the example.

¶ NOTE

The Finder uses the user immutable flag when it locks a file. Setting and unsetting the flag is the same as checking and unchecking the Locked box in the Finder's Get Info window.

ⁱ TIP

The append flag allows a file to be extended by adding text to the end of the file but not changing it in any other way. Because of the way most applications open and write to a file, append behaves just like immutable. You'll find, however, that append works well when applied to log files (Projects 41 and 42).

Let's create a file called `sys-immutable` and set the system immutable flag by using the `chflags` command. Only the root user may set system flags, so we issue `chflags` from the `sudo` command.

```
$ touch sys-immutable
$ sudo chflags schg sys-immutable
Password:
$ ls -ol sys-immutable
-rw-r--r--  1 saruman   saruman   schg 0 13 Aug 11:06
sys-immutable
```

As you might expect, we cannot delete the file, even as the root user.

```
$ sudo rm sys-immutable
override rw-r--r--   saruman/saruman schg for sys-immutable? y
rm: sys-immutable: Operation not permitted
```

To remove it, we must first unset the system immutable flag.

```
$ sudo chflags noschg sys-immutable
chflags: schange: Operation not permitted
```

This is *not* what we intended to happen. Even the root user is not allowed to unset the system immutable flag—or, therefore, to change or delete the file. Ever!

Here's why: When your Mac is running in multi-user mode (the normal operating mode; multiple users can share the system simultaneously), it's operating at *run level 1*. There are some operations that even root is not permitted to do at run level 1, such as turn off the system flags. The only way to achieve this is to run at *run level 0,* and the only way to run at level 0 is to operate in what's termed *single-user mode.*

Boot into Single-User Mode

To enter single-user mode, reboot your Mac, and hold down the `Command-s` key combination as it starts up. Keep the combination held down until you see a dark screen with scrolling white text. When the text stops scrolling, you'll have a root shell and will be running a minimal system. The root user in single-user mode (run level 0) is even more all-powerful than the root user in multi-user mode (run level 1).

Follow these instructions to unset the system immutable flag.

First, mount the file system as writeable (it's currently mounted as read only) by typing

```
$ mount -uw /
```

Next, change to the appropriate directory, and issue the `chflags` command.

```
$ cd /Users/saruman/...
$ chflags noschg sys-immutable
```

Finally, reboot by typing

```
$ reboot
```

When running normally again, you should be able to delete the file by typing

```
$ rm sys-immutable
```

ᵢ̈ TIP

If you have a file whose name contains odd characters that you cannot type, rename it by typing the first part of the filename and using tabbed completion to complete the filename.

```
$ mv cafe<Tab>
$ mv cafe\314\201 cafe
```

In situations where the typeable portion of the filename is not unique, discover the file's i-node with `ls` *and option* `-i`.

```
$ ls -i caf*
1073337 caf??   1073329
caf???
```

Then use a command such as

```
$ find . -inum 1073337 ¬
    -maxdepth 1 -exec ¬
    mv {} cafe \;
```

to rename it.

Project 70
Schedule Commands with at

"How do I schedule a shell script to run at 6:30 tomorrow morning?"

This project takes advantage of the Unix at command to schedule a job (a command or shell script) to run at a specific time. It shows you how to enable at, add jobs, and manage the jobs queue. It covers the commands at, atq, atrm and launchctl. Project 71 covers periodic scheduling with the system cron daemon. Project 72 covers periodic maintenance controlled by Apple's Launch Daemon.

The at Queue

The at command manages a queue of jobs, each scheduled to run on a particular date at a particular time. After each job is run, it's removed from the queue, so at is typically used for one-shot operations that need to occur at predetermined times. (Recurring tasks are better handled by the cron command, discussed in Project 71.)

You may add many jobs to the at queue, and each will be run at its scheduled time. If you change your mind about running a job, you can view the at queue and delete the job from it.

The default Mac OS X install has at disabled, so before we can use it, our first task is to enable it. How you enable at depends on whether you're running Mac OS X 10.4 (Tiger) or an earlier version of the operating system. We'll look at the Tiger case first.

The at command itself is scheduled to run every 5 minutes, at which time it checks its job queue for due jobs. It's launched by Apple's Launch Daemon, launchd, but is disabled by default "due to power-management concerns," according to the at man page. To enable it, we use the launchctl command, specifying subcommand load to load the configuration file for that service. The option -w removes the "disabled" key and writes the altered configuration file back to disk.

Type the following `launchctl` command, which you issue as the root user using `sudo`, and give your administrator password when prompted.

```
$ sudo launchctl load -w ¬
   /System/Library/LaunchDaemons/com.apple.atrun.plist
Password:
```

You might like to check the Launch Daemon configuration file for `at`, which is written to this file:

```
/System/Library/LaunchDaemons/com.apple.atrun.plist
```

Use a text editor, or if you have installed the Developer Tools, double-click the file to open it in the Property List Editor application. In either case, you'll see a property called `StartInterval` set to 300. This tells Launch Daemon to launch `at` once every 300 seconds (5 minutes). The default install also has a property called `Disabled` set to `Yes` or `True`, but we just removed it by issuing the `launchctl` command.

In versions of OS X before Tiger, `at` was enabled by the more traditional Unix method of adding a line to the system `cron` table. Add the following line to the file `/etc/crontab`. Edit the file as the root user.

```
*/5    *    *    *    *     root    /usr/libexec/atrun
```

(The line is probably already in the file but commented out. If so, remove the # character from the start of the line.)

Also, if it does not already exist, create the file `/var/at/at.deny` by typing

```
$ sudo touch /var/at/at.deny
```

Schedule a Job

Schedule a simple test command typed from the keyboard to test that `at` has been successfully enabled. Choose a time in the near future, and type the following (or something similar); then press `Control-d`,

ⓘ TIP

To disable `at`, *issue the same command you used to enable it, but specify subcommand* `unload` *instead of* `load`.

↗ LEARN MORE

`cron` **is discussed in Project 71.**

↗ LEARN MORE

Chapter 4 covers several Unix text editors.

TIP

The actual script that at generates to run a job resides in the directory /var/at/jobs. It's plain text, so you can display it by using cat or a similar command. You'll notice that each job is written as a shell script that reproduces the environment and current working directory at the time when the job was created.

which means "end of input." When the job runs, it creates a file called ~/at-is-running.

```
$ at  18:18
/usr/bin/touch ~/at-is-running
<Control-d>
job 1 at Sat Aug 13 18:18:00 2005
```

Check that the job is queued by issuing the atq command.

```
$ atq
1       Sat Aug 13 18:18:00 2005
```

Wait until the designated time (or up to 5 minutes after, because at itself is scheduled to run only every 5 minutes); then see whether the designated file was created.

Write the Job to a File

We can write a more complex job to a file and have at read the file. In the next example, we use the rsync command to copy updated files to a backup disk. Here's the file, called at-backup.

```
$ cat at-backup
/usr/bin/rsync  --delete --archive --update -E
/Users/saruman/Desktop/ /Users/saruman/Desktop2/
```

Add the job to the queue by using at with option -f, followed by the name of the file.

```
$ at -f at-backup 18:56
job 2 at Sat Aug 13 18:56:00 2005
```

Remove a Job

To remove a job from the queue before it's executed, use the atrm command, and give the job number as an argument.

```
$ atq
3       Sat Aug 13 19:10:00 2005
$ atrm 3
```

Capture Output from a Job

When a job is executed, any output it may produce is captured and mailed to you. Use the Unix `mail` command to view the mail, or simply view it directly with a text editor; you'll find it in a file called `/var/mail/your-user-name`. To throw away all output, redirect standard output and standard error to `/dev/null` by appending `&> /dev/null` to the end of the command.

To redirect output to a file, append `&> at.out` (or any other filename) to the end of the command. When the job executes, it sees the same working directory that was current when the job was scheduled.

Specify Dates

Here are some examples in which we specify dates and times for `at` to run jobs.

```
$ at -f at.example 10:15 14.08.05
job 9 at Sun Aug 14 10:15:00 2005
$ at -f at.example 10:15 Aug 15
job 11 at Mon Aug 15 10:15:00 2005
$ at -f at.example now + 1 hour
job 14 at Sun Aug 14 01:39:00 2005
```

⏌ LEARN MORE

Project 6 shows you how to redirect output.

Amusing at Anecdotes

Time travel:

```
$ at -f at.example ¬
   10:15 14.08.04
```

```
at: trying to travel
back in time
```

Pedantic, but the job is accepted.

```
$ at -f at.example ¬
   10:15 +1 days
```

```
at: pluralization is
wrong
```

```
job 10 at Mon Aug 15
10:15:00 2005
```

Project 71
Schedule Commands with cron

"How do I schedule a shell script to run at 8:30 every morning so my boss will think I arrive at work on time?"

This project uses the Unix cron daemon and the crontab command to schedule jobs to be run at periodic intervals. It shows you how to schedule both system jobs and jobs that belong to individual user accounts. Project 70 covers one-off scheduling with the at command. Project 72 covers periodic maintenance controlled by Apple's Launch Daemon.

Schedule a Job

The cron daemon is automatically enabled in a default Mac OS X installation. It runs continually and each minute checks its schedules (crontabs) to see whether any jobs are ready to run. When a job has been run, it's not removed from the schedule but remains to be executed at the next occurrence of the specified interval. We might schedule a job to run at a specific time, such as 8:30 a.m. every day, or every Monday, or on the first of every month.

To schedule jobs with cron, you need only edit or create a crontab specifying what to run and when to run it. Each user can create her own crontab; additionally, cron supports a system crontab in a file maintained by the root user.

Let's test cron by scheduling a simple command that creates the file /cron-on. We'll look at adding jobs to the system crontab first and then consider user crontabs. Here's what the system crontab looks like (it's empty except for comments that start with a # character).

```
$ cat /etc/crontab
# The periodic and atrun jobs have moved to launchd jobs
# See /System/Library/LaunchDaemons
#
# minute   hour    mday    month   wday    who      command
```

The last line is there to remind you of the required format of each job you add. We schedule a job by adding a line to this file, entering an appropriate value in each column to specify the time and date on which the job will be run, which user the job should be run as, and the job itself. The job may be a command written directly to the crontab or the filename of a shell script to execute.

Edit the system crontab file /etc/crontab, using a Unix text editor such as nano. Because the root user owns the system crontab file, we must issue the command by using sudo and give an administrator password when prompted.

```
$ sudo nano /etc/crontab
Password:
```

Choose a suitable time in the near future, and add a line such as the one shown in the following output. You may separate columns with spaces or tabs.

```
$ cat /etc/crontab
...
# minute hour mday month wday who   command
30       15   *    *     *    root /usr/bin/touch /cron-on
```

We scheduled our simple job to run at 15:30 hours. The three date columns contain stars, which are taken to mean *every*. Our job will be run at 15:30 every day. The job will be run as user root, executing the command /usr/bin/touch /cron-on. At the designated time, the file /cron-on should be created.

If you were to delete the file by typing

```
$ sudo rm /cron-on
```

it would be recreated tomorrow at 15:30. To cancel the job, edit the file /etc/crontab, and remove the line you just added.

cron in Tiger

Whereas versions of Mac OS X before version 10.4 (Tiger) launch cron at system startup, Tiger uses Apple's Launch Daemon to launch cron on demand. Under Tiger, cron won't run until you populate the system crontab file in /etc/crontab or a user defines her own crontab.

This difference is transparent to the user.

↗ LEARN MORE

Read the projects in Chapter 4 if you are not familiar with any Unix text editor.

↗ LEARN MORE

Project 6 shows you how to redirect output.

⌄ TIP

To throw away all output that's not redirected, instead of having it mailed, set the MAILTO *environment variable to null by adding the line* MAILTO="" *toward the start of* /etc/crontab.

⌄ TIP

You may prefix a command with @AppleNotOnBattery *to tell* cron *not to run the command when functioning on battery power.*

⌄ TIP

Learn all about the format of a crontab file by typing

```
$ man 5 crontab
```

Capture Output from a Job

When a job is executed, output is captured and mailed to you. Use the Unix mail command to view it, or simply view the mail directly with a text editor; you'll find it in a file called /var/mail/your-user-name. To throw away all output, redirect standard output and standard error to /dev/null by appending &> /dev/null to the end of the command. To run a backup script and throw away all output, including errors written to standard error, we might add a line such as

```
30 20 * * * root /usr/local/sbin/backup-script &>/dev/null
```

To redirect output to a file, append &> cron.out (or any other filename) to the end of the command. We might execute the date command, for example, and write the output to the file cron-date in the user's home directory. Note that in this case, we requested that the job be run as user saruman; consequently, the file will be written to that user's home directory and will be owned by saruman.

```
30    15    *    *    *    saruman    date &> ~/cron-date
```

Specify Dates

Here are some more examples that specify a time and date on which to launch a job.

Run job1 at 4:30 in the morning every Saturday.

```
30    4    *    *    6    root    job1
```

Run job2 at 5:30 in the morning on the first of each month.

```
30    5    1    *    *    root    job2
```

The time fields can be more complex than simple numbers. To run job3 at 11 a.m., 4 p.m., and 8 p.m., use

```
0    11,16,20    *    *    *    root    job3
```

To run job3 every n minutes, or hours, or days, and so on, use the notation */n in the appropriate column. To run job3 every 10 minutes, we might specify

```
*/10    *    *    *    *    root    job3
```

In place of the five number fields, cron can interpret special strings like "@weekly" to mean "once a week."

User Crontabs

You can maintain your own personal crontab. The format of its job line is the same as the system crontab's, except the who field is omitted; you may run a job only as yourself. Use the crontab command to define your crontab. I recommend that you maintain your crontab schedule in a file. You can edit the file whenever you want to change the cron schedule and then load the file into your personal crontab whenever it's changed.

Let's create such a file. We'll specify a single job that executes the date command every minute, writing the current time and date to the file ~/user-crontest. Here's our file.

```
$ cat my-crontab
*/1    *    *    *    *    date &>~/user-crontest
```

Now load the file into your crontab by typing

```
$ crontab my-crontab
```

To examine our crontab, type

```
$ crontab -l
*/1    *    *    *    *    date &>$HOME/user-crontest
```

To delete (remove) it, type

```
$ crontab -r
```

Rotating Log Files

To ensure that log files do not grow indefinitely, they are rotated. Rotation involves compressing the file and archiving it under a name such as system.log.gz.0. A formerly archived log file of that name is first renamed system.log.gz.1; the old 1 file in turn is renamed 2, 2 is renamed 3, and so on, thus keeping an archive of older log files. The oldest file is overwritten without being renamed. Type

```
$ ls /var/log
```

and you'll see the archived log files.

Project 72
Manage Periodic Maintenance

"Does Unix dust and polish?"

This project covers periodic maintenance. It shows you how Unix manages routine housekeeping tasks such as deleting temporary files and rebuilding databases; it also shows you how these tasks can be extended to include locally defined maintenance. Project 70 covers one-off scheduling with the at command. Project 71 covers periodic scheduling with the system cron daemon.

The Maintenance Scripts

A file system will become cluttered and dated if it is not cleaned periodically; Mac OS X has several shell scripts for this purpose. Specifically, it has daily, weekly, and monthly scripts that run (dare I say it?) daily, weekly, and monthly. The scripts are launched automatically, in the background and without user intervention. Even though this happens automatically, it's good to know how maintenance works and how to change or extend it when necessary.

The standard Mac OS X maintenance scripts perform the following tasks:

▶ Daily removes old crash-log files, temporary and junk files; backs up the local NetInfo database; rotates the system log files; and runs the local daily-maintenance script.

▶ Weekly updates the locate database (Project 15) and the whatis database (Project 3); rotates the ftp, lookupd, lpr, mail, netinfo, hwmond, ipfw, ppp, and secure log files in the directory /var/log; and runs the local weekly-maintenance script.

▶ Monthly rotates the wtmp, install, and fax log files, and runs the local monthly-maintenance script.

The periodic Command

Maintenance scripts are run as the root user from the `periodic` command. Apple's Launch Daemon issues the necessary commands at specific intervals as

```
periodic daily
periodic weekly
periodic monthly
```

The `periodic` command looks in the appropriate directory within `/etc/periodic` and executes all scripts it finds there. When given the argument *daily*, for example, it looks for scripts in `/etc/periodic/daily/`. List all such script files by typing

```
$ ls -R /etc/periodic
```

When a periodic script runs, it writes an audit trail to a file in `/var/log`: `daily.out`, `weekly.out`, or `monthly.out`. Examine these by using the `less` command or any text editor.

Add Your Own Maintenance

It's very easy to add your own maintenance tasks to the daily, weekly, and monthly scripts. Each script runs a corresponding local script called `/etc/daily.local`, `/etc/weekly.local`, or `/etc/monthly.local`. Commands added to those local files become part of the regular maintenance tasks. If the local script file does not already exist, create it.

Launching Maintenance Scripts

The way in which maintenance scripts are launched depends on whether you're running Mac OS X 10.4 (Tiger) or any system before Tiger. We'll look at Tiger first.

The `periodic` command is launched by Apple's Launch Daemon. You might like to check the Launch Daemon configuration settings that

---

⚉ TIP

The `periodic` command can be configured. It executes a script from the file `/etc/defaults/periodic.conf` to set up the environment before it executes each maintenance script. Find out more by typing

```
$ man 5 periodic.conf
```

◣ NOTE

Never change the Apple-supplied scripts when adding your own maintenance commands: Use the local versions in `/etc/*.local`. It's possible that the scripts supplied by Apple will be overwritten by a future software update.

⬈ LEARN MORE

Projects 9 and 10 introduce shell scripting, and the projects in Chapter 9 cover the subject in more detail.

⤢ LEARN MORE

**Project 40 talks about
process priority and the
nice command.**

⤢ LEARN MORE

**The cron daemon and
crontabs are discussed in
Project 71.**

run each of the three scripts. They are located in the following files in
the directory /System/Library/LaunchDaemons/.

```
com.apple.periodic-daily.plist
com.apple.periodic-weekly.plist
com.apple.periodic-monthly.plist
```

Use a text editor, or if you have installed the Developer Tools,
double-click a file to open it in the Property List Editor (PLE) application. In either case, you'll see a property called StartCalendar
Interval with subproperties Hour, Minute, Day, and Weekday. These
subproperties state the time and date on which the script will be run.
A property that is not specified is read as *every*. A missing Day property, for example, is taken to mean *every day*.

Examining these files, you'll see that the daily script is run at 3:15 in
the morning every day, because no day is specified. The weekly script
is run at 3:15 on a Saturday (day 6), and the monthly script is run at
5:30 on the first of every month. If your Mac is not switched on
when a script is scheduled to run, the script will be run when your
Mac is next started.

You'll also notice that other options are provided, such as running the
task at a low priority by specifying a *nice* value.

In versions of OS X before Tiger, periodic was scheduled by the
more traditional Unix method of adding lines to the system crontab.
You'll see the following lines in the file /etc/crontab.

```
# Run daily/weekly/monthly jobs.
15    3    *    *    *    root    periodic daily
30    4    *    *    6    root    periodic weekly
30    5    1    *    *    root    periodic monthly
```

The net effect is the same as for the Launch Daemon method
employed by Tiger, with one exception: If your Mac is switched off at
the scheduled times, the scripts will *not* be run later, and maintenance
will miss a beat. You'll have to run the scripts by hand, typing a command such as

```
$ sudo periodic daily
Password:

...
```

Add Your Own Scheduled Tasks

If you want to schedule recurring tasks at times other than those used for standard daily, weekly, and monthly maintenance, you can do so easily by configuring the Launch Daemon (introduced in OS X 10.4) or the system crontab (in any version of Mac OS X).

I scheduled custom backups of my server by adding the following lines to the system crontab in the file /etc/crontab.

```
# backup the server
00 5 * * * root /usr/local/sbin/bu-server ServerMadeData
30 5 * * 6 root /usr/local/sbin/bu-server UserAccounts all
00 6 1 * * root /usr/local/sbin/bu-server Partitions all
30 6 1 * * root /usr/local/sbin/bu-server SystemPartition
```

Alternatively, you may add a configuration file to Launch Daemon. Here's an example in which we add a new configuration file by copying and editing an existing one. We must always add local customizations to the directory /Library—never to /System/Library. Let's create a configuration to run a simple test command such as

```
/usr/bin/touch /my-daily-test
```

We choose to use the file com.apple.periodic-daily.plist as a starting point for our new file.

```
$ cd /Library/LaunchDaemons/
$ sudo cp /System/Library/LaunchDaemons/¬
    com.apple.periodic-daily.plist my-daily.plist
```

Next, we change the owner and permissions so that we (or any other administrator) can edit the file.

```
$ sudo chown root:admin my-daily.plist
$ sudo chmod g+w my-daily.plist
$ ls -l
-rw-rw-r-- 1 root admin 579 Aug 16 12:46 my-daily.plist
```

ℹ TIP

The format of the StartCalendarInterval *property follows the semantics of a crontab entry, and a missing subproperty is equivalent to a star in the crontab column. Project 71 covers the* cron *daemon and crontabs.*

Edit the file by using the OS X Property List Editor (in Developer Tools, if you've installed them) or any text editor. Here's an example, shown in **Figure 8.1**, in which we schedule our simple test command to run daily. Choose a time in the near future for testing purposes.

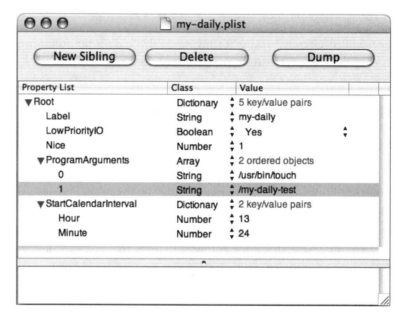

Figure 8.1 Apple's Property List Editor lets you view and edit XML-based plist files.

Finally, use the launchctl command to load the configuration for our new task and start it.

```
$ sudo launchctl load /Library/LaunchDaemons/my-daily.plist
$ sudo launchctl start my-daily
$ sudo launchctl list
...
my-daily
```

Wait until the scheduled time, and you'll see that the following file is created.

```
$ ls -l /my-daily-test
-rw-r--r--   1 root   admin   0 Aug 16 13:24 /my-daily-text
```

Project 73
Manage Network Settings

"How do I examine the current network location or the settings applied to my Ethernet connections?"

This project looks at commands to query and change network settings. It considers the commands `ifconfig`, `hostname`, `scselect`, and `ipfw`. Project 37 uses System Profiler to gather network information. Chapter 10 covers networking in general.

View and Change Interface Settings

You'll usually configure networking from the Network pane of System Preferences. Should you wish to configure a machine remotely or by running a shell script, however, Mac OS X provides several command-line tools that let you do so. First, we'll look at the command `ifconfig`, which is used to query and change the settings applied to network interfaces such as Ethernet.

To view the settings of all network interfaces, type

```
$ ifconfig
```

You'll see a list of interface names such as `en0`, each followed by its current settings. Interface `en0` is the first Ethernet connection; `en1` is the second, usually used by AirPort; `fw0` is TCP over FireWire; and `lo0` is the local loopback interface. View the settings for a particular interface—for example, `en1`—by typing

```
$ ifconfig en1
en1: flags=8863<UP,BROADCAST,SMART,RUNNING,SIMPLEX,
MULTICAST> mtu 1500
    inet6 fe80::210:a7ff:fe2e:b674 prefixlen 64 scopeid 0x5
    inet 10.0.2.4 netmask 0xffffff00 broadcast 10.0.2.255
    ether 99:10:a7:2e:b6:74
    media: autoselect status: active
    supported media: autoselectking interfaces, type
```

Interface lo0

The special interface lo0 is known as the *local loopback interface*. It's a software interface and responds to the IP address 127.0.0.1 as the address of the local machine. The host name localhost is mapped to the address 127.0.0.1.

⤴ LEARN MORE

For more information on using the sudo **command to issue commands as the root user, see "How to Become the Root User" in Project 2.**

The output from this command tells us that the IP address assigned to en1 is 10.0.2.4, and the subnet mask (netmask) is 255.255.255.0 (or 0xffffff00 in hexadecimal notation).

Switch an Interface Off and On

To reset an interface, or to turn it off or on, use ifconfig, stating the interface name and either down (off) or up (not off). All such commands must be issued as the root user. Let's reset the second Ethernet interface.

```
$ sudo ifconfig en1 down
Password:
```

(Where did all my iChat buddies go?)

```
$ sudo ifconfig en1 up
```

Multi-Home

To demonstrate how we might use ifconfig to change network settings, we'll multi-home en0. *Multi-homing* assigns a second IP address to an interface—a technique used when one host has to act temporarily as a backup for a second and must assume two network addresses.

First, let's check our current IP address, employing the grep command to display just the information in which we are interested.

```
$ ifconfig en0 | grep "inet "
inet 217.155.168.146 netmask 0xfffffff8 broadcast
217.155.168.151
```

To add an IP address, we specify the alias command to ifconfig, giving the new IP address and an appropriate subnet mask.

```
$ sudo ifconfig en0 alias 217.155.168.145 ¬
    netmask 255.255.255.248
```

Let's check that the command has worked.

```
$ ifconfig en0 | grep "inet "
inet 217.155.168.146 netmask 0xfffffff8 broadcast
217.155.168.151
inet 217.155.168.145 netmask 0xfffffff8 broadcast
217.155.168.151
```

To remove the second IP address (you probably don't want to keep it), use the -alias command.

```
$ sudo ifconfig en0 -alias 217.155.168.145
```

Check Host Names with hostname

You might find it useful when writing a script to check the host name of the current machine, perhaps to take specific action on a particular host. Do this with the hostname command. In the following example, we set two shell variables to be used by the script; domain is set to the full domain name of the host, and host is set to be just the host part.

```
$ domain=$(hostname)
$ host=$(hostname -s)
$ echo "I'm known locally as $host and globally as $domain"
I'm known locally as sauron and globally as
sauron.mayo-family.com
```

You may also use hostname, run as the root user, to assign a new host name to a machine.

Change Network Locations

Apple provides a command-line utility for switching network settings. This utility is equivalent to choosing a network location from the Location command in the Apple menu or from the Location pop-up menu in the Network pane of System Preferences.

TIP

Add IP addresses to lo0, and use them to test such things as IP-based virtual hosting on the Apache Web server.

```
$ sudo ifconfig lo0 ¬
    alias 127.0.0.2 ¬
    netmask 255.0.0.0
```

The command is called scselect. Issued without any arguments, it lists all locations.

```
$ scselect
Defined sets include: (* == current set)
   E5B52A04-857F-11D8-A6EA-000393B2D604 (carcharoth.zen)
   E5BBB531-857F-11D8-A6EA-000393B2D604 (sauron.zen)
 * E5A8E3FA-857F-11D8-A6EA-000393B2D604 (melkor.zen)
   E5C2A2A6-857F-11D8-A6EA-000393B2D604 (smeagol.zen)
   AC642A1F-84F1-11D8-A6EA-000393B2D604 (saruman.zen)
   0     (Automatic)
```

To change to a new location, name the location as an argument to scselect. To change to the location to saruman.zen, for example, type

```
$ scselect saruman.zen
CurrentSet updated to AC642A1F-84F1-11D8-A6EA-000393B2D604
(saruman.zen)
```

Eyeball the Firewall

Configuration of the firewall is beyond the scope of this project. We'll simply introduce the ipfw command and give some examples of how to use it.

Check the current firewall settings by typing the following command.

```
$ sudo ipfw list
02000 allow ip from any to any via lo*
02010 deny ip from 127.0.0.0/8 to any in
...
65535 allow ip from any to any
```

To configure the firewall manually, flush the existing rule set, and add your own set by using the add command.

```
$ sudo ipfw flush
Are you sure? [yn] y
Flushed all rules.
```

Let's add a rule to allow established connections.

```
$ sudo ipfw add allow tcp from any to any established
00100 allow tcp from any to any established
```

Next, we'll open port 80 so we can serve Web pages.

```
$ sudo ipfw add 00200 allow tcp from any to any 80 in
00200 allow tcp from any to any 80 in
```

Finally, we'll close all other ports.

```
$ sudo ipfw add 09000 deny tcp from any to any
09000 deny tcp from any to any
```

Check that the rules have been added as expected.

```
$ sudo ipfw list
00100 allow tcp from any to any established
00200 allow tcp from any to any 80 in
09000 deny tcp from any to any
65535 allow ip from any to any
```

The Unix man page for ipfw has a great deal of information on configuring the firewall.

ⵣ TIP

If you use the ipfw *command to configure the firewall by hand, System Preferences will disable its own firewall configuration. To change back to using System Preferences, you must flush all firewall rules by typing*

```
$ sudo ipfw flush
```

↗ **LEARN MORE**

Project 23 shows you how to use the grep **command.**

Project 74
System Tips

"How do I change the startup disk from the command line?"

This project gives you some handy tips and scripts for system administration.

Mount a Volume by Name

The diskutil tool (covered in Projects 67 and 68) mounts a volume identified by its disk identifier, such as disk1s5, or device node, such as /dev/disk1s5. If you wrote a script to mount a volume, you'd probably want to make life easier for whoever uses the script by letting him specify a friendlier volume name. To achieve this, you must translate a volume name into the disk identifier required by diskutil. Here's how we might go about this.

First, use diskutil to list all partitions and pipe its output to the grep command to search for a line containing the volume name. Here's an example.

```
$ diskutil list | grep -iw "macintosh hd"
   2:        Apple_HFS Macintosh HD          19.8 GB    disk1s3
```

Naturally, in a script we'd expect the volume name to be passed as a parameter, so we wouldn't use the literal string "macintosh hd". The options -iw passed to grep make the search case insensitive and match whole words only; we don't want to match volume backup against both backup and backup2.

Next, we extract the disk identifier disk1s3 from this line. The awk command is an obvious choice to extract a particular field, but in this case, we don't know which field the device identifier is; volume names that contain spaces appear to awk as though they occupy multiple fields. The cut command, however, will extract a specific character range. Careful counting, and allowing for a disk name of the form disknnsmm, suggests the command

```
$ diskutil list | grep -iw "macintosh hd" | cut -c 59-67
disk1s3
```

This rather cavalier approach will fail for long volume names that overrun the allotted column width. An alternative uses the `sed` command. We employ clever regular-expression trickery to match any of `disknsm`, `disknnsm`, `disknsmm`, or `disknnsmm` by using the expression `disk.\{1,2\}s.\{1,2\}`, and also capture the matching text by enclosing the pattern with `\(...\)`. The whole line is replaced by the captured text, which is represented by `\1`. The net effect is to extract the device identifier and display it onscreen. It could just as easily have been sent to the standard output for further use in a script.

```
$ diskutil list | grep -iw "macintosh hd" | sed -n ¬
    "s/.*\(disk.\{1,2\}s.\{1,2\}\).*/\1/p"
disk1s3
```

This isn't perfect, as it will match `macintosh` with the volume `macintosh hd`, but it's a good start.

Change the Startup Disk

To check or change the startup volume from the command line, Apple has blessed us with the `bless` command. Using `bless` with option `--setBoot` is equivalent to setting the Startup Disk in System Preferences.

To determine the current startup volume, type

```
$ sudo bless --getBoot
/dev/disk0s3
```

The `df` command confirms that this is indeed the current system disk mounted on /.

```
$ df -h
Filesystem      Size   Used   Avail  Capacity  Mounted on
/dev/disk0s3    234G    43G    190G     18%     /

...
```

⚲ LEARN MORE

Projects 59 to 62 cover the awk **and** sed **commands. Projects 77 and 78 show you how to form regular expressions.**

To obtain more information on the selected startup volume, type

```
$ bless --info
finderinfo[0]:   3048 => Blessed System Folder is
/System/Library/CoreServices
...
```

To choose another mounted volume as our startup volume, use `bless` in --mount mode, followed by the mount point of the new boot volume and the --setBoot operator. Applying --setboot to a volume writes the volume's ID to the Open Firmware boot-device variable.

To change the startup volume to another mounted volume, specify --mount followed by the volume's mount point and --setBoot to write that volume to the Open Firmware boot-device variable.

```
$ sudo bless --mount /Volumes/Macintosh\ HD/ --setBoot
```

Confirm that the startup volume has changed by typing

```
$ sudo bless --getBoot
/dev/disk1s3
```

or by checking the Startup Disk in System Preferences.

Try running `bless --info` again. Note that it reports on the selected boot volume—not necessarily the one that's running.

View the Open Firmware boot-device variable directly by typing

```
$ nvram -p | grep "boot-device"
boot-device fw/node@d04b5407023723/sbp-2@c000/@0:3,\\:tbxi
```

For a volume to be bootable, it must contain a Mac OS X system, and that system must be *blessed*—that is, the appropriate folder must be marked as a valid system folder. This will always be so when Mac OS X has been properly installed but might not be so on volumes created by cloning. To bless the appropriate folder, assuming that the potential boot volume is mounted at /Volumes/volname, type

```
$ sudo bless --folder ¬
    /Volumes/volname/System/Library/CoreServices/
```

If the device you wish to make your boot volume is attached but not mounted, specify `--device` instead of `--mount` and the device node instead of the mount point.

```
$ sudo bless --device /dev/disk1s3 --setBoot
```

Running `bless --info` confirms that the new boot volume has been selected and also reminds us that the device is offline.

```
$ bless --info
Volume for OpenFirmware path fw/node@d04b5407023723/sbp-
2@c000/@0:3,\\:tbxi is not available
```

Set the Date and Time

To set the system date from the command line, issue the `date` command as the root user. In the following example, we set the date and time to November 17, 15:35, year 2005.

```
$ sudo date 111715352005
```

The format for specifying a full date and time is `MMDDhhmmCCYY`, where `MM` is the month, `DD` is the date, `hhmm` is the hours and minutes, and `CCYY` is the century and year.

You may omit any field except the minutes, but if you specify the larger unit in any pair (date, time, or year), you must also supply its smaller counterpart. You'd confuse `date` by furnishing the month (`MM`) without the date (`DD`), for example.

To set the time to 15:31 without changing the date, issue the command

```
$ sudo date 1531
Wed Aug 17 15:31:00 BST 2005
```

➚ LEARN MORE

Project 38 illustrates the `nvram` **command.**

Learn Shell Scripting

9

This chapter covers many aspects of shell scripting. In keeping with the spirit of the book, it's not an A-to-Z tutorial on the subject. Rather, each project tackles a particular technology pertinent to writing shell scripts. The 13 projects cover the following topics:

Bash functions in a script, parameter expansion, here-documents, and script debugging

Regular expressions, both modern (extended) and obsolete (basic)

Shell quoting

Forming conditions for use in conditional expressions

Subshells and command blocks

Traps and handles, and how to implement them in a shell script

If you are not familiar with writing shell scripts, read Projects 9 and 10 for an introduction. See Project 4 for a discussion of shell and environment variables and how they differ in scope. Project 52 covers Bash functions.

The chapter focuses on scripting with Bash, the default shell for accounts created in Mac OS X. If your chosen interactive shell is not Bash, don't worry; you can still write and use the scripts you'll find here. Just make Bash execute them by making the first line of each script read `#!/bin/bash`. See Project 5 for a comparison of shells.

The projects in this chapter are fairly advanced. It's not a tutorial on writing shell scripts; rather, it presents useful and practical solutions to some of the most common scripting tasks. It's of most use to those who have grasped the basics of scripting and want to start writing real-world scripts.

↗ LEARN MORE

If you're not familiar with Bash functions, refer to Project 52.

ĭ TIP

Access an argument passed to a shell script from within a function by passing the argument to the function. To access the script's $2 from within function usage, *for example, call* usage *as follows:*

usage "$2" other
params...

Within usage, *the value of the main script's $2 can be accessed through the function's $1.*

Project 75
Use Functions in Scripts

"How do I avoid repeating the same piece of code in a shell script?"

This project demonstrates the use of Bash functions in shell scripts. It shows you how to use functions as a way of gathering commonly used code into blocks and demonstrates some handy tricks you can employ in your own code.

Functions' Power, Multiplied

In Project 52, we covered the technique of combining command sequences into functions that can be invoked from the command line. Within Bash scripts, functions work much the same way that functions do in other languages, such as JavaScript and C.

When functions are incorporated into a script, they usually are grouped at the top of the file, ahead of the main body of the code. When the script is invoked, Bash reads and parses the functions, which makes them available for use within the actual script. (Functions are not executed when they are parsed—only when they are *called* by the script.)

Like shell scripts, functions accept arguments, and both use the same syntax to refer to arguments. The first argument passed to a script or function is available in the variable $1; the second, in $2, and the *n*th, in variable $n. Bash also provides two special variables: $* expands to a list of all arguments, and $# expands to the total number of arguments passed.

Because of their shared syntax, arguments passed to a script are not accessible directly by the functions within it, but are available again when a function terminates and the main body of the script executes.

One point to be aware of: The variable $0 represents the script name in both the script and its functions. Use the special variable $FUNCNAME to access the name of the current function.

Write a Function

Most nontrivial shell scripts take arguments, and a well-written script will perform some validation on the arguments it receives. Validation methods can vary widely, depending on the nature of the arguments involved (testing for numbers versus text, for example), but most Unix commands and scripts respond the same way when incorrect arguments are passed: by writing a *usage line* to the terminal. In a script that does a lot of validation, handling this kind of repetitive task is an ideal candidate for a function.

Suppose that we are writing a script that does a lot of validation. We might write a simple function to be called from the many points of validation in our hypothetical script. The function would display usage information in the terminal window. Our example function, appropriately called usage, has been taken from a real-world script that creates a new Unix group.

```
usage ()
{
  echo "Create a new group"
  echo "  Usage: ${0##*/} groupname gid"
  if [ "$*" != "" ]; then echo "  Error: $*"; fi
  exit
}
```

In the new-group script, usage displays an informational message and a usage line, and (optionally) an error message preceded by the text Error: . Because this function is called in response to fatal errors, it also shuts down, or *exits*, the script. A function that simply completes and returns to the main body of the script should not finish on exit: An exit statement terminates the entire script.

Let's use our function to report an error when the number of arguments passed to a script is not two. Our script calls the usage function if the wrong number of arguments is passed.

```
if [ $# -ne 2 ]; then
  usage
fi
```

ⓘ TIP

A usage line traditionally displays the name of the script. Use the special variable $0 *instead of writing the script name literally. In this way, the name that's displayed always reflects that of the script, even if the script is renamed after it's written. The special variable expansion* ${0##*/} *truncates the leading pathname from the script name. If the script is called by a command line such as* /usr/local/bin/my-script, *the variable expansion becomes* my-script.

Project 76 covers Bash parameter expansion.

⚡ LEARN MORE

**Projects 9 and 10 show you
how to write simple Bash
shell scripts.**

⚡ LEARN MORE

**Project 6 covers the concepts
of redirection, standard
output, and standard error.**

⚡ TIP

*An often-used convention names
functions starting with a capital
letter, helping distinguish
functions from variables and
commands.*

To pass an error message to the function, call it like this.

```
if [ $# -ne 2 ]; then
  usage "Two arguments expected but $# received"
fi
```

Unix commands usually write error messages to standard error instead
of standard output. We can change our usage function to honor this
convention by using a redirection trick. Normally, the echo command
writes to standard output, but if we merge standard output into standard error by using the notation 1>&2, or the equivalent >&2, all output will be sent to standard error instead. As an example:

```
echo "  Usage: ${0##*/} groupname gid" 1>&2
```

Underline a String

Here's a handy function to underline a line of text. It accepts a line of
text as a single argument, displays the text on a line, and places a line
of dashes equal in length to the text on the line below it.

```
# Function Underline(string-to-underline)
# Display and underline a string.
# $1: the string to underline
Underline ()
{
  local -i len  # to hold the length of the string
  # write out the string and a '-' for each charater
  len=${#1}; echo "$1"
  while ((len!=0)); do echo -n "-"; len=len-1; done; echo
  return 0
}
```

Our function, named Underline, assigns the number of characters in
parameter 1 to the variable len by using the special notation ${#1}. It
then displays the text held in parameter 1 and loops to display the
appropriate number of dashes below the text. We employ a few more
tricks besides ${#1}. Passing option -n to echo stops it from displaying
each dash on a new line. Also, we declare len to be a local integer
variable in the line

```
local -i len  # to hold the length of the string
```

A local variable exists only while its defining function executes and prevents us from accidentally overwriting a variable of the same name from the main script. The option `-i` makes `len` an *integer* variable, allowing us to employ Bash integer expressions such as the condition in

```
while ((len!=0));
```

which loops for as long as the value of the variable `len` is not equal to 0; and the arithmetic expression

```
len=len-1
```

which subtracts 1 from the value of `len`.

We'd call `Underline` from the main body of the script in the following manner.

```
Underline "The Title"
```

yielding

```
The Title
---------
```

↗ LEARN MORE

Project 87 gives tips on declaring variables and Bash integer arithmetic.

↗ LEARN MORE

Project 81 covers Bash conditions.

ℹ TIP

To find out more about the `local` *command—which, when used within a function, is equivalent to the* `declare` *command—type*

```
$ help local
$ help declare
```

Project 76
Use Bash Parameter Expansion

"How do I perform string manipulation in Bash?"

This project covers the topic of parameter expansion. Parameter expansion is most often used to expand variables and arguments by means of the familiar $ notation: `$length` or `$1`. Parameter expansion, however, is more than simply the expansion of a variable or an argument into its value; it also involves manipulation of the value, such as pattern replacement and default initialization.

Basic Expansion

By now, the basics of parameter expansion are probably familiar. We give a variable a value.

```
$ title="101 Projects"
```

Later, we expand the variable to expose its value.

```
$ echo $title
101 Projects
```

Bash uses the terms *parameter* and *parameter expansion* not only for variables, but also for arguments passed to a script or function. Where Bash refers specifically to arguments such as `$1`, it uses the terms *positional parameter* and *positional parameter expansion*.

Positional parameter expansion works as follows: The first argument passed to a Bash script or function is available in the variable `$1`; the second, in `$2`; and the *n*th, in the variable `$n`. The special expansion `$*` expands to a list of all arguments passed, and `$#` expands to the number of arguments passed.

The special expansion `$@` is useful when enclosed in double quotes. To illustrate this, suppose that we pass two arguments to a script, both of which contain spaces.

```
$ ./tst "param one" "param two"
```

Whereas both $* and $@ expand to four items—"param", "one", "param", and "two"—the quoted versions behave differently.

▸   "$*" expands to one item: "param one param two".

▸   "$@" expands more usefully to two items: "param one" and "param two".

Complex Expansion

More complex parameter expansion lets us assign a default value to a parameter or change its value by cutting and replacing portions of its contents. Complex expansion uses the notation

```
${parameter-name<expansion-type>}
```

Set Default Values

Suppose that we have a script that takes one optional argument. We want to assign the value of argument (parameter) 1 to the variable level, but only if parameter 1 is given a value. If no argument is given when the script is called, we want the value of level set to equal the text string normal. We can take the conventional, long-handed approach and use an if statement.

```
if [ "$1" = "" ]; then
  level="normal"
else
  level="$1"
fi
```

Better, we can use the functionally equivalent complex expansion.

```
level=${1:-"normal"}
```

An alternate approach also initializes a parameter to a default value if the parameter is null. This technique doesn't apply to *positional* parameters (arguments), only to parameters (variables).

```
new_level=${level:="normal"}
```

ⓘ TIP

The special parameter $$ expands to the process ID of the shell. It provides an easy way to generate a uniquely named temporary file in a script. For example:

echo "Test" > $0$$.tmp

ⓘ TIP

Use the following technique to embed parameter expansion in text that might otherwise be confused with the name of the parameter. To expand an abbreviated day name, where day="Tues", *to* Tuesday, *we type*

${day}day

A third method causes a script to exit if a compulsory argument is not supplied. The following expansion displays an error message and aborts the script if no value is passed to $1; otherwise, it assigns the passed value to the variable level.

```
$ cat tst
level=${1:?Please supply a value}
```

If we run the script and fail to supply an argument, it displays the error message and aborts.

```
$ ./tst
./tst: line 1: 1: Please supply a value
```

Slice Strings

Bash can expand a *string variable* (a variable that contains text) to a fragment of the text. This process is called *slicing*. We might expand the variable $string by taking a slice starting from the 8th character (that's character 7, because the first character is 0) and returning the next 6 characters.

```
$ echo $hi
Hello, please slice me
$ echo ${hi:7:6}
please
```

Here's a practical application of slicing—a script that checks each of its arguments to see whether it's an *option flag* (an argument that starts with a - character). This technique is commonly used in connection with scripts for which option flags have been defined. Our example is part of a script that has two legal option flags: -p, which prompts the user for a password; and -v, which sets verbose mode. Any other option will cause the script to exit and report an error to the user.

We want to extract and compare the first character of each argument by slicing a substring one character long, beginning with the first character (character position 0). The following script uses the expansion ${1:0:1} to slice $1, where :0 specifies the start position and :1 specifies the number of characters to extract.

```
while [ "$1" != "" ]; do
  if [ "${1:0:1}" = "-" ]; then
    case "$1" in
      "-p") stty -echo; read -p "Password:" password
            stty echo; echo;;
      "-v") verbose=yes;;
      *) echo "invalid option $1"; exit
    esac
  else
    echo "Here we process non-option arguments..."
  fi
  shift
done
```

TIP

Use the command stty -echo
*to stop the user's input from
being echoed to the screen as
she types. This is useful when a
password or other such sensitive
information needs to be input.
The command* stty echo
puts things back to normal.

The script then tests to see whether the character is a dash (-). If so, it issues instructions depending on whether the dash is followed by p, v, or any other character (denoted by *); if not, it writes a message to the screen: Here we process non-option arguments...

The script demonstrates a few other useful techniques, too. It loops, processing each argument in turn. At the end of the loop, it uses the shift command to shift all positional parameters down one place, so $n becomes $n-1, $2 becomes $1, and $1 (which we just processed) drops off the end.

TIP

Use the special expansion
${#var} *to return the length
of a parameter, in characters.*

Top and Tail Strings

Bash provides a way to remove the head or tail of a string. We'll illustrate a few useful techniques on a Unix pathname written to the variable fullpath.

$ fullpath="/usr/local/bin/backup.user.sh"

In our first example, we remove the head of the string by specifying a parameter expansion in the form

${parameter##word}

The character combination ## instructs Bash to remove all characters, starting from the left (the start) of the specified parameter, that match word. We'll specify word as */, where * is matched by zero or more

✒ LEARN MORE

**Refer to Project 11 for a full
explanation of globbing.**

occurrences of any character and / represents itself. The star symbol is interpreted exactly as it would be for shell globbing. Our pattern, therefore, matches any string of characters from the start of the string, ending with /.

```
$ echo ${fullpath##*/}
backup.user.sh
```

You'll notice that the pattern matched the longest string it could, up to the *last* /. Try the same command, but type a single # to match the shortest string—up to the *first* /.

To extract the file extension, we type

```
$ echo ${fullpath##*.}
sh
```

To remove all characters starting from the right (the end) of the string instead of the left, specify % instead of #. The same convention of % versus %% applies. To remove the extension part (.sh) from fullpath, we require the shortest match, starting from the right (%), for the word .*.

```
$ echo ${fullpath%.*}
/usr/local/bin/backup.user
```

Here's an example script that splits a pathname into its component directories and the filename. We match the shortest string from the left and the longest from the right. Contrast this with the previous two examples. If you can figure out how it works, you've got topping and tailing down to a tee.

```
$ cat tst
#!/bin/bash
pathname=${1}"/"
while [ ! -z ${pathname#*/} ]; do
  pathname=${pathname#*/}
  echo ${pathname%%/*}
done
```

Let's try it on a pathname.

```
$ ./tst /usr/local/bin/command
usr
local
bin
command
```

Search and Replace

Bash gives us a means to search a parameter for a pattern, replacing each occurrence of that pattern with a new string. The syntax is

```
${parameter/match-pattern/replace-pattern}
```

Here are some examples in which we use the echo command to demonstrate search and replace.

Search for the first occurrence of Hello, and replace it with Goodbye.

```
$ message="Hello, Hello World"
$ echo ${message/Hello/Goodbye}
Goodbye, Hello World
```

Only the *first* occurrence of Hello is replaced: To replace *all* occurrences, specify a double slash instead if a single slash.

```
$ echo ${message//Hello/Goodbye}
Goodbye, Goodbye World
```

To match a pattern that must be at the very start of the string, introduce the search-and-replace expression with the character sequence /#.

```
$ echo ${message/#Hello/Goodbye}
Goodbye, Hello World
```

Similarly, to specify that the pattern must be at the end of the string, introduce the search-and-replace expression with the character sequence /%.

```
$ echo ${message/%World/Earth}
Hello, Hello Earth
```

✎ NOTE

Regular expressions are not the same as globbing (covered in Projects 11 and 12). Globbing is implemented by the shell and by commands such as find, *and matches a pattern against a list of filenames—usually, the files in the current directory. Regular expressions are more powerful and are used by text-processing commands to match against lines of text—usually, to search for and replace text.*

Project 77
Learn Regular Expressions

"How do I search for text that matches a specific pattern?"

This project shows you how to write regular expressions. A regular expression is formed to match a particular text pattern. Project 78 covers advanced use of regular expressions.

The Match Game

Regular expressions are widely used in Unix, and most text-processing tools support them. The most common uses include:

▶ Searching a text file for lines containing particular text

▶ Filtering the output from other commands for relevant lines

▶ Performing search and replace in text editors such as nano and TextWrangler, and in text-editing tools such as sed and awk

▶ Performing text manipulation in a programming language such as Perl or PHP

The simplest regular expressions are plain text sequences (such as index.html) that match other instances of themselves. More often, regular expressions contain a mix of wildcards, repetitions, and alternatives.

Unix supports three types of regular expressions, which unfortunately don't share a compatible syntax. The three forms are *modern* (also termed *extended*); *obsolete* (also termed *basic*); and *Perl regular expressions* (introduced by the Perl programming language). This project focuses on extended regular expressions, but a section at the end highlights how extended expressions differ from basic expressions. Perl regular expressions, the most powerful of all, are not generally supported by the Unix tools covered in this book.

Basic regular expressions are supported by the `grep` and `sed` commands. Extended regular expressions are supported by the `awk` command and by the extended variants of `grep` and `sed`—namely, `egrep` (or `grep -E`) and `sed -E`.

Regular expressions are employed in many of the projects in this book. Read this project to brush up on the theory, and you'll be ready to apply it in a more practical way to other projects.

Basic Rules

Depending on context, regular-expression matching is performed on a *string* (a sequence of characters) or a line of text. Matched text cannot span lines but must be wholly contained within one line. Matching is normally done in a case-sensitive manner, but most tools let you specify that matching should be case insensitive.

Regular expressions are greedy: Given a choice of several possible matches, they always choose the longest one. Consider the text

`backup.user.sh`

A regular-expression match against "anything followed by dot" will return `backup.user.` but the shorter match `backup.` will not be returned.

Regular-Expression Syntax

A regular expression consists of a sequence of atoms and repeaters.

An *atom* is any of the following:

▸ A character (most characters match themselves)

▸ . (matches any single character)

▸ ^ (matches the start of a line or string)

▸ $ (matches the end of a line or string)

▸ [...] (called a *bracketed expression*; represents exactly one instance from a group of possible characters and is explained more fully later in this project)

↗ LEARN MORE

Refer to Project 23 for examples of using the grep command.

↗ LEARN MORE

Refer to Projects 59 to 62 for more information on the sed and awk commands.

ⓘ TIP

Remember that the escaping character \ is a special character itself. To use it literally, escape it by typing \\.

TIP

When you enter a regular expression on the command line, remember that characters such as star have a special meaning to the shell and must be escaped from it. It's good practice always to surround regular expressions with single quotes.

TIP

A simple method of dry-running a regular expression uses the command `egrep` *(or* `grep` *for basic regular expressions). Type*

`$ egrep 'the-regular-¬`
`    expression'`

but give no filename. You can now experiment by typing lines of text, which `egrep` *will read from standard input. Lines that match the regular expression will be echoed back when you press Return; those that don't, won't. Press* `Control-d` *when you're finished.*

A *repeater* is any of the following:

- ▶ `*` (matches zero or more occurrences of the preceding atom)
- ▶ `+` (matches one or more occurrences of the preceding atom)
- ▶ `?` (matches zero or one occurrence of the preceding atom)

The syntax is explained by examples in the rest of the project. Project 78 covers advanced regular expressions, extending the syntax shown here.

To match a character such as star (`*`), which normally has a special meaning, you must *escape* its special meaning by preceding it with a backslash (\). The special characters that must be escaped in extended regular expressions are

`.  ^  $  *  ?  +  \  [  {  (  )  |`

Simple Regular Expressions

Let's form a very simple regular expression that we might use to match an incomplete crossword entry: *a p blank l blank*. In regular-expression language, a single-character *blank* is represented by a dot, so here's our regular expression.

`'ap.l.'`

When applied to a list of words, one per line, this expression will match lines that contain *apple, apply,* and *aptly.* It will also match lines that contain words such as *appliance, pineapple,* and *inapplicable.*

When applied to lines (or long strings) of text, the regular expression `'ap.l.'` will match lines such as *an apple a day* and *clap loudly* because those lines *contain* matches. It's not necessary to match the entire line or string.

Anchors

The special symbol caret (^) matches the start of a line or string; it matches a position rather than a character. Repeating our example from the previous section, we find that the regular expression

`'^ap.l.'`

matches lines that *start* with `ap.l.` and won't match *pineapple, inapplicable,* or *clap loudly.*

Similarly, the special symbol dollar ($) matches the end of a line or string, so the regular expression

`'ap.l.$'`

matches words that *end with* `ap.l.` and won't match *appliance* or *inapplicable.*

It's important to realize that anchoring applies to the whole line (or string), not to individual words. If we pass the line *red apple,* it will not match ^apple because caret anchors to the start of the line. It will match the line *apple mac.* Similarly, apple$ will match *red apple* but not a*pple mac.*

Finally, we match an entire line or string by applying both anchors. To match only *apple, apply,* and *aptly,* use the regular expression

`'^ap.l.$'`

Repeaters

To search for fixed patterns of text separated by arbitrary text, we must specify *any number of any character.* We do this by combining the atom dot (.) to mean *any character* and the repeater star (*) to mean *zero or more repetitions thereof.* Here are some examples that use a text file, paren.

```
$ cat paren
Here is (some text) in parentheses.
Here we have () empty parentheses.
Here we have (a) letter in parentheses.
Here we have no parentheses.
```

Let's search for lines that contain anything, including nothing, enclosed in parentheses. To do so, we create a regular expression that means (, followed by anything or nothing, followed by). We must

⚓ TIP

To match empty lines or strings, use the regular expression `'^$'`.

⚓ TIP

Pass the -w *option to* grep *to tell it to match only whole words.* "apple" *would match the string* "an apple a day" *but not the string* "a pineapple a day".

TIP

You may employ any number of repeaters in a regular expression.

LEARN MORE

Project 78 shows you how to apply finer control to repeaters and how to repeat constructs that are more complex than a single character.

escape the parentheses (and braces, too) because they are special characters (a topic discussed at greater length in Project 78).

```
$ egrep '\(.*\)' paren
Here is (some text) in parentheses.
Here we have () empty parentheses.
Here we have (a) letter in parentheses.
```

To exclude the empty parentheses, we specify one or more repetitions of any character by using the special character plus (+) instead of star.

```
$ egrep '\(.+\)' paren
Here is (some text) in parentheses.
Here we have (a) letter in parentheses.
```

To specify zero or one repetitions, we use the special character query (?).

```
$ egrep '\(.?\)' paren
Here we have () empty parentheses.
Here we have (a) letter in parentheses.
```

Repeaters can be applied to specific characters as well as to special characters like dot. Here are two regular expressions, the first matching two or more consecutive dashes (-); the second matching star, then one or two dots, and then star.

```
$ egrep -- '--+' test.txt
$ egrep '\*\.\.?\*' test.txt
```

The first example uses a trick to prevent the `egrep` command from thinking the regular expression is an option because it begins with a dash. A double-dash option preceding the regular expression signifies that no more options follow. The second example uses the special character \ to escape the star and dot characters.

Repeaters are summarized in "Regular-Expression Syntax" earlier in this project.

Bracket Expressions

To match any digit 0 to 9, or perhaps any letter, we list the alternative characters and have the text match exactly one of those characters.

Regular expressions provide *bracket expressions* for just such a purpose, whereby we list the alternative characters in square brackets. For example, the regular expression

```
'b[aeiou]g'
```

matches *bag, beg, big, bog,* and *bug.* It does not match *byg* or *boog.*

The following regular expression will match any line that starts with *a, b,* or *c* (uppercase or lowercase) immediately followed by a two-digit number.

```
'^[aAbBcC][0123456789][0123456789]'
```

To match all characters *except* a particular set, enclose the characters to be excluded in brackets, preceded by a caret (^) symbol. To match any character except a digit, specify the regular expression

```
'[^0123456789]'
```

Character Ranges

A *character range* is a bracketed expression with a start point and an end point separated by a dash. Here are some simple examples to illustrate this.

▶ All digits is '[0-9]' and equivalent to '[0123456789]'.

▶ All letters is '[a-zA-Z]'.

▶ All letters plus [ ] ^ and - is '[][a-zA-Z^-]'. To clarify, we specify the character set][a-zA-Z^- enclosed in square brackets.

In the last example, we employed a few tricks to include the special characters [, -, and ^ in the list. To include a] character, make it first in the bracketed list (or the second when you're negating the list with a caret symbol). A caret must not be the first in the list, and a dash character should be the last in the list.

Character Classes

Regular expressions provide special character classes to prevent the need to list many characters in bracketed expressions. To match all

⚓ **LEARN MORE**

Project 78 shows you how to choose alternatives that are more complex than a single character.

ⓘ **TIP**

All special characters lose their meaning inside bracketed expressions, where they should not (and in fact cannot) be escaped.

⚡ TIP

The sequence
`[[:alpha:]][[:digit:]]`
differs from
`[[:alpha:][:digit:]]`.
*The former specifies a letter
followed by a digit; the latter
specifies either a letter or
a digit.*

⚡ TIP

*To discover exactly which
characters are included in
a particular class, read the
Section 3 man page for the
corresponding library function.
The library function is named
like the class but starts with
`is`. To read about character class
`[:space:]`, for example, look
at the man page for `isspace`
by typing*

`$ man 3 isspace`

Basic Regular Expressions

Basic regular expressions do
not support the repeaters `?`
and `+`. The expression `'a+'` is
equivalent to `'aa*'`, however.
`'a?'` has an equivalent
functionality using bounds
(see Project 78). Also, `()` and
`{}` are not special characters
and need not be escaped.

letters and digits, for example, we specify the class `alnum` (alphanumeric). A class name should be surrounded by `[: :]` and enclosed in brackets.

Let's pose a matching problem and solve it by using character classes. We want to match lines starting with one or more digits, followed by one or more letters, followed by a colon, followed by anything. The line may optionally start with a white space. Here's an example.

```
42HHGG: Life, the universe, and everything.
```

We might describe our matching criteria by using a regular expression such as

```
'^[[:space:]]*[[:digit:]]+[[:alpha:]]+:'
```

The regular expression uses the character classes `space` (any white space, including tab), `digit` (0–9), and `alpha` (a–z, A–Z). The rest of the expression is formed with the now-familiar repeaters and anchors.

The following character classes are defined.

```
alnum alpha blank cntrl digit graph
lower print punct space upper zdigit
```

Project 78
Be Clever with Regular Expressions

"How do I search for text that matches a specific pattern?"

This project shows you how to write advanced regular expressions. A regular expression is formed to match a particular text pattern. Project 77 introduces regular expressions.

If you're not familiar with regular expressions, read Project 77, on which this project builds. This project introduces advanced techniques such as:

) Repeaters with bounds to state more precisely how many times a preceding atom must repeat

) Subexpressions to turn regular expressions into atoms, thereby making them subject to repeaters

) Branches to form choices more complex than the simple character alternatives offered by bracket expressions

Repeaters with Bounds

Project 77 introduced regular expressions and showed you how to use an *atom* followed by a simple *repeater* to say *match multiple occurrences of the specified atom.* But the alternatives offered by the simple repeaters *, +, and ? are not always adequate. We can specify to match *one or more letters* by using the expression

`'[[:alpha:]]+'`

but not *exactly nine letters* or *between five and nine letters, inclusive.*

To specify a precise number of matches, use a *bounded repeater,* which has the syntax {n,m}. You can use a bounded repeater wherever you'd otherwise use a simple repeater. We'll demonstrate the use of bounded

⚡ TIP

Attempting to specify a repeater such as {,9} to mean 9 or fewer is not legal syntax. Instead, use either {1,9} or {0,9} as appropriate.

repeaters by matching words of a particular length and words that fall within a particular length range. First, let's use `egrep` and a regular expression to match words of exactly nine letters. The input file contains a list of words, one per line.

To match all nine-letter words, we employ a bounded repeater in a regular expression such as

```
$ egrep '^[[:alpha:]]{9}$' /usr/share/dict/web2
...
pinealism
pinealoma
pineapple
pinedrops
pinewoods
pinheaded
...
```

(The file `/usr/share/dict/web2` contains a handy word list.)

The syntax element {9} is a bounded repeater that matches exactly nine occurrences of the preceding atom: a letter. Note that we've used a caret symbol and a dollar symbol to ensure that the expression matches a complete line; otherwise, the expression would also match a portion of all words more than nine characters in length.

To extract all words five to nine characters in length, we supply two comma-separated bounds.

```
'^[[:alpha:]]{5,9}$'
```

Whereas the first example matched words like *pineapple,* this example matches from *apple* through *dappled* to *pineapple.*

To search for nine *or more* occurrences, supply only the lower bound. The next example matches space-separated numbers of nine or more digits.

```
' [[:digit:]]{9,} '
```

Subexpressions

By enclosing a regular expression in parentheses, we turn it into an *atom* (see Project 77). Such an expression is termed a *subexpression*. A subexpression is seen as a single entity and, therefore, can be made the subject of a repeater.

Here's an example in which we check for valid IP addresses, which look like 10.0.2.120 or 217.155.168.147. We first construct a regular expression that matches one to three digits, followed by a dot.

```
'[[:digit:]]{1,3}\.'
```

Then we turn the regular expression into a subexpression, which allows us to repeat the whole expression three times with a repeater.

```
'([[:digit:]]{1,3}\.){3}'
```

Finally, we add the original expression to the end, but without the trailing dot. For good measure, we also assume an IP address to be surrounded by nondigit characters. This prevents matching an invalid address such as 1111111.2.3.4444444. Here's the final regular expression.

```
'[^[:digit:]]([[:digit:]]{1,3}\.){3}¬
    [[:digit:]]{1,3}[^[:digit:]]'
```

If you try this expression, you'll notice that it fails on IP addresses that fall at the start or end of a line. We need to delimit an IP address by *start of line OR not a digit* and *not a digit OR end of line*. We can achieve this by using branches, introduced in the next section.

Branches

Branches define sets of alternative matches. A regular expression may specify one or more branches separated by vertical-bar (|) symbols and will match anything that matches one of the branches. Each branch is itself a regular expression.

Here's a regular expression with seven branches that matches any one of the days of the week.

```
'monday|tuesday|wednesday|thursday|friday|saturday|sunday'
```

TIP

Any regular expression enclosed in parentheses becomes a subexpression. A subexpression is an atom and can be treated just like a simple character, which may be incorporated into a new regular expression. The new expression may be enclosed in parentheses and reduced in its turn to an atom. There is no effective limit to this process— at least not until your head starts to hurt!

NOTE

We must extend the definition of an atom given in Project 77 to include a subexpression.

Regular Expressions in a Nutshell

Technically, a regular expression is one or more *branches* separated by |. A branch is one or more *pieces* concatenated, and a piece is an *atom* optionally followed by a simple or bounded *repeater*. A *subexpression* encloses a regular expression in parentheses and makes it an atom.

This alone is limited, and an attempt to match a full date will not work. The following regular expression, for example, doesn't do what we probably intended.

```
'saturday|sunday jan|feb [[:digit:]]{1,2}'
```

It actually specifies a line that matches any of the three alternatives.

```
'saturday' OR 'sunday jan' OR 'feb [[:digit:]]{1,2}'.
```

To get around this problem, we employ subexpressions. Combining multiple branches as subexpressions within larger regular expressions enables complex and highly useful matches. We might use the following to pull out weekend events for January and February from an activities list.

```
'(saturday|sunday) (jan|feb) ([[:digit:]]{1,2})'
```

We might match days of the week by using the shorter regular expression

```
'(mon|tues|wednes|thurs|fri|satur|sun)day'
```

We'll conclude our look at branches by completing the IP address-matching example started in the preceding section. Recall that we wanted to delimit an IP address by *start of line OR not a digit* and *not a digit OR end of line*. We specify the former by using a two-branch subexpression such as

```
'(^|[^[:digit:]])'
```

Here's the full regular expression, split across three lines for clarity. It should be entered in Terminal on a single line and, obviously, as part of a command.

```
'(^|[^[:digit:]])
([[:digit:]]{1,3}\.){3}[[:digit:]]{1,3}
([^[:digit:]]|$)'
```

Capture Patterns

Suppose that we need to match a particular pattern and that that pattern must be occur twice. That's easy to do; we use the repeater {2}. However, if our requirement is for the text that matched the first time to be repeated verbatim the second time, that's not so easy. (Imagine a search that'd match *Monty Monty* and *Sugar Sugar* but not *Monty Python* or *Sugar Babes.*)

To pull off such a trick, we use *capture and playback*. Whenever a subexpression is matched, the matched string is captured in a buffer. The first string to be captured is held in buffer 1; the second, in buffer 2; and so on. This happens automatically. To replay a buffer, simply specify \1 or \2, and so on.

Here's an example in which we capture the entire expression and replay it.

```
'(b[aeiou]g)\1'
```

This expression will match *bigbig* and *bagbag,* but not *bigbag.* Remember that a pattern is captured only when it's a subexpression—that is, it's enclosed in parentheses.

Search and Replace

Capture patterns play an important role in search and replace. Editing tools such as sed support the capture-and-playback technique, allowing a pattern captured from the *search* string to be played back into the *replacement* string.

Here's an example in which we process a file that contains information about books. The entry for a book occupies one line in the file (shown split into three shorter lines in this book) and has the following format.

```
Level: Beginning/Intermediate/Advanced, "101 Projects",
 CBS Category: Macintosh/Unix, Covers: Mac OS X 10.4 Tiger,
 Price: $34.99, Author: Mayo.
```

TIP

When subexpressions are nested, capture and playback gets a bit confusing and is best avoided.

⚐ LEARN MORE

Projects 59 and 61 cover the
sed text editor.

Basic Regular Expressions

Basic regular expressions differ
in that branches are not
supported.

Also, () and {} are not special
characters and represent themselves. For subexpressions and
bounds, we must type \(\)
and \{ \}. This reverses the
meaning of () versus \(\)
and {} versus \{\} that we
see in extended regular
expressions. One day, it'll
catch you out!

Our mission, should we choose to accept it, is not so impossible. We
must extract the quoted title and price, and report them in the following format.

```
Cost 34.99 Title 101 Projects
```

To realize this, we match an entire line, capturing the title and price,
and replace the line with `Cost <price> Title <title>`.

Let's build the regular expression piece by piece. Start with `.*` to
match everything up to the title. Match the title with `".*"`, and capture it with `(".*")`. Then match intervening information with `.*`, and
match and capture the price with `(\$[0-9]{1,3}\.[0-9]{2})`. Note
that we escape `$` and `.` because they are special characters. Finally,
match the remainder of the line with `.*`.

The sed command's syntax for search and replace is

```
s/search-pattern/replace-pattern/
```

Our replace pattern is `Cost \2 Title \1`.

Putting this together, we get the following command.

```
$ sed -E 's/.*(".*").*(\$[0-9]{1,3}\.[0-9]{2}).*/Cost \2 ¬
    Title \1/'
```

Option `-E` to sed tells it to switch on extended regular expressions.
Let's try this command, adding a little extra sophistication to display
only matching lines with option `-n` (don't display input lines) and flag
`p` (display matching lines) placed at the end of the substitute function.

```
$ sed -En 's/.*(".*").*(\$[0-9]{1,3}\.[0-9]{2}).*¬
    /Cost \2 Title \1/p'
Level: Beginning/Intermediate/Advanced, "101 Projects",
 CBS Category: Macintosh/Unix, Covers:    Mac OS X 10.4
Tiger, Price: $34.99, Author: Mayo.
Cost $34.99 Title "101 Projects"
TEST"TITLE"TEST$111.22TEST
Cost $111.22 Title "TITLE"
<Control-d>
$
```

Project 79
Use Here-Documents in Scripts

↗ **LEARN MORE**

Project 6 covers the techniques of redirection and pipelining.

"How do I use an interactive command in a shell script?"

This project explores the use of here-documents in Bash shell scripts. Here-documents provide an easy way to display multi-line messages. They also offer a means of using interactive commands (that normally take input from Terminal) in a shell script by specifying that input will instead be found embedded in the script.

↗ **LEARN MORE**

Project 21 gives more information on the cat command.

"Talk" in a Script

A *here-document* is a clever Bash feature one can employ in shell scripts. It furnishes a technique for redirecting standard input not from a file or pipe, but from the text of the shell script itself. This is best explained by an example.

To display a sizeable message from a shell script, we could of course use the echo or cat commands to display text stored in a file. Instead, we'll use cat but supply the text inline as part of the shell script.

Redirect from a Here-Document

The cat command, in the absence of a filename, reads its input from standard input. In the next example, we use a here-document to redirect standard input to be from the text of the shell script.

The following example is taken from a shell script that creates a new Unix group, but for brevity of output, we show only the section that's of interest to us.

✎ NOTE

Remember to make the script executable (see Project 9).

🏹 LEARN MORE

Bash parameter expansion is explained in Project 76.

```
$ cat new-group
#!/bin/bash
cat <<EOS
The script creates a new Unix group within NetInfo
  Usage ${0##*/} groupname gid
  Neither the group name nor the group id must exist
EOS
$ ./new-group
The script creates a new Unix group within NetInfo
  Usage new-group groupname gid
  Neither the group name nor the group id must exist
```

The start of the region to be read as standard input is marked by <<word. The end of the region is marked by a line containing *only* word (in which even leading and trailing blanks are not permitted). In this example, the cat command reads the text between <<EOS and EOS and displays it on the terminal line.

Using a here-document has several advantages over just displaying the contents of a file. First, the shell script does not need to rely on or know the location of a second file. Second, you'll notice that the parameter ${0##*/} is expanded. All lines of a here-document are subjected to parameter expansion, command substitution, and arithmetic expansion.

We could achieve a similar effect by using the echo command, but here-documents have other advantages and uses, which are demonstrated next.

Nontrivial shell scripts usually employ indentation to highlight their structure and organization. Your here-documents can follow the natural flow of script indentation, without having that indentation reflected in the text they pass via redirection: Just set the indents within the here-documents using Tab characters, instead of spaces. To enable this useful feature, type <<- instead of << at the beginning of the here-document. Here's an example.

```
$ cat new-group
#!/bin/bash
        cat <<-EOS
        The script creates a new Unix group within NetInfo
          Usage ${0##*/} groupname gid
          Neither the group name nor the group id must exist
        EOS
$ ./new-group
The script creates a new Unix group within NetInfo
  Usage new-group groupname gid
  Neither the group name nor the group id must exist
```

Although tabs are stripped, spaces are not. This allows space-driven indentation within the here-document text, as in the example above. If you are in the habit of using spaces to indent your shell scripts, revert to using tabs within a here-document.

Control an Interactive Command

If you want to control an *interactive* command from a shell script, such as ftp to perform a file transfer, use a here-document to supply the command's input from the text of the script. An interactive command expects to receive its input from standard input (usually, in the form of a human at a keyboard).

Let's write a shell script that connects to an FTP server and issues three commands—user, ls , and exit—to ftp.

```
$ cat ftp-eg
ftp -n carcharoth.mayo-family.com <<-EOT
        user saruman mypassword
        ls
        exit
        EOT
```

ℹ TIP

Bash provides a here-string in which the expansion of a variable can be used as standard input. Try the following commands, and compare the results you get from the second and third lines.

```
$ text="This is a test ¬
   of a here-string"
$ cat $text
$ cat <<<$text
```

The third line is equivalent to

```
$ echo $text | cat
```

Here's what happens—automatically, with no user intervention—when we run the script.

```
$ ./ftp-eg
Connected to carcharoth.mayo-family.com.
220 carcharoth.mayo-family.com FTP server ready.
331 Password required for saruman.
...
150 Opening ASCII mode data connection for '/bin/ls'.
total 1
drwxr-xr-x    4 saruman    saruman      136 Jun 10 00:21 Public
drwxr-xr-x   27 saruman    saruman      918 Jun 28 13:17 Sites
226 Transfer complete.
221-
    Data traffic for this session was 0 bytes in 0 files.
    Total traffic for this session was 3573 bytes in 1 ...
221 Thank you for using FTP on carcharoth.mayo-family.com.
```

Here's a trick in which we use a here-document to form the standard input to a function, read_data, within a script, function-eg. The function requires three pieces of data.

```
$ cat function-eg
#!/bin/bash
read_data ()
{
  read make
  read model
  read color
}
read_data <<-HEREDOC
      BMW
      3 series
      Blue
HEREDOC
echo "Make: $make, model: $model, color: $color"
$ ./function-eg
Make: BMW, model: 3 series, color: Blue
```

Project 80
Understand Shell Quoting

"How do I selectively turn off the shell's interpretation and expansion of special characters?"

This project explores the art of quoting in the Bash shell. It shows how we force Bash to interpret characters literally in situations where they normally would be considered special characters.

Recognize Special Characters

The Bash shell expands a command line before the command line is executed. During the expansion phase, all special characters—such as wildcards, redirection symbols, and the dollar symbol used in variable expansion—are interpreted and replaced by their expansion text. To invoke a command and pass it text that includes any of those characters used in their literal senses (as in the strings M*A*S*H and $64,000 Question), the special characters must be *quoted* or *escaped* to prevent interpretation.

Before we can employ quoting, we need to know which characters must be quoted. **Table 9.1** is a handy reference listing all the special characters, and character combinations, that the shell is likely to interpret.

Table 9.1 Shell Special Characters

Symbol	Expansion or Interpretation
#	Introduce a comment
;	Separate commands
{...} (...)	Introduce a command block and subshell
&& ||	Logical AND and OR operators (placed between commands)
~	Home directory
/	Directory or filename separator
$var	Variable expansion
`...` $(...)	Execute a command and substitute the output
$((...)) ((...))	Evaluate an integer expression and condition
' " \	Strong quote, weak quote, escape next character
* [...] ?	Globbing
&	Background execution
< > | !	Redirection and pipelining
!	History expansion

Quote and Escape

Suppose that you want to echo the text

```
I want $lots
```

If no quoting is used, $lots will be taken as an instruction to expand the variable lots (which is currently unset). The result would be as follows.

```
$ echo I want $lots
I want
```

To prevent the dollar special character from being interpreted, escape it in one of three ways. First, precede it with a backslash.

```
$ echo I want \$lots
I want $lots
```

Second, enclose the entire string in single quotes, which are also called *strong quotes* because no special characters within them are interpreted.

```
$ echo 'I want $lots'
I want $lots
```

Third, use double quotes, also called *weak quotes* because most, but not all, special characters they enclose are escaped. The exceptions are

▪   The dollar symbol in all three forms : `$var`, `$(...)`, and `$((...))`

▪   The ! symbol in history expansion

In this example, we cannot use double quotes.

A First Escape Trick

Suppose that you want to echo a line such as

```
I want $1000000 (a lot of $)
```

We'll assume that the number of dollars is not fixed but is held in the variable `lots`. To illustrate the different forms of quoting, we'll examine what happens when each form is employed, starting with none.

```
$ echo I want $$lots (a lot of $)
-bash: syntax error near unexpected token `('
```

Employing single quotes prevents all forms of expansion.

```
$ echo 'I want $$lots (a lot of $)'
I want $$lots (a lot of $)
```

To achieve the intended result, we must employ double quotes, which prevent the parentheses from being interpreted but allow expansion of variable `$lots`.

```
$ echo "I want $$lots (a lot of $)"
I want 2324lots (a lot of $)
```

TIP

Don't be tempted to skip quoting because a command appears to work correctly. If your command attempts to pass the text note.* *to* grep *unquoted, for example, and no matching filenames exist in the current directory, the shell will not expand it. Your unquoted command will work—until the day you create a file with a name such as* note.1.

Closer, but this didn't quite work. It's still necessary to escape the first dollar symbol. If we don't, it attaches itself to the second dollar symbol and causes the shell to expand the special variable $$.

```
$ echo "I want \$$lots (a lot of $)"
I want $1000000 (a lot of $)
```

A More Daring Escape

Let's look at a trickier example. How might we quote this?

```
$ echo $5 - That's ok
```

We cannot use double quotes, because we don't want to interpret $5. Single quotes won't work either, because the text itself contains a single quote acting as an apostrophe. A first attempt might have us escaping the apostrophe.

```
$ echo '$5 - That\'s ok'
> Control-c
```

This fails because inside single quotes, no special characters are interpreted, including backslash. Hence, Bash sees the apostrophe as the closing quote and the last single quote as an unterminated open quote.

The simplest method involves converting the expression to two strings enclosed in single quotes, with the (unenclosed) apostrophe between them. Then we escape the apostrophe by using either a backslash or double quotes, as shown in the next two examples.

```
$ echo '$5 - That'\''s ok'
$5 - That's ok
$ echo '$5 - That'"'"'s ok'
$5 - That's ok
```

We could also use the following technique where two quoted parts are run consecutively.

```
$ echo '$5'" - That's ok"
$5 - That's ok
```

Consecutive Quotes

Suppose that we use the awk command to filter field number 4 (written as $4 in awk scripting) from the output of a ps command. We type the following, employing single quotes to escape $4 from the shell because we want it to be interpreted by awk.

```
$ ps xc | awk '{print $4}'
```

Suppose now that we want to do the same thing, but using the field number stored in a shell variable called field.

```
$ field=4
$ ps xc | awk '{print $$field}'
```

This won't work, of course. So how do we both allow Bash to expand $field to 4 *and* escape the first dollar so we pass, literally, $4 to awk? In this simple example, there are several ways, but you can apply a general solution to almost all quoting problems of this nature. It may seem trivial now, but remember it for the future; I've seen many people completely stumped trying to solve quoting dilemmas that are amenable to this particular solution.

We simply start and stop quoted regions as necessary. The first quoted region is '{print $'; the second is '}'. $field is not quoted and, therefore, is expanded by the shell.

```
$ ps xc | awk '{print $'$field'}'
```

Although not necessary in this example, the general rule would have quoted each region to prevent problems with spaces in expanded parameters.

```
$ ps xc | awk '{print $'"$field"'}'
```

Ensure that you don't include spaces between the quoted regions.

↗ LEARN MORE

Project 23 shows how to use
the grep command.

↗ LEARN MORE

Projects 39 and 40 explore
the ps command in detail.

Multi-Level Quoting

Let's write a command that uses grep to search a file for the sequence *a**. Here's our test file.

```
$ cat file
This line contains a*
This line does not
```

Because star is a special character in regular expressions, we must escape it, passing * to grep. Star and backslash are also special characters to the shell and must be escaped from it too, as \\ and *.

Therefore, we form the following command.

```
$ grep a\\\* file
This line contains a*
```

Quoting within Command Evaluation

Here's a tip that might save much head-scratching. Suppose that we have a command substitution such as

$(ps xc | grep "$target")

The variable $target may expand to include spaces, so we must double-quote it for the grep command to work correctly. If we then use the command substitution as a parameter to another command, we must enclose the whole substitution in double quotes. A naive attempt has us type the following.

$ grep "$(ps xc | grep "$target")" processes.txt

This shouldn't work, because as we have seen in previous examples, the expression forms two quoted regions : "$(ps xc | grep " and ")". Surprisingly, it does work, because Bash processes a command substitution ($(...)) as an independent syntactical element. It processes $(ps xc | grep "$target") and then considers the outer expression grep "..." processes.txt.

Project 81
Write Complex Bash Conditions

↗ LEARN MORE

Project 10 introduces basic shell scripting techniques and discusses the conditional statements supported by Bash.

"How does Bash interpret conditional expressions?"

This project looks at the many forms of conditional expression supported by Bash. It explains the differences of the forms and compares them with one another. It also presents some handy tricks and gives tips on how to avoid syntax errors and malformed conditions.

Understand Bash Conditions

Bash supports conditional expressions that are used in conditional statements such as if, while, and until. Here's an example in which we test whether 5 is less than 7 (we use -lt to mean *less than*). The condition is enclosed in [...] and evaluates to true or false. Ideally, Bash will find truth in such a condition.

```
$ if [ 5 -lt 7 ]; then echo "yes"; else echo "no"; fi
yes
```

Now let's examine this simple expression in more detail to discover how Bash interprets it, and explore the alternative forms of conditional expression offered by Bash.

There is more to Bash conditional expressions than is at first apparent. Let's look at how Bash interprets a conditional expression. This is key to understanding the different forms and being able to make the most of them.

When interpreting a conditional statement such as if, Bash does not expect to see a Boolean value (TRUE or FALSE), as other languages do, such as C and PHP. Rather, Bash expects to see an *executable command*. The syntax is effectively

```
if command; then ...
```

▼ TIP

Just as for any other command, white space must separate [and each of its parameters. You'll get a syntax error, or a conditional expression that evaluates incorrectly, if you omit the white space. The final parameter,], is required for syntactic completeness (or perhaps aesthetic value).

↗ LEARN MORE

Refer to Project 16 for more information on the type **command.**

Within such a command line, Bash executes the command that follows if and replaces it with whatever value the command returns. A return value of 0 is interpreted as TRUE; any other return value is interpreted as FALSE.

The [Command

In our example statement, you might well ask about the whereabouts of the command Bash requires following if. The answer is a little surprising: Bracket ([) is actually a built-in Bash command. When interpreting a conditional statement such as

```
if [ 5 -lt 7 ]; then ...
```

Bash first executes the bracket command, passing it the four parameters that form the remainder of the statement: 5, -lt, 7, and]. (The statement is terminated by a semicolon.) The bracket command (not Bash command-line interpretation) evaluates the conditional expression and returns 0 if the statement is true (as it is in this case) and 1 if it is false.

In our example, then, after it has executed the bracket command, Bash effectively sees the statement

```
if 0; then ...
```

and interprets it as if TRUE; then ....

We check the credentials of bracket with the type command.

```
$ type [
[ is a shell builtin
```

Equivalent to [is the test command. The two are identical except that test does not expect to see a closing bracket.

```
$ if test 5 -lt 4; then echo "yes"; else echo "no"; fi
no
$ type test
test is a shell builtin
```

To discover all the conditional operators supported by bracket and `test`, consult Bash's built-in `help` command by typing

```
$ help test
```

Several examples are given in the next section.

Here's a neat trick. A conditional statement may be given any command, not just `[` or `test`. We could test whether two files differ by directly testing the return value from the `diff` command.

```
$ if diff eg1.txt eg2.txt &> /dev/null
> then echo "Same"; else echo "Different"; fi
Same
```

Most commands return 0 (TRUE) for success or yes and 1 (FALSE) for failure or no. In the `diff` example, we took the precaution of throwing away all errors and other output by using the redirection `&>/dev/null` to prevent the shell script from writing unwanted text to the Terminal screen when it executes.

Example Conditionals

The bracket command has a number of primaries you can use to test file attributes, such as whether a file exists.

```
$ if [ -e no-file ]; then echo "Exists"; ¬
    else echo "No such file"; fi
No such file
```

or whether you own a particular file.

```
$ if [ -O eg1.txt ]; then echo "It's mine"; fi
It's mine
```

Bracket can compare strings for less than, greater than, equality, inequality, and emptiness. The next two examples demonstrate tests for equality and emptiness. The `-z` primary returns TRUE if the length of the string that follows is 0 (the string is empty).

⤴ LEARN MORE

Project 6 covers redirection and pipelining.

ℹ TIP

The return value of the last command to be executed is held in the special shell variable $?.

```
$ diff eg1.txt eg2.txt
$ echo $?
0
```

```
$ ans=""
$ if [ "$ans" = "yes" ]
> then echo "You agree"; else echo "You disagree"; fi
You disagree
$ if [ -z "$ans" ]; then echo "You didn't reply"; fi
You didn't reply
```

Integer evaluation is performed as demonstrated in previous examples, using -eq for equality, -ne for inequality, and so on. Type `help test` for more information.

Complex Conditions

You may specify more complex conditions by using AND, represented by -a; OR, represented by -o; and NOT, represented by !. We can test whether both the variables ans and default are empty by using the following complex condition.

```
$ if [ -z "$ans" -a -z "$default" ]
> then echo "I don't know what you want"; fi
```

Don't omit the spaces between operators and operands. In the next example, we have omitted the spaces around the = sign.

```
$ allow=""; user=""
$ if [ "$allow"="yes" -o "$user"="root" ]; ¬
    then echo "OK"; fi
OK
```

Omitting the spaces makes the conditional expression appear to be

```
 [ "non-null-string" -o "non-null-string" ]
```

This is how it should look and evaluate.

```
$ if [ "$allow" = "yes" -o "$user" = "root" ]; ¬
    then echo "OK"; fi
$
```

We form expressions that are more complex by employing parentheses to ensure that evaluation occurs in the correct order. Our first attempt does not work.

```
$ ans="yes"; allow="no"; user="root"
$ if [ "$ans" = "yes" -a ¬
    ( "$allow" = "yes" -o "$user" = "root" ) ]
-bash: syntax error near unexpected token `('
```

The syntax error is reported because the parentheses are parameters to the bracket command and must be escaped from the shell, as demonstrated in our next attempt.

```
$ if [ "$ans" = "yes" -a ¬
    \( "$allow" = "yes" -o "$user" = "root" \) ]
> then echo "OK"; fi
OK
```

Bash Boolean Operators

Compare the next two commands.

```
$ if [ "$allow" = "yes" -o "$user" = "root" ]; ¬
    then echo "OK"; fi
$ if [ "$allow" = "yes" ] || [ "$user" = "root" ]; ¬
    then echo "OK"; fi
```

The difference between the two statements is that in the first example, the built-in bracket command evaluates the whole expression. In the second example, we have two separated bracket commands, and it's Bash that performs the OR operation, using its own || operator. The two commands are functionally equivalent; which you choose is a matter of personal preference. Bash uses a more friendly and C language–like syntax. It provides OR (||), AND (&&), and NOT (!) operators.

We can employ Bash operators outside a conditional statement. For example:

```
$ command1 && command2
```

In such a command, command2 is executed if, and only if, command1 returns TRUE. This technique works because Bash does not evaluate the second part of an AND statement if the first part if FALSE; the

Built-In and External Tests

Both of the Bash built-in commands test and [have external equivalents in the directory /bin. These commands are used by older shells that do not have their own built-in equivalents.

TIP

To source a shell script if, and only if, it exists and is readable, use the following conditional syntax (shown here applied to an initialization script /sw/bin/init.sh).

```
[ -r /sw/bin/init.sh ]
&& source
/sw/bin/init.sh
```

result can only ever be FALSE. This behavior is known as *short-circuiting*. Similarly, we could specify

```
$ command1 || command2
```

In this example, command2 is executed if, and only if, command1 returns FALSE.

As a practical example, think of what happens if we type the following command line in a directory where no subdirectory named fred exists.

```
$ cd fred; ls
-bash: cd: fred: No such file or directory
Desktop     Library     Music      Public
...
```

Command cd returns an error, but ls executes anyway, listing the current directory.

To avoid executing the ls command when the cd command fails, we use the following trick, which relies on the fact that cd returns TRUE when it succeeds and FALSE when it fails.

```
$ cd fred && ls
-bash: cd: fred: No such file or directory
$
```

Use the [[Keyword

Bash provides a relatively new way of specifying a conditional expression, called an *extended conditional expression*. It uses the syntax [[...]] instead of [...] and is compatible with the older form. It is, in fact, a keyword like if and while, not a command like [and cd, and suffers fewer limitations. It also uses the more friendly syntax && and || for AND and OR. We may type a conditional expression such as

```
$ if [[ "$allow" = "yes" || "$user" = "root" ]]; ¬
    then echo "OK"; fi
```

Extended conditional expressions also spare you the trouble of escaping any parentheses they contain.

```
$ if [[ ("$allow" = "yes") || ("$user" = "root") ]]; ¬
    then echo "OK"; fi
```

Beware, however, that bare numbers within extended conditionals are treated as strings—text sequences without numerical value. You might be tempted to use this expression in the belief that Bash is employing integer arithmetic when evaluating the expression

```
$ if [[ (3 < 5) ]]; then echo "OK"; fi
OK
```

But it's not, as we can see by this example.

```
$ if [[ (3 < 15) ]]; then echo "OK"; fi
$
```

Use Bash Integer Conditions

When writing conditional expressions that involve integer values, use the Bash ((...)) construct. Like [[...]], it uses C language–like syntax. Although [[...]] is for general conditions, ((...)) operates only on integer values and variables.

Here's an example.

```
$ v1=3; v2=2
$ if (( $v1 < $v2 )); then echo "yes"; else echo "no"; fi
no
```

You may omit the $ normally required for variable expansion.

```
$ if (( v1 < v2 )); then echo "yes"; else echo "no"; fi
no
```

The Bash ((...)) construct provides a more friendly syntax by employing && and ||, unescaped parentheses, and < in place of -lt. We could write

```
$ if (( (a < b) && (b < c) )); then ...
```

or

```
$ while ((length!=0))
```

NOTE

The [[...]] *construct was introduced in Bash 2.02.*

TIP

To find out more about the [[...]] *construct, type*

```
$ help [[
```

or check the Bash man page by typing

```
$ man bash
```

and then type /\[\[exp *within the man page.*

TIP

To find out more about the ((...)) *construct, check the Bash man page by typing*

```
$ man bash
```

and then /^ARITHMETIC EVALUATION *within the man page.*

⌐ LEARN MORE

Project 45 covers Bash shell attributes.

⌐ TIP

If you write example scripts to try the debugging techniques, be sure to make the script executable (see Project 9).

Project 82
Debug Your Scripts

"My script doesn't work, and I can't figure out where it's going wrong. How do I debug it?"

This project looks at some useful attributes provided by the Bash shell to help in debugging a script. Projects 9 and 10 introduce the basics of shell scripting. Project 45 covers Bash shell attributes.

Use Bash Attributes to Troubleshoot

Suppose that you've just written a 100-line script. You run it, and it goes horribly wrong. It's time to start debugging. Bash provides several shell attributes to aid debugging. These attributes are normally switched off and are activated by the built-in **set** command. Multiple switches can be placed in a script so that attributes can be turned on and off selectively within specified sections.

To switch on an attribute—nounset, for example—type

```
$ set -o nounset
```

To switch off an attribute, type

```
$ set +o nounset
```

We'll write a simple shell script, complete with a couple of errors, to demonstrate some debugging techniques. Here's our script.

```
$ cat debug-me
#!/bin/bash
# debugging
set -o noexec

echo "Calculate the total cost"
price=12; quantity=10
total=((price*quantity))
echo "The total is $totl"
```

You'll notice on line 4 the statement `set -o noexec`, which sets the `noexec` attribute. This attribute instructs Bash to parse the script and check it for syntax errors, but without actually executing it. Setting `noexec` is probably the first step in testing a new script. We are able to eliminate syntax errors quickly, without ever executing the script (and potentially doing some harm if the script goes wrong).

Now let's test-run the script and check it for syntax errors.

```
$ ./debug-me
./debug-me: line 7: syntax error near unexpected token `('
./debug-me: line 7: `total=((price*quantity))'
```

One syntax error is reported; we'll correct it by changing line 7

```
total=$((price*quantity))
```

(This is the correct syntax for integer arithmetic evaluation.)

We'll run the script again, having removed the line that sets `noexec`.

```
$ ./debug-me
Calculate the total cost
The total is
```

Another bug has surfaced. Our variable `total`, which is supposed to hold the calculated total, seems not to do so. A rich area for bug catching is that of misspelled variable names. One way we can catch such errors is to request that Bash disallow the reading of unset variables. Near the top of the file, add the line

```
set -o nounset
```

(This reads *no unset,* not *noun set.*) Run the script again.

```
$ ./debug-me
Calculate the total cost
./debug-me: line 8: totl: unbound variable
```

That bug was easily spotted. After a quick correction, the script works.

```
$ ./debug-me
Calculate the total cost
The total is 120
```

Trace Script Execution

Our second example script contains some very simple branching. It's supposed to check whether an argument has been passed to the script and then print whichever of two messages is appropriate: An argument is required if none was passed or Ok if an argument was passed. Let's view and then run the script without giving it an argument.

```
$ cat debug-me2
#!/bin/bash
if [ "$1" = "" ]; then
 echo "Usage: An argument is required"
fi
echo "Ok"
$ ./debug-me2
Usage: An argument is required
Ok
```

Whoops! It printed both messages. Quantum mechanics aside, it can't have and not have an argument at the same time. Let's trace through the script by setting the verbose attribute. Every statement that's read will be echoed to the Terminal screen. Near the top of the file, add the line

```
set -o verbose
```

Now run the script.

```
$ ./debug-me2
if [ "$1" = "" ]; then
 echo "Usage: An argument is required"
fi
Usage: An argument is required
echo "Ok"
Ok
```

Following this through, we see each statement echoed as it's read. Interspaced with this debugging output is the actual script output Usage: An argument is required and Ok.

The problem (which is obvious in such a short script) is that we've missed the `exit` statement from just before the end of the `if` statement. We'll add the missing `exit` statement and (if it's not too presumptuous) switch off `verbose` and try again.

```
$ ./debug-me2
Usage: An argument is required
```

Now the script works.

Display Executed Statements

The shell attribute `xtrace` provides an alternative tracing facility. Like `verbose`, it causes statements to be displayed, but unlike `verbose`, it displays only those statements that are executed. Remember `verbose` causes statements to be displayed as they are read, whether they are executed or not. Additionally, `xtrace` echoes statements *after* the shell has expanded them, so you see the statements as they will be executed; that can be very useful when debugging. Let's try it out. Near the top of the file, add the line

```
set -o xtrace
```

We'll run the script twice, first without and then with an argument. Trace statements are shown preceded by a plus symbol.

```
$ ./debug-me2
+ '[' '' = '' ']'
+ echo 'Usage: An argument is required'
Usage: An argument is required
+ exit
$ ./debug-me2 hello
+ '[' hello = '' ']'
+ echo Ok
Ok
```

In the trace output, you'll see the `if` statement after expansion and the two alternative `echo` statements.

⍵ TIP

Set both the `xtrace` *and the* `verbose` *options to make it easier to follow a long script through execution. You'll see all statements echoed as they are read, plus those that are executed, expanded, and marked by a plus sign.*

⍵ TIP

Set the `xtrace` *option on the command line to aid the debugging of interactive commands. This technique can be especially useful when debugging shell or alias expansion, because each line is echoed* after *all the expansion has taken place, and you see exactly what the shell executes.*

Exit on Error

To terminate a script when it executes a command that fails, set the exit-on-error attribute, errexit,

```
set -o errexit
```

Whenever a command (mkdir or cp, for example) is executed and fails, the script terminates. This attribute relies on a command's return code. As discussed in Project 81, all commands return a number when they exit; a return code of 0 means success; nonzero return codes indicate errors; and different commands return different numbers depending on the type of error. Check a command's man page to find out what codes it's likely to return. This technique can be used to put the brakes on a script during debugging, ensuring that it doesn't continue after a failed command, executing potentially harmful statements.

Project 83
Batch-Process Files

"How do I adapt my scripts to operate on multiple files?"

This project shows you how to write a script that parses a list of filenames and processes each file in the list. It also shows you how to develop wrapper scripts that feed each filename in a list, one at a time, to scripts that accept only single filenames. Projects 9 and 10 cover the basics of shell scripting.

Discover Loops and Wrappers

Suppose that we write a script called `action` that performs some specified action on a text file. The script takes two option flags: -v for verbose and -a for action followed by an action name. We are not concerned with what the script actually does; it's presented merely as a vehicle to illustrate how to write a script that processes a list of filenames passed on its command line.

We might call the script to process all the text files in the current directory by typing

```
$ action -v -a squeeze *.txt
```

We rely on the shell to expand *.txt into a list of all the .txt files in the current directory. To succeed, our `action` script must be written to accept any number of files and to act on each file in turn. The script must parse the options, save them, and then loop to process each file listed on the command line.

A second approach sees us writing a general-purpose wrapper script. The wrapper script accepts many filenames and calls a simpler `action` script a number of times, each time passing it the next filename from the list. Such a wrapper script can also be used on scripts and commands over which we have no control and that do not accept a list of files. Project 58 introduced this technique when it considered how we might batch-edit files. The solutions presented in that project are similar but take advantage of Bash functions. In this project, we write Bash shell scripts.

↗ LEARN MORE

Project 52 explains Bash functions.

Process Multiple Files

Let's jump straight in with a sample script called action, which will take on the functionality described in the previous section.

$ cat action

```bash
#!/bin/bash

# This is our main function to process each file
Process () {
  echo "Processing $1, verbose: ${verbose:-n}, ¬
    action: ${action:-none}"
}

# This while loop extracts and remembers each option setting
while getopts "va:" opt; do
  case $opt in
    v) verbose="y";;
    a) action=$OPTARG;;
    *) echo "Usage: ${0##*/} [-v] [-a action] ¬
    filename..."; exit 1;;
  esac
done
shift $((OPTIND-1))

# This for loop processes each filename in turn
for filename in "$@"; do
  Process "$filename"
done
exit 0
```

The script is written to demonstrate batch-processing techniques. The actual processing is performed in the function Process, appearing at the top of the script. In the example script, this function does nothing more than echo the name of the file it's supposed to process and its understanding of the options.

Although the script does not perform a real-world task, it serves as a template from which you can build your own scripts.

We assume that the script takes two optional parameters. The first is -v for verbose output; the second is -a for action, followed by an action type. The default values for these options are *not verbose* and an action of *none*.

Process the Options

A script of any significance will accept options, and it's not possible to process the list of filenames without knowing where the options end and the filenames start. To ensure that the example script is a useful template, we'll first show you how to process and save the list of options.

The `while` loop processes the options. The code shown here may be used by any script that must parse a list of options. It takes advantage of the Bash built-in function `getopts` written to process a script's positional parameters (the arguments passed on its command line), looking for options and their associated arguments. In our example, the string `va:` in

```
getopts "va:" opt
```

tells `getopts` that we allow the options -v and -a, but no others. The colon following `a` tells `getopts` to expect an argument to follow. `getopts` writes the next option it reads to the variable `opt` (or whatever is named in the command) and any associated argument to the variable `OPTARG`. We employ a `case` statement to process each argument, setting the variables `verbose` and `action` as appropriate. `getopts` drives the `while` loop by returning TRUE when an option is found and FALSE when the list of options is exhausted. When the options are exhausted, we expect the list of filenames to follow. The `shift` statement immediately following the `while` loop shifts all parameters down such that the first filename is moved to the positional parameter `$1` and all the options we've just processed drop off the end. The value of `OPTIND` is set appropriately by `getopts` so that this works.

↗ LEARN MORE

Project 76 covers parameter expansion. The function Process employs parameter expansion with default values when it echoes the options.

ⓘ TIP

Consult the Bash man page or type

```
$ help getopts
```

to learn more about `getopts`.

Process the Files

The for loop extracts each filename from the remaining positional parameters, expanding "$@" to be the list of quoted filenames.

Note that the for loop uses "$@", which expands to "$1" "$2"... , ensuring that our script is able to cope with filenames that include spaces. Note that if we had used "$*", we'd have generated one long filename: "$1 $2...".

The variable filename is assigned the value of the next filename in the list each time around the loop. To process the file, we call the function Process. Remember, the point of this exercise is to write a script that processes a list of filenames; the actual processing performed on a file is incidental.

Here are some examples of what we might see when we run the script.

```
$ ./action -x
./action: illegal option -- x
Usage: action [-v] [-a action] filename...
$ ./action -v -a
./action: option requires an argument -- a
Usage: action [-v] [-a action] filename...
$ ./action -v -a list
$ ./action -v -a list *.txt
Processing letter.txt, verbose: y, action: list
Processing notes.txt, verbose: y, action: list
Processing three one.txt, verbose" y, action: list
```

Write a Wrapper Script

For scripts and commands that *don't* accept a list of filenames, and perhaps to avoid adding such functionality to your own scripts, write a wrapper script. The script, which we'll call **each**, accepts a wildcard pattern, such as *.txt, and a command to execute. It expands the wildcard into a list of filenames and applies the target command to each filename in turn. The target command, therefore, does not have to be written to process a list of filenames.

Here's our script, in which we assume that the first argument is a wildcard pattern; the remaining arguments form the command to execute and any options it requires.

```
$ cat each
#!/bin/bash
filetype=$1; shift
for file in $filetype; do
  $* "$file"
done
```

The first parameter (the wildcard pattern) is saved in the shell variable `filetype` for use later. The `shift` operator discards the first parameter, shuffling the remainder down. The `for` loop processes each file in the expanded wildcard pattern held in `filetype` (the shell automatically expands this for use, just as it does on the command line) by setting the variable `$file` to be the next filename in the list each time around the loop. The line that follows expands the remainder of the parameters into the target command and any arguments (`$*`) and the filename under consideration by the `for` loop (`$file`).

```
  $* "$file"
```

We'll try out our `each` script by using it with another script to rename all the text files in a directory, replacing their `.txt` extensions with `.txt.bak`. Recall that `each` simply feeds one file at a time to the target command (or script). The script that does the name-changing is named `rename`, and it contains just one command. It takes a filename as its only argument and changes the filename by tacking `.bak` onto the original filename.

```
mv "$1" "$1.bak"
```

To create a script that contains this command, simply echo it and redirect output to file `rename` (after making sure that no file of that name already exists in the working directory); then set execute permissions on the file.

```
$ echo 'mv "$1" "$1.bak"' > rename
$ chmod +x rename
```

✎ NOTE

You can't rename all .txt *files to* .bak *by using a command such as*

```
$ mv *.txt *.bak
```

because of the way the shell expands wildcard patterns on the command line.

Before we put each and rename to work, let's check the files in the current directory. Using wildcard pattern *.txt* with ls ensures that our list will include both normal text files (with extension .txt) and any that have been processed by rename (with extension .txt.bak).

```
$ ls *.txt*
letter.txt        notes.txt        three one.txt
```

Type the following to have each call and execute rename.

```
$ each "*.txt" ./rename
```

Now run ls again to check the results.

```
$ ls *.txt*
letter.txt.bak           notes.txt.bak                    three
one.txt.bak
```

For our next trick, we'll remove the extension we just added. This example pairs our each wrapper with a script called unrename, which uses "topping and tailing" strings during parameter expansion—a technique discussed at length in Project 76. In short, the parameter expansion ${1%.*} expands $1 and removes the final dot, and everything that comes after it, from any filename.

```
$ echo 'mv "$1" "${1%.*}"' > unrename
$ chmod +x unrename
$ each "*.bak" ./unrename
$ ls *.txt*
letter.txt        notes.txt        three one.txt
```

Finally, using each and a new script that applies techniques from rename and unrename, we'll change the extension of our .txt files to .bak.

```
$ echo 'mv "$1" "${1%.*}.bak"' > re-rename
$ chmod +x re-rename
$ each "*.txt" ./re-rename
$ ls *.txt*
ls: *.txt*: No such file or directory
$ ls *.bak
letter.bak        notes.bak        three one.bak
```

All the above are simply examples of what can be done. The each
script can be customized to your own preferences and used from the
command line or by another script.

Recursive Batch Processing

Here's a simple recursive version of each, which we call reach. It
searches a whole directory *hierarchy* for matching filenames.

```
$ cat reach
#!/bin/bash
filetype=$1; shift
find . -name "$filetype" -print0 | xargs -0 -n1 $*
```

To rename all .txt files to .bak, we employ the same rename script as
before, but use reach to apply the script to all .txt files in the current
directory *hierarchy*.

```
$ echo 'mv "$1" "${1%.*}.bak"' > rename
$ reach "*.txt" ./rename
```

⇱ LEARN MORE

**Project 18 shows what you
can do with** find **and** xargs.

↗ LEARN MORE

Project 5 compares the various shell flavors.

↗ LEARN MORE

Project 4 covers shell variables and environment variables, and how they differ.

Project 84
A Bash and Tcsh Reference

"What's the correct syntax for . . . ?"

This project looks at the syntax of common shell commands such as variable assignment, redirection, and shell scripting statements. It shows the syntax for Bash and Tcsh—the two shells that are used most often in Mac OS X Unix.

Set Variables

Table 9.2 shows you how to set shell variables and environment variables.

Table 9.2 Setting Variables

Set	Bash	Tcsh
Shell variable	`variable=value`	`set variable = value`
Environment variable	`ENVVAR=value; export ENVVAR`	`setenv ENVVAR value`
Environment variable (Bash only)	`declare -x ENVVAR=value`	

Redirection and Pipelining

Table 9.3 shows the syntax employed by both shells to express redirection and pipelining.

Table 9.3 Syntax for Redirection and Pipelining

Redirect or Pipe	Bash	Tcsh
stdout	cmd > file	cmd > file
stderr	cmd 2> file	(cmd >/dev/tty) >& file
stdout appending	cmd >> file	cmd >> file
stderr appending	cmd 2>> file	(cmd > /dev/tty) >>& file
stdout with clobber	cmd >| file	cmd >! file
stderr with clobber	cmd 2>| file	(cmd > /dev/tty) >&! file
Both to same file	cmd &> file	cmd >& file
Both to different files	cmd > out 2> err	(cmd > out) >& err
Merge stdout into stderr	cmd 1>&2	n/a
Merge stderr onto stdout	cmd 2>&1	n/a
stdin	cmd < file	cmd < file
Pipe stdout	cmd1 | cmd 2	cmd1 | cmd2
Pipe both	cmd1 2>&1 | cmd2	cmd1 |& cmd2

↗ LEARN MORE

Project 6 covers the concepts of redirection and pipelining.

Tee Time

To see the output of a command onscreen *and* redirect it to a file, use the tee command.

```
$ ls Sites | tee list.txt
images
index.html
$ cat list.txt
images
index.html
```

To redirect to multiple files, just type the names of the files as arguments. Apply option -a to append to the output files rather than overwrite them.

✎ NOTE

Noninteractive Bash shells do not execute any startup files.

↗ LEARN MORE

Project 47 covers the shell startup sequence.

Startup Files

The following script files are executed by the Bash shell when it starts up. For login shells (or shells started with the command `bash --login`), they are

▶   `/etc/profile`

▶   `~/.bash_profile`

For non-login shells, they are

▶   `/etc/bashrc` (though the Bash manual claims otherwise)

▶   `~/.bashrc`

The following script files are executed by the Tcsh shell when it starts up. For login shells (or shells started with the command `tcsh -l`), they are

▶   `/etc/csh.cshrc`

▶   `/etc/csh.login`

▶   `~/.tcshrc`

▶   `~/.login`

For non-login shells, they are

▶   `/etc/csh.cshrc`

▶   `~/.tcshrc`

Control Constructs

Syntax for each Bash and Tcsh control construct is illustrated in the following examples. All the scripts actually work, so you can play around with them.

The if Construct

```
#!/bin/bash
if [ "$1" = "positive" ]; then
  echo "Yes"
elif [ "$1" = "negative" ]; then
  echo "No"
else
  echo "Not sure"
fi

#!/bin/tcsh
if ("$1" == "positive") then
  echo "Yes"
else if ("$1" == "negative") then
  echo "No"
else
  echo "Not sure"
endif
```

The case/switch Construct

```
#!/bin/bash
case "$1" in
  "positive")
    echo "Yes"
  ;;
  "negative")
    echo "No"
  ;;
  *)
    echo "Not sure"
  ;;
esac

#!/bin/tcsh
switch ("$1")
```

code continues on next page

↗ LEARN MORE

Project 10 gives examples of control constructs in a shell script.

```
  case "positive":
    echo "Yes"
  breaksw
  case "negative":
    echo "No"
  breaksw
  default:
    echo "Not sure"
  breaksw
endsw
```

The for Loop

```
#!/bin/bash
for word in hello goodbye au-revoir; do
  echo $word
done
```

```
#!/bin/tcsh
foreach word (hello goodbye au-revoir)
    echo $word
end
```

The while Loop

```
#!/bin/bash
n=0
while [ ! $n = 10 ]; do
  echo $n
  n=$(expr $n + 1)
done
```

```
#!/bin/tcsh
set n = 0
while ($n != 10)
  echo $n
  set n = `expr $n + 1`
end
```

Project 85
Take Advantage
of Subshells

"How do I force a group of commands to execute in their own environment?"

This project discusses the use of subshells: what they are and how you might take advantage of their special features. It also introduces group commands, which are similar to subshells.

Subshells

A *subshell* is a new instance of a shell launched to run a single command, a *command list* (one or more commands separated by a semicolon), or a shell script.

To execute a command list in a subshell, enclose it in parentheses on the command line.

```
$ (cd /; ls)
```

This technique produces similar results to executing the command list in the normal manner except for one important difference: Because the command list runs in a new shell instance and not the current shell, it executes in a new environment. Recall that a new shell instance inherits environment variables from the current interactive shell, but *not* other settings, such as shell variables, attributes, and options. Further, no part of the subshell's environment is passed back to the parent shell. In our simple example, then, the built-in cd command executed in a subshell can't change the interactive shell's current working directory.

TIP

Use the environment variable SHLVL *to discover how deeply nested the current (sub-)shell instance is. Level 1 is the login shell, level 2 is a subshell, level 3 is a subshell launched by the subshell, and so on.*

LEARN MORE

Project 4 includes a section explaining shell and environment variables and their respective scopes.

TIP

A script is run by the executable named in the first line of the shell script—usually, #!/bin/bash. *The first line of a script may name any executable, not necessarily a shell. Here's a (pointless) illustration.*

```
$ cat myecho
#!/bin/echo
$ ./myecho Hello there!
./myecho Hello there!
```

⚑ LEARN MORE

Project 82 talks about the noexec **attribute.**

⚑ LEARN MORE

Project 86 shows you how to use a subshell to limit the scope of a signal handler in a Bash script.

Create Local Blocks of Code

The previous section explained that subshells execute in their own environments. We can take advantage of this when writing shell scripts. Enclosing a section of script code within parentheses, so that it executes in its own subshell, lets us set *local* shell variables and attributes that apply only to the enclosed code block. Such settings are not visible outside the code block and do not affect the remainder of the script when the code block has completed executing.

Here's a neat trick that uses a subshell to localize shell attributes. Suppose that we need to comment out a section of code and choose to use the noexec attribute to do so. Here's our first attempt, which doesn't work; line 3 is never echoed.

```
$ cat block-eg
#!/bin/bash
echo line 1
set -o noexec  # switch off execution to comment out
echo line 2
set +o noexec # switch execution back on
echo line 3
$ ./block-eg
line 1
```

The reason for the script's failure lies in the fact that the set +o noexec statement is never executed; we just switched off execution, and this includes execution of the built-in set command.

We get around this problem by placing the code to comment out in a subshell. Shell attributes set in a subshell—set -o noexec, in this example—are not passed back to the parent shell, so we don't need to turn execution back on. Clever!

```
$ cat block-eg
#!/bin/bash
echo line 1
( set -o noexec
echo line 2 )
echo line3
```

```
$ ./block-eg
line 1
line 3
```

Selectively Redirect Input and Output

We can group commands and apply selective input and output redirection. We might discard the standard error from several commands by writing them as a subshell. This technique averts the necessity to redirect the standard error individually from every command in the group.

```
$ cat redir-eg
#!/bin/bash
dir=$1; file=$2
( cd $dir
ls $file ) 2> junk
# more-commands ...
```

Here's another example that uses a subshell to redirect the standard input of a group of commands. The main script reads its input (name and age) from the terminal; the parenthesized section takes its input (code and membership) from the file autodata.

```
$ cat eg
#!/bin/bash
read -p "Name: " name
( read code
  read membership
  echo "Code: $code, membership: $membership"
) < autodata.txt
read -p "Age: " age
echo "Name: $name, age: $age"
```

The subshell reads from the file autodata.txt.

```
$ cat autodata.txt
ABC
123
```

When we run the script, we provide a name and (false ☺) age.

```
$ ./eg
Name: Adrian
Code: ABC, membership: 123
Age: 21
Name: Adrian, age: 21
```

As the script stands, the values read from the file autodata are lost when the subshell completes; the local shell variables code and membership are not passed back to the parent shell. Although this limitation stems from the rather simple example constructed to illustrate subshells, it provides a platform to illustrate some useful tricks.

The next code extracts shows you how to pass values back from a subshell to the main shell. New and changed lines are shown in bold.

```
$ cat eg
#!/bin/bash
declare -a autodata
read -p "Name: " name
autodata=($(
  ( read code
    read membership
    echo "$code $membership"
  ) < autodata.txt
))
read -p "Age: " age
echo "Name: $name, age: $age"
echo "Code: ${autodata[0]}, membership: ${autodata[1]}"
```

When we run the script, we see that the code and membership values are passed back to, and displayed from, the main script.

```
$ ./eg
Name: Adrian
Age: 21
Name: Adrian, age: 21
Code: ABC, membership: 123
```

How does this work? The whole subshell runs as a subcommand (enclosed in $(...)). As with all subcommands, Bash ultimately reads this expression as the value of its output—in this case, the value of subshell variables code and membership, which are echoed by the subshell before it completes. Furthermore, we capture that value (before the subshell disappears) by assigning the output of the subcommand to an array variable, autodata, using the expression

```
autodata=(value)
```

where value is the subshell run as a subcommand.

This example employs a few techniques, and you might have to experiment a little to follow how it works.

Redirect stdout with Tsch

The Tcsh shell is not able to redirect standard error independent of standard output. The Bash shell uses the following syntax to redirect only standard error.

```
cmd 2> file
```

In the Tcsh shell, we must apply the following trick.

```
(cmd >/dev/tty) >& file
```

The command is run in a subshell, and standard output is redirected back to the terminal. This has no effect except that the output from the subshell now contains only standard error. Then we specify Tcsh shell syntax to redirect both standard output (there's none, as it has already been redirected) and standard error to the file file.

Group Commands

A group command is like a subshell. To form a group command, enclose a command list, or a section of a shell script, in braces.

```
{ command; command; ...;}
```

The difference between a subshell and a group command is that the current shell, not a new instance of the shell, executes a group com-

↗ LEARN MORE

Project 87 covers Bash array variables.

↗ LEARN MORE

Project 55 shows how to launch commands to run in the background.

↗ LEARN MORE

Project 6 covers redirection.

❮ NOTE

The syntax to express a group command is quite fussy. The opening brace must be followed by a space, and a semicolon must terminate the last command.

⟟ TIP

A group command executes more efficiently than a subshell and is preferable whenever possible.

mand. This means that it does not execute in its own local environment, so some of the tricks employed using subshells do not work.

Let's revisit the standard-input example that we used earlier when illustrating subshells. In our new version, we employ a group command instead of a subshell. We need no longer use clever trickery to preserve the value of the variables `code` and `membership`, because they are no longer local to the enclosed block of code.

```
$ cat eg-group
#!/bin/bash
read -p "Name: " name
{ read code
  read membership
} < autodata.txt
read -p "Age: " age
echo "Name: $name, age: $age"
echo "Code: $code, membership: $membership"
$ ./eg-group
Name: Adrian
Age: 21
Name: Adrian, age: 21
Code: ABC, membership: 123
```

Project 81 shows how Bash operators are used outside a conditional expression to make execution of a second command dependent on the outcome of a first. For example:

```
$ command1 && command2
```

The `command2` is executed if, and only if, `command1` returns TRUE. This technique works because Bash does not evaluate the second part of an AND statement if the first part is FALSE. (There's no need to; if the first part returns FALSE, the result of the entire AND expression can only ever be FALSE.) This behavior is known as *short-circuiting*.

If either command is or both commands are a command sequence, you must make the sequence a group command for this technique to work.

```
$ { cmd1; cmd2; ...; } && { cmd3; cmd4; ...;}
```

Here's a useful trick that asks for root authentication.

```
sudo -p "Admin password " echo 2> /dev/null || ¬
    { echo "Incorrect" ; exit; }
```

The code is useful when placed at the start of a script that, later on, issues commands that require root permission obtained via sudo. The sequence will prompt for an administrator's password as soon as the script is invoked. Authentication resulting from a correct password lasts 5 minutes–plenty of time for most homemade scripts to run. If authentication fails, the second (group) command displays an error message and the script exits, before needless execution of the code that precedes an internal sudo command.

➐ LEARN MORE

Refer to Project 40, which lists the various signals and shows how you might send them to a running process by using the `kill` command.

⚡ TIP

Signals are frequently used by faceless background programs (daemons) to receive instructions from the user: There's no other simple means to communicate with them. You may use the same technique with your own background scripts. Project 55 covers background jobs.

Project 86
Trap and Handle Unix Signals

"How do I catch a signal sent to my Bash shell script?"

This project considers signals such as INT, HUP, and TERM, but from the receiving end. It shows how you might equip your Bash shell scripts with custom signal handlers (also called traps) to catch and handle signals sent to it. Project 40 considers signals from the other direction: how to issue them.

Understand Signals

Signals are a feature built into Unix. A signal is like an interrupt: Sending a signal to a process causes the process to stop what it's doing and to respond. Signals are used to tell processes to take a specific action, such as restarting, terminating, or temporarily halting.

Try this example.

```
$ sleep 1000
wake up
ok, you asked for it
<Control-c>
```

A running process that's not responding to keyboard input (wake up typed in the example above) somehow manages to respond when you press Control-c. How does this happen? When any process is launched, it's accompanied by some special code that manages signals, called a *handler*. A handler is executed whenever a signal is sent to its process. Some processes supply their own handlers; other processes rely on default handlers Unix automatically attaches as the process is launched.

You may send a signal to a process by using the `kill` command. A limited number of signals may also be sent by pressing control sequences such as `Control-c`, which instructs Terminal to send the appropriate signal.

There are many signals, and individual processes can elect to respond to some signals and ignore others. Each process may respond to a signal in its own particular way.

Catch Signals

Let's write a short Bash shell script that demonstrates how to catch and handle a specific signal. If you don't supply your own handlers, a script is launched with a default set of handlers. We'll override the default handler for a signal called `SIGINT` (or just `INT`), which can be sent from the `kill` command or from Terminal by pressing `Control-c`.

Here's an example script that loops indefinitely, going dotty.

```
$ cat signal-eg
#!/bin/bash
trap 'echo "Got INT"' INT
while true; do
  echo -n "."; sleep 1
done
```

Normally, we'd be able terminate the script by pressing `Control-c` in Terminal. The script catches the `INT` signal, however, by including the statement

```
trap 'echo "Got INT"' INT
```

This statement simply echoes the text `"Got INT"` and carries on regardless.

Let's run the script to see what happens when we press `Control-c` and when we send an `INT` signal from `kill`.

```
$ ./signal-eg
....^CGot INT      # <--here we typed Control-c (=INT)
......Got INT      # <--here we sent INT using command kill
......Terminated   # <--here we sent TERM using command kill
$
```

TIP

List the current settings for Terminal, including keystroke-to-interrupt mappings, by typing

`$ stty -e`

TIP

Discover the signals that a command or daemon respects by checking its man page. Search for the section titled "SIGNALS."

LEARN MORE

Refer to Projects 9 and 10 for basic shell scripting.

⬀ LEARN MORE

Project 40 shows you how to identify running processes and send signals to them.

⍑ TIP

trap is a Bash built-in command. To learn more about it, and to display a list of signals, type

```
$ help trap
$ trap -l
```

❧ NOTE

The signal KILL cannot be caught, because you can't override its default handler. This ensures that every process can be terminated by sending a KILL signal.

We sent an INT signal by using the line

```
$ kill -INT $(ps xww | awk '/\.\/signal-eg/{print $1}')
```

To stop the script, we must send a stronger signal, such as TERM, by typing

```
$ kill -TERM $(ps xww | awk '/\.\/signal-eg/{print $1}')
```

To honor the interrupt signal and exit the script, we would change our trap statement to read

```
trap 'echo "Got INT, bye bye."; exit' INT
$ ./signal-eg
....^CGot INT, bye bye.
```

Add Multiple Handlers

To add more than one handler, simply add more trap statements. To handle both the INT and TERM signals, for example, we would write

```
trap 'echo "Got INT, bye bye."; exit' INT
trap 'echo "Got TERM, bye bye."; exit' TERM
```

If more than one signal requires the same action, you may list them all in a single trap statement.

```
trap 'echo "Got INT or TERM, bye bye."; exit' INT TERM
```

Write a Complex Handler

If your signal hander is more complex than just a couple of statements, consider having a trap statement call a function. Here's an example that traps the HUP signal and performs some significant processing upon its receipt.

```
$ cat signal-eg
handlehup ()
{
  echo "Reloading configuration"
  # more statements here
  echo "Restart complete"
}
```

```
trap 'handlehup' HUP
while true; do
  echo -n "."; sleep 1
done
```

When a HUP signal is received, the function `handlehup` is called.

```
$ ./signal-eg
...Reloading configuration  # <-- we issued HUP using kill
Restart complete
.......
```

We issue the HUP signal by typing

```
$ kill -HUP $(ps xww | awk '/\.\/signal-eg/{print $1}')
```

Trap over a Block of Code

Suppose that you want to trap signals over a critical region of code but not over the whole script. This might be necessary in a script that writes information to a file in several steps, where an interrupt mid-way through the writing process would result in a half-written file.

We trap signals over the critical period, between opening and closing the file, by executing the critical region of code in a subshell and defining a handler that's local to the subshell. When the subshell completes, the handler ceases to be defined.

```
$ cat signal-eg
#!/bin/bash
# critical code - stop interrupts here
(
  trap 'echo "Caught by subshell"' INT
  echo "Critical code"
  a=100000; while ((a!=0)); do ((a--)); done
)
# normal code - allow interrupts from now on
echo "Normal code"
a=100000; while ((a!=0)); do ((a--)); done
```

✻ TIP

The HUP *signal is often interpreted by daemons as a request to reload their configuration settings and restart.*

↗ LEARN MORE

Project 52 covers Bash functions.

⊺ TIP

Switch off a handler by specifying null code to the **trap** *statement as a dash character.*

```
trap - SIG
```

This on/off technique can be used to limit a trap to a block of code in preference to using a subshell.

⬈ LEARN MORE

Project 85 covers subshells.

To illustrate this, both regions of code have a delay loop to make it possible to interrupt the script before it exits normally. After executing the script and pressing Control-c, we see that during execution of code in the critical region, the INT signal is caught and ignored. Thereafter, the INT signal terminates the script in the usual way.

```
$ ./signal-eg
Critical code
^CCaught by subshell
^CCaught by subshell
Normal code
^C
$
```

Project 87
Scripting Tips

"How do I write a function that returns an array of values?"

This project presents several tips that you might find useful when writing Bash shell scripts. It shows you how to declare variables and arrays, perform integer arithmetic, test if a value is numeric, return values from functions, and implement variable variables.

Declare Your Variables

This tip has nothing to do with the red channel at Customs. Declaring a variable is a way of telling Bash more about how you are going to use the variable. To declare a variable, use the Bash built-in command `declare`, followed by a type and variable name. Variable types include *integer* and *array,* both of which are described at greater length in this project.

In the next example, we declare the variable `count` to be an integer variable and perform some simple integer arithmetic, setting and incrementing `count`. First, by way of comparison, we try the sequence with an undeclared variable, which is taken by Bash to be a general-purpose string variable.

```
$ s=1
$ s=s+1
$ echo $s
s+1
$ declare -i count=1
$ count=count+1
$ echo $count
2
```

You may also `declare` variables read-only and export them as environment variables.

ℹ **TIP**

Display the names of all integer variables by typing

```
$ declare -i
```

To learn more about the `declare` *command, type*

```
$ help declare
```

Bash lets you declare a variable to be an array. An array variable holds many values, each accessed by its ordinal number (*index*). The following examples illustrate this.

Declare an array, and initialize it by specifying the option *-a* and listing the values you wish to assign within parentheses, separated by spaces. Enclose in double quotes any values that contain spaces.

```
$ declare -a products
$ products=(iBook iMac PowerBook PowerMac ¬
    "iPod shuffle" AirPort)
```

To retrieve a particular value, expand the array variable name, employing the syntax

```
${array-variable-name[index]}
```

To display the first value, which has an index of 0, and the fifth value, which has an index of 4, type

```
$ echo ${products[0]}
iBook
$ echo ${products[4]}
iPod shuffle
```

Display all values by giving an index of star.

```
$ echo ${products[*]}
iBook iMac PowerBook PowerMac iPod shuffle AirPort
```

To display the number of values in the array, type

```
$ echo ${#products[*]}
6
```

To display the length, in characters, of the second value in the array, type

```
$ echo ${#products[1]}
4
```

To create a list of all values, use a `for` loop to list all values one at a time.

```
$ for p in "${products[@]}"; do echo $p; done
iBook
...
iPod shuffle
AirPort
$
```

Enclosing the expansion in double quotes, and using an index @ (instead of *), ensures that each value is expanded to preserve spaces; without this, `iPod shuffle` expands into two values.

Use Integer Arithmetic Expressions

Bash provides a special syntax for integer arithmetic expressions and comparisons, in which variables are automatically expanded and assumed to have the type integer. Expressions are enclosed within `$((...))`, and conditions, within `((...))`. Within the double parentheses, you may employ expressions very much like those of the C programming language.

Here are a couple of examples.

```
$ i=7; j=35
$ echo $((i+j))
42
$ if (( (i*j) == 245)); then echo "yes"; fi
yes
```

As a trivial example, we might offer a thousand greetings in the following manner.

```
$ a=1000; while ((a!=0)); do echo -n "*hello*"; ¬
    ((a--)); done
```

↗ LEARN MORE

The difference between @ and * used as an array index affects expansion of the array in the same way that it affects expansion of positional parameters, explained in "Basic Expansion" in Project 76.

ℹ TIP

Learn about the Bash arithmetic expression allowed within `((...))` *and* `$((...))` *by typing* `/^ARITHMETIC EVALUATION` *within the Bash man page.*

Test for a Numeric Value

Here's a handy tip to determine whether a value is numeric. The line beginning with read generates a prompt, (Give a number) and assigns whatever you type to variable num. The line beginning with if tests num to see whether it's numeric.

```
$ read -p "Give a number: " num
Give a number: i23
$ if [ "${num//[0-9]/}" ]; then echo "Not numeric"; fi
Not numeric
$ read -p "Give a number: " num
Give a number: 123
$ if [ "${num//[0-9]/}" ]; then echo "Not numeric"; fi
```

Project 76 explains the parameter extension techniques we used in this trick.

Return Arbitrary Values

A Bash shell script or function may return an exit condition of 0 to 255, which is available in the shell special variable $?. To return an arbitrary value, we use the following trick, shown here applied to a Bash function.

The function return-eg returns a string value, simply set to Janet, to illustrate the technique. The function echoes its return value, and the calling script captures that value by calling the function and enclosing it in $(...). This syntax tells Bash to execute the function and replace it with its own output; thus, we assign the return value to the variable name.

```
$ cat return-eg
return-eg () {
  # processing here
  result="Janet"
  echo $result
}
```

```
name=$(return-eg)
echo $name
$ ./return-eg
Janet
```

If we combine the arbitrary-value trick with Bash array variables, we can write and call a function that returns many values.

```
$ cat return-eg
return-eg () {
  # processing here
  result="Janet Sophie"
  echo $result
}

declare -a guests
guests=($(return-eg))
for ((i=0; i<${#guests[*]}; i++)); do
  echo "guest $((i+1)) ${guests[i]}"
done
$ ./return-eg
guest 1 Janet
guest 2 Sophie
```

Variable Variables

Languages such as PHP implement *variable variables*. If you know what they are and would like to simulate their functionality in Bash, this trick is for you. Here's an example in which we echo the value of the variable detailsJanet.

```
$ echo $detailsJanet
Name: Janet Forbes, Country: England
```

Now we try the same exercise, except that the Janet part of the variable is itself held in a variable and, naturally, could be anything.

↗ **LEARN MORE**

Project 52 covers Bash functions.

```
$ read -p "Give name: " name
Give name: Janet
$ eval "echo \$details$name"
Name: Janet Forbes, Country: England
```

The built-in eval command tells Bash to expand the quoted command sequence and then to execute the expanded text as though it were the original command. The net effect is to expand the line twice before it's executed. After eval is executed, the command sequence in the example above becomes

```
echo $detailsJanet
```

Then this command is executed in the normal manner. If you were to give a different name, such as Sophie, in response to the Give name: prompt, the final statement would evaluate to

```
echo $detailsSophie
```

Network in Unix   10

This chapter covers some common networking tasks such as file sharing, Web serving, and network query tools. Although Apple provides graphical tools for administering the network, those tools do not afford the same freedom to configure services as their command-line equivalents. The eight projects cover the following topics:

Sharing files via AppleShare and NFS (Network File System)

Probing and testing networks, and querying the DNS (Domain Name System)

Configuring Apache, the Web server built in to Mac OS X

Configuring an FTP (File Transfer Protocol) server

Project 88
Mount Shares

"How do I access files shared from another Mac or a Unix Machine?"

This project shows you how to mount a share exported from another machine. It gives examples of mounting an AFP (Apple Filing Protocol) share exported by Apple's AppleShare, which is the default method of sharing files between Mac OS machines. Then the project shows you how to mount an NFS (Network File System) share. NFS is the industry-standard method of sharing files between Unix machines and is supported by Mac OS X's Unix core.

Switch on File Sharing

Before we mount a share on a client, we must enable file sharing on the server. To enable AppleShare, simply switch on file sharing by checking Personal File Sharing in System Preferences, pane Sharing, and tab Services. Mac OS X does not naturally export NFS shares the way it does AFP shares, but Project 89 shows you how to configure your Mac to be an NFS server.

Mount an AFP Share

You're probably familiar with mounting an AppleShare share from the Finder. Shares are shown by the Network icon in the top-left pane; you can also mount them by choosing Go > Connect to Server.

Naturally, a share can be mounted from the command line, too, via the `mount` command. To illustrate this, we'll mount an AppleShare share, choosing the home directory of `user jan` from the host (server) `saruman.local`. The syntax to mount an AppleShare share is

```
mount -t afp  afp://user:password@host/share mount-point
```

By default, the share takes on the name of the user account.

Here's our first attempt at mounting the share:

```
$ mount -t afp  afp://jan:pass@saruman.local/jan ~/jan
mount: realpath /Users/saruman/jan: No such file or dire...
```

That failed because we did not create the mount point at which the share was to be mounted—~/jan, in this example. The *mount point* is a directory that will contain all the files and directories of the share. (The files won't be physically copied, of course, but they will appear to be in that directory on the local machine.) You may create the directory at any point in the file system. We choose to mount jan (no sniggering, please) in the directory jan in our home directory. We type

```
$ mkdir ~/jan
$ mount -t afp  afp://jan:pass@saruman.local/jan ~/jan
mount_afp: the mount flags are 0000 the altflags are 0020
```

Let's check that the mount was successful by listing the mount-point directory, which should show the files from the mounted share.

```
$ ls ~/jan
Desktop     Library     Music       Public
Documents   Movies      Pictures    Sites
```

Use the mount command with no arguments to list all currently mounted file systems. We see our recently mounted share at the end of the list.

```
$ mount
...
afp_3vZVCw00srIR1Tstev72sQ5-1.2d000015 on /Users/saruman/jan
  (nodev, nosuid, mounted by saruman)
```

Access Shares Mounted by the Finder

When we mount a share with the mount command, we specify the directory at which the share is to be mounted. We have no such control of a share mounted by the Finder: It will always appear in a directory named /Volumes/name-of-share.

ͳ TIP

The command mount_afp *is equivalent to* mount -t afp. *Read its man page by typing*

```
$ man mount_afp
```

ͳ TIP

The mount *command reports that options such as* nodev *and* nosuid *are disabled; that's a security measure. Mount a volume as the root user to have those options enabled, and check the man page for* mount *to learn more about them. The SUID bit is explained by "The s-bit" in Project 8.*

⚡ LEARN MORE

"Hide History" in Project 48 shows you how to prevent sensitive commands, such as those that include passwords, from being recorded in the command-line history.

⚡ LEARN MORE

Project 66 discusses file systems, and Project 68 shows you how to mount and unmount a local volume.

⚡ LEARN MORE

Project 7 explains users, groups, UIDs, and GIDs.

Unmount a Share

To unmount a share, use the umount command naming the mount point.

```
$ umount ~/jan
```

There's no harm in leaving the mount-point directory for use the next time you mount the volume, but you may want to get rid of it. Depending on your version of Mac OS X, you may find that the Finder has already, and rather presumptuously, removed it for you.

Mount an NFS Share

As with AFP shares, you mount NFS shares from the Network icon in the top-left pane of the Finder or by choosing Go > Connect to Server.

From the command line, we mount NFS shares in much the same way as we mount AFP shares. One crucial difference is the method of authentication employed to ascertain file permissions. AFP requires a username and password just like a standard login. NFS compares user and group IDs (UIDs and GIDs), and assumes consistent UID and GID allocation across the server and all client machines. (In other words, your user account on all machines must be assigned identical UID and primary GIDs.)

This assumption holds true in a well-controlled network where a central server performs authentication, but not necessarily in an ad-hoc network. If your user accounts on the client and server machines are each assigned different UIDs (or GIDs), you'll not gain access to your own files on the server. Even worse, another user whose client credentials happen to match those of your account on the server *will* have access to your files. NFS is not designed for use in ad-hoc or hostile environments.

Assuming compatible IDs, let's mount an NFS share from the host sauron (IP address 10.0.2.3). The sauron host exports the directory /Users as a share called Users. We'll mount the share at the mount point /sauron on the client. The syntax for mounting an NFS share is

```
mount -t nfs host:/share mount-point
```

In this example, we choose to mount the share as the root user because we are mounting a system-level share (The directory /Users is owned by the system.)

```
$ sudo -s
Password:
# mkdir /sauron
# mount -t nfs -o nosuid 10.0.2.3:/Users /sauron
```

! WARNING

Mounting a share as the root user has security implications. Malicious users can take advantage of executables with the SUID or GUID bits set (called *suid* executables and explained in "The s-bit" in Project 8) to escalate their permissions. It's advisable to specify the option -o nosuid to the mount command to disable the effect of the s-bit, especially when you're mounting the user account space or any directory to which nonprivileged users can write. If you are mounting shares that have legitimate suid programs, such as those in /bin, /sbin, and /usr, don't specify the option.

Once mounted, the share is accessible from the directory /sauron. List this directory, and you'll see all the user directories that reside on the host sauron.

```
$ cd /sauron
$ ls -l
total 24
drwxrwxrwt   5  root      wheel      170 Jul 16 11:54 Shared
drwxr-xr-x  16  loraine   loraine    544 Jul  3 17:35 loraine
drwxr-xr-x  26  saruman   saruman    884 Sep  6 11:19 saruman
drwxr-xr-x  14  505       505        476 Aug 26 15:49 sharing
```

You'll notice that the directory sharing is shown with numeric user and group IDs of 505. This is because the server sauron has a user and group called sharing with a UID and GID of 505, but the client does not. Therefore, the client cannot map IDs to names. However, both client and server have the two user accounts saruman and loraine with consistent ID-to-name mappings.

↗ LEARN MORE

Refer to "How to Become the Root User" in Project 2 for more information on the sudo command.

↗ LEARN MORE

Project 8 covers file permissions and the s-bit.

⚡ LEARN MORE

Refer to the projects in Chapter 4 if you are not familiar with using any of the Unix text editors.

❗ WARNING

NFS does not support HFS+ resource forks. When you copy files using NFS, all such metadata is lost.

Unmount a Share

To unmount an NFS share, use the umount command.

```
# umount /sauron
```

If the umount command reports the device as busy, check that no files are open and that your current working directory is not in the mounted share.

Automount Shares

By adding an appropriate entry to the file /etc/fstab, we cause the client to mount an NFS share automatically when it boots. You must edit the file as the root user, creating it if it does not already exist. To automount the share /Users, we would add the entry

```
sauron.local:/Users /sauron nfs -b,-i,-P 0 0
```

We used a hostname instead of an IP address in this example.

Show in the Finder

Mounting an NFS volume with the Unix mount command does so behind the Finder's back. To get the mounted volume to show up in the Finder, refresh the list of mounted volumes by typing

```
$ disktool -r
```

Project 89
Set up an NFS Server

↗ **LEARN MORE**

Project 7 explains users, groups, UIDs, and GIDs.

"How do I share my files with other Unix machines?"

Mac OS X does not naturally export NFS shares the way it does AFP shares. This project shows how to configure your Mac to be an NFS server, thereby allowing other Unix machines to share your files. Project 88 shows how we might mount an NFS share on a client machine and, although written for Mac OS X, applies to any Unix client.

Set up a Simple NFS Server

NFS (Network File System) is the industry-standard method of exporting and mounting shares in a Unix environment. Its role is roughly equivalent to that of AppleShare in a Mac OS environment.

NFS is much more complex and capable than this simple example suggests. Indeed, whole books have been written on the subject. The project provides only a minimal example, being just enough to export a share that can be mounted by a Mac OS X or Unix client.

NFS does not employ password authentication but relies on user accounts having consistent user and group IDs (UID and GID) across the server and all clients.

! WARNING

NFS is not inherently secure and should be used only for trusted local networks.

⊋ LEARN MORE

Refer to "How to Become the Root User" in Project 2 for more information about issuing commands as the root user.

⊋ LEARN MORE

Refer to the projects in Chapter 4 if you are not familiar with using any of the Unix text editors.

Define Exports

On the server, we must define the shares that are to be made available to NFS clients. We can use Apple's NetInfo Manager application or edit the Unix *flat files* in the directory /etc. We'll choose the latter method, as it's more traditionally Unix.

Let's create a share by *exporting* the directory /Users, thereby making the home directory of each user available to NFS clients: This complements the mount example given in Project 88. To create a share, we need only change (or create) the file /etc/exports, which we must do as the root user. The syntax to define an NFS share is (all on one line)

```
directory-to-share -alldirs -maproot=nobody
-network=ip-address -mask=subnet-mask
```

For example, we might add the line

```
/Users -alldirs -maproot=nobody -network=10.0.2.0 ¬
    -mask=255.255.255.0
```

Let's examine this line:

▶ /Users is the full pathname of the directory we want to share.

▶ Option -alldirs makes all subdirectories of /Users available to clients.

▶ Option -maproot=nobody tells NFS that the root user on the client machine *does not* have root permissions on files in the mounted share. Recall that authentication is done by UID and GID, and that the root user will have IDs of 0 on both the client and server. Change this option to -maproot=root to allow full root access to the share from client machines.

▶ Option -network=10.0.2.0 says that *only* machines on the specified (local) network may mount the share, thereby protecting the share from clients outside your local network. You might instead specify a network such as 192.168.0.0, depending on the IP range of your local network.

▶ Option -mask=255.255.255.0 defines the extent of the local subnet in the usual "netmask" manner. In our example, we allow access to all clients with an IP address in the range 10.0.2.0 to 10.0.2.255 (or 192.168.0.0 to 192.168.0.255).

To activate the share, reboot your Mac. The NFS server daemon will now be running, and the share Users will be available to any NFS client whose IP address lies in the allowed range.

Enable a Pre-Tiger system

In versions of Mac OS X before 10.4 (Tiger) you'll probably have to enable flat-file mounts. To do so, type

```
# mkdir /etc/lookupd
# echo "FF NI DS" >> /etc/lookupd/mounts
```

Avoid Rebooting

It's possible to start the NFS server by hand. As the root user, type

```
# mountd
# nfsd -t -u -n 6
```

In versions of Mac OS X before 10.4 (Tiger), in which you had to create the file mounts in the directory /etc/lookupd, also type

```
# kill -HUP $(head -n1 /var/run/lookupd.pid)
```

If you make changes to /etc/exports after the NFS daemons have been launched, you must either reboot or reload the mountd daemon by typing

```
# kill -HUP $(head -n1 /var/run/mountd.pid)
```

Mount a Share

Refer to Project 88 if you want to know how to mount the share Users on a client machine.

Starting NFS

The NFS server is started automatically when your Mac boots if shares are defined in either the file /etc/exports or Apple's NetInfo Manager application. The Startup Item NFS, in the directory /System/Library/StartupItems, takes care of this: It launches two daemons called mountd and nfsd. The mountd daemon services mount requests, and nfsd services all other NFS calls.

⚓ TIP

Debug your NFS server by starting the NFS daemon by hand and putting it in debug mode by typing

```
# mountd -d
```

If the daemon is already running, kill it first by typing

```
# kill -KILL $(head -n1 ¬
    /var/run/mountd.pid)
```

Other Share Examples

To export the entire system volume, add the following line to /etc/exports.

```
/ -alldirs -maproot=nobody -network=10.0.2.0 ¬
    -mask=255.255.255.0
```

To export the shared home directory /Users/Shared to the whole world, add the following line to /etc/exports.

```
/Users/Shared  -ro -mapall=nobody
```

The option -ro says to make the share read only. We have mapped all users to the user nobody to increase security further. We do not specify a network, thus opening the share to all clients, no matter what their IP addresses are.

Project 90
Probe Networks

"How do I discover more information about my network?"

This project provides some useful tricks for probing networks. It covers the commands `ping`, `appleping`, `traceroute`, `netstat`, and `arp`, and Apple's port scanner. Project 91 considers utilities for querying the Domain Name System, and Project 73 shows you how to manage network settings.

Unix Utilities Power Apple's Tools

Apple's Network Utility application provides several useful tools for probing and testing networks. It's actually a front end to the equivalent Unix command-line utilities, which we'll explore in this project. *Network,* for the purposes of these utilities, can mean anything from a two-machine home network to the Internet. The results you see from typing the examples will usually differ in the details from those shown in the book.

First, let's *ping!*

Ping a Host

The venerable `ping` utility sends network packets to a remote host and waits for a response. It's a handy way to check whether a particular host is responding to network connections or your own network connection is live.

In the example below, we ping `apple.com`. The fifth line of output marks where we pressed `Control-c` to stop `ping`; otherwise, it would have kept running forever. The response times give a good indication of the responsiveness of the connection between your machine and the destination host.

```
$ ping apple.com

PING apple.com (17.254.3.183): 56 data bytes
64 bytes from 17.254.3.183: icmp_seq=0 ttl=41 time=177.021 ms
64 bytes from 17.254.3.183: icmp_seq=1 ttl=41 time=181.916 ms
64 bytes from 17.254.3.183: icmp_seq=2 ttl=41 time=181.250 ms
^C
--- apple.com ping statistics ---
3 packets transmitted, 3 packets received, 0% packet loss
round-trip min/avg/max/stddev = 177.021/180.062/181.916/2.168
ms
```

Use option -i to change the interval between ping transmissions and option -c to tell ping to send a specific number of packets before exiting. To ping your server once a minute (specified as 60 seconds) for 30 minutes, for example, type

```
$ ping -i 60 -c 30 myservername.local
```

Ping Bonjour (Rendezvous)

Here's a neat trick, but it'll only work only if you have a local network with several Macs connected and running Bonjour. Type the following command (for which you'll get different results from those shown).

```
$ ping  224.0.0.251
PING 224.0.0.251 (224.0.0.251): 56 data bytes
64 bytes from 217.155.168.146: ... time=0.213 ms
64 bytes from 217.155.168.149: ... time=0.553 ms (DUP!)
64 bytes from 217.155.168.150: ... time=0.855 ms (DUP!)
```

You'll wonder what's responding to the IP address 224.0.0.251 and why three responses were received. This address is reserved for *multicast DNS (Domain Name Server)* queries. Apple's Bonjour technology uses this feature to resolve hostnames that end in .local into IP addresses. A machine running Bonjour may send a hostname such as sauron.local to this broadcast address, and the machine with that hostname will respond with its IP address. In our example, each Bonjour-enabled Mac on the local network has responded to the ping.

Ping All Hosts

Call all hosts on the local network by pinging the network's *broadcast address.* In this example, we have assumed that machines on the local network have IP addresses in the range 10.0.2.1 to 10.0.2.254 (typical of an AirPort network); therefore, the broadcast address is 10.0.2.255. This example won't work if your Mac is not part of a local network.

```
$ ping 10.0.2.255
PING 10.0.2.255 (10.0.2.255): 56 data bytes
64 bytes from 10.0.2.3: ... time=0.247 ms
64 bytes from 10.0.2.4: ... time=246.945 ms (DUP!)
64 bytes from 10.0.2.1: ... time=247.011 ms (DUP!)
```

The broadcast address is the highest IP address on the local network. If your IP address is in the range 192.168.x.x with a subnet mask of 255.255.0.0, for example, the broadcast address is 192.168.255.255. Similarly, for an IP address in the range 192.168.10.x with a subnet mask of 255.255.255.0, the broadcast address is 192.168.10.255.

Find the Router

Your router *might* respond to this ping.

```
$ ping 0
PING 0 (0.0.0.0): 56 data bytes
64 bytes from 217.155.168.150: ... time=1.234 ms
```

Use Bonjour Names

Every Bonjour-enabled Mac answers to its Bonjour hostname (local hostname), which looks like computername.local. Your Macs' local hostname is shown in the System Preferences Sharing pane, in the Services tab. We can use this local hostname in all the usual places. For example:

```
$ ping sauron.local
PING sauron.local (10.0.2.3): 56 data bytes
64 bytes from 10.0.2.3: icmp_seq=0 ttl=64 time=1.571 ms
```

Zero Configuration

Bonjour is Apple's proprietary implementation of an Internet standard called Zero Configuration Networking. Any machine that implements the technology should respond to the IP address 224.0.0.251.

Bonjour was called Rendezvous in versions of Mac OS X before 10.4 and wasn't available in versions of Mac OS X before 10.2.

⚓ TIP

If you have older Macs still sharing over AppleTalk, use the command appleping *instead of* ping. *Issued with no parameters, the command displays a quick use summary.*

To browse a Mac that's running Personal Web Sharing, use an address such as `http://sauron.local/` instead of its IP address. Bonjour operates over the local subnet only: Don't expect to be able to connect over the Internet by specifying a local hostname.

Local hostnames are resolved by `mDNSResponder`, the multicast DNS daemon (see "Ping Bonjour (Rendezvous)" earlier in this project). Check whether this daemon is running by typing

```
$ ps -auxww | grep mDNS
root  39  0.0  0.1  28068 1200  ??  Ss Tue01PM 0:02.73
/usr/sbin/mDNSResponder -launchdaemon
```

Trace a Route

The `traceroute` command reports on the route a network packet may take when traveling from your machine to a destination host. It does so by sending the destination host *control packets* with a limited lifetime. The lifetime is measured in network *hops* (the number of nodes the packet must pass through to get to its destination). The first packet sent is given a lifetime of one hop. When the packet expires, the machine at which it expires (usually, a router) sends a control packet back to your machine to report the packet's demise. Each subsequent packet that's sent has a lifetime one hop greater than that of the previous packet, allowing `traceroute` to map the machines between your Mac and the destination. `traceroute` may or may not work, depending on how cooperative the intervening machines are in returning a response to an expired packet.

As an interesting exercise, use `traceroute` when you have a machine connected to a couple of local subnets (like a wired Ethernet and an AirPort network), and see what route packets are taking between your machine and the local server. For example:

```
$ traceroute carcharoth.mayo-family.com
traceroute to carcharoth.mayo-family.com (217.155.168.149),
64 hops max, 40 byte packets
 1  middle-earth (10.0.2.1)  3.855 ms  3.546 ms  2.116 ms
 2  my.router (192.168.1.1)  7.483 ms  2.832 ms  2.018 ms
 ...
```

Examine Routing Tables

Your Mac maintains a network routing table for communication with other hosts on the local network. This table translates an IP address, which is the usual way of identifying another host, into an Ethernet address, which is how hosts are actually identified on the local network.

The netstat Command

Check Internet-to-Ethernet routing by using the netstat command with option -r.

```
$ netstat -r
Internet:
Destination         Gateway           Flags Refs Use Netif Exp
default             valinor.mayo-fam  UGSc  10   325 en0
10.0.2/24           link#5            UCS   3    0   en1
middle-earth.wless  0:d:93:cd:be:74   UHLW  0    0   en1  723
sauron.wless        localhost         UHS   0    10  lo0
saruman.wless       0:10:a7:2e:b6:74  UHLW  0    3   en1 1045
...
```

The arp Command

The arp command displays (and modifies) the Internet-to-Ethernet address translation tables. Use option -a to display all the current table entries. You'll probably never edit these tables unless you're a networking wizard!

```
$ arp -a
middle-earth.wless (10.0.2.1) at 0:d:93:cd:be:74 on en1
[ethernet]
saruman.wless (10.0.2.4) at 0:10:a7:2e:b6:74 on en1
[ethernet]
smeagol.mayo-family.com (217.155.168.148) at
0:3:93:1b:fc:de on en0 [ethernet]
carcharoth.mayo-family.com (217.155.168.149) at
0:3:93:1b:fc:de on en0 [ethernet]
valinor.mayo-family.com (217.155.168.150) at
0:50:7f:6:82:34 on en0 [ethernet]
...
```

⚓ TIP

Use the netstat *command to show many other network statistics besides Internet-to-Ethernet routing. Read its man page to discover a whole host of options.*

Scan Ports

Port scanning is a method of probing a host to find out what services it provides; an open port implies an active service. A host running a Web server, for example, will have port 80 open. Port scanning is often used to check for weaknesses in your own network, preferably before other people find them. Port scanning is also used by e-vandals with no social lives and, therefore, time on their hands to play at breaking into other people's computers.

Grab an Open-Source Port Scanner

One of the best network scanners (or *mappers*) is nmap from Insecure. org (www.insecure.org/nmap/). It's not supplied as standard in Mac OS X but can be built from scratch or installed from one of the popular ports such as Fink (http://fink.sourceforge.net/) or Darwin Ports (http://darwinports.opendarwin.org/).

Steal Apple's Port Scanner

Apple's Network Utility application includes a port scanner called stroke. It's possible to call this from the command line or copy it to a new file such as /usr/local/bin/portscan. Type the following to grab a copy.

```
$ sudo cp /Applications/Utilities/Network\ Utility.app/¬
    Contents/Resources/stroke /usr/local/bin/portscan
```

To scan a machine, type portscan and the machine's hostname, followed by the start and end numbers (between 1 and 65,535) for the range of ports you want to scan.

```
$ portscan carcharoth.mayo-family.com 75 85
Port Scanning host: 217.155.168.149
          Open TCP Port:     80          http
```

Project 91
Resolve Hostnames

"What's the IP address of `jan.1dot1.com`*?"*

This project shows you how to query the Domain Name System (DNS) to translate domain names and hostnames into IP addresses. The DNS is used to discover other information, too, such as which hosts handle email for a particular domain. It covers the commands `host` and `dig`.

Learn What's in a (Domain) Name

The *Domain Name System* is a distributed database that resolves domain names and hostnames into their assigned IP addresses. Mac OS X includes a DNS server distribution called Bind that lets you set up your own DNS server (called `named`), but we'll be considering just how to query a DNS server, not how to set one up.

Consider a domain name such as `bbc.co.uk`. You can think of it as a pathname, but in reverse, rather like this.

`/uk/co/bbc`

Performing a DNS search to resolve `bbc.co.uk` into its IP address involves starting from the root of the DNS system and asking the *root servers* about `uk`. The root servers point to other servers that are authoritative for the domain `uk` and that tell you about `co.uk`. Those servers in turn point you to still other servers than can answer for `bbc.co.uk`.

Hostname resolution is the responsibility of your nominated DNS servers named in the Network pane of System Preferences. The servers are most likely those of your Internet Service Provider (ISP), but it's possible to run your own. If you obtain your IP address by using DHCP (Dynamic Host Configuration Protocol), your DNS servers will be configured automatically; therefore, it's not necessary to name them in the Network pane.

Hostnames and Domain Names

A *hostname* is a name given to an individual machine. A *domain name* usually is a starting point from which to name many hosts. `1dot1.com` is a domain name, but it might also be a hostname if I choose to call my only machine in that domain `1dot1.com`. So what's `jan.1dot1.com`? To the outside, it's academic; only the administrator of the domain knows whether it's merely a name assigned to a particular Web site or also the name of a particular machine.

A hostname must have an IP address, but a domain name need not.

ᵢ̈ TIP

Use the special type any *to grab any (all) information available.*

$ host -t any 1dot1.com

Option -a *is similar to* -t any *but provides verbose output.*

ᵢ̈ TIP

Request a zone transfer by typing

$ host -t axfr 1dot1.com

Most servers will deny this request, but the technique is useful in checking your own server configuration should you ever run a DNS server.

Look up DNS Information

To look up the IP address of jan.1dot1.com, use host. The host command forms a DNS query and sends it to one of your nominated DNS servers for resolution. Type

```
$ host jan.1dot1.com
jan.1dot1.com is an alias for 1dot1.com.
1dot1.com has address 217.155.168.149
```

The first line tells us that jan.1dot1.com is the same machine as 1dot1.com. The second line gives the IP address of the machine (and both domains) as 217.155.168.149. This simple query searched for *A records*, which hold the IP address of a host or domain. It's equivalent to specifying the option -t (for type) followed by a designator a (for A records).

```
$ host -t a jan.1dot1.com
```

We can query for other information, too. We might be interested in the servers that gave us the A records—called the *name servers* for the domain. We ask for name-server information by specifying the type designator ns.

```
$ host -t ns 1dot1.com
1dot1.com name server smeagol.mayo-family.com.
1dot1.com name server carcharoth.mayo-family.com.
```

Other information includes the Start of Authority (SOA) record for a domain, which gives administrative information such as the time in seconds for which the domain information should be cached after being fetched.

```
$ host -t soa 1dot1.com
1dot1.com SOA carcharoth.mayo-family.com.
hostmaster.1dot1.com. 2004111505 7200 3600 604800 3600
```

Mail Exchange (MX) records hold the IP addresses of the hosts that handle mail for the domain.

```
$ host -t mx 1dot1.com
1dot1.com mail is handled by 20 saruman.mayo-family.com.
1dot1.com mail is handled by 10 carcharoth.mayo-family.com.
```

Configure DNS Lookup

As you may already know, we nominate DNS servers by using System Preferences, selecting the Network pane and then the TCP/IP tab for each interface (**Figure 10.1**). You can also define *search domains* from System Preferences, which allows you to specify relative hostnames. Having defined `mayo-family.com` as a search domain, for example, we can name the individual hosts in that domain by specifying just their hostname. The following would be equivalent.

```
$ host carcharoth
carcharoth.mayo-family.com has address 217.155.168.149
$ host carcharoth.mayo-family.com
carcharoth.mayo-family.com has address 217.155.168.149
```

If you specify a domain name with a trailing dot, the name is taken to be absolute and will never have the search path added.

```
$ host carcharoth.
Host carcharoth not found: 3(NXDOMAIN)
```

ⓘ TIP

If `localhost` *is being treated as a relative hostname and does not resolve correctly, specify it as an absolute hostname by ending it with a dot, as in* `localhost..`

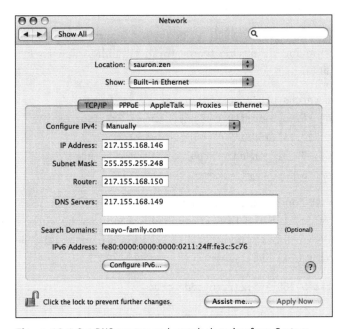

Figure 10.1 Set DNS servers and search domains from System Preferences.

↗ **LEARN MORE**

Project 19 explains Unix symbolic links.

ᵢ̆ TIP

To learn more about configuration settings that can be specified in /etc/resolv.conf, *type*

$ `man 5 resolver`

ᵢ̆ TIP

If your Mac has no active network connection, Mac OS X will remove the file /var/run/resolv.conf. *This does not matter normally, but if you run your own DNS server and rely on it to resolve multiple hostnames to 127.0.0.1 (you might implement virtual hosting by using the Apache Web server) simply replace the file that was removed.*

Configure from Unix

System Preferences maintains a Unix configuration file called /etc/resolv.conf. Display this file, and you'll see that it reflects the DNS servers and search domains set in System Preferences or configured by DHCP.

```
$ cat /etc/resolv.conf
search mayo-family.com
nameserver 217.155.168.149
```

Although it's possible to maintain the file by hand, be warned that System Preferences may overwrite it should any network settings change. The file is actually a Unix symbolic link to /var/run/resolv.conf.

Use Reverse Mapping

Reverse mapping is looking up a hostname from an IP address. It employs the same DNS system as forward mapping, starting from a top-level domain called arpa and a subdomain called in-addr.arpa for the Internet address space.

Here's an example in which we perform a forward and then a reverse query, moving from a hostname to an IP address and back to the original hostname.

```
$ host carcharoth.mayo-family.com
carcharoth.mayo-family.com has address 217.155.168.149
$ host 217.155.168.149
149.168.155.217.in-addr.arpa domain name pointer
carcharoth.mayo-family.com.
```

The host command lets us type an IP address in the more familiar form of 217.155.168.149, although this is not a valid entry in the reverse-map DNS system. Strictly, we should have typed a domain name that looks like this.

```
$ host 149.168.155.217.in-addr.arpa
$
```

This format reverses the order of the familiar four-part IP address, in which the address starts with the largest network (217) and ends with an individual host (149). It uses the DNS convention of placing the host first, then subdomains, and then the largest domain. You'll notice, however, that this command elicits no response. Recall that the host command assumes we want A records unless we specify otherwise from the -t option. To obtain a hostname from an address, we need a *pointer record*, denoted by type designator ptr. Thus, the full command is

```
$ host -t ptr 149.168.155.217.in-addr.arpa
149.168.155.217.in-addr.arpa domain name pointer
carcharoth.mayo-family.com.
```

Dig for Information

The dig (Domain Information Groper) command is an alternative to host. It's more comprehensive and is the preferred tool among DNS server administrators. The output from dig is more comprehensive and verbose than that from host.

Let's revisit some of the examples we used to illustrate host, but this time, we'll employ dig to grope jan.1dot.com.

```
$ dig jan.1dot1.com
; <<>> DiG 9.3.0 <<>> jan.1dot1.com
;; global options:  printcmd
;; Got answer:
;; ->>HEADER<<- opcode: QUERY, status: NOERROR, id: 5665
;; flags: qr rd ra; QUERY: 1, ANSWER: 2, AUTHORITY: 2,
ADDITIONAL: 2

;; QUESTION SECTION:
;jan.1dot1.com.                  IN  A

;; ANSWER SECTION:
jan.1dot1.com.   24868  IN  CNAME  1dot1.com.
1dot1.com.       24868  IN  A      217.155.168.149
```

output continues on next page

NOTE

The older nslookup *command is depreciated in favor of* dig.

✎ NOTE

Unlike host*, dig does not use the search domains unless explicitly told to so do by the inclusion of the* +search *option.*

```
$ dig +search carcharoth
```

✸ TIP

List all the root name servers by typing

```
$ dig @a.root-¬
    servers.net ns .
```

✸ TIP

To request a domain transfer type the following (replacing 1dot1.com *with the relevant domain name):*

```
$ dig 1dot1.com axfr
```

```
;; AUTHORITY SECTION:
1dot1.com.          111268 IN  NS  smeagol.mayo-family.com.
1dot1.com.          111268 IN  NS  carcharoth.mayo-family.com.

;; ADDITIONAL SECTION:
smeagol.mayo-family.com. 24868    IN  A  217.155.168.148
carcharoth.mayo-family.com. 46537 IN  A  217.155.168.149
...
```

As you can see, dig answered more questions than were asked. It returned related and useful information, such as the name servers for the domain and their IP addresses.

Look up Additional Information

dig has many options to query for information other than A records, equivalent to the host command's -t option. Here are some examples you might like to try.

```
$ dig ns 1dot1.com
$ dig +multiline soa 1dot1.com
$ dig mx 1dot1.com
$ dig any 1dot1.com
```

The dig command displays useful additional information, including the questions it asked of the DNS server. Specify the +noall option to turn off the display of additional information; then selectively switch on exactly what you want to see. In the next example, we ask for only the direct answer (option +answer) to our query for the A record of 1dot1.com.

```
$ dig +noall +answer  a 1dot1.com
1dot1.com.          86400   IN  A   217.155.168.149
```

We can specify a particular name server rather than have dig use those specified in System Preferences. To use the (fictional) name server ns1.example.com in querying the domain apple.com, type

```
$ dig @ns1.example.com apple.com
```

Trace a DNS Chain

To follow the chain of DNS servers that were queried to resolve a hostname, specify the option +trace.

```
$ dig +trace news.bbc.co.uk
```

Use Reverse Mapping with dig

dig will not automatically recognize a reverse-map request unless you specify the option -x or supply the proper reverse-map address. Type either of the following.

```
$ dig -x 217.155.168.149
$ dig ptr 149.168.155.217.in-addr.arpa
```

Project 92
Configure Apache

"How do I enable Apache to serve the main Web site from my home directory?"

This project shows you how to configure the Apache Web server that is part of a standard Mac OS X install. It describes how to start and stop Apache, and how to change the document root. Project 93 shows you how to enable features such as PHP support, server-side includes (SSI), and CGI (Common Gateway Interface) scripts. This project assumes that you are familiar with the concept of a Web server and are able to write simple HTML files.

Set Up Your Own Web Server

Apache is an open-source Web server (more strictly, an HTTP server) maintained by the Apache Software Foundation (www.apache.org). Apache is supplied as part of Mac OS X, so you can serve Web pages straight out of the box. It's easy to start Apache from System Preferences: Select the Sharing pane, click the Services tab, and check Personal Web Sharing. Use the Computer Name at the top of the Sharing pane in place of `computer-name` in the examples below.

The default configuration has Apache serving documents from the directory `/Library/Webserver/Documents`. Users can view the Web site from a Web browser by entering one of the following URLs.

- `http://computer-name.local/`

- `http://localhost/`

- `http://127.0.0.1/`

In addition to the main site, each user account has a personal Web presence. The user `saruman`, for example (we'll assume this user throughout the rest of the project), maintains a personal Web site at `/Users/saruman/Sites` (`~/Sites`), accessible by entering the URL

- `http://computer-name.local/~saruman/`

Try these example URLs now. If you've enabled Personal Web Sharing, you'll see a placeholder Web site answering to your Mac's IP address or hostname, plus a Web site answering to each user account. Note that the main site looks different from the personal sites; you'll need to remember this for later.

Configuration of Apache from System Preferences is limited to turning Apache on and off. That's a shame, because Apache is a very powerful and highly configurable server. However, and as you might have guessed, we can configure Apache and take full advantage of its many features from the Unix command line. Let's look at a few examples of what we can achieve.

The Apache daemon, which runs as httpd, is owned by the root user. The Apache configuration file is also owned by root. For the remainder of this project, we'll assume the status of the root user by issuing the command

```
$ sudo -s
Password:
#
```

Start and Stop Apache

We can enable, start, stop, and restart Apache from the command line. First, let's enable Apache. Once it's enabled, Apache will start automatically every time your Mac boots.

Edit the file /etc/hostconfig, using a Unix text editor such as nano. Look for a line that starts with WEBSERVER, and set it to equal -YES-

```
    WEBSERVER=-YES-
```

Reboot your Mac, and Apache will start automatically.

To disable Apache at startup, set

```
    WEBSERVER=-NO-
```

↗ LEARN MORE

Refer to "How to Become the Root User" in Project 2 for more information about the sudo command.

↗ LEARN MORE

Refer to Chapter 4 if you are not familiar with any of the Unix text editors.

ᵢ̈ TIP

*The file /etc/hostconfig
enables other services, such as
Personal File Sharing and
Windows Sharing. As for
Personal Web Sharing, these
setting are honored when your
Mac boots, but changing them
during normal operation will
have no effect.*

ᵢ̈ TIP

*If you maintain a live Web site
and don't want to disrupt the
experience of clients who may
already have connections, restart
Apache gracefully by typing*

apachectl graceful

Alternatively, to start Apache at any time, no matter what WEBSERVER is set to, type

apachectl start

To stop Apache, type

apachectl stop

Configure Apache

All Apache configuration directives you'll want to change are in a single file called /etc/httpd/httpd.conf. We'll be editing this file throughout the project. Remember to edit it as the root user.

Change the Document Root

Changing the *document root* is a common configuration requirement. The document root tells Apache where you've placed the HTML files that make up the main Web site. In a standard configuration, the document root is the directory /Library/WebServer/Documents.

Let's change it to the Sites directory in our home directory. Edit the file /etc/httpd/httpd.conf, and search for the DocumentRoot directive. You'll find it currently naming the default directory root.

```
DocumentRoot "/Library/WebServer/Documents"
```

In the examples that follow, we assume the username saruman, but you should type your own username. Replace the line above with the following line.

```
DocumentRoot "/Users/saruman/Sites"
```

There's one more change we must make. The document root must be configured—permissions and options set—by a Directory directive. We'll see some examples of changing options in Project 93. For now, locate the current setting that configures the old document root.

```
<Directory "/Library/WebServer/Documents">
```

Replace it with this one, which configures the new document root.

```
<Directory "/Users/saruman/Sites">
```

Don't change any of the actual settings—just the name of the document root specified in the `Directory` directive. The `Directory` directive is brought to a close by the following line.

```
</Directory>
```

Always ensure that Apache, which runs under the user and group www, has read access to the files it is supposed to serve. This is best achieved by granting read permission (but not write permission) to others.

Remove Clashing Sites

The last line of the configuration file is

```
Include /private/etc/httpd/users/*.conf
```

This line loads several additional configuration files into Apache to configure the document root for each user's personal Web site. The user saruman's personal Web site now clashes with our new main document root (because we just set the main document root to be /Users/saruman/Sites), so we must remove the file /etc/httpd/users/saruman.conf.

Alternatively, we could serve the main site from a different directory, such as ~/MainSites. You may also remove the entire <Directory "/Users/saruman/Sites"> directive from the main configuration file and maintain the version in the file saruman.conf, but be warned that this represents a more advanced configuration task that may cause you problems.

Test the New Configuration

First, because we changed the configuration file, we must restart Apache by typing

apachectl restart

⏻ **LEARN MORE**

Projects 7 and 8 cover users, groups, and permissions.

⏻ **TIP**

Lines in the configuration file that start with the hash (#) symbol are comments, and Apache ignores them. When changing the file, you might want to leave the original lines in but comment them out by preceding them with a hash.

**Personal Web Sharing
Document Roots**

The document root for
personal Web sites (those
with URLs in the form
`http://computer-
name.local/~username/`)
is controlled by the `UserDir`
directive, not by the
`DocumentRoot` directive.

ᵢ̈ TIP

*Sometimes, a browser's caching
habits obscure configuration
changes made to Apache. If you
make a configuration change
that appears to have no effect,
click the reload button.*

↗ LEARN MORE

Project 21 explores the `tail`
command.

ᵢ̈ TIP

*Read the Apache manual at the
URL* `http://localhost/
manual/`. *Don't leave out the
trailing forward slash when
entering the URL.*

Reload the main Web site from the URL `http://computer-
name.local/`. Click the browser's reload button to ensure that it does
not display a cached page. If everything has worked correctly, you'll
see a new main Web site that sports the same look as the personal
Web site. That wasn't our intention; we'd now replace the placeholder
Web site with a real Web site. Our intention was to be able to populate the directory `~/Sites` instead of `/Library/Webserver/Documents`.

If the changes have not worked, check Apache's log files, as described
in the next section.

Check Apache's Log Files

Apache writes information to two log files, often used to monitor
hits on your site or debug configuration changes. You'll find Apache's
log entries in the two files

`/var/log/httpd/access_log`
`/var/log/httpd/error_log`

View them with the `tail` command by typing

`$ tail -f /var/log/httpd/access_log`

Project 93
Configure Apache More

"How do I configure Apache to enable PHP support?"

This project shows you how to configure the Apache Web server that is part of a standard Mac OS X install. It shows how to enable features such as PHP support, server-side includes (SSI), and CGI (Common Gateway Interface) scripts. The project continues Project 92, which describes how to start and stop Apache and how to change the document root. It doesn't teach you how to write Web sites but assumes that if, for example, you want to enable CGI scripts, you know what a CGI script is.

Configure Apache

If you're not familiar with basic Apache configuration, read Project 92 first.

All the Apache configuration directives you'll want to change reside in a single file called /etc/httpd/httpd.conf. We'll be editing this file throughout the project as the root user. For the remainder of this project, we'll assume the status of the root user by issuing the command

```
$ sudo -s
Password:
#
```

Enable PHP Support

To enable PHP support, uncomment the following lines by removing the leading hash symbols.

```
#LoadModule php4_module     libexec/httpd/libphp4.so
#AddModule mod_php4.c
```

Restart Apache by typing

`apachectl restart`

Write a test file called `index.php`, and put it in the directory `~/Sites` (or whatever directory is your document root). This simple script tells PHP to generate a test page that reports on the PHP configuration (**Figure 10.2**).

```
$ cat ~/Sites/index.php
<?php
  phpinfo()
?>
```

Load the test page from the URL `http://localhost/index.php` or any of the equivalent URLs.

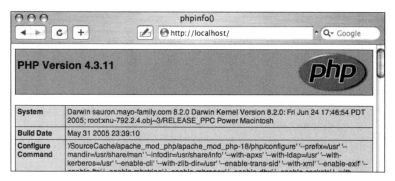

Figure 10.2 You'll see this test page if you have successfully enabled PHP support in Apache.

For older versions of Mac OS X, it may be necessary to add the following lines at the end of the configuration file but before the `Include` directive. Check first to see whether you already have them.

```
<IfModule mod_php4.c>
    AddType application/x-httpd-php .php
    AddType application/x-httpd-php-source .phps
    DirectoryIndex index.html index.php
</IfModule>
```

Search for Index.html

How does Apache know which filenames to search for when none is specified—for example, in a URL such as `http://localhost/`? To answer this question, search for the `DirectoryIndex` directive in Apache's configuration file. There probably are two of them, and you'll want the second, which looks like this.

```
DirectoryIndex index.html index.php
```

The directive tells Apache to check for a file named `index.html` and serve it if found; otherwise, serve `index.php`. If neither is found, Apache lists the contents of the document root directory.

Enable Server-Side Includes

Server-side includes (SSI) are commands interpreted by the Apache HTTP server as it serves a page. The Apache manual has a short tutorial on SSIs. We'll simply enable them and present a test page to write the current date and time to a Web page as it is served.

Uncomment the following lines to make them active. They tell Apache to treat files whose names end with `.shtml` as SSI scripts.

```
AddType text/html .shtml
AddHandler server-parsed .shtml
```

Next, change the options on the directory that serves as the document root. If you followed the steps in Project 92, you'll be looking for the following line (except that it names your home directory).

```
<Directory "/Users/saruman/Sites">
```

Otherwise, the directory root will be defined by the line

```
<Directory "/Library/WebServer/Documents">
```

Shortly after this line, you'll see an `Options` directive.

```
Options Indexes FollowSymLinks MultiViews
```

Add the option `Includes` to enable SSI.

```
Options Includes Indexes FollowSymLinks MultiViews
```

TIP

To tell Apache to load the file `index.php` *in preference to* `index.html` *where they both exist, swap the order in which the two files are listed in the* `DirectoryIndex` *directive. If two* `DirectoryIndex` *directives are present, remove one of them.*

TIP

Read the Apache manual at the URL `http://localhost/manual/`. *Don't leave out the trailing forward slash when entering the URL.*

ⓘ TIP

Check the syntax of a configuration file by typing

apachectl configtest

Restart Apache by typing

apachectl restart

Finally, we must write a test file, which we'll call index.shtml, and place it in the directory ~/Sites (or whatever you have chosen as your root directory). This simple script tells Apache to generate a page that displays the current date and time (**Figure 10.3**).

```
$ cat index.shtml
  <p> SSI Test: <br />
  <!--#config timefmt="It is now %k:%M on %A %e %B" -->
  <!--#echo var="DATE_LOCAL" -->
  </p>
```

Load the test page from the URL http://localhost/index.shtm or any of the equivalent URLs.

If you encounter problems in getting this to work, check the Apache log files and review "Remove Clashing Sites" in Project 92.

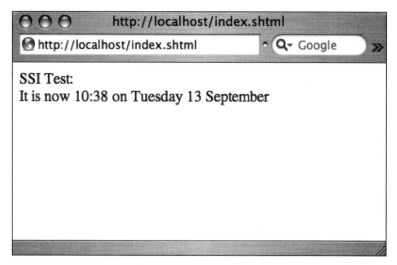

Figure 10.3 You'll see this test page if you've successfully enabled SSI support in Apache.

Disable Personal Web Sites

To disable personal Web sites that answer to URLs that look like `http://computer-name.local/~myusername/`, comment out the following lines in `/etc/httpd/httpd.conf` and then restart Apache.

```
LoadModule userdir_module  libexec/httpd/mod_userdir.so
AddModule mod_userdir.c
Include /private/etc/httpd/users/*.conf
```

Control Bonjour (Rendezvous)

To control the way that the main and personal Web sites are advertised over Bonjour, search for the following directive.

```
<IfModule mod_bonjour.c>
```

In Mac OS X versions before 10.4 (Tiger), search for

```
<IfModule mod_rendezvous_apple.c>
```

Switch on and off the advertising of all user sites, customized user sites, and the main site by activating or commenting out the relevant directives. The options available in versions of Mac OS X before Tiger are more limited.

Enable CGI

The default Apache configuration serves CGI (Common Gateway Interface) scripts from the directory `/Library/WebServer/CGI-Executables/`. CGI scripts placed elsewhere are not executed but simply displayed as text in the generated Web page. CGIs are enabled by the `ScriptAlias` directive, which in the default configuration looks like this.

```
ScriptAlias /cgi-bin/ "/Library/WebServer/CGI-Executables/"
```

The `ScriptAlias` directive tells Apache two things. First, when a URL mentions any directory starting with `/cgi-bin/...`, Apache should actually look in `/Library/WebServer/CGI-Executables/...` *no matter what the document root may be*. Second, it says that files in the

⁚᷇ TIP

The ScriptAlias *directive may map any alias to any target directory. The target directory does not even have to be in the document root (but must exist).*

⁚᷇ TIP

Check out the Alias *directive. It maps a directory mentioned in a URL to any other directory. The difference between* ScriptAlias *and* Alias *is that* ScriptAlias *additionally enables CGI execution on the target directory.*

named directory (and its subdirectories) should be interpreted as executable scripts. In response to the URL http://localhost/cgi-bin/test.pl, for example, Apache will grab *and execute* a script called /Library/WebServer/CGI-Executables/test.pl.

Serve CGI from Elsewhere

To serve CGI scripts from elsewhere, you must add more ScriptAlias directives. Assuming that ~/Sites is our new document root, let's serve CGIs from the directory ~/Sites/cgi. First, we'll create the necessary directory. Issue the commands as your own user, not the root user, because you are working in your home directory. Type

```
$ mkdir ~/Sites/cgi
```

We'll borrow a simple Perl test CGI from the default document root, typing

```
$ cp /Library/WebServer/CGI-Executables/test.pl ¬
    ~/Sites/cgi/
```

Edit this test file to work with directories that do actually exist in Mac OS X! The Apple-supplied file we just copied is somewhat flawed. For example, change the line

```
my $path = "/usr/local/ncbi/";
```

to

```
my $path = "/usr/local/";
```

Next, add a new ScriptAlias directive, and optionally remove the existing directive. Remember to replace the document root given in the example with your own.

```
  ScriptAlias /cgi/ "/Users/saruman/Sites/cgi/"
```

As ever, restart Apache, and load the URL http://localhost/cgi/test.pl. Apache will load the file /cgi/test.pl from /Users/saruman/Sites/cgi/test.pl and interpret it as a script that should be run by the Perl interpreter.

CGI from Anywhere

You can execute a CGI script from an arbitrary directory and are not limited to those directories named by ScriptAlias directives. To do so, you must add the appropriate the handlers and an option to the document root. Search for the following line in Apache's configuration file.

```
#AddHandler cgi-script .cgi
```

To run a simple Perl test CGI, named with an extension of .pl, add the following AddHandler directive after the one we just searched for.

```
AddHandler cgi-script .pl
```

Next, add the option ExecCGI to the Options directive of the root directory. (We added Includes to the same line when we enabled SSI earlier.)

```
Options ExecCGI Includes Indexes FollowSymLinks MultiViews
```

After restarting Apache, copy the test Perl script we used earlier to anywhere in the document root; then browse for it with the appropriate URL. If we copy the script to ~/Sites by typing

$ cp ~/Sites/cgi/test.pl ~/Sites/

we would use the URL http://localhost/test.pl.

❧ NOTE

Enabling CGIs to run from anywhere in the document root is a security risk compared with limiting them to specific directories.

Project 94
Configure the FTP Service

"How do I configure my FTP server?"

This project shows you how to enable and configure the FTP (File Transfer Protocol) server that is part of a standard Mac OS X install. It describes how to enable the server, open the necessary ports, and configure it to be a little more secure. This project assumes that you are familiar with the concept of FTP and are able to use an FTP client.

Enable FTP

Mac OS X provides both an FTP server and an FTP client. FTP is a not a service most people need to run, so the server is disabled by default. It's easily enabled, which causes the FTP server to be launched on demand when a client connects.

It's easy to start the FTP server from System Preferences: Select the Sharing pane, click the Services tab, and check FTP Access. This enables the FTP server and opens port 21 in the firewall. (In systems before Mac OS X 10.4 [Tiger], other ports are opened, too.)

Unfortunately, Apple's firewall rules don't open all the ports necessary for the FTP server to support passive FTP (discussed later in this project). We must open those ports manually. After enabling FTP access, click the Firewall tab and then the New button. In the resulting drop-down sheet, select Port Name Other, enter **1024-65535** in the TCP Port Number(s) box, and add a description such as **FTP Passive**. The new rule will automatically be checked, meaning that our newly enabled server is able to accept connections from an FTP client in Passive mode. No ports need be opened on the client.

Test the server by connecting to it from another machine. Use the hostname or IP address of the server, and type a command such as

```
$ ftp myhostname
```

You must have a Unix account to connect to the FTP server.

System Preferences doesn't provide a mechanism to configure the FTP server. That's unfortunate, because the server can be configured in many ways, not the least of which is to increase security. However, and as you might have guessed, we can configure FTP from the Unix command line.

Active and Passive FTP

To run an FTP server, we must open port 21. A client connects to this port to send control information (commands such as `ls` and `get`). We can choose to support active connections, or passive connections. Active and Passive modes use different ports for transferring data (such as files from the `get` command or the results of issuing the `ls` command). To use passive mode, we must open additional ports in the firewall.

Active mode operates as follows. Data is sent over a connection established by the server. It moves from port 20 on the server to a high-numbered port (>=1024) on the client. The client must open ports 1024 through 65535 but accepting connections originating from only port 20.

Passive mode is preferred because it does not involve opening ports on the client. It operates as follows. Data is sent over a connection established by the client; it moves between a high-numbered port on the client and a high-numbered port on the server. The server must open ports 1024 through 65535, accepting connections originating from all high-numbered ports.

Summary of open ports necessary for Active mode:

▶ Server: Port 21

▶ Client: Ports 1024 through 65535 from 20

Summary of open ports necessary for Passive mode:

▶ Server: Port 21, Ports 1024 through 65535

▶ Client: None

⚓ TIP

To test your server configuration, use the command-line FTP tool, appropriately called `ftp`. *Alternatively, many graphical clients are available, such as Transmit from Panic (http://panic.com/).*

⏻ LEARN MORE

Refer to "How to Become
the Root User" in Project 2
for more information about
the sudo **command.**

⏻ LEARN MORE

Project 72 covers Apple's
Launch Daemon and shows
how you might add your own
tasks to its configuration.

ᵢ TIP

To disable FTP, issue the same
launchd *command as you did*
to enable it, except specify the
subcommand unload *instead*
of load.

Enable FTP from Unix

Let's enable FTP and add the necessary firewall rules to allow clients
to connect to our server in Passive mode. What we'll do is the command-line equivalent to checking FTP Access in System Preferences
and adding the new firewall rule—therefore, reverse the steps we
took earlier in the project so that we start from a clean sheet.

Enabling and configuring FTP, and configuring the firewall, require
root permissions. For the remainder of this project, we'll assume the
status of the root user by issuing the command

```
$ sudo -s
Password:
#
```

The FTP server itself is launched on demand by Apple's Launch Daemon. To enable a service, we use the launchctl command, specifying
subcommand load to load the configuration file for that service and
option -w to remove the disabled key and write the altered configuration file back to disk.

Type the following command.

```
# launchctl load -w /System/Library/LaunchDaemons/ftp.plist
```

Apple's Launch Daemon was introduced in Mac OS X 10.4 (Tiger).
For versions before Tiger, you must enable FTP by changing the configuration of xinetd. Edit the file /etc/xinetd.d/ftp, and change the
line disable = yes to be disable = no. Restart xinetd to make it
reread the changed configuration by typing

```
# kill -HUP $(cat /var/run/xinetd.pid)
```

Next, we'll configure the firewall by adding rules to open the ports
described in "Active and Passive FTP" earlier in this project. **Note:
It's better that you configure the firewall from System Preferences,** because after you've tampered with its settings, System Preferences disowns the firewall, and you'll have to maintain it by hand
(until you reboot). If you still want to configure the firewall from the
command line, type the following.

```
# ipfw add 3000 allow tcp from any to any dst-port 21 in
# ipfw add 3010 allow tcp from any to any dst-port ¬
    1024-65535 in
# ipfw show
```

The rule numbers (3000 and 3010) shown here should not clash with any of those already used. To delete a rule such as 3000, type

```
# ipfw delete 3000
```

Test the FTP server from another machine, which need not have any ports open and which should connect by using the default Passive mode. Specify the hostname or IP address of the server, and type a command such as

```
$ ftp myhostname
```

Configure FTP

Let's look at an example FTP configuration. First, display the file /etc/ftpusers. This file gives the default setup for a Mac OS X installation, and you'll see that it lists users who are *not* allowed to connect via FTP. We can improve on this blacklist policy with a white-list policy in which we list all users who *are* allowed to connect via FTP and then disallow all others. Here's our new white-list ftpusers.

```
# cat /etc/ftpusers
# all admin users are set to class 'free'
*:admin allow free

# other accounts that can ftp are set to class 'restricted'
loraine allow restricted
jan allow restricted

# all other users are denied ftp access
* deny
```

ȚTIP

If you use the ipfw *command to configure the firewall by hand, System Preferences will disable its own firewall configuration. To change back to using System Preferences, you must flush all firewall rules by typing*

```
# ipfw flush
```

You might have to close and reopen System Preferences for it to resume responsibility for the firewall. This trick averts rebooting.

⟋LEARN MORE

Project 73 covers firewall configuration in a little more detail.

Lines that start with a hash (#) symbol are comments and ignored by
the FTP server. The first (proper) line says to allow all (represented by
*) administrator users (those belonging to the group admin) to con-
nect. The next lines allow the users loraine and jan (who are not
administrators) to connect. The last line denies all users not otherwise
mentioned.

You'll notice the free and restricted tags attached to user entries.
They are *classes* used by FTP to define the capabilities and restrictions
applied to the associated users. By using classes, we avoid the necessity
to repeat ourselves for every user.

We define classes (among other things) in the file /etc/ftpd.conf.
Let's create such a file to define the two classes we previously
assumed. It should look like this.

```
# cat /etc/ftpd.conf
# users of class 'free' (see /etc/ftpusers) chroot to /
#  with their ftp home directory set to their login home
chroot  free /
homedir free %d

# users of class 'restricted' chroot to their home directory
#  with their ftp home directory set to their new root
#  (ie their login home)
chroot  restricted %d
homedir restricted /
```

The first two configuration commands specify that members of the
class free have access to the entire file system, from the root directory
down (chroot free /), and that their FTP home directory is the
same as their Unix account home directory (homedir free %d). This
setup is actually no different from the usual (and unrestricted) configuration any FTP connection would enjoy. (The FTP home directory
is the directory in which a user is placed when she connects; it need
not be the same as her Unix account home directory.)

We'd like to give nonadministrative users a little less freedom by restricting their view of the file system to their Unix account home directory. We do this by writing the configuration line `chroot restricted %d`. Such users cannot move outside their home directory; consequently, the FTP command

```
$ cd /
```

takes them to their home directory.

The next configuration line, `homedir restricted /`, sets these users' FTP home directory to be the file system root *as the users now see it:* their Unix account home directory.

Finally, we must specify that all users be subject to *chrooting* (or be *jailed*) according to the `chroot` configuration applied to their class. To do this, we must mention all users in the file `/etc/ftpchroot` or, better, use star (*) to mean all users.

```
# cat /etc/ftpchroot
# all users are chrooted (see /etc/ftpd.conf)
# according to the their class (see /etc/ftpusers)
*
```

Reduce Open Ports

When we configured the firewall, it was necessary to open all high-numbered ports on the server. In passive FTP, the server tells the client which port the client should connect to when opening the data channel. The server normally chooses a port within the range 1024 to 65535, but by limiting this range, we also limit the number of ports that must be open in the firewall. Add the following lines to the file `ftpd.conf`.

```
# set port range for passive for all classes
portrange all 40000 40999
```

⤤ LEARN MORE

Refer to Chapter 4 if you are not familiar with any of the Unix text editors.

↗ LEARN MORE

Project 8 covers Unix permissions and the umask.

↧ TIP

To lean more about FTP configuration, consult the following Unix man pages:

$ man ftpusers
$ man ftpd.conf

↗ LEARN MORE

Project 21 explores the tail **command.**

Now we need open only ports 40000 to 40999, which we do by deleting the original firewall rule and reissuing it with the reduced port range.

```
# ipfw delete 3010
# ipfw add 3010 allow tcp from any to any dst-port ¬
    40000-40999 in
```

Change the Default umask

If you find the permissions of FTP-created files to be too restrictive, and find that they differ from those you would normally expect to see, set FTP's *umask* to reflect the permissions enjoyed by a normal Unix account. Add the following lines to the file ftpd.conf.

```
# change the umask from the FTP default 027 for all users
umask all 022
```

Check the Log Files

The FTP daemon writes information to a log file. This information is useful for monitoring who has connected to your server. You'll find the log entries in the file /var/log/ftp.log.

View them with the tail command by typing

```
$ tail -f /var/log/ftp.log
```

Project 95
Networking Tips

"How do I automate FTP transfers in a script?"

This project gives a few tips on grabbing files from across a network. It covers the `curl` command. It shows how `curl` is used to grab files from a Web site by using the HTTP protocol or from an FTP server by using the FTP protocol. It also shows how you might look up dictionary definitions by using the DICT protocol.

The `curl` command transfers data to or from a server by using one of many protocols: HTTP, FTP, DICT, GOPHER, TELNET, LDAP, HTTPS, or FTPS. We'll show how to transfer files and data by using the HTTP, FTP, and DICT protocols.

The `curl` command can be incorporated into scripts to fetch files without user intervention. It's a very comprehensive tool, but we'll touch on only the basics.

Grab via HTTP

Let's grab a page from a Web site. We grab the index page from Jan's site by issuing the following command.

```
$ curl http://jan.1dot1.com
```

If you try this command, you'll see raw HTML code written to your Terminal window. To capture the output in a file named `jan.html`, type

```
$ curl -o jan.html  http://jan.1dot1.com
  % Total % Received % Xferd  Average Speed  Time  Time ...
                              Dload  Upload  Total Spent...
100  2873 0  2873     0     0  6707      0  --:-:-- --:-:-...
```

☞ TIP

If you experience difficulties connecting to FTP servers, make sure that you have enabled Passive Mode by checking Use Passive FTP Mode in the Proxies tab of each network port configuration shown in the System Preferences Network pane.

We may fetch any page from the site. In the next example, we fetch the page `object.php` from the directory `tails`. By specifying option -O, we tell `curl` to write the fetched page to a file of the same name (`object.php`).

```
$ curl -O  http://jan.1dot1.com/tails/object.php
```

The `curl` command also supports the HTTP `get` and `post` methods, and can fetch and set cookies. As ever, `man curl` is your friend when you require more information on `curl`.

Grab and Upload via FTP

`curl` provides an easy way to download and upload files to an FTP server. Because it requires no user interaction, this functionality is easily incorporated into shell scripts to automate FTP transfers.

Let's grab from an anonymous FTP server (one that does not require you to have an account and password). In this example, we'll simply list the files and directories at the root of the anonymous FTP account.

```
$ curl ftp://ftp.apple.com
drwxrwxrwx    3 ftpprod   ftpprod    102 May   7   2003 Apple_...
drwxrwxr-x  20 ftpprod    ftpprod    680 Mar   8   2005 developer
drwxrwxr-x  37 ftpprod    ftpprod   1258 May  18   2004 emagic
drwxrwxr-x  11 ftpprod    ftpprod    374 Mar   9   2004 filemaker
drwxrwxrwx  10 ftpprod    ftpprod    340 Apr   7   2003 research
```

To list a directory such as **research**, name the directory, and add a trailing slash.

```
$ curl  ftp://ftp.apple.com/research/
drwxrwxrwx    5 ftpprod   ftpprod    170 Nov 12   1997 eg
drwxrwxrwx    4 ftpprod   ftpprod    136 Nov 19   1997 goe
...
```

To grab a file such as /research/goe/goe4mac.sea (whatever that might be), type

```
$ curl -O ftp://ftp.apple.com/research/goe/goe4mac.sea
```

The options -o and -O have the same meanings as they did for the HTTP protocol.

Connect to an FTP Account

To connect to an FTP account that requires a username and password, we simply supply the necessary information on the command line. To grab a file named `test` from our account `saruman` on the FTP server `ftp.mayo-family.com`, we would type

```
$ curl -O ftp://saruman:pass@ftp.mayo-family.com/test
```

Upload Files

FTP servers let you upload files as well as download them (though usually only if you have a proper account). Upload a file with the option -T.

Here, we upload a file named `test` to our FTP home directory.

```
$ curl -T test ftp://saruman:pass@ftp.mayo-family.com
```

To rename the file at its destination, type

```
$ curl -T test ftp://saruman:pass@ftp.mayo-family.com/new
```

We may also upload the file to a specific directory by specifying a pathname after the server name. To upload a file named `test` to the directory `Documents` and call it `t01`, type

```
$ curl -T test ftp://saruman:pass@ftp.mayo-family.com/¬
    Documents/t01
```

Use option -v to see the FTP transcript that `curl` executes in performing its allotted task.

```
$ curl -v -T test ftp://saruman:pass@ftp.mayo-family.com/¬
    Documents/t01
* About to connect() to carcharoth.mayo-family.com port 21
...
> USER saruman
< 331 Password required for saruman.
```

output continues on next page

⚡ LEARN MORE

To prevent a command line that contains sensitive information, such as a password, from entering the Bash command-line history, refer to Project 48.

↗ LEARN MORE

Refer to Project 52 to learn about Bash functions.

```
> PASS pass
...
> CWD Documents
< 250 CWD command successful.
...
> STOR t01
< 150 Opening BINARY mode data connection for 't01'.
...
```

Query a Dictionary

A site named dict.org (among others) understands the DICT dictionary protocol. Look up the definition of *apple* by typing

```
$ curl dict://dict.org/d:apple
220 aspen.miranda.org dictd 1.9.15/rf on Linux...
250 ok
150 2 definitions retrieved
151 "Apple" gcide "The Collaborative International
Dictionary of English v.0.48"
Apple \Ap"ple\ ([a^]p"p'l), n. [OE. appel, AS. [ae]ppel,
   [ae]pl; akin to Fries. & D. appel, OHG, aphul, aphol, G.
...
```

We might define a handy Bash function to encapsulate this functionality by typing

```
$ defn () { curl dict://dict.org/d:$*; }
```

and use it to look up *Unix* by typing

```
$ defn Unix
220 aspen.miranda.org dictd 1.9.15/rf on Linux  ...
250 ok
150 1 definitions retrieved
151 "UNIX" wn "WordNet (r) 2.0"
UNIX

     n : trademark for a powerful operating system
           [syn: {UNIX system}, {UNIX operating system}]
...
```

Discover More Commands   **11**

This chapter introduces some special-purpose Unix tools that can be both useful and fun. Its six projects will help you do the following:

Discover Unix utilities such as a calendar and a unit converter.

Bridge the gap from Unix to OS X, by running some Mac applications from the command line and using custom Unix commands specific to the Mac OS.

Brush up on Unix with a reference that covers every major command.

Have a laugh, with a sampling of Unix humor and trivia.

Project 96
Discover Useful Utilities

"What cool Unix commands might I have missed?"

This project presents miscellaneous Unix tools and utilities that you might find useful, including a calendar, a calculator, and a units converter. It covers the commands cal, bc, units, dc, and banner.

Display a Calendar

Display the current month in calendar form by typing

```
$ cal
     September 2005
 S   M  Tu  W  Th   F   S
                1   2   3
 4   5   6  7   8   9  10
11  12  13 14  15  16  17
18  19  20 21  22  23  24
25  26  27 28  29  30
```

To see the whole year, type

```
$ cal -y
                             2005
       January              February              March
 S  M Tu  W Th  F  S   S  M Tu  W Th  F  S   S  M Tu  W Th  F  S
                 1          1  2  3  4  5          1  2  3  4  5
...
```

The cal command displays any month of any year, too. You might be surprised, for example, by September of 1752.

```
$ cal 9 1752
    September 1752
 S  M Tu  W Th  F  S
        1  2 14 15 16
17 18 19 20 21 22 23
24 25 26 27 28 29 30
```

(That's a bug in the month of September, not in cal!)

Calculate

When you want to do big math, Unix gives you an arbitrary-precision calculator called bc. *Arbitrary precision* means that if bc were a traditional handheld calculator, it would have a very wide screen.

Here are some examples.

```
$ bc
2^8
256
2^1024
17976931348623159077293051907890247336179769780942306572734\
30081157732675805500963132708477322407536021120113879871390\
33576587897688144166224928474306394741243777678934248654850\
27630221960124609411945308295208500576883815068234246288140\
73913110540827237163350510684586298239947245938479716304830\
53563296242241370216
quit
```

Two to the power 1024 is very big math!

Set a variable called scale to specify the significant number of decimal digits. Initially, bc assumes integer arithmetic and truncates the fractional part.

```
$ bc
1/3
0
```

TIP

Use the cal command to discover the weekday on which you were born.

ⓘ TIP

If you know Reverse Polish notation, try the dc *command.*

```
$ dc
2 2+ 4 3+*p
28
quit
```

To see 30 decimal places of precision—enough for most people but nowhere near the limit of bc—type

```
scale=30
1/3
.333333333333333333333333333333
```

The bc command understands complex expressions that use parentheses, variables, and in fact a whole C-like programming language. In the next example, we write a simple bc program to a file named sum, and then invoke bc, passing it the file. The sum program sums all the numbers from 1 to 10.

```
$ cat sum
sum=0
for (i=1; i<=10; i++) {
  sum+=i
  print "Number = ", i, ", sum = ", sum, "\n"
}

$ bc sum
Number = 1, sum = 1
Number = 2, sum = 3
...
Number = 9, sum = 45
Number = 10, sum = 55
quit
```

Convert Units

The units command converts pretty much anything to anything else. We're not talking lead to gold or any other form of alchemy, but units such as gallons and ergs to other compatible units. At some time, for example, we've all wondered how many scruples there are in a gram (haven't we?). The answer to this burning question—and to many other, more sensible questions, too—lies in using units.

Let's ask units how to convert feet to meters (or even metres).

```
$ units
500 units, 54 prefixes
You have: feet
You want: meters
        * 0.3048
        / 3.2808399
Control-d
```

The units command told us to multiply the number of feet by 0.3048, or divide it by 3.2808399, to convert to meters.

Here are some more examples.

```
$ units
You have: kilo-litres
You want: gallons
        * 264.17205
        / 0.0037854118

You have: zetta-ergs
You want: joules
        * 1e+14
        / 1e-14
Control-d
```

And, of course.

```
You have: scruples
You want: grams
        * 1.2959782
        / 0.77161792
```

Finally, you may convert combinations of units such as feet per minute to meters per second by specifying feet/minute and metres/second or, my personal favorite,

```
You have: furlongs/fortnight
You want: metres/second
        * 0.00016630952
        / 6012.8848
```

ĭ TIP

To discover all the units supported by units, *examine the file* units.lib *in the directory* /usr/share/misc.

ĭ TIP

Type the following:

```
$ banner -w80 ":-)"
```

Or go for a hard copy if you have a printer available.

```
$ banner  hello | lpr
```

We might convert the speed of light, which is 3*10e8 meters per second, to furlongs per fortnight by using

```
You have: 3e8*metres/second
You want: furlongs/fortnight
        * 1.8038654e+12
        / 5.5436508e-13
```

Project 97
Connect with Aqua

↗ **LEARN MORE**

Project 6 covers standard input, standard output, redirection, and pipelining.

"How do I cross the great divide between Mac OS X graphical applications and the command line?"

This project shows you some techniques for sharing data and services between Aqua (Mac OS X graphical) applications and command-line utilities. It covers the commands `pbcopy` and `pbpaste`. Project 98 shows you how to open graphical applications from the command line.

Copy and Paste

All graphical applications use the *pasteboard* (also called the *clipboard*) to save text between copy and paste operations (`Command-c` and `Command-v`). The `pbcopy` command reads text from its standard input and writes it to the pasteboard, providing a way to copy Terminal output directly to the clipboard.

To copy an entire file to the clipboard, we might type

```
$ cat ~/Sites/index.html | pbcopy
```

In a graphical text editor such as Apple's TextEdit, we need only press the familiar `Command-v` to paste the copied file `~/Sites/index.html` into the current document.

Even more useful, we can copy the output from any Unix command directly to the clipboard. Let's copy the output from the `cal` command, covered in Project 96, and paste it into a Microsoft Word document. We issue the `cal` command and pipe its output to `pbcopy`.

```
$ cal | pbcopy
```

In Word, we type `Command-v` to paste the copied text into the current document (which is exactly how the following example was generated).

```
September 2005
 S   M  Tu   W  Th   F   S
                1    2   3
 4   5   6   7   8    9  10
11  12  13  14  15   16  17
18  19  20  21  22   23  24
25  26  27  28  29   30
```

Going in the other direction, to copy the contents of the clipboard to standard output, use the pbpaste command. Copy a section of text in TextEdit by selecting it and typing Command-c, for example. Then use pbpaste to write the text to the Terminal screen or, more usefully, pipe it to the standard input of a Unix command.

Let's count the number of lines, words, and characters in the copied text by piping the clipboard contents to the wc command.

```
$ pbpaste | wc
      28      80      857
```

Drag and Drop

Apple's Terminal recognizes when a file, folder, or application is dropped onto the Terminal window. It responds to the drag and drop by writing the full pathname of the dropped entity on the command line. Terminal doesn't write contents to the command line—just names.

Use this technique whenever a command requires a filename. For example, type

```
$ cd
```

followed by a space. Drag a folder from the Finder or the Desktop to the Terminal window. The command line will be completed with the full pathname of the dropped folder.

```
$ cd /Users/saruman/1dot1/Peachpit/101-projects-book/archive
```

Now press Return to set your home directory to the folder you just dropped.

Double-Click a Shell Script

Apple's Terminal recognizes a file that contains a shell script. Double-clicking such a file launches a new Terminal window in which the script is automatically executed. A simple script will illustrate this. We write a standard shell script and save it to a file whose name includes the extension .command. The example script that follows displays the names of all files in your Documents folder that were modified less than a day ago.

```
$ cat mod.command
#!/bin/bash
echo "All Documents modified less than a day ago"
find ~/Documents  -mtime -1
```

The script must be made executable before it can be executed by double-clicking.

```
$ chmod +x mod.command
```

To run the script, select the file mod.command in the Finder, and double-click it. A new Terminal window opens and immediately starts executing the script. The window remains open so that you can view the results, which are followed by logout and [Process completed].

⬈ LEARN MORE

Refer to Project 9 if you are new to writing shell scripts.

⬈ LEARN MORE

Project 44 shows many Terminal tricks.

↗ **LEARN MORE**

Project 18 shows you how to use the find **and** xargs **commands in combination.**

🛈 **TIP**

Use open *to open a folder that's normally hidden by the Finder. For example, open* /etc *by typing*

`$ open /etc`

Project 98
Open Aqua Items

"How do I open a Mac OS X application from the command line?"

This project is all about the open command. It's the command-line equivalent of double-clicking, used to open files and folders and to launch Mac OS X graphical applications.

Open a Folder

To open a folder into a Finder window from the command line, use the open command, passing the name of the folder. Open your Documents folder, for example, by typing

`$ open ~/Documents`

A Finder window opens, showing the contents of your Documents folder in Icon view.

Although this command is not very useful on its own, you could use open in a script to open a set of commonly used folders or as part of another command. You could search for folders named backup and open them all in a single command by typing

`$ find ~ -type d -iname backup -print0 | xargs -0 open`

Make a commonly used and deeply nested folder the subject of an alias for quick and easy opening.

`$ alias archive="open ~/Documents/101/Chapter11/archive"`

Open an Application

The open command simulates a double-click action and can be used to launch any of the applications in the /Applications directory. To launch Calculator, type

`$ open /Applications/Calculator.app`

An application written to Apple's guidelines is part of a package. Although it looks like an application icon in the Finder, a package is really a folder with a `.app` extension. The executable itself is located within the package, as are other resources, including the application's icon, displayed instead of the usual blue folder icon. Explore a package such as `/Applications/Calculator.app`: You'll find the executable code in the subdirectory `Contents/MacOS/Calculator`.

Older (Carbon-based) applications are not implemented as Mac OS X packages and don't have an `.app` extension. If, for example, your publishers were to insist that you use Microsoft Word, launch it by typing

```
$ open "/Applications/Microsoft Office X/Microsoft Word"
```

The `open` command will launch an application's executable directly if you specify the `-a` option. To launch the Calculator executable instead of double-clicking its package, type

```
$ open -a /Applications/Calculator.app/¬
    Contents/MacOS/Calculator
```

An executable can also be launched directly—without using `open -a`—just like a Unix command. (Remember to launch it as a background job so that it returns control of the Terminal immediately.)

```
$ /Applications/Calculator.app/Contents/MacOS/Calculator &
[1] 22820
$
```

This technique does not work for Carbon-based applications such as Microsoft Word, because the executable is not in the native format required by Mac OS X. Although you'd probably use `open` to launch such an application, here's how to launch its executable directly.

```
$ /System/Library/Frameworks/Carbon.framework/Versions¬
    /Current/Support/LaunchCFMApp ¬
    "/Applications/Microsoft Office X/Microsoft Word" &
```

Short and snappy!

➚ **LEARN MORE**

Project 55 covers background jobs.

Clicking and Launching

The `open` command issued without option `-a` simulates double-clicking, whereas with option `-a`, it launches an application directly. The difference is subtle, but you'll see it in effect if you apply option `-a` to a package or omit option `-a` when launching an executable directly.

✐ **TIP**

Run two or more Calculators at the same time by double-clicking (or using open *without option* –a) *the executable instead of the package.*

◣ NOTE

Although it's possible to pass an application's alias to the open command, this will not work when used in combination with the option -a.

ᵢ̈ TIP

The open command option -e is shorthand for

-a /Applications/
TextEdit.app

Open a File

The open command can be used to open a document in the default application for the document type. To open a screen shot that has the extension .png, in the default application Preview, for example, type

```
$ open ~/Desktop/Picture\ 1.png
```

You may use wildcards, of course, to open multiple files.

```
$ open *.png
```

Like double-clicking, open uses Launch Services to determine which application to launch to open a document. To have a document open in an application other than the default, specify the -a option, and name the application. To open the same screen shot in Adobe Photoshop 7 instead of Preview, type

```
$ open -a "/Applications/Adobe Photoshop 7/¬
    Adobe Photoshop 7.0" ~/Desktop/Picture\ 1.png
```

A handy option, -f has open read text from its standard input, or a pipe, and open the text in TextEdit. To open this year's calendar using the cal command covered in Project 96, type

```
$ cal -y | open -f
```

Alternatively, specify an application other than TextEdit.

```
$ cal -y | open -a "/Applications/Microsoft Office X/¬
    Microsoft Word" -f
```

Open URLs

Try the following commands, which demonstrate that open understands URLs.

```
$ open ftp://ftp.apple.com
$ open http://www.apple.com
```

You can even connect to a server. To mount an AFP share called saruman from a host called carcharoth, for example, type

```
$ open afp://carcharoth/saruman
```

Project 99
OS X–Specific Commands

"What Mac OS X–specific commands might I find useful?"

This project illustrates miscellaneous and useful commands that are specific to Mac OS X Unix. It covers the `ditto`, `screencapture`, `SetFile`, `GetFileInfo`, `defaults`, and `plutil` commands.

Other Mac OS X–specific commands are covered elsewhere in this book. They are

- `pmset` to report and change power management settings (Project 37)

- `system_profiler` to report on the hardware and software configuration of your Mac (Project 37)

- `softwareupdate` to update Mac OS X from the command line (Project 38)

- `nvram` to report and change NV-RAM settings (Project 38)

- `dscl`, `nifind`, and `nireport` to operate on information in the Directory Services database, such as user-account details (Project 65)

- `diskutility` to manage locally mounted disks (Projects 67 and 68)

- `pbcopy` and `pbpaste` to copy and paste text between the command line and the pasteboard, or clipboard (Project 97)

- `open` to open Mac OS X files, folders, and graphical applications from the command line (Project 98)

Copy with ditto

The `ditto` command recursively copies directories and files, preserving permissions and timestamps in a similar way to the Unix command `cp -pr`. In versions of Mac OS X before 10.4 (Tiger), `ditto` *must* be used in preference to `cp` to copy files that have resource forks, which the Unix `cp` command did not preserve.

⤴ LEARN MORE

Refer to Project 2 to learn about recursion and how to copy directories recursively by using the cp command.

❧ NOTE

In Mac OS X 10.4, the --rsrc option is switched on by default. In previous versions, it was switched off by default.

In the next example, we copy the entire letters directory and any subdirectories it contains to a new directory called letter.bak, preserving resource forks by passing the option --rsrc.

```
$ ditto --rsrc letters letters.bak
```

In Mac OS X 10.4, ditto is less useful because cp, and most other Unix commands, now preserve HFS+ metadata, including resource forks. In a role reversal, ditto can be used to strip HFS+ metadata when passed the option --norsrc. Use this feature to trim the fat when preparing files for transfer to non-HFS+ file systems.

The ditto command provides other useful options. Specify -V (verbose) to tell ditto to echo the name of each file as it is copied. Options also create and extract Unix cpio archives and PKZip archives for Windows compatibility: Read the man page for more details on these options.

A difference in the ways that ditto and cp behave can cause confusion. Both create the target directory when it does not exist. When the target directory does exist, ditto performs the copy in exactly the same way. The cp command, however, creates a new directory within an existent target directory, named after the source directory, and copies into that instead.

If you've installed Apple's Developer Tools, you'll find a command called CpMac, which copies files preserving resource forks and attributes just as ditto does.

```
$ /Developer/Tools/CpMac
```

```
usage: CpMac [-r] [-p] <source-path> <dest-path>
       CpMac [-r] [-p] <source-path>... <dest-dir>
```

CpMac has a Unix man page, but remember to type man CpMac and not man cpmac.

Snap with Screen Capture

The screencapture command provides functionality equivalent to pressing Command-Shift-4, taking a snapshot of the screen. It has many options, including an interactive mode, but of greatest use for the command line and scripting is its "hands-free" mode, in which it operates without user intervention. To take a screen shot, specify option -x to silence the sound effects and provide a filename. For example:

```
$ screencapture -x ~/Desktop/p1.png
```

The default image format is PNG (Portable Network Graphics)—hence, our chosen file extension.

Other useful options include -C to capture the cursor and -c to capture to the clipboard (in which case a filename is not necessary). Also, change the format of captured images by passing the -t option. Here are some examples, in which you can guess the chosen image format.

```
$ screencapture -xC -ttiff ~/Desktop/p1.tiff
$ screencapture -xC -tjpeg ~/Desktop/p1.jpg
$ screencapture -xC -tpdf ~/Desktop/p1.pdf
```

To check that the file format is as expected, use the file command.

```
$ file ~/Desktop/p1.tiff
```

```
/Users/saruman/Desktop/p1.tiff: TIFF image data, big-endian
```

Just for fun, here's a trick in which we take a snapshot of the login screen while logged out. Issue the following command and then log out, allowing Terminal to terminate. Make sure that the login screen is showing 60 seconds after issuing the commands.

```
$ sudo -s Password:
(admin password here)
$ nohup bash -c "sleep 60; ¬
    screencapture ~/Pictures/screen.pdf"
```

To create time-delayed screen shots, use screencapture in combination with the at command (see Project 70).

Manage HFS+ File Attributes

If you've installed Apple's Developer Tools, you'll have two commands that view and set HFS+ file attributes. Such attributes include a file's Mac OS type and creator codes, and the hide-file-extension attribute (where the Finder hides the file's extension). We won't explain the meanings of HFS+ attributes; we'll just present examples showing how you might view and set them.

To display a brief usage summary, issue the SetFile command with no parameters.

```
$ /Developer/Tools/SetFile
Usage: SetFile [option...] file...
 -a attributes # attributes (lowercase = 0, uppercase = 1)*
 ...

        E    Hidden extension*
 ...

        Z    Busy*
 ...
```

Display the HFS+ attributes for a file named p1.jpg by typing

```
$ /Developer/Tools/GetFileInfo p1.jpg
file: "/Users/saruman/Desktop/p1.jpg"
type: ""
creator: ""
attributes: avbstclinmEdz
created: 10/17/2005 10:11:12
modified: 10/17/2005 10:11:12
```

The capital E in the attributes list tells us that the extension is hidden (the hide-file-extension attribute is switched on), and the filename shows as p1 in the Finder. To make the extension visible, type

```
$ /Developer/Tools/SetFile -a e p1.jpg
```

A lowercase letter e switches off the hide-file-extension attribute. View the file in the Finder, and you'll see that its name now shows as p1.jpg. (You might have to click the file icon to make the Finder refresh before the extension shows.)

To switch the attribute back on and hide the extension, type

```
$ /Developer/Tools/SetFile -a E p1.jpg
```

Read and Set Preferences Files

Your personal preference settings are stored in *plist* files (files with the extension .plist) in the directory ~/Library/Preferences. System preferences applicable to all users are in the directory /Library/Preferences. In versions of Mac OS X before 10.4 (Tiger), preferences are stored in XML (eXtensible Markup Language) format. Preferences in Tiger are stored in binary format.

It's possible to examine and change preferences settings from the command line with the defaults command. To examine preferences, such as your personal preferences settings for iChat, type

```
$ defaults read ~/Library/Preferences/com.apple.iChat
{
    ABDirectoryResultColumnTitle = "Instant Messaging";
    AccountSortOrder = ("90AFA166-D274-4514-9358-136AEF...
    AutoReplyWithAway = 0;
    AutosaveChats = 1;
    AwayOnFastUserSwitch = 1;
    BuddyInfoSelectedTab = 0;
    "BuddyList.EnableGroups" = 0;
    "BuddyList.Visible" = 1;
...
```

(Notice that we don't include the extension in the filename given to defaults.)

Most of the preferences settings can be related to those in the application's Preferences window, accessed from its Preferences menu. In the next example, we set the preference AwayOnFastUserSwitch to 0 (off or FALSE).

```
$ defaults write ~/Library/Preferences/com.apple.iChat ¬
    AwayOnFastUserSwitch 0
```

You'll have to explore preferences files to determine what settings an application has and what values they can be set to.

TIP

Some preferences are not shown in an application's Preferences window but can be discovered and changed with defaults. *If you want to try experimental settings, be sure to save a copy of the original preferences file first.*

Manage Preferences Files

Use the `plutil` command to check and convert preferences files. The next example checks all preferences files in the directory ~/Library/Preferences for signs of corruption. Specify the -lint option to `plutil` and option -s to report only on preferences files that fail the check.

```
$ plutil -lint -s ~/Library/Preferences/*.plist
2005-10-17 11:57:22.847 plutil[6653] CFLog (0):
    CFPropertyListCreateFromXMLData(): plist parse failed;
    the data is not proper UTF-8. The file name for this
    data could be:
    com.apple.help.plist
    The parser will retry as in 10.2, but the problem should
    be corrected in the plist.
    com.apple.help.plist:
Conversion of data failed. The file is not UTF-8, or in the
encoding specified in XML header if XML.
```

This command provides a handy integrity check of application preferences, to be run when applications start to act strangely or fail to start up.

To convert a preferences file's contents between XML and the new Tiger binary format, specify the -convert option. We might want to make a binary Tiger preferences file readable in a text editor by converting it to XML.

```
$ plutil -convert xml1 ¬
    ~/Library/Preferences/com.apple.TextEdit.plist
```

A Tiger application can read both formats, but tests show that applications rewrite their preferences files in binary format.

To convert back to binary format manually, type

```
$ plutil -convert binary1 ¬
    ~/Library/Preferences/com.apple.TextEdit.plist
```

Project 100
Unix Command Reference

"Is there a quick reference for Unix commands?"

This project lists a large number of Unix commands, each with a brief description of its purpose. The commands are organized in categories and grouped by functionality. Where a command is covered by a project in this book, the project number is shown in parentheses. In some cases where multiple projects are listed, numbers in bold are used to indicate the most significant coverage. Apple-specific commands are shown at the end, in "Use Mac OS X–Specific Commands."

Use Basic Commands

The following are stock commands that you'll use all the time.

ls	list the contents of the current directory (2)
cp	copy files and directories (2)
mv	move or rename files and directories (2)
rm	delete files and directories (2)
mkdir	create a new directory (2)
rmdir	delete a directory (2)
touch	create a file/modify access times (**2**, 17)
ln	make a link to a file (19)
cd	change working directory (2, **13**)
pwd	display working directory (2)
pushd	change working directory and stack it (14)
popd	move back to last pushed working directory (14)
dirs	print working directory stack (14)
chmod	change file and directory permissions (8)
chown	change owners of files and directories (3)
chgrp	change group owners of files and directories (7)
chflags	change file flags (69)
man	consult the Unix manual (3)
apropos	equivalent to man -k (3)
whatis	equivalent to man -f (3)
makewhatis	(re-)build the whatis database (3)
info	consult the GNU info system (3)

View Files

The following are commands to view and edit files, including compressed and binary files.

cat	display a file (**21**, 63)
head	display first 10 lines of a file (21)
tail	display last 10 lines of a file (**21**, 41)
less	display a file page by page (21)
lesskey	specify key binding for less
more	display a file page by page (21)
pr	display files with pagination (21)
lp	print a file (21)
file	report the type of a file (11, **29**)
hexdump	display binary files (22)
xxd	display binary files (22)
strings	search a binary file for printable strings (22)
vis	display nonprintable characters (21)
unvis	reverse the output from vis (21)
zcat, zmore	cat, more for zipped files (22)
bzcat,bzless, bzmore	cat, less, more for bzipped files (22)
nano	simple text editor (30)
emacs	powerful text editor (31)
vi/vim	powerful text editor (**32**, 33, 34, 35)
visudo	safe edit /etc/sudoers

Search for Files and Commands

The following are commands to search the file system for files and directories, and Unix executable files.

find	find files matching many criteria (15, 17, 18)
locate	search database for filenames (15)
locate.updatedb	update the locate database (15)
type	find an executable (bash) (16)
which	find an executable (csh and tcsh) (16)
whereis	find an executable (search system path)

Search File Content

The following are command s to search the contents of text files for specific text or patterns of text that match regular expressions.

grep	search a file for text (23)
egrep	equivalent to grep -E (23)
fgrep	equivalent to grep -F (23)
wc	count lines, words, and characters (23)
bzgrep, zgrep	grep for bzipped, zipped files (23)
bzegrep, zegrep	egrep for bzipped, zipped files (23)
bzfgrep, zfgrep	fgrep for bzipped, zipped files (23)

Change File Content

The following are commands to change file content programmatically and to format file content.

awk	search and change file content (**60, 62**, 23)
sed	search and change file content (**59, 61**, 23)
tr	translate one character into another (57)
col	strip chars
cut	filters columns from files
expand	expand tabs to spaces (57)
unexpand	compress spaces to tabs (57)
fmt	format a text file (29, 57)
fold	fold long lines (29, 57)
sort	sort the lines of a file in alphabetical order (26)
uniq	filter out repeated lines from a file (26)
comm	display lines common to two files (26)
join	perform a database join on files
split	split a file into multiple smaller files (63)
paste	merge corresponding lines from two files (63)

Compress and Archive File Content

The following are commands to compress files and to place multiple files in a single file archive.

bzip2, bunzip2	uses a better compression algorithm (27)
gzip, gunzip	GNU version of zip (27)
zip, unzip	compress/uncompress files and folders (27)
tar	archive files into a single file (28)
cpio	copy file archives in and out

Compare Text Files

The following are commands to compare the differences between two files and to create patches that can be applied to update older files.

diff	compare two files and display differences (24)
diff3	compare two files relative to a third (24)
sdiff	compare and merge two files into a third (24)
patch	update file from differences (24, 25)
bzdiff, zdiff	diff for bzipped, bzipped files (24)

Query and Manage Processes

The following are commands to view, manage, and delete running processes.

kill	stop/restart processes by PID (40)
killall	stop/restart processes by name
ps	list running processes (39, 40)
top	display information on running processes (39)
nice	execute a process with a given priority (40)
renice	alter the priority of an existing process (40)
nohup	execute a command immune to HUP signals

Query and Manage Users

The following are commands for, and to get information about, user accounts.

login	log into a machine
su	switch to another user's identity (15)
sudo	execute a command as root (2)
exit	close a non-login shell
logout	close a login shell
id	display identity of current user (64)
groups	display groups to which a user belongs (64)
last	list all logins with date, time, and status (64)
users	display who is currently logged in
who	as users but with more detail (64)
w	as who but with more detail (64)
whoami	useful for amnesiacs (64)
talk	chat to another user
write	send a message to another user
wall	send a message to all logged-in users
mesg	allow/disallow messages from other users

Schedule Tasks

The following are commands to schedule one-off and periodic commands.

at	execute a command at a specific time (70)
atq	list the pending at jobs (70)
atrm	remove an at job from the queue (70)
leave	remind you when it's time to leave
calendar	scheduling and reminder service
crontab	create user cron tasks (71)
periodic	run system-maintenance tasks (72)

Use Shell and Scripting Commands

The following are commands used to change shell settings and manage shell jobs, as well as miscellaneous commands useful for writing shell scripts.

Shell Environment and Settings

alias	alias a command line to a keyword (4, **51**)
unalias	remove an alias (4, **51**)
declare	declare a shell variable or array (4)
unset	remove a shell variable
env, printenv	display environment of current shell
history	display command history (4, **48**)
set	set a shell attribute (45)
shopt	set a shell option (45)
umask	display and set the file-creation mask (8)
bind	to change shell key functionality (53)
function	assign a function to a keyword

Shell Jobs and Processes

fg	bring a background job to the foreground (55)
bg	place a job in the background (55)
jobs	list active shell jobs (55)
batch	execute commands in nonbusy periods
exec	execute a command in place of the shell
source	execute a script with current shell (47)
script	make a transcript of a Terminal session
time	time the execution of a command

Shell Scripting Commands

`echo`	display arguments (2, 4, 63)
`printf`	formatted display arguments (56, 63)
`expr`	evaluate an expression
`expect`	script a dialogue with interactive programs
`getopts`	get and parse command-line options (83)
`sleep`	pause processing of a script
`tee`	split a pipe into streams
`xargs`	form a command line from arguments (18)
`mktemp`	generate a unique temporary filename
`lockfile`	block file access by more than one process

Tcsh–Specific Commands

`bindkey`	to change shell key functionality (53)
`set`	set a shell variable (4, 45)
`setenv`	set an environment variable (4, 50)
`unsetenv`	remove an environment variable

Commands to Control the Terminal

`clear`	clear the Terminal window
`reset`	reset the Terminal display
`resize`	resize X11 window (for example, `resize -s 25 80`)
`sty`	change the setting for the Terminal
`tty`	display the user's current Terminal

Employ Useful Utilities

The following are other useful commands.

`banner`	create banner text (96)
`bc`	arbitrary-precision calculator (96)
`dc`	arbitrary-precision reverse-polish calculator (96)
`cal`	display a monthly or yearly calendar (96)
`units`	convert quantities between units systems (96)
`openssl`	manage TLS/SSL certificates
`certtool`	create new key pairs for certificates

Query and Mount File Systems

The following are commands to report on and manage file systems, including those on local disk drives and those on servers.

df	display disk free information for all disks (66)
du	display disk use statistics (66)
lsvfs	list the known virtual file systems (66)
mount	mount and query drives (68) and shares (88)
umount	unmount drives (68) and shares (88)

Access Network Services

The following commands are attached to and query network services.

ssh	start a secure shell on a remote machine
scp	secure copy files to/from a remote machine
sftp	secure version of FTP
curl	grab a URL from a remote server (95)
fetchmail	get mail from SMTP, POP, IMAP, and so on
ftp	File Transfer Protocol (94)
telnet	connect using the Telnet protocol
apachectl	control the Apache HTTP server (92, 93)
dig	look up DNS information (91)
host	look up DNS information (91)
ntpq	query NTP time server
ntptimeset	set network time

Report and Configure Network Settings

The following are commands to configure network interfaces, report on their current settings, and report traffic.

hostname	set or display the hostname (73)
ifconfig	configure network interfaces (73)
ipconfig	set the IP mode of an interface
ipfw	query and set the firewall (**73**, 94)
arp	maintain address-resolution protocol tables (90)
route	maintain network routing tables
ping	contact a remote host (90)
traceroute	report on the route network packets take (90)
netstat	display network status (43, 90)
tcpdump	dump TCP activity (43)

Manage the System

The following are commands to reports on various aspects of the system, including the processor and file-system activity.

arch	display machine architecture (37)
hostinfo	display information on the host (37)
machine	display processor type (37)
uname	display OS name, version, and processor type (38)
dmesg	display system message buffer (43)
logger	write to the system-log daemon syslogd (42)
date	display and set the system date (74)
uptime	report how long system has been running (43)
fs_usage	display live file system usage (43)
lsof	list open files (43)
vm_stat	display virtual-memory statistics (43)
sc_usage	display live system call stats (43)
latency	display context switches and interrupts (43)

Manage the Kernel

The following are commands to examine the kernel settings.

ktrace	perform kernel tracing (43)
kdump	display a human-readable `ktrace.out` file
sysctl	display and set kernel-state variables (43)
zprint	display information on kernel zones
kextload	kernel extension load
kextunload	kernel extension unload
kextstat	display kernel extension statistics

Use Mac OS X–Specific Commands

The following commands are specific to Mac OS X and supplied by Apple. They are not found in other Unix-based distributions.

Manage Disks

bless	bless a system folder, set boot disk (74)
diskutil	repair, journal discs (**67, 68**, 74)
drutil	interact with CD and DVD burners
hdiutil	manipulate disk images
pdisk	partition table editor
vsdbutil	read/write enable permissions on HFS+ volumes

Manage HFS+ Files

CpMac	copy with resource forks (99)
ditto	copy files/sync folders with resource forks (99)
GetFileInfo	get attributes of HFS+ files (99)
SetFile	sets attributes of HFS+ files (99)

Manage the System

system_profiler	generate detailed system information (37)
softwareupdate	command-line version of S/W update (38)
scselect	change network location (73)
launchctl	manage Apple's Launch Daemon (70)
scutil	manage configd
syslog	manage the system log facility (42)
nvram	view and change Open Firmware variables (38)
pmset	set power-management parameters (37)
ioreg	display IO registry hierarchy

Manage User Accounts

dscl	Directory Services command-line utility (65)
nifind	find a NetInfo directory (65)
nireport	print tables from NetInfo (65)
nicl	NetInfo command-line utility
nidump	dump NetInfo information in Unix FF format
nigrep	perform a regular-expression search on NetInfo
niload	load NetInfo information from Unix FF format
niutil	read and write domain in plain text

Manage Useful Utilities

pbcopy	copy text to the pasteboard (97)
pbpaste	paste text from the clipboard (97)
open	open a file as though double-clicked (98)
screencapture	screen and window capture (99)
opendiff	open two files and compare
say	text-to-speech converter
defaults	read and write .plist files (99)
plutil	.plist file utilities (99)
sips	scriptable image processing system
lsbom	interpret bom files; see man 5 bom
otool	examine object files (Unix ldd)

Project 101
Have Fun

"Know any good jokes?"

This project shows some amusing responses from Bash and Tcsh, and tells you how to cheat at crosswords.

Bash Humor

Type the following commands exactly as given.

```
$ %earn-easy-money
-bash: fg: %earn-easy-money: no such job
```

```
$ man woman
No manual entry for woman
```

```
$ awk 'The ship is leaking:'
awk: syntax error at source line 1
 context is
        The ship is >>>  leaking: <<<
awk: bailing out at source line 1
```

Create a trick file to confuse your (less clever) colleagues. Call the file README, and make its contents that of the error message reported when the same file does not exist.

```
$ echo "cat: README: No such file or directory" > README
```

Prove that the file exists.

```
$ ls -l README
-rw-r--r--   1 saruman  saruman  39 Oct 14 19:45 README
```

Show that it (apparently) cannot be found by the cat command.

```
$ cat README
cat: README: No such file or directory
$
```

Q. How do you pronounce "1000 000 000 000 000 000 000"?

A. Type

```
$ say "1000000000000000000000000"
```

And, even sillier,

```
$ say -v "Bad News" "77777777777777777777777777777777"
```

Tcsh Humor

If you're running the Bash shell, start a Tcsh shell to run these examples by typing

```
$ tcsh
%
```

Type the following commands exactly as given.

```
% "How good looking am I?
tcsh: Unmatched ".
```

```
% Got a light?
tcsh: Got: No match.
```

```
% ^^How did the sex change operation go?
tcsh: Modifier failed.
```

```
% man: Why did you get a divorce?
tcsh: man:: Too many arguments.
```

Cheat at Crosswords

Take advantage of the `grep` command, regular expressions, and the dictionary that's supplied with a standard Mac OS X install. The dictionary is in the directory /usr/share/dict/. Read the README file for more information (it's not a trick README ☺).

```
$ ls /usr/share/dict/
README    connectives    propernames    web2    web2a    words
```

ⅰ TIP

Do you know that "eleven plus two" is a mathematically correct anagram for "twelve plus one"?

↗ **LEARN MORE**

Refer to Project 23 for more information on the grep command and Project 77 to learn regular expressions.

↗ **LEARN MORE**

Project 95 covers the curl command in detail.

To search for all the words that match "b blank blank b blank blank z blank blank," type

```
$ grep "^b..b..z..$" /usr/share/dict/web2
bamboozle
```

If several words match the pattern, and you don't know the meaning of them all, look up a meaning by using an online dictionary and the curl command.

```
$ curl dict://dict.org/d:bamboozle
220 aspen.miranda.org dictd 1.9.15/rf on Linux 2.4.27...
...
Bamboozle \Bam*boo"zle\ (b[a^]m*b[=oo]"z'l), v. t. [imp.
 {Bamboozled} (b[a^]m*b[=oo]"z'ld); p. pr. & vb. n.
 {Bamboozling} (b[a^]m*b[=oo]"zl[i^]ng).]
 [Said to be of Gipsy origin.]
 To deceive by trickery; to cajole by confusing the senses;
 to hoax; to mystify; to humbug. [Colloq.] --Addison.
```

Trivial Pursuits

Other useful directories are at /usr/share. Many calendars, including U.S. holidays and computer-related dates, are there for the grepping.

When are the spring and autumn equinoxes?

```
$ grep -sh "Equinox" /usr/share/calendar/calendar.usholiday
03/20*  Vernal Equinox
09/22*  Autumnal Equinox
```

When was Apple Computer founded?

```
$ grep -swh "Apple" /usr/share/calendar/calendar.*
01/03   Apple Computer founded, 1977
06/10   First Apple II shipped, 1977
```

When was Sir Paul McCartney born?

```
$ grep -sh "Paul McCartney" /usr/share/calendar/calendar.* ¬
    | grep born
06/18   Paul McCartney born in Liverpool, England, 1942
```

Appendix: Unix Terminology Reference

This appendix lists the Unix terminology, techniques, and concepts covered in the book. Each term is cross-referenced to the projects(s) that cover it. When several projects are shown, those that provide the most significant coverage are shown in bold.

Project 100 lists Unix commands and the projects in which they are covered.

. and .. as directory entries—Projects 2, 19 (as hard links), 50 (in the PATH variable)

~—see tilde expansion

AFP, Apple Filing Protocol and mounting shares—Project 88

aliases—Projects 4 & **51** (Unix shell aliases), 19 (Mac OS X Finder aliases)

append-only directories and the sticky bit (the t-bit)—Project 8

arguments—Project 1 (passed to commands), Project 10 (passed to shell scripts). See also positional parameters.

auto-completion of a command line, also called tabbed completion—Project 4

background jobs—Projects 15 (running find in the background), **55** (launching and controlling background jobs

batch processing techniques—Projects 58 (using Bash functions), 83 (using Bash shell scripts)

Bonjour (formerly known as Rendezvous), Apple's zero configuration networking technology—Project 90

case sensitivity in filenames in Unix's UFS and Apple's HFS+ filesystems—Project 1

character classes and ranges in globbing—Project 11

command line editing—Projects 4, **53**

Index

Symbols

A